Augustus Jessopp

**One Generation of a Norfolk House**

A Contribution to Elizabethan History. Second Edition

Augustus Jessopp

**One Generation of a Norfolk House**
*A Contribution to Elizabethan History. Second Edition*

ISBN/EAN: 9783744767699

Printed in Europe, USA, Canada, Australia, Japan

Cover: Foto ©ninafisch / pixelio.de

More available books at **www.hansebooks.com**

# ONE GENERATION

OF

# A NORFOLK HOUSE:

A Contribution to Elizabethan History.

BY

AUGUSTUS JESSOPP, D.D.

HEAD MASTER OF KING EDWARD THE SIXTH'S SCHOOL, NORWICH,
EDITOR OF "DONNE'S ESSAYS IN DIVINITY,"
ETC. ETC.

*SECOND EDITION.*

LONDON: BURNS AND OATES.
1879.

SI QUID

IN HOC LIBELLO

VEL PRÆSENS VEL POSTERA ÆTAS

CEDRO HAUD INDIGNUM

JUDICAVERIT

MEMORIÆ VIRI HONORABILIS

FREDERICI WALPOLE,

NAUTÆ MILITIS SENATORIS

AMICI NUNQUAM NON DESIDERATI

TRIBUTUM SIT.

# PREFACE.

IT is sixteen years since I heard for the first time of Henry Walpole the Jesuit Father, who was put to death at York in 1595. Under his portrait, as it hung in the Library at Rainthorpe Hall, the conversation would often turn to that strange phase of the conflict with Rome which was exhibited in the latter half of Queen Elizabeth's reign—which for the most part historians have slurred over so carelessly, and yet about which there is still so much to learn.

It was in 1866 that the Hon. Frederick Walpole seriously suggested to me that I should undertake the writing of the Jesuit Father's life. I had by this time begun to see clearly that it would be impossible to narrow the subject to the limits of a single biography, unless the significance of the incidents related and their bearing upon the history of the time were first explained and clearly apprehended.

The further I proceeded in my inquiries the more evident it became that my task would require me to elucidate the merely personal narrative by dwelling on matters which I had good reason to believe were but little known to us of the Church of England; and it was the more necessary to do this, because no historian of any mark, except Dr. Lingard, has yet dealt with that portion of Queen Elizabeth's reign which was subsequent to the Armada, and because even Mr. Froude curiously ignores much that was going on during the last few years with which his volumes are professedly concerned.

In 1873 I edited, with somewhat copious notes, a collection of nineteen letters of Henry Walpole, the originals of which are now in the archives of Stonyhurst College. Some will be disappointed that these letters are not given fully in this volume. They were in the first instance printed only for private circulation at Mr. Walpole's sole expense, and it was his wish that the collection should always remain a "Book-rarity." On such a point his wishes are to me law; nevertheless, the substance of this collection has been incorporated in the following pages, and it must be confessed that the literary value of the letters themselves is but small.

In the notes appended to the several chapters I have made my acknowledgment to those who have so readily and so liberally assisted me in the course of my work. Only they who have themselves had occasion to leave the beaten track and to grope among manuscripts, consult original sources, and hunt up for evidence and information in holes and corners, know how generous and how chivalrous scholars and men of learning are when they find that a student is honestly unsparing of himself, and is not satisfied with being a superficial compiler. To me the right hand of fellowship has been held out in no grudging fashion by men of European reputation who yet had never heard my name till I applied to them for such help as only they could afford. I have never applied in vain.

There is one, however, to whom I am under deeper obligations than to all others—less for any direct and special aid than for that sort of influence which the master exercises over the scholar, the veteran over the tyro. This book would have been more worthy of its subject if Mr. RICHARD SIMPSON had lived to watch its progress through the press. His enormous knowledge, his vigorous and sagacious criticism, his wonderful memory and minute acquaintance with the undercurrents and byeways, the buried secrets and curious tangles of Elizabethan history, were possessions which belonged to him pre-eminently, and which he seemed to value chiefly as they qualified him to assist others in the pursuit of historical truth.

In the course of the same week death snatched him from us

and that other the nobly-born but yet nobler-hearted friend to whom this volume is inscribed.

One of the greatest difficulties which I have had to contend with has been the extreme rarity of some of the books which it has been necessary to consult, and the consequent difficulty of procuring them at any cost, or even of obtaining a sight of them at any library. Of all the works mentioned in Dr. Oliver's *Collections* as written by Michael Walpole, not one is to be found either in the British Museum, the Bodleian, or the Cambridge Libraries. There are probably not ten copies of More's *History of the English Province* at this moment in England. As to Cresswell's little *Life of Henry Walpole*, it is probably unique; and more than one of Parsons' minor works even a Bibliomaniac would count himself fortunate in obtaining twice in a lifetime.

It was with a painful recollection of my own mistakes, loss of time, bootless journeys, and provoking waste of money, that I determined to append the short list of the rarer books which I have had occasion to use and refer to. A solitary student with limited resources, and cut off from access to the larger libraries, except at intervals of some months, works at very great disadvantage, and I would gladly spare others some of the trouble I have gone through in the long process of simply learning *where to look* for information. The list is after all a meagre one, and I have not named such works as any one can consult almost anywhere; but I must warn those who may feel any inclination to go at all deeply into the history of the period with which this volume deals, that they must make up their minds to be book buyers, and not be frightened at the prices they will have to pay. It was at the peril of a man's life that he ventured three hundred years ago to be in possession of some of the books which this list contains, and if we want to possess them now we cannot hope to get them below their market value.

A volume of little more than three hundred pages will perhaps appear to some but a small result of nearly fifteen years of research. How much easier it would have been to double the bulk they know best who are best qualified to act as my critics. To tell what somebody else has told before is easy: my ambition has been to make some small additions to our previous knowledge, or at least to throw some little gleam of light upon what heretofore was obscure, misrepresented, or misunderstood.

THE SCHOOL HOUSE, NORWICH,
*June* 1878.

# PREFACE TO THE SECOND EDITION.

THE reception accorded to the First Edition of this volume was to me a great surprise: I was prepared for anything but a literary success. Practical men assured me that for a book whose very title seemed to promise that its main interest would be local, and the prominent personages in it, members of a single family, I could expect but a very limited circulation. Prudence suggested that no more copies should be printed than were subscribed for, and the first issue was limited to one hundred and sixty.

I discovered too late my mistake, and can only express my regret to my many friends and correspondents for the disappointment it occasioned.

As the original Edition did not and could not cover its expenses, and as I could not afford to publish another at so costly a rate, I am glad that an enterprising Publisher has been found willing to bring out the book in a cheaper and more convenient form.

In this re-issue, some errors have been corrected and some few omissions supplied. I shall be grateful for suggestions or intelligent criticism, whether friendly or hostile.

THE SCHOOL HOUSE, NORWICH,
   1st *March* 1879.

# A LIST OF SOME OF THE RARER BOOKS REFERRED TO IN THE NOTES.

ABBOT, ROBERT.—A Mirrour of Popish Subtilties; Discovering sundry wretched and miserable evasions and shifts, which a secret cavilling Papist in the behalf of one Paul Spence, Priest, yet living and lately prisoner in the castle of Worcester, hath gathered . . . Written by Rob. Abbot, Minister of the Word of God in the city of Worcester . . . . London, 1594, 4to.

[The author was brother of Archbishop Abbot, and became eventually Bishop of Salisbury. Spence was one of those ordained *Deacon* in Queen Mary's reign. He received Priest's Orders at Douai, and returned to England as a Missioner; but the fact of his having received his first Orders here before the accession of Elizabeth seems to have served to extenuate his subsequent indiscretions.]

ALLEN.—De Justitia Britannica sive Anglica, quæ contra Christi Martyres Continenter exercetur. Ingoldstadii, Ex officina Typographica Davidis Sartorii, Anno 1584.

[See under Burleigh.]

―― Cardinal Allen's Defence of Sir William Stanley's Surrender of Deventer. Edited by Thomas Heywood, Esq., F.S.A. Printed for the Chetham Society, MDCCCLI.

―― A Briefe Discoverie of Doctor Allen's Seditious Drifts, conteined in a Pamphlet written by him, concerning the Yeelding vp of the towne of Deuenter (in Ouerrissel) vnto the King of Spain, by SIR WILLIAM STANLEY. (By G. D.) London, Imprinted by I. W. for Francis Coldock, 1588, 4to.

AQUEPONTANUS (Bridgewater) JOANNES.—Concertatio Ecclesiæ Catholicæ in Anglia adversus Calvino-papistas, et Puritanos sub Elizabetha Regina quorundam hominum doctrina et sanctitate illustrium renovata . . . Augtæ: Trevirorum, 1588, 4to.

[Bridgewater was a Yorkshireman. He was elected Rector of Lincoln

College, Oxford, in 1563, being then Archdeacon of Rochester, and holding other valuable preferment. He resigned it all and left England in 1574. The "Concertatio" was first published in 1583. ". . . . one Joh. Gibbon a Jesuit, and John Feune, having taken a great deal of pains in writing the lives and sufferings of several Popish martyrs, with other matters relating to the Roman Catholic cause . . . . many things therein being wanting or defective, one other, Bridgewater, took more pains in enlarging and adding to it other matters, with an account of 100 or more Popish martyrs . . . ."
—Wood, *Ath. Oxon.*, Bliss, i. 626. The book is hard to meet with, and of great value for the information it contains.]

BAGSHAW, CHRISTOPHER.—A True Relation of the Faction began at Wisbeach by Father Edmonds, alias Weston, a Jesuit, 1595, and continued since by Father Walley, alias Garnet, the Provincial of the Jesuits in England, and by Father Persons in Rome. 4to, 1601.

[Though I have not dwelt on the business of the Appellant Priests in my volume, yet it is impossible to understand the relations of the Catholic hierarchy in England towards the Jesuits, without obtaining some acquaintance with the history of the remarkable dispute which divided the Catholic body in England at the close of the sixteenth century. Much light has been thrown upon this subject lately by the publication of the letters of Father Rivers in Mr. Foley's *Records of the English Province*, series i. Dr. Bagshaw was a personal enemy of Father Parsons all his life.]

BARTOLI.—Dell' Istoria della Compagnia di Giesu. L'Inghilterra parte dell' Europa descritta dal P. Daniello Bartoli della medesima Campagnia. 4to, Bologna, 1676.

[I have always referred to this edition, the original folio was published at Rome in 1667.]

BELL, THOMAS.—The Anatomy of Popish Tyrannie: Wherein is conteyned a plaine Declaration and Christian Censure of all the principall parts, of the Libels, Letters, Edictes, Pamphlets, and Bookes, lately published by the Secular priests and English hispanized Jesuites, with their Jesuited Arch-priest: both pleasant and profitable to all well affected readers. London, 4to, 1603.

―――― The Catholique Triumph, conteyning a Reply to the pretended Answere of B. C. (a masked Jesuit), lately published against the *Tryall of the New Religion* . . . . . At London, printed for the Companie of Stationers, 4to, 1610.

[One of the coarsest books of its class, but invaluable as giving many of the abominable stories which were current at the time.]

BERINGTON, JOS.—The History of the Decline and Fall of the Roman

Catholic Religion in England, during a period of two hundred and forty years, from the reign of Elizabeth to the present time; including the memoirs of Gregorio Panzani . . . . by the Rev. Joseph Berington. 8vo, 1813.

[The book was *printed* in 1793, but, I believe, was not *published* till twenty years afterwards. The introduction, extending to 111 pages, is concerned in great part with giving the history of the dissensions between the Secular Priests and the Jesuits in England at the close of the sixteenth and beginning of the seventeenth century. The author, a Catholic priest, was vehemently assailed by Charles Plowden, a Jesuit father, and others, for the ground he took up in this introduction, and is still denounced as 'unorthodox.' His book is never likely to be republished, and is getting rarer every year.]

tr. Bristow.—Richardi Bristoi, Vigornensis, eximii suo tempore sacræ Theologiæ Doctoris et Professoris, Motiva. . . . Atrebati, 4to, 1608.

[There is a brief life of the author prefixed to this book, which was prepared for the press by Dr. Worthington. Scattered up and down through the volume are curious scraps of personal history which one would hardly expect to find there.]

Cecil, Lord Burghley.—The Execution of Justice in England for maintenance of publique and Christian peace, against certaine stirrers of sedition . . . London, 4to, 1583.

[It has frequently been reprinted and translated; it was answered by Cardinal Allen in "A true, sincere, and modest defence of the English Catholics, that suffer for their faith both at home and abroad, against a slanderous libel entitled 'The Execution of Justice in England.'" 12mo, 1584.]

——— A Declaration of the favourable dealing of her Majesties Commissioners appointed for the examination of certaine Traitors, and of Tortures unjustly reported to be done upon them for matters of religion 1583, 4to.

Certamen Seraphicum Provinciæ Angliæ pro sancta Dei ecclesia.
In quo breviter declaratur, quomodo Fratres Minores Angli calamo et sanguine pro Fide Christi Sanctaque eius Ecclesia certarunt.
Opere et labore R. P. F. Angeli a S. Francisco Conventus Recollectorum Anglorum Duaci Guardiani, Provinciæ suæ Custodum Custodis, ac. S. Theologiæ Lectoris Primarij concinnatum. Duaci Typis Baltasaris Belleri, sub circino aureo. Anno 1649.

[The copy now in my possession was sold some years ago at Sotheby's for seventeen guineas!]

Challoner.—Memoirs of Missionary Priests as well Secular as Regular;

and of other Catholics of both sexes, that have suffered Death in England on Religious Accounts, from the year 1577 to 1684. Gathered partly from the printed accounts of their lives and sufferings, published by cotemporary authors in divers languages, and partly from manuscript relations. . . . 2 vols. 8vo, 1741 and 1742.

[The author was titular Bishop of Debra, and his work is invaluable as a collection of authentic memorials of the unfortunate persons whose sufferings it details. A new edition in 4to, with some hideous engravings, has lately been published, with an introduction of some considerable merit by Mr. Law, late of the London Oratory.]

CRESWEL, JOSEPH.—Histoire de la vie et ferme constance du Pere Henri Valpole, &c. . . .
[See p. 168, n. 5.]

DE BACKER.—Bibliothèque des Écrivains de la Compagnie de Jésus, ou Notices Bibliographiques, 1° de tous les ouvrages publiés par les Membres de la Compagnie de Jésus, depuis la Fondation de l'Ordre jusqu'à nos jours ; 2° des Apologies, des controverses religieuses, des critiques littéraires et scientifiques suscitées à leur sujet. Par les PP. Augustin et Alois de Backer, de la même Compagnie. Liége, 7 vols. 8vo, 1853-1861.

This is one of the most remarkable bibliographical works ever published, and is essential for the student. The first edition cited above is somewhat awkward to refer to, as there are two indexes, one at the end of the fourth, and one at the end of the seventh volume. The new edition, in 3 vols. folio, is a considerable improvement upon the first. The first volume was sent out in 1869 ; the final sheets have only just been issued. Unfortunately this important edition, which (after the death of the last of the brothers de Backer) was completed by their learned associate Charles Sommervogel, is limited to two hundred copies.]

DESTOMBES.—La Persécution Religieuse en Angleterre sous le règne d'Élizabeth. Par l'Abbé C. J. Destombes, Supérieur de l'Institution Saint-Jean, à Douai. Paris, 8vo, 1863.

[A respectable compilation, on which the author must have bestowed some pains and labour. It is of course written entirely from the Catholic point of view.]

—— Mémoire sur les Séminaires et Colléges Anglais, Fondés à la fin du xvi° siècle dans le Nord de la France, et sur les services qu'ils ont rendus à la Religion Catholique en Angleterre ; par l'Abbé C. J. Destombes, Directeur au petit Séminaire de Cambrai. Cambrai, 1852.

DODD, CHARLES.—The Church History of England, from the year 1500 to the year 1688, chiefly with regard to Catholics ; being a complete account of the divorce, supremacy, dissolution of monasteries, and first attempts for reformation under Henry VIII. . . . together with the various fortunes of the Catholic cause during the reigns of King James I., Kings Charles I. and II., and King James II., particularly the lives of the most eminent Catholics, Cardinals, Bishops, inferior Clergy, Regulars and Laymen, who have distinguished themselves by their piety, learning, or military abilities . . . Brussels, 1737, 3 vols. folio.

[This is the original edition, and is very difficult to meet with. A new edition was commenced by the Rev. M. A. Tierney, F.S.A., and carried down to the end of James I. It extended to 5 vols. 8vo. At this point the work ended abruptly, and since then Tierney's papers and books have been dispersed, and will never be collected again. Even "Tierney's Dodd," by which title I have quoted the book, is now difficult to procure.]

ECLESHAL.—Relacion de un Sacerdote Ingles, escrita a Flandres, à un cavallero de su tierra, desterrado por ser Catolico : en la qual le dacuenta de la veinda de su Magestad a Valladolid, y al Colegio de los Ingleses, y lo que alli se hizo en su recebimiento. Traduzida de Ingles en Castellano, por *Tomas Ecleshal*, cavallero Ingles. 12mo, Madrid, 1592.

[The date of the license for printing is 15 Oct., 1592.]

FITZHERBERT.—Nicolai Fitzherberti De Antiquitate et Continuatione Catholicæ Religionis in Anglia, et de *Alani Cardinalis* Vita Libellus. Ad Sanctissimum D. N. Paulum Quintum Pontificem Maximum. *Romæ*, Apud Guillelmum Facciotum, M.D.C.VIII. sm. 8vo.

[The author appears to have been Cardinal Allen's secretary, and was of the family of Fitzherbert of Padly. He was a conspicuous adversary of the Jesuits, and "virulently opposed Father Parsons at Rome."—Dr. Oliver.]

GEE.—The Foot out of the Snare : With a Detection of Sundry Late Practices and Impostures of the Priests and Jesuits in England. Whereunto is added a Catalogue of such Books as in the Author's knowledge have been vented within two years last past in London by the Priests and their Agents. As also a Catalogue of the Romish Priests and Jesuits, together with the Popish Physicians now practising about London. By John Gee, Master of Arts, of Exon. College in Oxford, 4to, London (3rd edition), 1624.

[". . . Printed four times in the said year, 1624, because all the copies, or most of them, were bought up by R. Catholics before they were dispersed, for fear their lodgings, and so consequently themselves, should be found out and discovered."—Wood, *Ath. Ox.* ii. 391, Ed. Bliss.]

——— New Shreds of the Old Snare, containing the Apparitions of two new Female Ghosts ;—The Copies of Divers Letters of late intercourse concerning Romish Affairs ;—Special Indulgences purchased at Rome, granted to Divers English Gentle-believing Catholicks for their Ready Money ;—A

Catalogue of English Nuns of the late Transportation within these two or three years. By *John Gee*, Master of Arts . . . London, 4to, 1624.

HARPSFIELD.—Dialogi sex contra summi Pontificatus, Monasticæ Vitæ, Sanctorum, Sacrarûm imaginum oppugnatores et Pseudomartyres : Ab Alano Copo Londinensi editi . . . Antverpiæ, 1573.
[The real author of this work was Nicholas Harpsfield. It is curious for containing the account of the miracle of the Cross said to have been found in a tree in Sir Thomas Stradling's park in 1559. The story caused great excitement at the time. There is a plate at p. 360 professing to give an accurate representation of this Cross, but it is rarely that copies of the book are to be found which contain this plate.]

HAZART, CORN.—Kerckelycke Historie van de Geheele Werelt, naemelyck vande voorgaende ende Tegenwoordige Eeuwe, Beschreven door den Eerw. P. Cornelius Hazart, Priester der Societeyt Jesu.  4 vols. folio, Antwerp, 1667.
[Valuable only for the magnificent portraits it contains of Parsons, Campion, and others, and for its brilliant engravings.]

JOUVENCY.—Historiæ Societatis Jesu pars quinta. Tomus posterior ab anno Christi 1591 ad. 1616. Auctore Josepho Juvencio Societatis ejusdem Sacerdote. Romæ, 1710, folio.
[Jouvency was one of the literary giants of the Society. Professor of Rhetoric at Paris, he edited Juvenal, Persius, Horace, Terence, the Metamorphoses of Ovid, and many other works, which have still a certain value. He was born in 1643, and died at Rome in 1719. His thirteenth book is occupied with the history of the Jesuits in England, Scotland, and Ireland, from 1591 to 1616. The most valuable portion of this book is the Appendix, which gives some curious incidents in the lives of some Jesuits who ". . . post graves ærumnas in Angliæ toleratas, pie placideque mortui, ab anno 1591 ad 1616."]

MORE, HENRY.—Historia Missionis Anglicanæ Societatis Jesu, ab anno salutis MDLXXX ad [M]DCXIX, et Vice Provinciæ primum, tum Provinciæ ad eiusdem sæculi annum XXXV. Collectore *Henrico Moro*, eiusdem societatis sacerdote. Andomari : typis Thomæ Gevbels, MDCLX.
[Father Henry More was a great-grandson of Sir Thomas More, the Chancellor. He was for some years chaplain to Lord Petre ; was "Minister" of the College at Valladolid in 1615 ; came to England about 1620 ; became Provincial in 1635, and continued to reside in England till 1649. Of all the works which treat of the history of the labours of the Jesuits in England down to the year 1635, Father More's is by far the most valuable, and unfortunately one of the rarest.]

Muñoz.—Vida y Virtvdes de la Venerable Virgen Doña Luisa de Carvajal y Mendoça. Su jornada a Inglaterra, y sucessos en aquel Reyno. Van al fin Algvnas Poesias espirituales suyas, parto de su devocion, y ingenio. Al Rey Nuestro Señor por el Licenciado Luis Muñoz. Con Privilegio, En Madrid, En la Imprenta Real, 1632.

[The following is sometimes bound up with Munōz' *Vida*, as in my copy.]

Copia de una Carta, Que el Padre Francisco de Peralta de la Compañia de Jesus, Rector del Collegio de los Ingleses, de Sevilla. Escriuio al Padre Rodrigo de Cabredo, Provincial de la Nueua España. En que se da quenta, *De la dischosa muerte que tuuo en Londres la sancta señora doña Luysa de Caruajal. Y algunas cosas de las muchas, que por su medio Dios nuestro Señor obrō En Inglaterra, en nueue años que estuuo en aquel Reyno. Y de las honras* Que se le hizieron, en la yglesia de San Gregorio Magno, Apostol de Inglaterra : En el Collegio Ingles de Seuilla, en 11 de Mayo, de 1614.

Nichols.—A Declaration of the Recantation of John Nichols (for the space almost of two yeeres the Pope's Scholar in the English Seminarie or Colledge at Rome), which desireth to be reconciled and received as a Member into the true Church of Christ in England. London, 1581.

[Parsons answered this book in his "Discoverie of J. Nichols, Minister, misreported a Jesuite, lately recanted in the Tower of London . . . by John Howlett." 8vo, Douai. Dudley Fenner answered Parsons.]

Oliver.—Collections towards illustrating the Biography of the Scotch, English, and Irish Members, S. J. Exeter, 1838.

Parsons, Robert.—Elizabethæ Reginæ Angliæ Edictum promulgatum Londini 29 Novemb. Anni MDXCI Andreæ Philopatri ad idem Responsio. 8vo, pp. 361.

[Doubtful whether published at Paris or Rome.]

———— The Judgment of a Catholic Englishman living in banishment for his religion, showing the Oath of Allegiance to be unlawful. St. Omers, 4to, 1608.

———— A Conference about the next succession of the Crowne of England, divided into two Partes. Published by R. Doleman. Imprinted at N., with License, 1594, 12mo.

[The object of the book was to support the title of the Infanta against that of James I. It was made High Treason to possess a copy of this book. Copies with the folding genealogical table are very rare.]

———— *Anon* [Attributed to Father Parsons.] De Persecutione Anglicana Commentariolus, A Collegio Anglicano Romano, hoc anno Domini 1582, in urbe editus, et iam denuo Ingoldstadii excussus. Addītis Literis S. D. N. D. Gregorii Papæ XIII. hortatoriis ad subveniendum Anglis, &c. Ex officina Weissenhorniana apud Wolffgangum Ederum, Anno eodem.

[The Roman edition I have not seen, but I believe this one contains all to be found therein, and the Papal Letters besides. Another edition was published at Paris the same year, "Apud Thomam Brumennium." This tract is comprehended in Bridgewater's *Concertatio*, Part I.]

—— *Anon* [Parsons.] Historia del Glorioso Martirio di Sedici Sacerdoti Martirizati in Inghilterra per la cōfessione & difesa della fede Catolica, l'anno 1581, 1582, & 1583. Con una prefatione che dichiara la loro innocenza. Composta da quelli, che son essi praticauano mentre erano vivi & si trouorno presenti al lor giuditio & morte . . . In Milano . . . 1584.

[Another edition of this was published next year, "In Macerata, Apresso Sebastiano Martellini," with considerable additions, *e.g.*, the account of William Hart is nearly twice as long, and the narrative of George Hadock's execution is given for the first time.]

—— [Parsons.] A Briefe Apologie and Defence of the Catholike Ecclesiastical Hierarchie, and Subordination in England, erected these later yeares by our Holy Father Pope Clement the Eighth; and impugned by certaine libels printed and published of late both in Latin and English; by some unquiet persons under the name of Priests of the Seminaries. Written and set forthe for the true information and stay of all good Catholikes, by Priestes united in due subordination to the Right Reverend Archpriest, and other their Superiors. [1601.] Sine loco aut anno, 12mo.

Possoz.—Vie du Père Henri Walpole, mort pour la Foi en Angleterre, sous Elizabeth. Par le R. P. Alexis Possoz de la Compagnie de Jesus. Casterman, Tournai, 1869.

Rainoldes.—The Somme of the Conference between John Rainoldes and John Hart: touching the Head and Faith of the Church. \* \* \* London, 1609.

[John Hart has been the puzzle of friends and foes for three hundred years: he was one of Campion's associates; condemned to death in 1581, and pardoned for some reason shortly after. This conference was not published till twenty-eight years after it took place, and in the meantime Hart had returned to his Jesuit friends, and been received apparently without any suspicion. There is much about him in Simpson's Campion.]

Ribadeneyra.—Historia Ecclesiastica del scisma del Reyno de Inglaterra Recogida de diversos y graues Autores, por el Padre Pedro di Ribadeneyra, de la Compañia de Jesus. En Emberes, 1588.

Sanders, Nic.—Nicolai Sanderi de Origine ac Progressu Schismatis Anglicani Libri tres . . . Olivæ, 1690.

[This edition contains a Diary kept in the Tower, from 1580 to 1585, by Edmund Rishton the editor, which, though short and meagre, contains some curious information.]

SIMPSON.—Edmund Campion: a biography by Richard Simpson. Williams and Norgate, 8vo, 1867.

[Beyond comparison the most important contribution which has yet appeared to the knowledge of the history of the Jesuit Mission to England in 1580.

SLINGSBY.—The Lady Falkland: her Life, from a MS. in the Imperial Archives at Lille. Also a memoir of Father Francis Slingsby, from MSS. in the Royal Library, Brussels. London, Dolman, 1861.

[This work was printed from a transcript of the original MS. made by Mr. Richard Simpson.]

SMITH, RICHARD.—Vita piissimæ ac Illustrissimæ Dominæ *Magdalenæ Montis-Aucti* in Anglia Vice-Comitissiæ: Scripta per Richardum Smitheum Lincolniensem, Sacræ Theologiæ Doctorem, qui illi erat a sacris confessionibus. Ad Edwardum Farnesium, S. R. E. Card. Illustrissimum, et Angliæ Protectorem. S. loc. et ann. 16mo.

[I have seen it stated that this curious and precious little book was printed at Rome. Lady Montagu died in 1608. Her house was called "Little Rome;" it was the resort of priests during the whole of Queen Elizabeth's reign, the peers' houses being still privileged. The account given of the domestic arrangements and the religious life in this house is most curious and almost unique.]

STAPLETON, THOMAS.—Apologia pro Rege Catholico Phillippo II. Hispaniæ et cæt: Rege. Contra varias et falsas accusationis Elizabethæ Angliæ Reginæ. Per Edictum suum 18 Octobris Richemundiæ datum, et 20 Novembris Londini promulgatum, publicatas et excusatas . . . Authore Didymo *Veridico Henfildano*. Constantiæ apud Theodorum Samium. 12mo, 1592.

[The title, Henfildanus, refers to his being born at Henfield in Sussex. This is the fiercest and most powerful attack upon Queen Elizabeth which was ever written. Nothing that has ever appeared from the pens of the Jesuits—and Stapleton was not a Jesuit—can be compared to it in eloquence, earnestness, and force; moreover, it is singularly free from the vulgar scurrility which only too often characterises such attacks. Stapleton was, perhaps, a greater loss to the Church of England than he was a gain to the Church of Rome, but the same may be said of many of the exiles.]

TANNER.—Societas Jesu usque ad Sanguinis et vitæ profusionem militans . . . Sive Vita et mors eorum qui ex Societate Jesu in causa Fidei et Virtutis propugnatæ, violenta morte toto orbi sublati sunt, Auctore R.P. Matthia Tannero, S. J. . . . Pragæ, 1675, folio.

[The book is remarkable for the illustrations, many of them of great merit, but ghastly enough to awaken horror rather than pleasure. Perfect copies are very scarce, as it has been a practice to cut out the plates and sell them as edifying pictures for the faithful. I have seldom had the opportunity of consulting the original Latin edition, and have been compelled to content myself with a German translation, published also at Prague, in folio, 1683: in this the plates are much worn. This work must not be confounded with another work (also in folio) of the same author, published in 1694, "Societas Jesu Apostolorum Imitatrix." The plates alone, without note or comment, of this work were published in 4to, under the title "Societas Jesu usque ad sudorem et mortem pro salute proximi laborans," without date, by the University of Prague, probably the same year as the original work. The copy in my possession is the only one I have ever seen.]

VERSTEGAN.—Theatrum Crudelitatum hæreticorum nostri Temporis. *Antverpiæ*, 1587, 4to.

[Ant. à Wood gives a long and curious account of Verstegan: he was for many years the chief instrument for carrying on communications between the English exiles in Belgium and their friends at home. The Fathers of the London Oratory intend, I believe, to publish a collection of his letters at some future time. In this work, which is one of very great rarity, there are eight plates of the sufferings of the Catholics during Elizabeth's reign.]

WATSON, WILLIAM.—A Decacordon of Ten Quodlibeticall Questions concerning Religion and State: Wherein the Authour framing himself a Quilibet to every Quodlibet, decides an hundred crosse Interrogatorie Doubts, about the generall Contentions betwixt the Seminarie Priests and the Jesuits at this present. Newly imprinted 1602, 4to.

[The book contains a great deal of curious information, more or less true. On Watson's plot against James I. (for it was his) see Gardiner's *History of England*, 1603-1616, vol. i. p. 81. He was hung for High Treason, December 1603. There is a long and curious letter of his in Goodman's *Court of King James*, vol. ii. p. 59-87.]

—— A Sparing Discovery of our English Jesuits, and of Father Parsons' Proceedings under Pretence of Promoting the Catholic Faith in England. 4to, 1601.

[No place. A very *unsparing* attack upon the Jesuits by one of the Secular Priests, who were opposed to the influence of the Society.]

—— A Dialogue betwixt a Secular Priest and a Lay Gentleman, Concerning some points objected by the Jesuiticall faction against such Secular Priests as have showed their dislike of *M. Blackwell* and the Jesuits' proceedings. Printed at Rhemes, 1601, 4to.

YEPEZ.—Historia Particular de la Persecucion de Inglaterra, y de los martirios mas insignes que en ella ha auido, desde el año del Señor, 1570. En la Qval se Descubren los efectos lastimosos de la heregia, y las mudanças que suele causar en las Republicas : con muchas cosas curiosas, y no publicadas hasta aora, sacados de Autores graves. Recogida Por el Padre Fray Diego de Yepes, de la Orden de S. Geronimo, Confessor del Rey don Felipe II. de gloriosa memoria, Obispo de Taraçona. Dirigida Al rey don Felipe III. *Nuestro Señor.* En Madrid, Por Luis Sanchez Año MDXCIX. 4to.

# TABLE OF CONTENTS.

|  | PAGE |
|---|---|
| INTRODUCTORY | 1 |
| NOTES | 11 |

## CHAPTER I.

| THE WALPOLES OF HOUGHTON | 19 |
|---|---|
| NOTES | 28 |

## CHAPTER II.

| SCHOOL AND COLLEGE DAYS | 36 |
|---|---|
| NOTES | 51 |

## CHAPTER III.

| THE EXCOMMUNICATION AND ITS RESULTS | 58 |
|---|---|
| NOTES | 78 |

## CHAPTER IV.

| THE JESUIT MISSION TO ENGLAND | 86 |
|---|---|
| NOTES | 103 |

## CHAPTER V.

| THE KINSMEN | 113 |
|---|---|
| NOTES | 123 |

## CHAPTER VI.

| JOHN GERARD | 130 |
|---|---|
| NOTES | 145 |

## CHAPTER VII.

| THE MISSIO CASTRENSIS | 154 |
|---|---|
| NOTES | 168 |

## CHAPTER VIII.

THE RETURN TO ENGLAND . . . . . 173
    NOTES . . . . . . . 192

## CHAPTER IX.

FATHER GERARD'S "MUCH GOOD" . . . . 194
    NOTES . . . . . . . 211

## CHAPTER X.

CAPTURE AND IMPRISONMENT . . . . 222
    NOTES . . . . . . . 244

## CHAPTER XI.

THE TOWER AND THE RACK . . . . . 246
    NOTES . . . . . . . 264

## CHAPTER XII.

THE TRIAL AND THE SCAFFOLD . . . . 270
    NOTES . . . . . . . 284

## CHAPTER XIII.

THE GATHERING OF THE FRAGMENTS . . . 287
    NOTES . . . . . . . 310

**INDEX** . . . . . . . 319

# ONE GENERATION OF A NORFOLK HOUSE.

## INTRODUCTORY.

ON the 17th of November, 1558, as the first grey dawn was gaining upon the darkness of the night, Mary Tudor, Queen of England, ceased to breathe. Two days later Reginald Pole, Cardinal and Legate of the Holy See, Archbishop of Canterbury, and the last Englishman who is known to have been a candidate for the Papacy, died at his palace at Lambeth: Sovereign and Primate receiving the last rites of the Church according to the ritual of the See of Rome. And thus—as Mr. Froude puts the matter—"the reign of the Pope in England and the reign of terror closed together."

"The reign of the Pope in England" certainly did close then, and closed for ever. Whether "the reign of terror" ended, is another question, the answer to which is not to be given hastily. Among those best qualified to decide, some put that question from them as one too much surrounded with shameful associations to admit of being answered pleasantly, and some reply to it with indignant and passionate denial.

We are apt to say that in our days events follow one another with unexampled rapidity. We affirm, not without a touch of self-complacency, that "we live fast." Fifty years have seen the passing of the Reform Bill, the Emancipation of the Slaves, the Repeal of the Corn Laws, the Disestablishment of the Irish Church, and the annulling of a host of statutes that were a reproach upon our legislation. But it may be doubted whether any twenty years since the Peace of Amiens—fruitful as they may have been in measures exercising a profound influence upon our daily lives and habits of thought—can be compared, in the tremendous consequences they involved, with the twenty years which closed with the death of Queen Mary.

By a single act of the Legislature—we may almost say by a single sweep of the King's pen—at least a twentieth part of the best land in England had been made to change hands. ([1]) Upwards of six hundred religious houses in England and Wales alone were given over to pillage; ([2]) the dwellers in precincts once held sacred, counting, it must be remembered, by thousands, were turned adrift to live as they could, scantily pensioned, and sometimes exposed to actual penury and want. ([3]) Hundreds of men, gentlemen by birth and education, ([4]) with the student's tastes and the student's retiring habits, whose lives had been spent in harmless, if unprofitable, seclusion—not seldom, too, spent in acts of piety and devotion—found themselves cast out, homeless and strange, to become suddenly the scorn and derision of the fickle mob or the coarse and brutal fanatics who were now let loose upon them.

The vulgar time-servers of the monasteries, the men whose god was their belly, easily accommodated themselves to the change; they were soon absorbed in the multitude with whom their sympathies lay, and, being of the earth earthy, had lost but little, perhaps had gained something on the whole. But it was precisely the best and most devout, the purest and gentlest spirits, upon whom the full force of the blow fell. The hypocrites could take care of themselves; the religious and conscientious men were the real sufferers. These, clinging still to their monastic dress (for they held themselves still bound by their vows), were assailed by jeers and insults wherever they appeared; ([5]) in the streets they were hooted at and stoned, the ribald clamour growing to such a height that at last a special proclamation was issued to restrain the violence of the disorderly. Meanwhile the vast estates so rudely confiscated were tossed about almost at random. Upstarts, enriched by spoils that surpassed their wildest dreams, played the part of gamblers: the chances of the cards had brought them wealth, but not the power to use it wisely. Sometimes a creature of the Court would get a grant of lands which he had neither the means to cultivate, nor even the funds to pay for the expense of entering upon. The market was glutted with estates that were to be had for a song. But while the lawyers throve and made colossal fortunes, the recklessness of the gambling-table clung to the adventurers who seemed to be clutching their gains. What came lightly went as lightly. Hungry Italians or notorious profligates grasped manor after manor only to let them slip: the booty seemed to the vultures about the Court inexhaustible, yet it came to an end. ([6])

In 1536 the smaller monasteries were suppressed; in 1539 the larger ones shared the same fate; nine years later followed the dissolution of the chantries, collegiate churches, and hospitals, to the number of nearly three thousand more; ([7]) and two years later, as though this were not enough, the churches were stripped of their vestments, chalices, ornaments, and bells, and the very college libraries plundered of the jewelled binding of their books, if any such remained for the spoiler.

Henry VIII. died in January, 1547, King Edward in July, 1553. The utter break-up of the ancient ecclesiastical institutions of the kingdom had taken barely seventeen years. The overwhelming character of the revolution is even now difficult to realise, impossible adequately to describe; the shock which the moral sentiment of the nation experienced has never yet been duly appreciated: its effect upon the religious tone and habits of the people can hardly be exaggerated. The ordinary restraints of religion had been suddenly and violently torn away; the clerical police was disarmed; the pulpits silent; the universities menaced, and warned that their time was coming next; learning and literature were smitten as with palsy; thoughtful men looked out upon the future with dismay, almost with despair. ([8])

6 July, 1553. Such was the state of affairs in England when Queen Mary ascended the throne. Less than a month before, she had been declared illegitimate and incapable of succeeding to the crown by letters patent, the draught of which her brother had prepared with his own hand.* At the moment when Edward breathed his last, her life was believed to be in imminent peril; and no sooner did the tidings of his decease reach her at Hunsdon, in Herts, than she fled as fast as relays of horses could carry her, and rode night and day without halt for a hundred miles, to Kenninghall, twenty miles from Norwich, a castle of the Howards.† Three weeks more and she is riding into London as Queen; her sister Elizabeth, escorted by two thousand horse and a retinue of ladies, waiting to receive her outside the gates.‡ Three days after Mass was sung by Gardiner, Bishop of Winchester, in the chapel of the Tower; and in another month, to the joy of three-fourths of the people, the Catholic ritual was generally restored throughout the land.

Recklessly as the confiscated property of the monasteries had been flung about, some still remained undistributed. In the third year of her reign Mary determined to make such restitution as was still possible. In October, 1555, a Bill was laid before Parliament to authorise the surrender of all the abbey lands remaining in the possession of the Crown. All rectories, impropriations, and ecclesiastical possessions were resigned, the total annual revenue, amounting to not less than £60,000, being set apart for the augmentation of small livings, the maintenance of preachers, and the providing exhibitions for poor scholars at

---

\* Froude, v. p. 500 et seq.     † Ibid., vi. 82 and 310.

‡ ". . . . queen Marie's grace came to London the 3 daye of August, beinge broughte in with her nobles very honorably & strongly. The number of velvet coats that did ride before hir, as well strangeres as otheres, was 740, and the nomber of ladyes and gentlemen that followede was 180. The Earle of Arundell did ride next before hir bearinge the sworde in his hande, and Sir Anthony Browne did beare up hir trayne. The ladye Elizabethe did followe hir next, and after hir the Lord marques of Excter's wyfe."—*The Chronicles of Queen Jane* (Camden Society, 1850), p. 14.

the two Universities. (⁹) By the same Act the Statute of Mortmain was suspended for twenty-one years, that all who were so inclined might have the opportunity of making some amends for the wholesale spoliation that had been carried on. Nor was this all; a beginning was actually made in the direction of restoring the monastic bodies. Once again an abbot of Westminster ruled in the venerable cloister over a score or so of Benedictine monks collected under his crozier: once again Dominican friars were settled at Smithfield, and Observant friars at Greenwich, and nuns of the order of St. Bridget, were summoned to take possession of their old home at Sion. (¹⁰)

The legislation of the past few years had been so violent and so sweeping that only the most passionate and thoroughgoing reformers could keep pace with it. With the accession of Mary a reaction set in, the force of which none could estimate. There can be no doubt that the bulk of the nation witnessed the return of the old ritual with unmixed thankfulness and joy. (¹¹) What course events might have taken but for that miserable Spanish marriage it is idle now to speculate upon; it is certain that as yet the doctrines of the Reformers had made very little impression indeed upon the religious convictions of the people of England. Very soon a cry of discontent and bitter hostility was raised. From over the sea, in the refuge at Geneva, book after book came forth filled with furious denunciations of the new Queen. John Knox, Goodman, Becon, Ponet, Traheron, and many another whose name has gone down into silence, shrieked at her in language which for coarseness and scurrility stands unparalleled in literature. She was a bastard;* she was a woman, and so unfit to reign; she was Jezebel; she was Athaliah; she was "this ungodlie serpent Marie, the chief instrument of all this

---

* Even Ridley had not scrupled to proclaim this at Paul's Cross. ". . . . the nexte Sonday after [July, 1553] prechyd the Bysshoppe of London, Nicholas Reddeele, and there callyd bothe the sayde ladys [Mary and Elizabeth] bastarddes, that alle the pepull were sore anoyd with his worddes, so uncherytabulle spokyne by hym in so opyne ane awdiens."—*Chronicle of the Grey Friars,* p. 78.

present miserie in England." Volume and pamphlet and broadsheet came pouring forth in a never-ceasing stream. Every resource of furious rhetoric was exhausted, the polemics goading one another on to the wildest frenzy of hatred and disappointed rage. (¹²) Safe in their Swiss asylum, they had nothing to fear for themselves, nothing to lose and everything to gain by fomenting discontent and sedition at home.

Irritated by the hornets' nest which she could not reach, and perplexed in the maze of questions which she could not solve; her life one long dreary disappointment; in her childhood sickly and ailing; in her girlhood a forlorn and anxious recluse; in her womanhood a neglected and forsaken wife,—the unhappy Queen sought for comfort, vainly, in the dark and morose fanaticism of her French and Spanish directors, and the stern persecution took its course, which slander and malice and vituperation had done much to provoke, and which her own religious melancholy aggravated.

Over that deplorable chapter in Queen Mary's history the most faithful apologists of the Church of Rome must needs be content to cast a veil.* And God forbid that any Christian man should seek to excuse or palliate the enormities of that terrible time, or should look back upon them with any other feeling than horror. Nevertheless, this fact has been passed over quite too lightly by Protestant writers, viz., that religious persecution was no novelty on the one side or the other, that the Reformers' hands were deeply stained in the blood of the Anabaptists, and that a restless and malignant band of malcontents, from their hiding-places beyond the seas, were from the very first stirring heaven and earth to make the Queen's crown a crown of thorns upon her brow. This uncompromising faction, whose one and only bond of union was their community

---

* "The foulest blot on the character of this queen is her long and cruel persecution of the Reformers. The sufferings of the victims naturally begot an antipathy to the woman by whose authority they were inflicted."—Lingard, v. 259.

in hatred of their sovereign, stood to her precisely in the same attitude as that adopted subsequently by the Seminarists to her successor. They differed only in this, that the Protestants had no discipline, no great unity of principle, no grand unselfish aim. As a rule they were eminently plebeian; socially they belonged to a rank several grades lower than that of the men who in the next generation filled the Colleges of Rheims, Valladolid, and Douay; ([13]) but in their restless activity in plotting and slandering they were more than a match for their Romish successors; and whatever excuse may be found for the persecution by Elizabeth in the fierce attacks of Parsons and his fellows, is fairly to be allowed for the atrocities of Mary's reign in the abominable scurrilities of Becon and Knox.

Meanwhile, in these years which intervened between the suppression of the monasteries and the accession of Mary, the condition of affairs in the Church of England was beyond measure deplorable. Parsonages were bestowed upon grooms and menials, a share of the income being reserved for the patron of the benefice; the curates were the scorn of their parishioners, and the "rude lobs of the country" jeered at the illiterate "lack-Latins who slubbered up their services, and could not read the humbles." ([14])

In the country parishes the eye was greeted at every turn by gaunt stone walls crumbling to ruin, sumptuous buildings untenanted, shrines that were once the treasure-houses of a district and the resort of thousands of pilgrims who, in their journeyings, had circulated countless sums of money among the inhabitants of the district, ([15]) stripped bare and plundered to the very lead upon their roofs or the brasses in their pavements. A chill horror had begun to haunt the ruined cloisters, and shudderings of a superstitious fear, lest the curse should light upon such as even slept upon the desecrated ground.*

---

\* ".... those that enjoyed them did not inhabit or build upon the lands, but forsook them for many years, till [in] the time of Queen Eliza-

Men saw, or fancied they saw, with perplexity and amazement that the spoilers who had seized the bulk of the plunder were none the richer for their booty. The old resident county families were not they whose broad acres were increased by any share of the abbey lands;* to them the spoliation was almost an unmixed loss. The prior or abbot of some neighbouring monastery might be wanting in that fervent devotion which the monk was theoretically supposed to exhibit, but he was at any rate socially the country squire's equal, often a man of education and taste, sometimes too a cadet of a "knightly family," and even if addicted to hunting and hawking (not to mention more reprehensible and immoral pursuits), yet in the main a genial companion whose society and hospitality made him an accession in provincial circles, while his undeniable open-handedness to the poor materially lightened the burdens which would otherwise have pressed heavily upon the landlord class. It was all very well for the great nobles about the court to go on their way as if the dissolution had never taken place, they saw little or nothing of the actual working of the mighty change; but in remote districts, in villages far away from the towns—villages to which the abbey *was* the town; the gentry were brought face to face with the tremendous magnitude of the social revolution that had been effected; and as, in their case, there had been no change of religious conviction, the discontent among them was sullen, deeprooted, and all but universal.

In the dark chimney corner during the long dull winter evenings, while the Christmas logs were sending up their lazy smoke, as his children gathered round him and stared at the fire, many an old squire, still but a little past his prime, would

---

both a great plague happening, the poor people betook themselves into the remainder of the houses, and finding many good rooms, began to settle there, till at length they were put out by them to whom the grants of the leases and lands were made."—Spelman, p. 239, ed. 1853.

* This is abundantly clear by Spelman's lists, &c.

tell of this or that prior or monk who used to drop in in the old days and bring some relief to the monotony of their isolated lives; he would not seldom mutter his curse upon the ribald recklessness of the parvenus who had ousted their betters and made the grand old places desolate. Sometimes, too, he would sigh for a priest of the old school, into whose practised ear he might pour out his soul and seek remission of sins that pressed sorely upon his burdened conscience. How bitterly he would mourn for "the good old times," and denounce the wild havoc that had been wrought. Generous lads heard the laments and brooded over them: they got to believe that their parents' lives had been saddened and their own estates seriously damaged by that which they had been taught from childhood to regard as sacrilege, and the rising generation were in the mood to hope for little in the future and to regret very much in the past. About that past, already becoming well-nigh heroic, there clung a certain romance and mystery which, to the enthusiasm of youth, it seemed supremely desirable to revive.

There was yet another reason why the country gentry should feel soreness and irritation at the new order of things. When all has been said that can be said to the discredit of the "Regulars," it should never be forgotten that the whole machinery of education had for centuries been in their hands. (16) That education may have been as meagre and unsatisfactory as the exaggerations of Erasmus and Reuchlin strove to exhibit it, but such as it was, it was the only education offered. The dissolution of the monasteries meant the shutting up all the great schools in the kingdom, and leaving fathers of families to create their own supply under the pressure of the sudden demand. The country gentry saw with dismay that the old seminaries had been swept away. It was no longer possible to send a daughter to a neighbouring convent school or a son to the nearest abbey. The country clergy were as ignorant as the mechanics from whom, in a vast number of cases, they had sprung; and though here and there some monk or friar would be driven to earn his bread by taking service in the layman's family as private tutor ([17]), (and there were many instances of this), yet the supply of these men fell off every year, and in the after times the arrangement exposed the households to serious pains and penalties if any suspicion attached to the too conscientious retainer.

Mary's accession to the crown was to the "Country party" a promise of return to the better way. The abbey lands were gone—gone irrecoverably (even the Pope and his legate were compelled to confess so much), but new endowments might be forthcoming, and in numberless instances a comparatively small outlay would suffice to restore the buildings that as yet had scarcely had time to fall into decay. There seemed some probability, there certainly was a hope, that a revival would sooner or later set in. At any rate the beaten side could not bring itself to acquiesce in defeat, and the "logic of facts" was lost upon it. As yet men had not learned to recognise in the force of the mighty current which had swept away the abbeys, an outcome from that perennial source of discord, the antagonism between town and country,—the one, greedy for change which might bring incalculable profit; the other, clinging to the past lest it should lose all that was worth having.

Just when the country gentry began to be sanguine, Mary died; and before a year had passed their dreams of a restoration of the "old order" were rudely dispelled. How the bitter disappointment told upon them; how the irritation of blighted hopes drove them to passionate outbursts of rage and abortive attempts at rebellion; how the new Queen, with that mighty oligarchy, her council, tightened the curb, and plunged in the rowels, and laid on the lash with a heavier hand the more restive and furious the team became that she was breaking to submission; how the townsmen beat the countrymen, and the traders the squirearchy, and the new men were too strong for the old houses,—will be illustrated, I trust, by the narrative in the following pages.

# NOTES.

(1) *Page 2, line 8.* There are few questions more difficult to decide than the amount of landed property in the hands of the monasteries at the time of the dissolution. The estimates given by various writers differ as widely as guesses usually do when they are made without sufficient knowledge and suggested by violent prejudice. The estimate adopted in the text is that of Hume, who certainly had no predilections in favour of the monks: he came to the conclusion that the aggregate of all the ecclesiastical property in the kingdom at the date of the suppression yielded one-tenth of the national rental, and that this was about equally divided between the "secular" clergy and the "regulars." The subject has been very ably discussed by a writer in the *Home and Foreign Review* for January, 1864. He shows conclusively (1) that so far from monastic bodies having increased in wealth during the 14th and 15th centuries, they had certainly declined; (2) that the sequestration and suppression of monasteries had been always going on to a far greater extent than is commonly believed. No less than 146 Alien Priories were appropriated by Henry V.; 29 of the lesser monasteries were granted to Cardinal Wolsey alone, and more than half of the monastic foundations which had at some time or other been endowed in Hampshire, had disappeared before 1536. In Scotland, where might was always stronger than right, the monasteries appear to have been despoiled according to the caprice of the reigning sovereign, and their estates dealt with in a peculiarly arbitrary manner.—(See Historical MSS. Commission, 5th Report, pp. 647, 648.) As to the fiction in Sprot's *Chronicle*, that William the Conqueror divided England into 60,000 knights' fees, and that the clergy held 28,000, and that there were then 45,000 churches in the country, it has been rightly described as "a mythical estimate which ought never to have been accepted by historians."

See the preface to Tanner's *Notitia* by Nasmith; Taylor's *Index Monasticus*, Introduction; Lingard, *History of England*, vi., note E.; Collier, *Ecclesiastical History*, B. 7, c. xv., p. 650. There is a very suggestive table in Appendix A, p. 138, of Bishop Short's *Church History*, giving the number of religious houses founded in each reign since the Conquest.

(2) *Page 2, line 10.* Take the following as one indication among a thousand of the wholesale character of the spoliation:—"England had been largely replenished with bell metal, since the dissolution of the monasteries; and vast quantities of it were shipped off for gain. Nor was the land yet

(1547) emptied of it, for now it was thought fit to restrain the carriage of it abroad; especially having so near an enemy as France, that might make use of it for guns against ourselves. Therefore, July 27th, a proclamation was issued out, forbidding the exportation of that and other provisions, lest the enemy might be supplied, and our own country and army want."—Strype's *Memorials*, Edw. VI., B. 1, c. vi., 845. For the spoils in the shape of jewels and plate, removed from WALSINGHAM, see Heylin's *Hist. Reform.*, fo. 10.

(3) *Page 2, line* 13. "But those that were appointed to pay these poor men, were suspected to deal hardly with them by making delays, or receiving bribes and deductions out of the pensions, or fees for writing receipts; as it appeared afterwards they did, which occasioned an Act of Parliament in behalf of these pensioners."—Strype's *Memorials*, Edw. VI., B. 1, c. xv., fo. 118.

(4) *Page 2, line* 14. "The ignorance of the Monks" has, until very lately, been taken for granted by all popular writers; and yet that, as a body, they were *less* learned than the secular clergy appears on examination to be almost infinitely improbable: the very contrary might be proved to demonstration if it were worth while. During the last ten years of Henry VIII.'s reign the king appointed to twenty-eight bishoprics in England and Wales. In no less than fifteen cases were the vacancies supplied by ecclesiastics who had been superiors of monastic bodies. The list of these men is suggestive, and, as far as I know, has not been given elsewhere.

| Name. | Office. | Bishopric. | Date of appointment. |
|---|---|---|---|
| 1. Barlow, William | Prior of Haverfordwest | St. Asaph | 1536 |
| 2. " " | " " | St. David's | 1536 |
| 3. Bird, John | Provincial of White Friars | Chester | 1542 |
| 4. Bushe, Paul | R. of the College of Bonhommes at Eddington, Wilts | Bristol | 1542 |
| 5. Chambers, John | Abbot of Peterborough | Peterborough | 1542 |
| 6. Hilsey, John | Prior of Dominicans | Rochester | 1535 |
| 7. Holbech, Henry | Prior of Worcester | Lincoln | 1541 |
| 8. " " | " " | Rochester | 1544 |
| 9. Holgate, Robert | Prior of Watton | Llandaff | 1537 |
| 10. King, Robert | Abbot of Osney | Oxford | 1542 |
| 11. Kitchin, Anthony | Abbot of Einsham | Llandaff | 1545 |
| 12. Rugg, William | Abbot of St. Benet's, Hulme | Norwich | 1536 |
| 13. Salcot, John | Abbot of Hyde | Salisbury | 1539 |
| 14. Wakeham, John | Abbot of Tewkesbury | Gloucester | 1541 |
| 15. Warton, Robert | Abbot of St. Saviour's, Bermondsey | St. Asaph | 1536 |

Of these I have collected the following notices :—

BARLOW...."When he was Bishop of St. David's, laboured for the disposing of Aberguilly College to Brecknock, whereby provision being made for learning and knowledge in the Scriptures, the Welsh rudeness might have been formed into English civility.... he wrote several books against Popery...."—Strype's *Memorials*, Edward VI., B. ii. c. xxvi. Concerning his learning and writings, see Wood, *Ath. Ox.* i. 365; see too Heylin's *Hist. Reform.*, p. 54.

BIRD...."Educated in theologicals in the house or college of the Carmelites (he being one of that order) in the University of Oxon, where making considerable proficiency in his studies ... he wrote and published Lectures on St. Paul, &c., &c."—Wood, *Ath. Ox.* i. 238; see too Strype's *Cranmer*, B. I, c. xvi. § 61.

BUSHE was "well skilled in physic as well as divinity, and wrote learned books." Wood says "he was numbered among the celebrated poets of the university," and that he was "noted in his time for his great learning in divinity and physic."—*Ath. Ox.* i. 269. [He was deprived under Queen Mary.]

CHAMBERS graduated both at Oxford and Cambridge. He has been credited with the revision of the Book of Revelation in the Bishops' Bible, but there is some doubt whether truly or not. In either case the story proves the estimation in which he was held by his contemporaries.—Cooper, *Ath. Cant.* i. 142.

HILSEY "being much addicted from his childhood to learning and religion, nothing was wanting in his sufficient parents to advance them."— *Ath. Ox.* i. 113, where an account of him and his writings may be found.

HOLBECH was "a true favourer of the Gospel, and made much use of in the reforming and settling of the Church."

KING. "While he was young, being much addicted to religion and learning, was made a Cistercian monk.... In Queen Mary's reign.... he did not care to have anything to do with such that were then called heretics, and therefore he is commended by posterity for his mildness."— *Ath. Ox.* ii. 775.

KITCHIN was the *one single* Bishop in the kingdom who consented to take the oath of allegiance to Queen Elizabeth, and to assist at her coronation.

Perhaps the most memorable instance.of a monk becoming a protestant martyr is that of Bishop Hooper. Who that reads Foxe's account of him (*Acts and Mon.* vol. vi. p. 636 and seq.) would suspect that Hooper was for some years *a Cistercian monk* at Gloucester?—Strype, u.s. Stow's *Survey*, 1633, p. 533.

(5) *Page* 2, *line* 32. Tierney's *Dodd*, Pt. I., art. iv.

(6) *Page* 3, *line* 14. Spelman, *History and Fate of Sacrilege*, ch. vi. The chapter is entitled "The particulars of divers Monasteries in Norfolk, whereby the late owners since the Dissolution, are extinct or decayed or

overthrown by misfortunes and grievous accidents." Sir Henry Spelman began to write his book in the year 1612.

(7) *Page* 3, *line* 18. Henry VIII. has sins enough to answer for; but if the pillage of "the Terror," as Mr. Green justly calls this period of our history, had not been followed by the far more sweeping robberies of the following reign, it is conceivable that no very great harm would have been done, for sooner or later something like a dissolution of the Monasteries was inevitable; but the spoliation of the Hospitals was an almost unmixed evil, and the wholesale destruction of the Colleges, Chantries, and Free Chapels was vehemently opposed by Cranmer in the House of Lords. The Hospitals, Chantries, and Free Chapels had been given to the king by a statute passed in the 27th of Henry VIII., but this had never been put in force, possibly through Cranmer's intercession. In the 2nd of Edward VI. they were again condemned. By this act no fewer than 110 Hospitals, 90 Colleges, and 2374 Free Chapels "were thus conferred upon the king by name, *but not intended to be kept together for his benefit* only."—(Heylin.) The "Free Chapels" in many cases appear to have approximated to what are now *Nonconformist places of worship;* they were "free" in the sense that they were exempt from Episcopal Jurisdiction, and frequently had something like a special ritual.—(Tanner's *Notitia*, Preface; Fuller's *History of Abbeys;* Taylor's *Index Monasticus*, Introduction; Heylin's *Hist. Reform.* Anno 1547.) Perhaps the most outrageous and inexcusable robbery of all was the stripping of the Guilds. It is astonishing that historians have passed over this shameful measure with so little notice. The plunder derived from the ecclesiastical corporations was so prodigious, that it has served to draw off men's attention from the consequences which the abolition of the Guilds involved. In Taylor's *Index Monasticus* there is a list of no less than 909 Guilds given over to the spoilers *in Norfolk alone.* In the very valuable volume of *Ordinances of Early English Guilds*, published by the "Early English Text Society," there are 46 more or less complete Ordinances of Norfolk Guilds that sent in returns to the King in Council in the 12th year of Richard II. The Guilds were merely Benefit and Burial clubs supported by the subscriptions of the members, and enriched from time to time by small bequests of their members. At the meetings of the Guild of St. Christopher at Norwich, a very beautiful prayer was used, which may be found at p. 23 of the volume referred to. These meetings were almost always of a convivial character, and legacies are frequently left to furnish a dinner for the brethren : thus WILLIAM WALPOLE, of Great Shelford (in Cambridgeshire), by his will, dated 20th March, 1500, leaves "To the prefects of the Gylds in Great Shelford, viz. :—our Lady and Saint Anne to each of them a Ewe. Item, to the prefect of the Gylde of all Halloweys in Starston, a Bullock and two quarters Barley."—[Peterborough Register, Probate Court, E. 6.]

(8) *Page* 3, *line* 35. As I am not writing the history of the spoliations in the reigns of Henry VIII. and his son, I am unwilling to give chapter and verse for all the statements made in the text. My readers must accept my assurance that there is abundance of authority ready at hand to support any and every assertion put forward. I cannot, however, resist the temptation to print the following Proclamation, which, as far as I know, has never yet been referred or alluded to by historians of this period. It will be news to some of my readers that *the earliest Pigeon Matches on record were shot off in St. Paul's Cathedral !*

" A Proclamation for the reformation of quarrels and other like abuses in the Church.

" The Kings Maj<sup>y</sup> considering that Churches holy Cathedrals and others which at the beginning were godly instituted for common prayer for the word of God and the ministration of Sacraments be now of late time in many places *and especially within the city* of London irreverently used and by divers insolent rash persons sundry ways much abused so far forth that many quarrels riots, frays bloodsheddings have been made in some of the said Churches besides *shootings of hand guns to doves*, and the common bringing of horses and mules in and through the said churches making the same which were properly appointed to God's service and common prayer like a stable or common Inn, or rather a den or sink of all unchristliness to the great dishonour of God, the fear of his Majesty, [and] *disquiet of all such as for the time be then assembled for common prayer and hearing of God's word* (!)

" Forasmuch as the insolency of great numbers using the said ill demeanes doth daily more and more increase, His Highness by the advice of the Lords and others of his privy council, straitly chargeth and commandeth that no manner of person or persons of what state or condition soever he or they be, do from henceforth presume to quarrel, fray or fight, shoot any hand gun, bring any horse or mule into or through any cathedral or other church or by any other ways or means irreverently use the said Churches or any of them upon pain of his highness' indignation and imprisonment of his or their bodies that so shall offend against the effect of his present proclamation . . . . . . "EDWARD VI."

*Cotton MSS., Titus*, B. ii. 39.

In the Bishop's Registry at Norwich there is a fragment of a volume of the Records of the Commission for the trial of causes ecclesiastical, from which I extract the following curious parallel to the above :—

" ix° die Martii Anno Dñi 1597 coram Rever<sup>do</sup> in Chro : patre ac dũo : Willielmo providentia Dei Domino Norvicens̃ Epc̃o. . . . . AMMON DE BISSON comperuit. . . . . who being charged to have let into the Palace chapel (where the French people by the said Reverend father his licence do resort to have divine service) a man having a piece [a gun], *who there did shute to kill pigeons* not only to the profaning of the place of prayer, but also to the endangering of the whole palace by fire and terrifying of some within the same; the said Ammon confessed that he had so done, &c., &c. . . . ."

(9) *Page* 5, *line* 1. Tierney's *Dodd*, vol. iii. p. 114; Burnet's *Reformation*, p. 587.

(10) *Page* 5, *line* 11. Tierney's *Dodd;* Heylin's *Reformation*, p. 236 and seq.; Aungier, *History and Antiquities of Syon Monastery*, p. 96 and seq.

From that curious and very rare book, the *Certamen Seraphicum Provinciæ Angliæ*, 4to. Duaci, 1649, it appears clearly that on the re-establishment of the order not only were the old monks reinstated, but great numbers of recruits took the vows. One of these persisted in retaining the Franciscan habit till his death. He lived the life of a hermit at Layland in Lancashire, protected by the Earl of Derby. He came at last to be regarded as a saint, and was supposed to work cures in his retreat, not only upon men and women but cattle. He went by the name of "Father John, the old beggar man," and to the end consistently refused to touch money, though he lived on the contributions of the neighbourhood. He died at Layland about 1590, and lies buried near the north of the chancel porch.— *Cert. Seraph.* p. 13.

(11) *Page* 5, *line* 17. "Meantime the eagerness with which the country generally availed itself of the permission to restore the Catholic ritual, proved beyond a doubt that, except in London and a few large towns, the popular feeling was with the queen."—Froude, c. 30, vol. vi. p. 83. See too Maitland's *Essays on the Reformation*, Essays viii. and ix.

(12) *Page* 6, *line* 5. Goodman quoted by Maitland, *Essays on the Reformation*, p. 138.

PONET was actually "engaged as a leader, if not as an original plotter and instigator, in Sir Thomas Wyatt's insurrection," and narrowly escaped being taken with Sir Thomas on the 7th February, 1554. Maitland (u.s. p. 93) gives in his text the passage from Stow which details the circumstances.

GOODMAN too was implicated in the same rebellion.

TRAHERON's foul language is like the ravings of a filthy madman. See Maitland, p. 84. What must that passage be like which "is so gross that it must be omitted"? One is tempted to think that nothing *could* be worse than the previous paragraph.

All these men were deeply implicated in the treasonable plots of Mary's reign.

(13) *Page* 7, *line* 8. Simpson's *Campion*, p. 46, and Allen's *Apology for Seminary Priests* there referred to.

(14) *Page* 7, *line* 22. Strype apud Tytler, *England under the Reigns of*

*Edward VI. and Mary*, vol. i. p. 322. See too Becon's Preface to *The News out of Heaven*, p. 5 (Parker Society). "Your wisdoms see what a sort of unmeet men labour daily to run headlong into the ministry, pretending a very hot zeal, but altogether without necessary knowledge. . . . The smith giveth over his hammer and stithy; the tailor his shears and metewand; the shoemaker his malle and thread; the carpenter his bill and chip-axe . . . and so forth of like states and degrees . . . so that now not without a cause the honourable state of the most honourable ministry, through these beastly belly-gods and lazy lubbers, is greatly defamed, evil spoken of, contemned, despised, and utterly set at nought." . . .

(15) *Page* 7, *line* 28. See *Statutes of the Realm*, 35 Henry VIII. c. 13. —"The King's Imperial Majesty, most benignly calling to his gracious remembrance that his town of LITTLE WALSINGHAM, otherwise called NEW WALSINGHAM, which heretofore, as well through the great and continual trade of all manner of merchandise in times past then used and practised, as also by and through *the populous concourse and resort of his people from all parts of this Realm in times past within the said Town frequented and continued*, was grown and commen to be very populous and wealthy and beautifully builded, is at this present by the great decay and withdrawing of the said trades and merchandise there, and by divers other sundry occasions of late happened, *like to fall to utter ruin and to be barren, desolate, and unpeopled* . . . *&c.*"

(16) *Page* 9, *line* 23. See the very valuable Preface to "The Babee's Book," by Mr. Furnival, "Early English Text Society," 1868.

(17) *Page* 10, *line* 2. I give the following instances, from a host that might be adduced, because I suspect that the Thomas Woodhouse here named was a cadet of the Kimberley family; and because Ralph Crockett was for some time engaged as a private tutor in Norfolk. The title "Sir" (Sir Thomas Woodhouse) was the ordinary designation of a parish priest.

"SIR THOS. WOODHOUSE was made priest in the time of Queen Mary, a little before her death, and presented to a parsonage in Lincolnshire, which he enjoyed not a whole year, by reason of the change of religion which he could not be contented to follow; wherefore, leaving his living, he went into Wales, where for a while, in a gentleman's house, he taught his sons, but could not continue there unless he would dissemble his conscience. He left that place, and within a while was taken and sent prisoner to the Fleet in London, &c. &c."—*Stonyhurst MSS., Angl.*, A, vol. i.

"Ralph Crockett examined, saith he was first brought up in Christ's College in Cambridge, where he continued about three years . . . from thence he went to TIBNAM LONGROWE in Norfolk, where *he taught children a year or more*, &c. &c."—P.R.O. *Domestic MSS.*, Eliz., No. 214.

Crockett was hung at Chichester, in Sept., 1588 ; Woodhouse at Newgate. Add to these—

"George Lingam. . . . The said Lingam harboured and lodged at one Mr. Wiltcot's, at Englefield . . . and *under colour of teaching the Virginals*, goeth from Papist to Papist : is thought also to be a priest, so made in Queen Mary's time, and like to be the man that was kept in the top of the said Parkyns' house at a time when her majesty was but ill served by her officers in a search there made."—*Cotton MSS., Titus*, B. iii. 63.

CHAPTER I.

# THE WALPOLES OF HOUGHTON.

THE family of Walpole has been settled in the county of Norfolk for at least six hundred years. Whether any faith is to be placed in the tradition which tells of an ancient charter bestowed upon some remote ancestor by Edward; whether there be Norman blood in their veins;([1]) whether the founder of the house were some adherent of the Conqueror who, after the revolt of the Fenmen in 1070, received a grant of lands for his services in that dreary but fertile district through which the Ouse finds its way sluggishly into the Wash, and where Hereward the Englishman made his last gallant stand;([2])—are questions which must for ever remain unanswered. Certain it is that under the Plantagenets the ancestors of this ancient Norfolk family were seated at Walpole St. Peter's, where they had a manor and lands, which they retained in their possession as late as the year 1797, when an Act of Parliament compelled them to sell both the one and the other, after the decision of the great Houghton lawsuit.

They appear to have migrated from Marshland in the reign of Henry II., ([3]) and to have taken up their residence at Houghton, where Sir Henry de Walpole held one knight's fee of the fee of Blaumister, and the fourth part of a knight's fee of the Honour of Wermegay; and in the reign of King John either he or another Henry de Walpole occurs as one of those who paid a fine of £100 for release from prison, on giving security for his allegiance to the king in time to come. Another of the name figures as a supporter of Simon de Montfort in the barons' war, and as taking a leading part in the rebellion; while in the thirteenth century the Walpoles, then a "knightly family," appear on more than one occasion to have held office in the royal Court. Throughout this century, too, they are conspicuous as ecclesiastics.([4]) Edmund de Walpole was Abbot of St. Edmund's Bury from 1247 to 1256, at a time when,([5]) thanks to the genius and administrative ability of Abbot Sampson, St. Edmund's was one of the most wealthy and important abbeys in England; and Radulphus de Walpole was successively Bishop of Norwich and Ely from 1288 to 1302, his tomb being conspicuous in the cathedral of the latter see, standing before the high altar of the church at the present day. In 1335 Simon de Walpole was Chancellor of the University of Cambridge,([6]) about the same time that his kinsman, Sir Henry de Walpole, was returned as one of the Knights of the Shire to serve in the Parliament summoned to meet at York in the 7th year of Edward III. All through the fourteenth and fifteenth centuries the Subsidy Rolls, which still exist in the Record Office, show the Walpoles to have been residing at Houghton, and to have been men of substance and influence in the Hundreds of Smethdon, Freebridge, North Greenhow, and Brothercross; their manor of Houghton being handed down from father to son, and their possessions gradually increasing as time went on. Two members of the family ([7]) appear to have attained to eminence as judges in the reigns of Edward III. and Richard II., one of them being even Chancellor, if, as seems highly probable, Mr. Rye's conjecture regarding Adam de Houghton be founded on fact.

An offshoot of the Norfolk family became early established in Lincolnshire; and the Walpoles of Pinchbeck were for centuries one of the leading families in the county: another branch acquired lands in Suffolk, the Walpoles of Brockley being seated there from the time of Edward I. down to the end

## THE WALPOLES OF HOUGHTON.

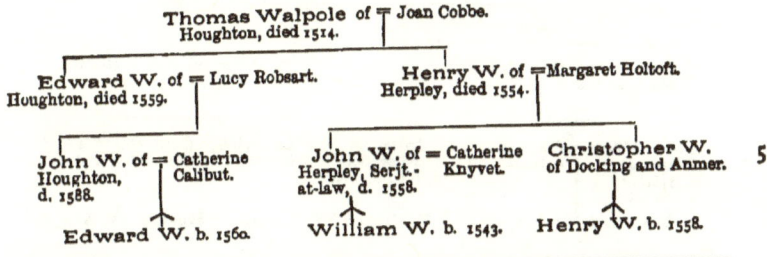

of the fifteenth century; (⁸) and I meet with three generations of them as owners of considerable estates and a capital mansion called Walpole's Place in Cambridgeshire, where they were evidently the chief landowners in Great Shelford and the contiguous parishes.(⁹)

On the 24th January, 1513-14,(¹⁰) Thomas Walpole of Houghton, Esq., was gathered to his fathers. He left behind him two sons, and divided his estates between them; the manors descended to Edward, the elder son; the outlying lands were left to Henry, the second; who, though his Lincolnshire estates were larger than those in Norfolk, appears to have resided at Herpley, where he died in 1554.

It is with the grandsons of these two men that the present work is chiefly concerned.

Edward, the elder son, had taken to wife Lucy, daughter of Sir Terry Robsart of Siderston, a parish contiguous to Houghton, and with her appears to have obtained a sufficient marriage portion. Sir Terry Robsart had only one other child, John, or as he is usually called, Sir John Robsart,(¹¹) who twice served the office of High Sheriff for his native county. Sir John Robsart resided at Stanfield Hall near Wymondham; and when Dudley, Earl of Warwick, was sent down to suppress the formidable rebellion of Kett "the Norfolk Tanner," it seems that the earl, with his son the Lord Robert Dudley, passed the night at Stanfield Hall, and there Lord Robert, probably for the first time, saw the beautiful Amy Robsart, whom he married on the 4th June of the following year, the king being

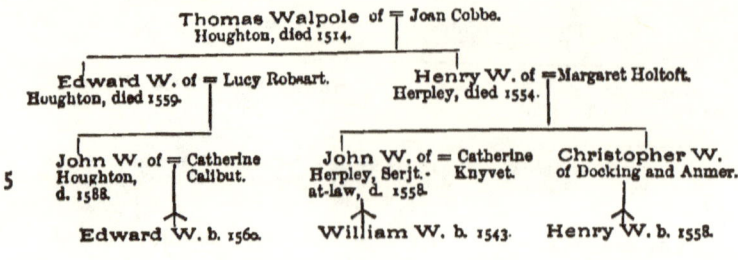

present at the ceremony, which was carried out with great magnificence. Upon the newly-married pair the Manors of Siderston and Bircham, and other property, were settled, with remainder, failing issue, to the right heirs of Sir John; in other words, if Amy Robsart should prove childless, the offspring of Edward Walpole of Houghton would in right of their mother inherit the Robsart property.

Henry Walpole, the younger brother of this Edward, had married a Lincolnshire heiress, ([12]) one Margaret Holtoft of Whaplode, and with her he came into large and valuable estates. As an equivalent, his father had settled upon him a considerable landed property in Herpley, Rudham, and the adjoining parishes.

Edward Walpole of Houghton, though his wife had been no portionless damsel, was by no means so rich a man as his brother; nevertheless by prudent management he contrived to increase rather than diminish his resources, and at his death, in 1559, he was able to make ample provision for three sons,— John, Richard, and Terry.

John, the eldest son, succeeded his father at Houghton in the first year of Queen Elizabeth. He too had married well. His wife was Catherine, eldest daughter of William Calibut of Coxford, Esq., ([13]) a man of wealth and substance, whose ancestors had been for some generations large landowners in this part of Norfolk, but, as he had no son, his inheritance would devolve at his death upon his daughters. For some time it looked as if the Houghton estate would pass away to the Herpley Squire, for daughters only were at first the fruit of the marriage. It was not till the beginning of 1560 ([14]) that a son appeared. The child was named after his grandfather, Edward, and in the following year another son was born, who was called after his mother's surname, Calibut.

Not many months after the birth of the elder son Amy Dudley died, and died childless; and thus, when the year 1560 ends, we have John Walpole of Houghton tenant for life of the Norfolk and Suffolk manors, owner in fee-simple of an extensive property in the former county, and heir-at-law to all the Robsart estates at the death of Lord Robert Dudley, afterwards Earl of Leicester, a man of vigorous constitution, and not yet thirty years of age. ([15])

Meanwhile, as has been said, Henry Walpole of Herpley had died six years before, leaving behind him three sons, with two of whom only have we much concern. ([16]) His eldest son had died before his father, leaving, however, issue who inherited the Lincolnshire estates. The second son was John Walpole of Herpley, one of the most successful barristers of his time. He was of Gray's Inn, and was appointed Lent Reader of that society in the third year of Edward VI. In the first year of Queen Mary he was returned M.P. for Lynn; the next year he was raised to the degree of Serjeant-at-law, and Dugdale has left us an account of the magnificent feast which was given at the Inner Temple on the occasion of his receiving the coif. ([17]) It is evident that his practice was extensive and his income correspondingly large, and as fast as he made his money he proceeded to buy land in Norfolk, and especially in his own part of the county. ([18]) But while he was adding manor to manor, and in the midst of a career which must have led to the highest honours and emoluments of his profession, he was cut off in the prime of life, leaving behind him an only son, William, a boy of thirteen, and four daughters, all unmarried and under age.

Christopher Walpole, the serjeant's younger brother, and third son of Henry Walpole of Herpley, had been amply provided for

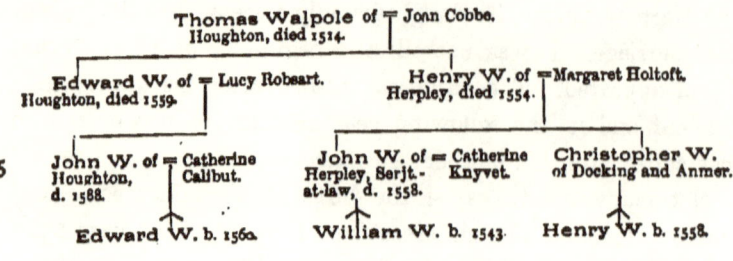

by his father's will. At the end of Queen Mary's reign he was settled at Docking Hall, a house about five miles from Houghton. He had married Margery, daughter of Richard Beckham of Narford, and with her appears to have obtained something like a fortune, for prudent marriages seem always to have been the characteristic of the race. A few months after his brother the serjeant's death Christopher's first child was born. ([19]) The boy was baptized at Docking in October, 1558, and took the name of his grandfather, Henry. This is he who is the central figure in the narrative of the following pages.

The Docking family was increased by a fresh child almost every year, and at the close of 1570 it consisted of six sons and three daughters, one son, John, having died in infancy ten years before.

The household at Docking had become too large for the house, and an opportunity having occurred for purchasing the neighbouring estate of Anmer Hall, ([20]) with a large tract of land in Anmer and Dersingham, Christopher Walpole removed his family to the new residence in 1575; his estate lying immediately contiguous to his cousin's domain at Houghton on the one side, and to his nephew's property at Herpley on the other.

First and last the possessions of the three squires stretched over a tract covering not much short of fifty square miles. It was wild heath and scrub for the most part, where huge flocks of sheep roamed at large; except where the "common fields" of arable land and the small patches of meadow and pasture, supplied with cereals and fodder the population of villages

which were then perhaps more thickly inhabited than now.
The peasantry were dismally ignorant, timid, and slavish; each
man's village was his world, and he shrank from looking beyond
it. The turf or the brushwood of the parish gave him fuel: the
bees gave him all the sweetness he ever tasted: the sheep-skin
served him for clothing, and its wool, which the women spun,
served for the squire's doublet and hose. The lord of the manor
allowed no corn to be ground save at his own mill; and he who
was so fortunate as to own some diminutive salt-pan was the
rich man of the district. ([21]) It is very difficult for us to throw
ourselves back in imagination to a time when nothing was too
insignificant to be made the subject of a special bequest. Not
only do we meet with instances of bed and bedding, brass pots,
a single silver spoon, a table, and the smallest household utensils
left in the wills of people of some substance and position; but
old shoes, swarms of bees, half a bushel of rye, and as small a
sum as sixpence, are common legacies even down to the end of
the sixteenth century. The "cottage" of the labourer, a creature as much tied to the soil as his forefather the "villein" (who
had passed with the land as a chattel when an estate changed
owners), was nothing but a mud hovel with a few sods for roof,
and, as a dwelling, incomparably less comfortable than the
gipsy's tent is in our own days. The manor-house, on the other
hand, small though it were, exhibited a certain barbaric pro-
digality. Foreigners were amazed at the extent of English
households, out of all proportion to the accommodation provided
for them. ([22]). In the latter half of Elizabeth's reign the fashion
of building large houses in the country parishes prevailed to a
surprising extent, and this, with other causes, hastened the ruin
of many an old county family which had held its own for
generations; but at her accession the houses of the landed gentry
were very small and unpretending, and their furniture almost
incredibly scanty; while for the agricultural labouring classes,
there were tens of thousands of them who, as we understand the
words, had never in their lives slept in a bed. ([23]) Roads there

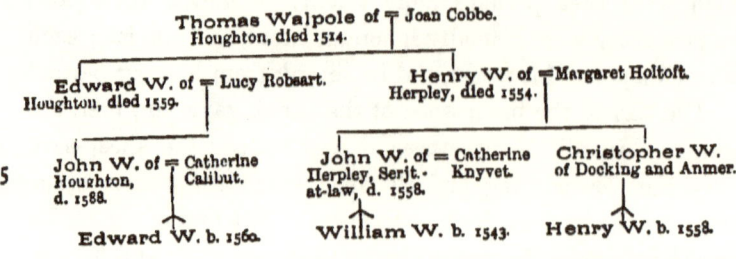

were none. Fakenham, the nearest town to Houghton, was nine miles off as the crow flies, and Lynn was eleven or twelve. As men rode across the level moors, now and then starting a bustard on their way,([24]) or scaring some fox or curlew, there was little to catch the eye save the church towers, which are here planted somewhat thickly; but Coxford Abbey, not yet in ruins—indeed part of it actually at this time inhabited ([25])— and Flitcham Priory, a cell of Walsingham, frowned down upon the passer-by,—the desolate ghosts of what had been but twenty years before.

The great man of the family at this time was young William Walpole, the serjeant's son and heir, though his Norfolk cousins could have known but little of him. When his father was made serjeant in 1554,([26]) he entered his son at Gray's Inn, I presume in compliment to the Inn, although the boy was only in his twelfth year. He had been left to the guardianship of Thomas Thirlby, Bishop of Ely, to whom, during the minority, the Manor of Felthams in Great Massingham was left to defray the charges of his ward's education; and though on the accession of Queen Elizabeth ([27]) the wardship was bestowed upon his mother, and subsequently, on her marriage with Thomas Scarlett the serjeant's friend and one of his executors, was transferred to him and Robert Coke, Esq., of Mileham, father of Sir Edward Coke, afterwards Lord Chief Justice; yet the provisions of the will were faithfully carried out, and Bishop Thirlby became *de facto* guardian, and superintended the lad's early education according to his father's desire.

Thus, in this district, lying between Fakenham and Ely, there was no family at the beginning of Queen Elizabeth's reign at all to be compared with this Walpole clan in the extent of their possessions and the width of their local influence and resources. For the young heir of Herpley any future might be in store, and the family connections had been extended with great prudence by the marriages of the daughters with the leading gentry of the county round,—the Cobbes of Sandringham, the Russels of Rudham, and other substantial squires.

While young William Walpole was away in London, his mother, with her second husband, kept up the establishment at Herpley, and as the boys at Houghton and Anmer grew, there must have been almost daily intercourse between the several households. And now that question, which had begun to be a very serious one for many a country gentleman at this time, began to press upon such men as Christopher and John Walpole —men with eight sons between them, and doubtless not without ambition which their prospects or their pride of parentage might well be supposed to justify. If these growing boys were to take their place in the world, and make their way to distinction,—perhaps even follow in the steps of their uncle the serjeant, and raise the family to all that shadowy greatness which the traditions of the house were not likely to diminish,— where and how was their education to be carried on?

# NOTES TO CHAPTER I.

(1) *Page* 19, *line* 5. The names of members of the family which occur in the twelfth and thirteenth centuries indicate a Norman origin, *e.g.*, *Reginald de Walpole*, Henry I.; *Joceline de Walpole*, Richard I. *Lemare de Walpole* and *Beatrix* his wife, about the time of King John, assign lands to the prior of Lewes, the deed being executed first in St. Nicholas Chapel, Lynn, and afterwards in the churchyard of Castleacre.—(Blomefield, viii. 504). We meet also during this period with the names EGELINE, CLARICE, ALAN, and OSBERT WALPOLE. See Collins, and especially Mr. Rye's Paper, "Notes on the Early Pedigree of Walpole of Houghton," in the *Norfolk Antiquarian Miscellany*, part i. p. 267 *et seq.*

(2) *Page* 19, *line* 11. Freeman's *Norman Conquest*, vol. iv. p. 463 *et seq.*

(3) *Page* 19, *line* 19. Collins's *Peerage*, s.v., "Walpole Lord Walpole." It is evident that Collins had access not only to charters and family documents which since his time have perished, or at least disappeared, but that the registers of Houghton and many of the adjoining parishes were placed at his disposal, and laid under contribution. I suspect that these latter were never returned to the several churches to which they belonged : there is an unusual absence of *early* parish registers within a radius of five or six miles round HOUGHTON. In every case where I have had an opportunity of testing his work, I have found Collins scrupulously accurate, and my own researches have only served to increase my confidence in him as an antiquary and genealogist of a very high order. Of course the vast wealth of manuscript sources now open to students at the Record Office and other depositories were not accessible to inquirers in Collins's days, and I believe the Subsidy Rolls, which are a rich mine for the genealogist, were not known or even discovered till comparatively lately.

(4) *Page* 20, *line* 7. *Rye*, u.s. p. 279.

(5) *Page* 20, *line* 8. See *Chronica Jocelini de Brakelonda* (Camden Society, 1840). This charming volume is the basis of Mr. Carlyle's *Past and Present*.

(6) *Page* 20, *line* 15. Le Neve's *Fasti Eccles. Anglic.* vol. iii. 598. WILLIAM WALPOLE was elected Prior of Ely some time before 10th August 1397. He was in possession of that office 20th September 1401 (at which time the church was visited by Archbishop Arundel), and resigned soon after.—Rymer, *Fœdera*, viii. p. 9, quoted in Bentham's *History of Ely Cathedral*, 4to, Camb. 1771.

(7) *Page* 20, *line* 26. Rye, u.s. They certainly were both Norfolk men, but can scarcely have been father and son, as Mr. Foss (*Judges*, vol. iii. p. 447, and iv. p. 59) suggests.

(8) *Page* 21, *line* 9. Gage's *History of Thingoe Hundred* (4to, 1838), pp. 94 and 359; Gardner's *History of Dunwich* (4to, 1754), p. 197.

(9) *Page* 21, *line* 13. See Note 7, page 14.

.(10) *Page* 21, *line* 14. For the date, his Inquisition p.m. is the authority. —*Chancery* Inq. (P.R.O.) 6° Henry VIII. *Norfolk*, No. 49.

(11) *Page* 21, *line* 27. In his will he calls himself "JOHN ROBSART, *Esquier*." In the inquisitions taken at Ipswich on the 13th November, and at Diss in October, 1554, he is described as a knight, as he is also in the contracts entered into between himself and John Earl of Warwick, in May, 1550. He was twice High Sheriff for the counties of Norfolk and Suffolk, and bore for arms, *Vert, a lion rampant or, vulned in the shoulder.*

The terms of the marriage contract between him and the Earl of Warwick are curious. The earl settles all that the *reversion* of his site, circuit, and precinct of the late PRIORY OF COXFORD, and of all that the manor of COXFORD in the county of Norfolk, . . . and of the rectories and churches of EAST RUDHAM, WEST RUDHAM, BROWNSTHORPE, and BARMER; and the moiety of the rectory of BARNHAM, and also of the manors and farms of EAST RUDHAM, WEST RUDHAM, BARMER, TITTLESHALL, SIDERSTON, THORPMARKET, and BRADFIELD, with all their rights . . . "*being parcell of the Possessions and Revenues of Thomas, late Duke of Norfolk, of high treason attainted*" . . . upon his son ROBERT DUDLEY and AMY, daughter of Sir JOHN ROBSART, and upon their issue, and in default of such issue, upon the right heirs of Lord ROBERT. He further settles an immediate annuity of £50 on ROBERT and AMY, to be paid out of his manor of Burton Lisle in the county of Leicester; such annuity to cease *on the death or marriage* of "the lady Mary's grace, sister to y⁹ King's Majesty." Besides this the earl covenants to pay to Sir JOHN ROBSART "at the sealing of these presents" *the sum of two hundred pounds.*

Sir JOHN on his part settles the manors of SIDESTERN and NEWTON juxta BIRCHAM in the county of Norfolk, and the manor of GREAT BIRÇHAM in the said county, and the manor of BULKHAM in the county of Suffolk, "upon himself and his wife, the LADY ELIZABETH," for life, and after their death upon the said ROBERT and AMY and their issue; in default of issue the remainder to revert to the right heirs of SIR JOHN, who covenants moreover to pay an annuity of £20 a year to ROBERT and AMY, and at his death to leave them a legacy of "three thousand sheep to be left in a stock going on the premises in Norfolk and Suffolk aforesaid." The earl signs and seals on the 25th May, 1550.

Great as the advantages *appear to be* on the face of these documents, as conferred by the Earl of Warwick upon his son, they proved in the issue very small indeed. The attainder upon Thomas, third Duke of Norfolk, was reversed at the accession of Queen Mary, and his lands were restored to him. The annuity of £50 ceased at the marriage of Queen Mary, and Lord Robert and his wife must have been in great measure dependent upon Sir John Robsart during the whole of Mary's reign; for it must be remembered that Warwick (then Duke of Northumberland) perished on the scaffold on the 22d August, 1553.

In addition to all that Lord ROBERT obtained with his wife in the counties of Norfolk and Suffolk (and the Siderston property alone amounted to more than four thousand acres, with thirty-six "messuages," and fifteen "cottages") there was another manor in Shropshire, OLDBURY, which Amy inherited, and the reversion of which JOHN WALPOLE of Houghton sold in 1566 to ARTHUR ROBSART, an illegitimate son of Sir John's, for £350.—*Close Rolls*, 8 Elizabeth, No. 706. This son was living at OLDBURY HALL in 1595, and had then been married for about thirty years to MARGARET, relict of ANTHONY COCKET of SIBTON co. SUFFOLK, Esquire. She is described as "nunc uxor Arthuri Robsarte, gen., de Oulbery Hall alias Blakely Hall, in Com. Salopiæ."—*MS. in the Bishop's Registry, Norwich.*

The original of the marriage settlement is at Longleat, in the possession of the Marquis of Bath, and appears to have been discovered there some years ago by the Rev. J. E. Jackson, F.S.A. The grant of the annuity of £20 by Sir John Robsart is at the Record Office (*Miscell. Augment.* vol. vii. 112, Edward VI.), as are the p.m. inquisitions (1 and 2 Philip and Mary, co. Suff. 62, co. Norf. 63). The account of the marriage of Lord Robert and Amy Robsart is to be found in the Diary of King Edward VI. in the British Museum.—*Cotton MSS.*, No. 110.

(12) *Page* 22, *line* 17. Blomefield, and they who follow him, all assert that she was a daughter of GILBERT HOLTOFT, second Baron of the Exchequer, who died long before she was born. It is quite certain that she was not descended from the judge at all. I have printed GILBERT HOLTOFT's will, in the *Original Papers, Norf. and Norw. Archæol. Soc.*, vol. viii. p. 179. He had not an acre of land at Whaplode. On the other hand,

in a Subsidy Roll of the reign of Henry VII. (?) now in the Record Office, containing the names of persons in the county of Lincoln holding lands or rents of the value of £40 a year, I find among the twenty-two names that of "WILLS. HALTOFT de Quaplode, Sen.," by which it appears he had probably a son named William, who lived at Whaplode at the close of the fifteenth century, from whose daughter, MARGARET, the Whaplode property came to the Walpoles. The similarity in the form of the name *Guilielmus*, often written *Gilelm* and *Gilbert*, will account for the mistake. At the death of JOHN WALPOLE of Whaplode, Esq., in 1590, without issue, the estates were sold according to the instructions of his will, and the great bulk of his property was left to his widow, who survived him forty years. By her will (P.C.C. Scroope, f. 15), dated 20th October, 1629, she directed that a monument to her first husband's memory should be erected in Prestwold Church, co. Leicester, which I believe still exists there.—Nichols, *Hist. Leic.* iii. 359.

(13) *Page* 22, *line* 31. Though the Calibuts had been settled in Norfolk from a very early period, their name does not occur in the lists of gentry of the county returned by the Commissioners to Henry VI. in 1433, (Fuller's *Worthies*, iii. 460). The family appear to have first risen to wealth and importance through the success of one of its members at the bar: FRANCIS CALIBUT was a Governor of Lincoln's Inn in the 16th and 24th years of Henry VII., and was Autumn Reader of that Society in the 7th and 12th years of the same reign (Dugdale, *Orig. Jur.*). He died on the 5th March, 9 Henry VIII., seized of the manor of FOXES alias SANDARS in Castle Acre, and about three thousand acres in Castle Acre, West Lexham, East Lexham, and the adjoining parishes, with the manor of West Lexham, the advowson of Little Dunham, and a great deal else which is specified. His son John married Bridget, daughter and heir of Sir John Boleyn, and died on the 20th February, 1553. This JOHN left behind him two sons, JOHN CALIBUT of Castle Acre, [who died at Upton, in Northamptonshire, 23d October, 1570, leaving four daughters, who divided his inheritance;] and WILLIAM CALIBUT of Coxford, Gent., father of CATHERINE WALPOLE, and other daughters. I suspect this WILLIAM was "learned in the law:" he certainly was a man of wealth and consideration, and he lived for some time at COXFORD ABBEY. By his will, dated 1st August, 1575, it appears he spent his last days at Houghton, and he leaves 20s. to the "household servants" there.

In the will of his daughter CATHERINE WALPOLE, dated 16th June, 5 James I., she leaves to her granddaughter ELIZABETH WALPOLE, " my chain of gold sometime WILLIAM CALIBUT'S my father's, deceased, by estimation worth one hundred marks." WILLIAM CALIBUT'S own will, to one who can "read between the lines," betrays an unfair and cruel disposition of his property in favour of the Walpoles, and indicates that he was a person of strong Puritan tendencies.

What Blomefield means by talking of an EDGAR CALIBUT who was Serjeant-at-law, I cannot understand. No such name appears in Dugdale. There was an EDWARD CALIBUT, with whom ROGER ASCHAM kept up a correspondence for many years. Some of Ascham's letters to him have been printed, but there are several still unpublished in the possession of Matthew Wilson, Esq. of Eshton Hall.

A ROBERT CALIBUT, of St. John's College, took his B.A. degree at Cambridge in 1551, and HENRY CALIBUT was parson of CRANWICH, co. Norfolk, from 1533 to 1560; he left some liberal legacies behind him, but in his will he mentions no relatives of his own name. There were CALIBUTS at *Grimeston* in 1594, and on the 24th November of that year EDWARD the son of JAMES CALIBUT was baptized there. As late as 1640 I find an ANDREW CALIBUT, who marries DOROTHY CURZON at St. Martin's at Palace Norwich, on the 29th June.—Francis Calibut's p.m. inq. *Chancery*, 9 Henry VIII., No. 125; John Calibut's the elder, u.s. 2 and 3 Philip and Mary, No. 52; John Calibut's the younger, *Wards and Liveries*, 12 Elizabeth, vol. xii. No. 74; William Calibut's will, *Reg. Norvic. Ep. Cawston*; Catherine Walpole's will, u.s. *Reg. Coker*.

(14) *Page* 23, *line* 2. Collins, who had seen the register, gives the date of his baptism at Houghton 28th January, 1559-60.

(15) *Page* 23, *line* 13. He was born 24th June, 1532 or 1533.—*Adlard*, p. 16.

(16) *Page* 23, *line* 16. His will, dated 15th June, 1549, and proved at Norwich 2d May, 1554, is in the Registry at Norwich (*Wilkins*, fo. 255). His *eldest* son was Thomas Walpole, who died before his father, leaving behind him two sons, Henry and John. Henry died under age, as appears by his mother's will, which was proved in P.C.C., 26th January, 1579-80 (*Arundel*, fo. 3). She married twice after her first husband, THOMAS WALPOLE'S death, first to Thomas Fleet of Whaplode, co. Linc., Gent., and second to—Horden of Camberwell, whom also she survived. Her second son, JOHN, inherited the Lincolnshire estates, and at his death they were sold in obedience to his will, P.C.C., 13th October, 1590 (*Drury*, fo. 62), of which we shall hear more hereafter. The great bulk of the Lincolnshire property was left to CHRISTOPHER WALPOLE to enjoy till such time as his nephew Henry, or, in the event of his death, till his nephew John should have arrived at the age of twenty-six years. CHRISTOPHER WALPOLE must have had the usufruct of the property for at least twenty years. The fourth son, *Francis, i.e.*, the third alive at the death of HENRY WALPOLE of Herpley, appears to have died early.

(17) *Page* 23, *line* 25. See Dugdale's *Origines Juridicæ*, ch. xlviii. The account is too long to give *in extenso* here, but will well repay perusal by

those who have access to the book. The sum total of the expenses incurred by the incoming Serjeants amounted to the enormous sum of £667, 7s. 7d., which represents at least £5000 at the present time. The feast was held in the Inner Temple Hall, on the 16th October, 1555. In the "Bury Wills" (Camden Society, 1850) there is an inventory of the goods of MARGARET BAGSTER of HUNDEN, with the date 14th October, 1521, whereby it appears that even thus early Mr. WALPOLE was in practice, and had already learnt the art of getting fees out of his clients. Serjeant Walpole's coat of arms was to be seen in the large semicircular window of Gray's Inn Hall in Dugdale's time; and also in one of the windows of the Refectory of Serjeants' Inn in 1599, but it had disappeared from the latter place in 1660. —Dugdale u.s. (ed. 1671) pp. 302, 320, 321.

(18) *Page* 23, *line* 29. He had before his death immensely increased his landed property. He is owner of manors in Wymbottsham, Great and Little Massingham, Hillington, Congham, Depdale, and elsewhere, and of lands and houses all over the county of Norfolk, but principally in the north. His p.m. inquisition is a long document.—*Chancery, Norf.* 5 and 6 Philip and Mary. His will is at Somerset House.—P.C.C. *Reg. Moody*, fo. 6. His executors are MARTIN HASTINGS, Esq., HENRY SPELMAN, Gent., ROBERT COKE, Gent., GEFFREY COBBE, CHRISTOPHER WALPOLE, and THOMAS SCARLETT.

(19) *Page* 24, *line* 15. The extracts from the parish register of Docking will be found later on.

(20) *Page* 24, *line* 23. Blomefield, viii. 395. By a curious chance the original Sheriff's order for the surrender of a portion of the Anmer estate (Blomefield, u.s. 334) came into my possession with a parcel of similar documents some years ago. They were bought for me at a sale in London.

(21) *Page* 25, *line* 10. The WALPOLES had some salt works at WALPOLE, which appear to have been of some importance, as they are frequently mentioned in the wills and inquisitions of members of the family, in the fifteenth and sixteenth centuries.

Strype, in his *Memorials of Archbishop Parker* (i. p. 408), writes as follows:—"This year (1565) was a project for salt works in Kent set on foot by several persons of quality; one whereof was the Earl of Pembroke, and amongst the rest the Secretary Cecil and the Queen herself. . . . He [ABP. PARKER] told Secretary Cecil that he doubted not but that they had well considered the likelihood of the matter, wishing it good success, *better than he knew the like to take place about thirty years past in his county, about* WALSINGHAM *side. From whence came to* NORWICH *by cart great plenty. So that the price of the bushel fell from sixteenpence to sixpence. But after experience, they ceased of their bringing, and fell to their old salt again, three pecks whereof went further than a bushel of that white, fair, fine salt."*

(22) *Page 25, line 27.* See the very interesting collections published by Mr. W. B. Rye, entitled *England as seen by Foreigners*, 4to, Lond. 1865, pp. 70, 110, and especially the note on p. 196. In the Household Books of the L'Estranges of Hunstanton I find, under the year 1519, an account for *Liveries of thirteen servants.* In 1530 there is another account for wages paid to sixteen servants.—*Archæologia*, vol. xxv. pp. 424 and 493. Hunstanton Hall appears by these Household Books to have been as full of visitors for the greater part of the year as a large hotel. A regular list of "Strangers" was kept, and their names appear duly recorded. The house steward apologises for the largeness of his weekly bills in a somewhat plaintive strain, but modern housekeepers would be glad indeed if they could keep their expenses down to the sixteenth century figures. Take the following as an example. It is actually the largest weekly bill at Hunstanton in the year 1533.

" The xx[th] Weke. Straungers in the same weke."
" Mestrys Cobe & hyr syster, w[t] other off the cūtreye, and so the sm̃ of thys weke besyde gyste & store . . . xxviijs. ijd."

(23) *Page 25, line 35.* The following from Harrison's Preface to *Holinshed's Chronicle* (1577) is quoted in a note (p. 103) in Miss Sneyd's translation of *A Relation of the Island of England*, published by the Camden Society in 1847. "There are olde men yet dwelling in the village where I remayne, who have noted some things to be marvellously altered in Englande within their sound remembrance. One is the great amendment of lodging: for, sayde they, our fathers and we ourselves have lyen full ofte upon straw pallettes covered only with a sheete under coverlettes made of *dogswain* or *hop harlots* (I use their own terms) and a good round logge under their heads insteade of a bolster. If it were so that our fathers or the good man of the house had a materes or flockbed, and thereto a sacke of chafe to rest hys heade upon, he thought himselfe to be as well lodged as the lord of the towne, so well were they contented. Pillows were thought mete only for women in childbed. *As for servants, if they had any shete above them, it was well, for seldom had they any under their bodies, to keepe them from the pricking strawes, that ranne oft thorow the canvas and razed their hardened hides."* But see Mr. Furnival's "Forewords" to the *Babees Book*, E.E.T.S. 1868, p. 64 *et seq.*

(24) *Page 26, line 12.* The Great Bustard continued to haunt this part of Norfolk till this century. Mr. H. Stevenson, an authority on all matters of ornithology, assures me that "the last Great Bustard killed in Norfolk,

*and the last of the local race*, was a female, shot at LEXHAM in May 1838; another having been killed at DERSINGHAM in January of the same year. The extinction of the bustard in Great Britain dates from 1838." See Mr. Stevenson's *Birds of Norfolk*, vol. ii. p. 1-42, for a complete and interesting discussion of this subject.

(25) *Page* 26, *line* 15.   Blomefield, vii. 155.

(26) *Page* 26, *line* 22.   His name may be seen in the Lists of Admissions of Gray's Inn, 1521-1677.—*Harleian MSS.* No. 1912.   Students entered at the "Inns" much earlier in those days than now.

(27) *Page* 26, *line* 28.   *Entries of Preferments and Sales of Wards*, from 1 Mary to 1 Elizabeth, Com. Norff., Philip and Mary, 3 and 4.—P.R.O. This document sells the wardship to his mother.   By the *Lit. Pat.*, dated 30th October, 2 Elizabeth, *Court of Wards*, it is assigned to ROB. COOKE, Esq., and THOS. SCARLETT, Gent.   An allowance, which was then liberal, is made for his education.

## CHAPTER II.

## SCHOOL AND COLLEGE DAYS.

WHEN Queen Elizabeth came to the throne, there was only one Grammar School in the county of Norfolk, that, viz., which her father had intended to found, and which her brother actually did found, in the city of Norwich.(¹) When the free chapels were "suppressed," the chapel of St. John the Evangelist, in the precincts of the Cathedral Close, with the houses and premises thereto belonging, were granted to Sir Ed. Warner, Knight, and Richard Catline, Gent., who sold their rights to the Mayor and Commonalty of the city of Norwich.(²) Here the newly-established Grammar School was intended to be carried on, and probably was carried on in a languid, careless manner. The citizens appear to have been far more anxious to make the most of their Hospital Charter in the way of patronage and doles, than to use any portion of its revenues to secure to themselves a really efficient school, and, as the natural consequence of this policy, one of the first things we hear of is that when a Grammar School was set up at Yarmouth, in 1551, the corporation of that town found no difficulty in inducing "Mr. Hall, grammarian of Norwich," to leave his post and to remove to a better-paid mastership at the more attractive seaport.(³) The school would seem to have been closed for the next year or two; but in the third year of Queen Mary, "at an assembly holden and kept within the Guildhall,"(⁴) John Bukke, B.A., was appointed master of the Grammar School of the city, and under him appears to have been an usher or sub-master, one Henry Bird, who, whatever became of his chief, continued to discharge his duties as master during the whole of Mary's reign; (⁵) but the school was evidently starved by the city magnates, and the buildings were allowed to fall into decay. With the accession of Matthew Parker to the Primacy, a better day dawned. Mr. Walter Haugh or Hawe, a member of Archbishop Parker's own college, and a Master of Arts of eight years' standing, was appointed to the head-mastership, and a subscription was raised among the leading citizens and some of the county gentry to put the place into complete repair.(⁶) The school soon became famous, and among its earliest scholars was one who was destined to play an important part hereafter in the politics of England, and to earn from posterity the reputation of having been one of the ablest judges that ever sat upon the bench, and perhaps the profoundest lawyer of his time. Edward Coke, the future Chief-Justice of the Common Pleas, was for seven years a boy at Norwich School, and left it for Trinity College, Cambridge, in September, 1567. (⁷) Nor was he the only boy at Norwich at this time who afterwards attained to some celebrity: Nicholas Faunt (⁸) was there, who is said to have brought to England the first news of the St. Bartholomew massacre, and who, as secretary to Sir Francis Walsingham, was familiar with all the intrigues of Queen Elizabeth's court; and Robert Naunton,(⁹) author of the famous *Fragmenta Regalia,* a work which, as a wise and sagacious critique upon the reign of Elizabeth, by one who knew personally all the actors in the drama, stands alone in English literature. Contemporary, too, with these, but a very different notable, was the riotous and profligate Robert Greene, that audacious and prolific genius who even presumed to regard Shakspere as a rival dramatist. (¹⁰)

Among others who sent their sons to Norwich School at this

time were Christopher Walpole of Docking, and John Walpole of Houghton. In the brief account which both one and the other give of themselves when they entered the Noviciate at Tournay many years after, each speaks of himself as having been brought up in grammar and the *litteræ humaniores* "in patria," (¹¹) *i.e.*, in his own county—Edward says, for four years; Henry, *aliquamdiu*, *i.e.*, for some considerable time. Henry Walpole probably entered at the school in 1566 or 1567, for in those days boys were sent to the grammar schools at seven years of age. His first master was Mr. Hawe, who has been mentioned above, who died in 1569, and was buried in Norwich Cathedral. (¹²) To him succeeded a scholar of some eminence in his day, one Stephen Limbert, of Magdalen College, Cambridge. Magdalen College at this time was presided over by Roger Kelke, a leading spirit among the Puritan faction then very strong at the university. (¹³) Limbert had followed in the master's steps, and was ready and eager to show himself no half-hearted disciple. In the year 1565 a violent agitation had been raised in the university against the wearing of the surplice or any academical or ecclesiastical habit, and the feeling against everything that approximated to Romish fashions in garb or ritual had displayed itself in more than one noisy and extravagant outbreak. This feeling Limbert had brought with him from Cambridge to Norwich; and as he had probably witnessed the great surplice riot in the university, so he was quite prepared to join in a similar protest against vestments, or stained glass, or organ music at Norwich, if the opportunity presented itself. In the very year he came to Norwich there had been a violent anti-ritual demonstration in the Cathedral, headed *by five of the prebendaries* "and others with them;" who, in the absence of the dean, but apparently with something like connivance on the bishop's part, thought proper to march in a kind of procession into the choir, and after committing various unseemly outrages, ended by breaking down the organ, and doing their best to stop the continuance of the choral service. The bishop would have been glad enough to pass over the affair, disgraceful as it was, without notice, but when the news of these proceedings came to the ears of the Queen she was extremely indignant, and wrote a very severe letter of censure upon the bishop for his negligence, and ordered the offenders to appear before Archbishop Parker and give account of themselves for their evil behaviour. No harm, however, seems to have come upon any of the parties concerned, and it is to be presumed that the organ was repaired, and that things went on pretty much as before. (14) But not many days after Henry Walpole left Norwich School, previous to his entry at Cambridge, *a second riot* occurred, and this time we read that " Innovation was suddenly brought about into the Cathedral ... at evening service ... by *Limbert, Chapman, and Roberts*, then of this church. These, in the time of reading the lessons, had inveighed against the manner of the singing them, and termed it *disordered*, and wished it utterly thence to be banished. And one of them starting up at that time, *took upon him to use another and a new form of service*, contrary to that ordered by her Majesty and the book." By this time one at least of the previous malcontents had learned his lesson: Dr. Gardiner, though he had been at the head of the former disturbance, had now succeeded to the deanery, and was not without hopes of even greater preferment, for Parkhurst was reported to be in declining health, the bishopric might fall vacant any day, and the dean was too shrewd a courtier not to have an eye to his own interest. Accordingly he " stood up and confuted the reasons the others had brought," and even committed one of the offenders to prison; but with characteristic astuteness he managed to insinuate that some of the blame of these mutinous irregularities rested upon the bishop, through whose laxity mainly such things had come to pass. (15) One would have supposed that such indecent violence would have been visited with severe censure and punishment. But no! the rioters were mildly reproved and warned against any repetition of such a scandal; and there the matter seems to have ended, and the bishop, if he called the offenders to account, seems to have troubled them no more.

Dr. John Parkhurst, who was at this time Bishop of Norwich, had been a fellow of Merton and tutor of Bishop Jewell. "Better for poetry and oratory than divinity," says Wood. He had put forth in youth a volume of Latin verse which he republished in his later years, though the critics said there were in those poems things that were at least unseemly. In Queen Mary's time he joined the exodus, and crossed the sea; and he appears to have suffered more privations than some others of the fugitives. In Switzerland he was highly esteemed and held in honour for his learning and piety. He had settled at Zurich, not Geneva, and henceforth Zurich and its ecclesiastical constitution were very dear to his heart. As firm and resolute as any man in his opposition to Romanism, Zuinglius, and not John Calvin, was his master and pattern, and his rule he would have been glad to carry out in his own diocese. ([16])

Dr. Gardiner's predecessor in the Deanery was John Salisbury, a man of learning and some mark. He had been a student at both universities, and a Benedictine monk at Bury St. Edmund's. Here he incurred the suspicion of heresy, and for some years was kept under restraint in the abbey by order of Cardinal Wolsey. Henry VIII. appointed him Prior of the monastery of St. Faith at Horsham, near Norwich, and subsequently, in 1536, Suffragan Bishop of Thetford. In 1537 we find him Archdeacon of Anglesey; in 1538 a Canon of Norwich Cathedral; next year he was installed Dean. His deanery he continued to hold with the archdeaconry and other rich preferments, till the accession of Queen Mary, when he was deprived for being married. At the accession of Queen Elizabeth he was restored. About the year 1565 he preached a sermon in Norwich Cathedral which created at the time a great sensation, and so much provoked the gentry of the county that he was accused of favouring the old religion, and was for a time suspended once more from his deanery. He managed to defeat the machinations of his enemies, and in 1571 received a dispensation from Archbishop Parker to hold the bishopric of Sodor and Man, the Deanery of Norwich, the Archdeaconry of Anglesey, and the Rectories of Thorpe-super-Montem in the Diocese of Lincoln, and of Diss in the Diocese of Norwich, all which he seems to have retained till his death. ([17])

There were six canons or prebendaries belonging to the Cathedral Chapter at this time. Of these, Edmund Chapman was apparently the most pronounced as a zealous Puritan of the advanced iconoclastic school. He appears as one of the leaders of the riot in the Cathedral in 1570 and again in 1575, and his irrepressible temperament made him a somewhat troublesome personage to the authorities. At last his erratic and defiant habits, and his reluctance to submit to any discipline, could no longer be borne, and he was deprived of his canonry for non-conformity in 1576. Bishop Aylmer, when compelled to proceed against him, was inclined to show him great leniency, and suggested that he should be sent to some remote part of the kingdom, where he might be kept from doing much harm, and be, possibly, employed in doing some good as a preacher against Popery. ([18])

Thomas Fowle, another of the prebendaries, was implicated in the same disturbances with Chapman. He, too, was a vehement Puritan, and when, in 1572, a commission was issued for proceeding against the popish recusants in Norfolk, his name was put upon the commission as that of a man who was not likely to spare the recalcitrant gentry. ([19])

Entirely of the same mind, and quite as conspicuous as the other members of the chapter on the occasion of the first riot, was Dr. John Walker, a somewhat famous preacher among the Puritan clergy of the time. He, too, got into trouble in the sequel for non-conformity, but nevertheless was rewarded with substantial preferment, and when the farce of a conference with

Campion was carried out in 1580, he was one of those who took a leading part in the discussion. ([20])

The last of that band of zealots was George Gardiner, a pluralist among pluralists even in those days. He had been a fellow of Queen's College, Cambridge, and it was alleged that in Queen Mary's time he had been conspicuous as a persecutor of the gospellers in Cambridge. Whether it was so or not, he showed no sign of any Romish tendencies from the time he became a Minor Canon of Norwich Cathedral in 1561, till his death as Dean in 1589. He appears never to have lost an opportunity for advancing himself and his own interest, and held at various times no less than fourteen pieces of preferment: at his death he was Dean, Chancellor, and Archdeacon of Norwich, and Rector of Ashill, Blofield, and Forncett, besides holding one or two other benefices scarcely less valuable. ([21])

Only two more of the Canons of Norwich remain to be mentioned, Nicholas Wendon and Thomas Smith, who held their stalls for ten years, but were deprived at last, when it was found that *they were both laymen!* ([22])

Thus a schoolboy at Norwich in these times was of necessity reared in a very heated atmosphere. If daily and hourly tirades against the Pope and Babylon could make a lad a sound Protestant, few schoolboys in England could have been in a more favourable position for arriving at such a frame of mind. Unfortunately there is in some boys' nature a certain perversity of will which leads them to revolt from influences forced upon them too obtrusively; and when a youth is subjected to a hard and repressive discipline ([23])—never cheered by a gleam of sympathy or softened by a word of tenderness— a time is apt to come when he turns out a stubborn rebel, and the reaction from habitual submission sets in at last in a form which his elders least desire to see, and are least prepared to expect.

Moreover, though bishop, and dean, and chapter, and schoolmaster were all of one mind, it must not be supposed that there was no minority who — "popishly inclined" — were sulkily and obstinately clinging to their own opinions with a troublesome and uncompromising tenacity. The Norfolk gentry were almost unanimous in their dislike of Puritanism. The conflict with Rome in the latter half of the sixteenth century was a war of classes; it was almost precisely of the same character as the conflict with the Crown became a century later. In both cases, speaking generally, the "optimates" were on one side, the "plebeians" on the other, and the smouldering jealousy of class against class displayed itself at times in other than religious bickerings. Very significant is the story of that mad conspiracy of sundry of the *gentlemen of the county* and others in the year 1570, which had for its object the forcible expulsion of the strangers in Norwich "from the city and the realm," and which ended in the indictment of ten of these gentlemen for high treason, three of whom were hung, drawn, and quartered, and the rest kept in jail, with the forfeiture of their goods and lands, for life. ([24]) The gentry of England were at this time almost a caste; not a whit less arrogant, haughty, and overbearing because they must have known that their order had been fearfully broken in upon of late, and knew, only too well, that they were poorer and weaker than their sires.

It must be remembered, too, that though the towns had preachers enough and to spare, and though the town churches were served by a ministry, some of whom were men of eloquence, zeal, and power, whose earnestness was patent and their piety sincere and glowing; yet in the country villages, and among the agricultural population, far out of the reach of the pulpit agitators, the tidings that came at times of all this turmoil of religious excitement only served to perplex and amaze. To the villager it seemed as if chaos had come again. The townsmen were going on too fast for the "lobs of the country." How could these latter unlearn the lessons of their youth so easily? The quick-witted citizen looked down with contemptuous pity at the slow-thinking rustic and the heavy squire, and these returned the sneer with a sullen scowl of their own. What had all these changes of the last twenty years done for *them?* What were they likely to do? When King Edward died, the county clergy had been turned out of their Norfolk livings by hundreds. ([25]) When Queen Mary died, the Marian priests forsook their cures in shoals. What would be the next thing? There had been no peace since the old order had changed. How pressing the need of new clergy was is plain from the fact that the very week after Archbishop Parker's consecration he ordained twenty-two priests and deacons at Lambeth,([26]) and two months afterwards no less than one hundred and fifty-five at a single ordination. It was made a matter of special provision that the newly-ordained clergy should be required to serve more than one cure.([27]) A new order was instituted, that of "Readers," who were only allowed to read the service, but forbidden to preach or even administer the sacrament of Baptism; but these men were a miserable makeshift, and upon trial the newly-ordained clergy, as a rule, were found deplorably wanting. Very soon it became necessary to address to the bishops a letter forbidding them to ordain any more mechanics, and the Ecclesiastical Commissioners put forth certain Articles to enforce at any rate the semblance of discipline, and, among other things, "abstinence from mechanical sciences" was enjoined "as well to ministers as to readers."

But not only was the religious destitution of the country parishes patent and deplorable, but to earnest and thoughtful men in the large towns things were not at all as they should be. To a lad of any refinement of feeling, and reverence for the sacred associations of the past, there must have been something very shocking in all this organ-breaking and glass-smashing. Was it likely that men whose zeal burst forth in these vulgar and passionate outbreaks would be likely to command the respect and esteem of the gentler and more affectionate among the rising generation? They, too, had their fund of enthusiasm. How if that enthusiasm should find vent for itself in quite other expressions than those in which the passions of the mob were now exhausting themselves? How if these coarse excesses of the dominant faction should defeat their own object and make many a young man begin to think that there might be worse things even than "monkery"—that a sour "presbyter" was, after all, but the "priest writ large," and that it was quite possible to conceive a tyranny more galling and odious even than that of the Pope of Rome?

Meanwhile there were other scenes which a schoolboy must have witnessed in those days, which were not calculated to make him feel at ease. At Norwich itself, religious fanaticism in every form was rampant. Upwards of 4000 Flemings had their own peculiar worship, their sects, their "views," their broils, almost their faction-fights; crazy prophets rose up in the streets, claiming to be inspired; "Anabaptists" propounded new theories of the rights of property, and even were for introducing a reformed code of morals. Whispers were heard of a real new revelation, whose apostle or high priest none could name, whose adherents called themselves by a strange title, to be heard of by and by often enough when David George's rhapsodies should have become translated into English jargon, and when the "family of love" should have had its martyrs and confessors who suffered they scarce knew why. ([28])

In the face of all this wild confusion, it is not to be wondered at if there was a party in England who had no love for the new learning,—a party, too, that, in the upper ranks of English society, was rather increasing in weight, influence, and numbers, though the "great middle class," the tradesmen and the "common people," were all on the other side.

Looking at the matter from our present point of view, we are too ready to regard the excommunication of Elizabeth as nothing but a stupendous blunder. It was a blunder because it failed; but to the statesmen of that day, to those who were not the least sagacious and far-sighted of their generation, the issuing of the Bull seemed a very bold and skilful move, which called for the utmost determination, promptitude, and resolve to meet it. To them it was nothing less than the menace of a new crusade, and a call to the territorial aristocracy of this country to join in a holy league, not only for the restoration of the faith but for the reconstitution of society. What the enormous power of the sovereign had done in Spain, what the noblesse with the Guises at their head seemed in a fair way of doing in France, that the papal advisers believed might be effected by the gentry of England. A counter reformation which should end in stamping out heresy was regarded as a consummation not only devoutly to be wished but even likely to be achieved. How much the Bartholomew massacre, following so close as it did upon the promulgation of the Bull, contributed to strengthen the hands of the English government, it would be difficult to say. Certainly when the penal laws were enacted, they were directed against the gentry almost exclusively; fines and forfeiture of goods were terrible only for those who had something to lose, and it soon became a point of honour with the squirearchy to stand up for the old religion, and to throw in their lot with the *gentlemanly* sufferers for conscience' sake; the "good old Tories" of this time clung stubbornly to the past, and would not accept the logic of facts; but the gauntlet which the Pope threw down was taken up with a grim satisfaction by the Queen and her council, and from henceforth there was no hesitation and no mercy.

Had there been no provocation? Was there not a cause? Assuredly there was. It is not for a wise man to defend the one side or the other, least of all to defend the audacious and irritating aggressions which made the conflict an absolute necessity and compromise impossible. But now that that struggle may be said to be practically at an end,—at any rate so far at an end that the political ascendancy of the Papacy over this country at any future time is simply inconceivable,—

it may be well to remind readers ignorant of the fact, that there were two sides in Queen Elizabeth's days, and that for young men of enthusiastic temperament and chivalrous nature, for men who instinctively chose the weaker side and threw in their lot with the persecuted rather than the persecutors, there would be an absolute fascination in the creed that seemed to them to be now remorselessly assailed, and a vehement opposition arose to the statesmanship which perhaps had been driven, and at any rate seemed pledged, to a war of extermination.

. . . . . . . . .

At last the school days came to an end, and on the 15th of January, 1575, Henry Walpole matriculated at Cambridge. He entered at St. Peter's College, at that time presided over by Dr. Andrew Perne.

Dr. Perne was a Norfolk man, and his family were possessed of some landed property at Pudding Norton, not far from Houghton. He was notorious through life as a trimmer, whose astute accommodation of himself to the prevailing winds and currents of opinion had made his name proverbial among the wits of the time. (29) In King Henry's days he had been preferred to the rich living of Walpole St. Peter, and to that of Pulham, in his native county. As one of Edward VI.'s chaplains, he was appointed to preach the doctrines of the Reformation through the remote parts of the kingdom. He signed without a murmur the Catholic Articles of Queen Mary in 1555, and the Thirty-nine Articles of Elizabeth in 1562; in 1573 he preached at Norwich against the Puritans, and in 1580 he was engaged in a conference with Feckenham, Abbot of Westminster, at Wisbeach. Witty, genial, urbane, and learned, he had a rare faculty of being able to carry off his frequent tergiversations with a grace and courtesy which any diplomatist might envy, and which actually gained him a certain measure of confidence from both sides. A latitudinarian, who professed to see the good in everything, he could tolerate Papist and Puritan alike. He could even make some efforts to abate the violence of the persecutor's zeal and to moderate the rancour of polemics. His college appears to have been the natural place of resort for extreme men, who might count on the protection of the master's broad shield so long as his own interests and prospects were not compromised. He would certainly "leave his men alone," and would not worry them by too prying scrutiny, or harass them with too strict a discipline; and the college throve as the master prospered. (³⁰)

On the same day that Henry Walpole entered at Peterhouse, another young man of diametrically opposite proclivities was admitted at the same college. Dudley Fenner was the eldest son of a Kentish gentleman, and heir to a large estate; he was almost exactly of the same age as his fellow-collegian, and the subsequent career of the two men offers some remarkable parallels. Fenner was from the outset a rigid and fervent Puritan; Walpole as earnest and devoted a Catholic. Fenner was suspected of being concerned in the Marprelate books; Walpole certainly had a hand in Parsons' writings. Neither proceeded to a degree at the university, both being deterred by the tests and engagements which every graduate was compelled to submit to. Both were driven into exile for conscience' sake; both were imprisoned; both exercised their several ministries in Belgium, the one as a Puritan preacher, the other as a Jesuit priest; both were for a time employed in the same town of Antwerp, at no very long interval; and when Dudley Fenner lay upon his deathbed at Middlebwrg in the winter of 1589, Henry Walpole was lying in prison at Flushing, scarcely five miles off, in hourly peril of losing his life too as an exile in a foreign land. How little could either of these young men have guessed what was in store for them as they attended the same lectures, dined in the same hall,—both of them, too, for different reasons shirking the same "chapels," and, doubtless, fiercely arguing with one another on the profoundest points of controversy, for which they were both in the sequel to suffer so cruelly, and to labour so long!

Among the Ordinances drawn up by Archbishop Parker for Norwich School, special provision was made for the teaching of Greek.([31]) It is almost incredible how few at Cambridge even professed a knowledge of the language or literature of Hellas. Baker tells us that at this time no more than two fellows of St. John's were "Grecians;" and it is pretty certain that almost as few knew anything about it as now do of Sanscrit.([32]) But at Peterhouse Charles Horne, who was elected to a fellowship in Henry Walpole's second year, was a distinguished Grecian, and doubtless gave lectures in the college. There, too, was Richard Bainbrigg the antiquary, already making collections, and Degory Nichols, a divine, who scandalised people by his gay attire— "too fine for scholars." The two Bacons were fellow-commoners at Trinity—Anthony and Francis the great; while at Pembroke, across the street, so near that a child might toss a biscuit from one college to the other, Spenser, by this time an M.A., whom the undergraduates would regard with some little awe, was writing his *Shepherd's Calendar*, Kirke and Gabriel Harvey already recognising in him a poet for the ages.

A year after Henry Walpole entered at St. Peter's, his cousin Edward matriculated at the same college, and along with him came four more of their kindred or close neighbours—Edward Yelverton of Rougham, one of the Cobbes of Sandringham, Philip Paris of Pudding Norton, and Barclay (otherwise Bernard) Gardiner of Coxford Abbey. Of these young men now studying together at the same college, three were to become eventually members of the Society of Jesus, and another, Edward Yelverton, was destined to suffer through all his life for his obstinate adherence to the Romish cause.([33])

This is not the place to dwell upon the subject of Cambridge studies during the period we are engaged with, the less so as neither Henry nor Edward Walpole proceeded to any degree at the university. That both young men were diligent students seems clear from the facility with which they obtained admission to the Society of Jesus, and we are expressly told that Henry Walpole was regarded as a man of learning and promise when he first presented himself at the College of Rheims.([34]) His name appears on the buttery books of the college for the last time on the 17th April 1579. He had already been entered at Gray's Inn the year before.([35]) His university career had come to an end, and it remained for him now to qualify himself for a career at the bar. Whether Edward Walpole remained behind at Cambridge, or had already left the university, we cannot tell.

# NOTES TO CHAPTER II.

(1) *Page* 36, *line* 5. The Charter of Edward VI. was first printed in Burton's *Antiquitates Capellæ D. Johannis Evangelistæ hodie Scholæ Regiæ Norvicensis*, which was published among Sir Thomas Browne's posthumous works. The stipend of the head-master was at first £10 a year, with a house free of all charges : the stipend of the usher was £6, 13s. 4d., with a house. The head-master's stipend was doubled in 1562, and again doubled in 1610. It continued to be £40 a year till Mr. Lovering's appointment in 1636, when the head-master received £50 a year and a house, the usher £30 and no house. Burton's work was reprinted with some additions in 1862 by the late John Longe, Esq. of Spixworth Park.

(2) *Page* 36, *line* 10. See Blomefield, iv. 59. Burton has printed the Award upon the dispute between the Dean and Chapter and the Corporation, which Blomefield refers to.

(3) *Page* 36, *line* 21. Manship's *History of Yarmouth*, vol. i. p. 232. He seems to be identical with the Walter Haugh mentioned below. He stayed only two years at Yarmouth.

(4) *Page* 37, *line* 1. The document is preserved among the *Miscellaneous Deeds and Documents*, in the archives of the Corporation of Norwich. Already the city magnates had begun to evade the conditions of their Charter *by dividing the schoolhouse between the head-master and his usher*, though they were bound to provide a house for each of them. " . . . . And also we do give, grant, and confirm to the said John Bukke for the exercising of the said office of Schoolmaster all that the crypt of the late Chapel and house of St. John within the precincts of the Cathedral Church of the Holy Trinity of Norwich, and all those houses, buildings, outer yards, and gardens whatsoever, being occupied or used as part or parcel of the said soil of the said Chapel or Charnel House. . . . *Except and always reserved within the foresaid charnel or house a sufficient habitation and dwelling for such person as now is or any time hereafter shall be Usher of the same school for the time being to live and inhabit in.*"

(5) *Page* 37, *line* 6. Strype prints from the Baker MSS. a highly-interesting paper, of which a copy is to be found in the Registry at Norwich.

"Articles to be inquired of in the Metropolitical Visitation of the most reverend Father in God, Matthew, by the providence of God, Archbishop of Canterbury . . . in all and singular cathedral and collegiate churches within his province of Canterbury." The replies for Norwich were sent in by Mr. George Gardiner, then one of the prebendaries, and disclose a deplorable state of affairs. In reply to the question, "Whether your grammar school be well ordered? &c."—a question which assumed that every cathedral chapter was expected to maintain a grammar school—Gardiner says, " . . . this respondent saith, that there is no grammar school at all within their house, saving, that, as he saith, they allow xx marks by year *to one Mr. Bird* who teacheth a grammar school in the city, and receiveth such scholars as they send him, of which he knoweth not one, as he saith. And the whole order of the school is left to Mr. Bird's discretion, which he thinketh to be well done, as he saith; and believeth that he bringeth up them that are under him in the fear of God."—Strype, *Parker*, B. iii. No. 54. This paper belongs to the spring of 1567. Five years after this Mr. Bird was associated with Sir Nicholas Bacon, the Bishop of Norwich, Thomas Lord Wentworth, and some of the most considerable people of the county, in a commission for examining suspected Papists. When Dean Salisbury died in 1573, "great suit was made" to get the deanery for Mr. Bird, and we read that "the city of Norwich had written up for one Mr. Bird, a very godly man, and well-learned." Mr. Gardiner, however, obtained the preferment.

(6) *Page* 37, *line* 13. See Blomefield, iv. 60. There is a fuller account of the restoration in Burton's *Antiquitates*. Some of the stained glass still remained in the windows on the north side as late as Blomefield's time (1744). In the archives of the city in the Guildhall, I came upon a memorandum, dated 24th September 1747, of some dispute between the Corporation and Mr. Redington, the head-master of the school at that time, in which it is said, "Corporation have repaired the glass in the windows, *which are frequently broke by the scholars, and are expensive.*"

(7) *Page* 37, *line* 21. His father, Robert Coke of Mileham, was one of Serjeant Walpole's executors.—See n. 18, chap. i.

(8) *Page* 37, *line* 23. He was probably a son of Robert Fonde or Faunt, who was Vicar of Kimberley in 1569. He matriculated at Caius College, Cambridge, in June 1572. There are several letters of his in Birch's *Elizabeth.*—See Cooper's *Athenæ Cant.*

(9) *Page* 37, *line* 27. Sir Robert Naunton set up a monument to his old schoolmaster (Limbert) at Norwich, with an inscription upon a brass plate (which existed in Blomefield's time), when he was already advanced in life. This was after he was knighted in 1615.

(10) *Page* 37, *line* 34. There is a complete list of Greene's Works in Cooper's *Athenæ Cant.*, where, too, may be found the best account of him.

(11) *Page* 38, *line* 6. The *Album of the Tournai Noviciate* is now in the Royal Library at Brussels (*MS. No.* 1016). I have printed Henry Walpole's account of himself written with his own hand, " Circa Natalem Dni. A°. 1591," in the *Walpole Letters*, 4to, Norwich, 1873. Edward's autobiography given in the same MS. will be found *infra*.

(12) *Page* 38, *line* 12. The inscription upon his monument in the cathedral is given by Blomefield, iv. 62. He entered at Corpus Christi College, Cambridge, in 1552, having probably been elected to a scholarship from some other college. He graduated B.A. in 1554. Master's *History of Corpus*, by Lamb.

(13) *Page* 38, *line* 16. See Cooper's *Annals of Cambridge*, vol. ii. p. 218 *et seq.*, and Baker's *History of St. John's College*, edited by Prof. Mayor, vol. i. p. 162. Baker's brief account of the condition of St. John's at this time is long enough to convince us of the degradation of the college. Prof. Mayor has collected the notices of the Surplice Feuds and other disorders of the time in the exhaustive way which is characteristic of all his work.— (Vol. ii. p. 586 *et seq.*)

STEPHEN LIMBERT was entered as a sizar at Magdalen College, Cambridge, 12th November 1561. On the death of Mr. Haugh he succeeded to the head-mastership of Norwich. He married Katherine Sutton of Frettenham on the 27th April 1573 (P.R.), and by her had a family of ten children, whose baptisms are recorded in the register of St. Mary in the Marsh, Norwich, where also we find the entry of his burial, 10th October 1598. Cooper (*Athenæ Cantab.*), led astray by a misprint in Blomefield, asserts that he was a master at Norwich in 1555, which is certainly incorrect. In the MSS. of the University Library at Cambridge there is a mysterious letter of his addressed to Bishop Parkhurst, proving him to have been on intimate terms with the Bishop; but he appears never to have taken Orders, which accounts for his not getting preferment. In Whitney's *Emblems*, 4to, Leyden, 1580, there are some verses addressed to him by the author, and some prefatory verses by Limbert. When Elizabeth came to Norwich in 1578, Limbert was very graciously received by the Queen, to whom he was deputed to make a Latin speech. It is printed in Blomefield, and is a pedantic and pretentious harangue. Sir Robert Naunton's monument to Limbert has disappeared.

(14) *Page* 39, *line* 10. Strype, *Parker*, ii. 36. This first riot took place about the middle of September 1570. The letter of Queen Elizabeth to Bishop Parkhurst on the subject is dated 25th September 1570.—*P.R.O. Domestic*, Eliz., vol. lxxiii. n. 68.

(15) *Page* 39, *line* 32. Strype's *Annals*, vol. II. i. 485. The Limbert riot occurred some time in January. Parkhurst died 2d February 1574-5. It is evident that Bp. Freake lost very little time, after his appointment to the See of Norwich, in attempting to reform his diocese, and that he carried things with a high hand. Among *Lord Calthorpe's MSS.* vol. cx. fo. 133, there is a curious "Petition of certain aggrieved ministers" at Norwich, who protest against slanders, defaming them as schismatics, and on their part denouncing *Jesuits* (*five years before any Jesuit had ever set foot in England*), Anabaptists, Libertines, Family of Love, &c. " . . . And if the Bishop proceed to urge them as he hath begun, surely it will bring a wonderful ruin to this Church here in Norwich and round about. There be already xv or xx godly exercises of preaching or catechising put down in this city *by the displacing of three preachers.*" . . . . The document is dated 25th September 1576. Freake was elected Bishop of Norwich, 15th July 1575. His election was not *confirmed* till the 14th November. Bishop Freake had been an Augustinian monk at Waltham Abbey, and was one of those who received a pension of £5 a year.

(16) *Page* 40, *line* 19. Wood, *Athen. Oxon. Ed. Bliss*, vol. i. 412. Strype's *Annals*, II. i. 425. Archbishop Parker evidently had but a mean opinion of Parkhurst, and a tone of something like contempt is observable in his letters to him. Bishop Parkhurst had incurred the suspicion "even of the best sort for his remissness in ordering his clergy" as early as 1561. See a letter of Cecil in the *Parker Correspondence*, p. 149.—(Parker Soc.)

(17) *Page* 41, *line* 8. Wood's *Athenæ Oxon*. ii. 808; Cooper's *Athenæ Cant*. i. 318; Strype, *Parker*, ii. 80.

(18) *Page* 41, *line* 23. Cooper, *Athenæ Cant*. i. 382; Strype, *Aylmer*, p. 36. He appears to have been deprived of his stall at Norwich in 1576, for Launcelot Thexton succeeded in February 1576-7.—Le Neve, *Fasti*.

(19) *Page* 41, *line* 29. He was a Fellow of St. John's College, Cambridge, and appears to have obtained his stall at Norwich through Sir Nicholas Bacon. He had hardly been installed before an attempt was made to induce him to resign in favour of John Foxe the Martyrologist. This he declined to do, and he held his canonry till 1581. Strype, *Annals*, I. ii. 44; and Cooper's *Ath. Cant.* i. 452.

(20) *Page* 42, *line* 2. He became eventually Prebendary of St Paul's. There is much about him in Strype's *Parker*. See, too, Cooper, *Ath. Cant.* vol. ii. p. 37.

(21) *Page* 42, *line* 15. Cooper's *Ath. Cant.* ii. 55. He obtained the

Deanery by the intercession of Robert Earl of Leicester.—Strype, *Annals*, II. i. 448. Archbishop Parker tried to get the Deanery for his chaplain, Mr. Still, but in vain.—*Parker Correspondence*, p. 451.

(22) *Page* 42, *line* 19. Parker gives a deplorable account of the state of the Norwich Chapter, and, indeed, of the whole diocese, in a letter to Lady Bacon, dated 6th February 1567-8.—*Correspondence*, p. 311. Five years afterwards he again speaks with some bitterness on the same subject: "the church is miserable," he says. In the former letter Parker relates his interview with Smith, whom he advised to resign his stall or take Orders. Smith declined to do either the one or the other. Nicholas Wendon, besides being a canon of Norwich, was actually Archdeacon of Suffolk and Rector of Witnesham. In 1576 he became a professed Romanist, and slipped away to the Continent, where he probably ended his career.—Le Neve's *Fasti*; Cooper's *Athenæ Cant.* i. 384; Strype's *Parker*, iii. 159.

(23) *Page* 42, *line* 28. How cruel and pitiless the treatment of schoolboys was at this time is abundantly proved by such a weight of evidence as would be wearisome to the reader even to refer to. Roger Ascham's *Scole master* and Brindley's *Grammar School* may be regarded as protests against the brutality of the sixteenth century pedagogues.

(24) *Page* 43, *line* 18. Blomefield's *Norfolk*, iii. 284; *P.R.O., Domestic*, Eliz., vol. lxxi. No. 60, 61, 62, and vol. lxxiii. No. 28.

(25) *Page* 44, *line* 6. I have gone carefully through the Bishop's Register for the Diocese of Norwich, for the year ending 25th March 1554, and I find no fewer than two hundred and twenty-eight new incumbents presented in the twelve months to benefices *in the County of Norfolk alone*. Only twenty-six of these were occasioned by the death of the previous holders of the livings. This subject requires a more thorough examination than it has yet received. I *conjecture* that in many instances the monks dispossessed by Henry VIII. were presented to benefices by Queen Mary.

(26) *Page* 44, *line* 12. Strype's *Parker*, i. 229. Strype (*Aylmer*, p. 21) says, "Many of the old Incumbents (1577) and Curates were such as were fitter to sport with the timbrel and pipe than to take in their hands the book of the Lord." Grindal ordained nearly ninety persons in 1559.— Strype's *Grindal*, p. 53. See, too, *Annals*, I. i. 233.

(27) *Page* 44, *line* 15. Strype, *Annals*, I. i. 265; Parker, i. 180, 194; ii. 85.

(28) *Page* 45, *line* 25. Froude, *Hist. England*, x. p. 112; Blomefield, iii. 364; *Parker Correspondence*, p. 247; Fuller, *Church History*, B. ix. s. ii. § 10.

See especially his account of the Familists, s. iii. § 36. "These Familists (besides many monstrosities they maintained about their communion with God) attenuated all Scriptures into allegories; and, under pretence to turn them into spirit, made them airy, empty, nothing. They counterfeited revelations; and those, not explicatory or applicatory of Scripture (such may and must be allowed to God's servants in all ages), but additional thereunto, and of equal necessity and infallibility to be believed therewith. In a word, as in the small-pox (pardon my plain and homely, but true and proper, comparison), when at first they kindly come forth, every one of them may severally and distinctly be discerned; but when once they run and matter, they break one into another, and can no longer be dividedly discovered; so though at first there was a real difference betwixt Familists, Enthusiasts, Antinomians (not to add high-flown Anabaptists), in their opinions, yet (process of time plucking up the pales betwixt them) afterwards they did so interfere amongst themselves, that it is almost impossible to bank and bound their several absurdities." Strype (*Parker*, ii. 69, and *Annals*, II. i. 487) gives a good account of the Brownists and their eccentric founder. Fuller, u.s. B. ix. sect. vi. § 3, says, "For my own part (whose nativity Providence placed within a mile of this Brown's charge [*i.e.*, benefice]), I have when a youth often beheld him." He proceeds to tell a story of his having been carried to jail at Northampton, where he died, in a "cart with a feather bed provided to carry him." His offence was an assault upon a rate collector.—*Cf.*, too, *Annals*, II. i. 483.

There is a long and curious account of the Brownists in Ephraim Pagitt's *Heresiography; or, a Description and History of the Heretics and Sectaries sprung up in these times.* London, 1661. Hanbury gives nearly twenty pages to Browne and his doctrines. *Historical Memorials relating to the Independents*, vol. i. p. 19 *et seq.*

(29) *Page* 47, *line* 22. "*Jack.* What Doctor Pearne? Why, he is the notablest turncoat in all this land, there is none comparable to him. Why, every boy hath him in his mouth; for it is made a proverb, both of old and young, that if one have a coat or cloak that is turned they say it is *Pearned.*" From "A Dialogue, wherein is plainly laide open, the tyrannical dealing of the Lord Bishop against God's children," &c. This is one of the Marprelate Tracts, and was originally published in 1589, and "Reprinted in the time of the Parliament," 1640.

(30) *Page* 48, *line* 10. There is an exhaustive account of him in Cooper's *Athenæ Cant.* In 1573 there were sixty pensioners at St. Peter's.—Cooper, *Annals*, ii. 315.

(31) *Page* 49, *line* 5. I discovered these "ordinances" in the archives of the city of Norwich, and transcribed them in 1862. They are too long

## SCHOOL AND COLLEGE DAYS.    57

to reprint here. The Greek authors appointed to be read are *Lucian's Dialogues, Hesiod, Homer,* and *Euripides,* and the head-master is required to see that the boys of the sixth form "attain to some competent knowledge of the Greek tongue."

(32) *Page* 49, *line* 9. See Baker's *History of St. John's,* by Prof. Mayor, p. 171 and 180, and the notes on the last passage, p. 598.

(33) *Page* 49, *line* 31. I am indebted to the Registrar of the University, Rev. H. R. Luard, for permission to search the documents in his custody, and to make the necessary extracts from them. I find that in the January of 1579-1580 the following, among others, were admitted to the B.A. degree, and I give the names here because they will occur again in the course of my narrative. EDWARD YELVERTON (of Rougham, co. Norfolk); ROBERT REMINGTON (whom Henry Walpole calls his tutor); MILES SANDS (who took part in the disputation at York, 1594); GEORGE STRANSHAM (*alias* POTTER, who subsequently became a Catholic priest and got into trouble); ARTHUR DAUBENY (of Sharington, mentioned by H. Walpole in his examination); PHILIP PARIS (of Pudding Norton, a Recusant); JOHN COBBE (of Sandringham).

EDWARD WALPOLE matriculated as of St. Peter's in May 1576. DUDLEY FENNER was a Fellow Commoner of the college. BARTLEY [*sic*] GARDINER matriculated as a pensioner in March 1577-8.

(34) *Page* 50, *line* 5. 1582, 7° die Julii. Ex Anglia ad nos venit D. Hen. Walpoole, disertus gravis et pius. *Douay Diary.*

(35) *Page* 50, *line* 7. I have to thank the Rev. J. Porter, now Master of St. Peter's, for this information, taken from the Books of the College. The entry of Henry Walpole at Gray's Inn is to be found in *Harl. MSS.* 1912 (*Lists of Admissions of Gray's Inn,* 1521-1677).

## CHAPTER III.

# THE EXCOMMUNICATION AND ITS RESULTS.

"We must now take, and that of truth, into observation, that until the tenth of her reign, her times were calm and serene, though sometimes a little overcast, as the most glorious sunrisings are subject to shadowings and droppings in: for the clouds of Spain and vapours of the Holy League began then to disperse and threaten her serenity. . . . For the name of Recusant began then, and first to be known to the world; and till then the Catholics were no more than church Papists, but were commanded by the Pope's express letters to appear, and forbear church going as they tender their Holy Father, and the Holy Catholic church their mother." . . .
—NAUNTON's *Fragmenta Regalia.*

HITHERTO our attention has been mainly given to such incidents as may be supposed to exercise a direct influence upon the development of a thoughtful and intelligent lad, born into the world with a certain bias of his own, and some of that spirit of unrest and melancholy and discontent which leads a man to the conviction that the times in which he lives are "out of joint," and urges him passionately to set them straight again. But our characters are not formed only by the direct influences which are brought to bear upon them, nor our opinions adopted only from the things we see with our own eyes and hear with our own ears. Rather is it the indirect influence of events which are going on around us in that outer circle with which we have no personal contact, that affects us most profoundly in the period when boyhood is passing into manhood. And, therefore, if we would understand the error or the heroism, the weakness or the nobleness, the fervour or the infatuation of such a life as we are engaged in reviewing, it is essential that we should endeavour to estimate the significance of those larger questions and those more stirring events which were agitating the minds of men during these eventful times.

. . . . . . . .

The year 1569 is a memorable one in the history of Queen Elizabeth's reign. Mary Stuart was a prisoner in England, and on her as the next heir to the throne the eyes of all politicians turned. Should any one of those numberless chances occur to which we are all liable,—and to which in times of great excitement and uneasiness men are apt to believe that sovereigns must be peculiarly liable,—the Queen of Scots, it was thought, would certainly ascend the English throne, and as certainly attempt to bring back the days of the Papal dominion, and the doctrine and ritual of Rome.

In the northern counties of England, more than anywhere else, the great bulk of the population were averse to the Protestant faith; and almost all the more powerful families were vehemently and conscientiously in favour of the mass as against the new doctrines which were being slowly but steadily forced upon them. In the temper of men's minds at this time, it needed very little to stir them up to deeds of violence, and it was almost inevitable that sooner or later the long-suppressed but widely-fermenting discontent should prove altogether irrepressible, and passion grown reckless should drive on angry people to defy the terrors of the law. In November of this year, 1569, the Northern Rebellion blazed forth under the leadership of the Earls of Northumberland and Westmoreland.([1]) By Christmas it had run its course, had collapsed, and the vengeance had begun. Whoever likes may read the account of that atrocious massacre, for it deserves no better name, as it is set down in the pages of Mr. Froude's work; and he will scarcely think the historian has been too severe upon his heroine when he tells us that "the retribution inflicted upon the northern insurgents shows undoubtedly that anger and avarice had for a time overclouded Elizabeth's character."

There can be no question but that the Northern Rebellion was a religious war. As an attempt to restore the old order of things, or to put the Catholic party in a better position, the revolt of the northern earls was an utter failure; but its effects did not soon pass away. There was deep discontent and horror: the "Mass Priests" were among the sufferers, upon whom signal severity appears to have been exercised, and the lower orders were remorselessly butchered, but *the gentry's lives were spared that their lands might be forfeited.* A host of high-born paupers were thus thrown upon the resources of their relatives and friends: discontent smouldered, but it did not die.

While "the hanging business went on," and Sir George Bowes was "stringing them leisurely upon the trees in the towns and village greens," the Queen herself was being tried in the Papal Court at Rome on certain grave charges affecting her right to retain possession of her kingdom and her crown. Twelve Englishmen, exiles for their religion, were examined as witnesses, and their depositions taken in due form. The court considered its verdict, and finally decided that the Queen was guilty, and had incurred the canonical penalties of heresy. On the 25th February 1570 the sentence was pronounced, and the Bull of Pope Pius V., called "*Regnans in Excelsis,*" was signed, and launched forth on its disastrous mission. On the 15th May, when quiet people rose in the morning to pursue their ordinary duties, lo! nailed to the door of the Bishop of London's Palace appeared a strange document—it was the Papal Bull declaring the Queen of England excommunicated, "deprived of all dominion, dignity, and privilege whatsoever," and her subjects not only absolved from all oath of allegiance, but forbidden to render to her any homage or obedience! ([2])

Only they who have little or no acquaintance with the conflict of sentiment and opinion raging in England during Elizabeth's reign, will commit the error of supposing that the Excommunication was an event of trifling importance. The truth is, it was the turning-point in the history of the Reformation. Hitherto it had been possible for "good Catholics" to keep up some sort of conformity, and to bow in the house of Rimmon, in the hope of some turn in affairs; now they were placed between two fires. The Excommunication was nothing less than a challenge thrown down by the Pope defying Protestant Europe to a conflict à l'outrance, which had for its object the absolute subjection of the intellects and consciences of mankind to the decrees of the Council of Trent (which had closed its sittings seven years before); a conflict in which all Europe should be forced to take one side or the other without hesitation or reserve, on pain of forfeiting peace in this world and salvation in the next; a conflict in which, while it lasted, all laws were to be abrogated, and even the ordinary conditions of warfare ignored; a conflict in which mercy was to be forgotten till victory was sure, and neutrality to be reckoned criminal and dealt with as treasonable.

War was declared, and the struggle began. The Papacy, as has been said, hoped for the support of the great territorial lords, and of all who had more sympathy with the old order of things than with a present in which they were compelled to acquiesce against their wills. How little the Papal advisers knew of the temper of the people,—how profoundly ignorant they were of the social and intellectual revolution that had been going on in England,—how utterly they misunderstood the spirit of the age and misread the signs of the times,—the event sufficiently proved. The landed interest had had its day; the townsman's turn had come; he was for progress. What was the past to him? He was ready to break with it root and branch; his cry was 'Reform;' at any rate he was bent upon change; he was still loyal to the name and person of the sovereign; as for the nobles, his reverence for them had been for some time very much on the wane. Times had altered since the very name of Duke had inspired some little awe. There was but a single duke in England now, and yet Norwich cared as little for the Duke of Norfolk as Exeter did for the Earl of Devon. Henry VIII. had shown the towns how little account need be taken of a peer of the realm, and how loosely his head clung to his shoulders. Even the spoliation of the monasteries had been a gain rather than a loss to the townsmen; trade and commerce could get on well enough without the religious orders. Men were richer, more self-reliant, more independent, and less inclined to submit to restraints, moral or religious; as for any other restraints, say social and political ones, they did not yet see that these too must go some day; nevertheless that day was coming. Already, through many wide districts in England, and nowhere more than in the eastern counties, the town and country parties were in sharp antagonism; the one did not know its strength, nor the other its weakness; but the elements of dissension were slowly and ceaselessly fermenting through every grade of society. Revolutions may be sudden and spasmodic elsewhere: with us the nation is not roused to frenzy in an hour. When Charles I. set up his standard at Nottingham that crisis came, which a hundred years of discontent and exasperation on the one side, and wounded pride, disappointed ambition, and a desperate clinging to shadows when the substance had perished, on the other, had been leading up to; and the sword once drawn, the issue was not doubtful long.

The first Act of Parliament passed in the reign of Queen Elizabeth was one " to restore to the Crown the ancient jurisdiction over the *estate ecclesiastical and spiritual*, and abolishing all foreign powers repugnant to the same." By the nineteenth clause of this Act it had been enacted that all ecclesiastical persons whatsoever, all civil servants of the Crown, all magistrates, and all taking any degree in the universities, should be required to swear allegiance to the Queen in a form of oath which declared her to be supreme "as well in all *spiritual or ecclesiastical things or causes* as temporal." It is hardly too much to say that on those two words "spiritual things" the differences between the Catholic party and the government in England turned. Sir Thomas More had calmly laid his head upon the block rather than bind himself by an oath less explicit and precise, and, at the accession of Elizabeth, there were not wanting many men of conscientious convictions who would have boldly faced the scaffold rather than acknowledge the claim of the *spiritual* supremacy of the sovereign. Granted that this was taking offence at a word—yet, can we forget that some of the most momentous struggles that the world has ever known have been about a mere word which has grown to be the war-cry of millions? Be it as it may, the oath in its new form became the cause of deep and widespread offence. A very large proportion of the English gentry refused to swear allegiance in the terms prescribed, and by their refusal forfeited at once any office or preferment they might happen to hold, and debarred themselves for the future from all positions of emolument and all distinctions conferring any social status. These men were from this time known as the *Recusants*, or refusers of the oath, and the stigma and inconvenience attaching to the term began then first to be felt in its odious force.

But the next Act of the same Parliament was one which touched the Catholics in a different way. The re-establishment of the mass in Queen Mary's reign had caused immense joy throughout the land, and ever since the death of King Edward no other form of administration of the eucharist had been permitted in the churches; now it was enacted that the Book of Common Prayer alone should be used, and "to *sing or say* any common or open prayer, or to *minister any sacrament* otherwise . . . than is mentioned in the said book . . . in any cathedral or parish church or chapel, *or in any other place*," subjected the offender to forfeiture of his goods, and on a repetition of his offence, to imprisonment for life. The mass was felt to be, and known to be, the one great and precious mystery which every devout Catholic clung to with unspeakable awe and fervour, and to rob him of that was to rob him of the one thing on which his religious life depended; that gone, it was imagined all else would go with it.

But this was not all. It was bad enough for the Catholic gentry to be condemned to political extinction; worse that they should be denied freedom of worship and the enjoyment of what was to them the highest Christian privilege; but there was yet another clause in this Act, which was even more galling and hateful than the others. The fourteenth clause enacted that any person not resorting to his parish church on Sundays and holydays was to forfeit twelvepence for every offence, the money to go to the poor of the parish; the churchwardens were bound to 'present' offenders to the Ordinary, but as these had little to gain and much to lose by embroiling themselves with the Recusant squires, and where they did so, the fine could be paid without any great inconvenience, the Catholic gentry during the first twelve years of the Queen's reign could afford to hold aloof from the Church services without experiencing any great pressure, or suffering from much except the sense of vexation and annoyance. But when the Papal Bull was launched, things began to assume a more threatening aspect.

A few weeks after the excommunication had been pronounced Parliament assembled. One of the first Acts which it passed was one " against the bringing in or putting in execution bulls, writings, or instruments, and other superstitious things from the See of Rome." By this statute it was enacted (i.) that "if any person, after the 1st day of July next coming, shall use or put in use in any place within the realm any bull, writing, or instrument . . . obtained or gotten . . . from the Bishop of Rome . . . . he *shall suffer pains of death,* and also lose and forfeit all his lands, tenements, and hereditaments, goods and chattels, as in cases of high treason." It may fairly be said that, under the circumstances, and considering the issues involved and the dangers apprehended, the severity of this clause of the Act was at least morally justifiable. But there was another clause which affected the Catholics much more seriously. As a party they were now much divided upon the question whether or not they would or could accept the Bull of Excommunication; if they had been let alone, the probability is that hatred of Spain and loyalty to England, feelings which were steadily on the increase, would have sooner or later done more than all these penal laws could effect; but the statute did not stop at pronouncing the severest penalties upon those who should assist in promulgating the Bull: it added that "if any person after the same 1st July shall take upon him to *absolve or reconcile* any person ... or if any shall willingly *receive and take any such absolution or reconciliation*," he should be subject to exactly the same penalties as in the former case. Furthermore, by the seventh clause of the statute it was enacted that "if any person ... shall bring into the realm any tokens, crosses, pictures, beads, or such like vain superstitious things, from the Bishop or See of Rome ... and shall deliver the same to any subject of the realm ... then that person so doing ... as well as every other person as shall *receive* the same ... shall incur the penalties of the Statute of Præmunire." By virtue of this clause, any Catholic priest admitted to his orders on the other side of the Channel, and venturing to exercise his functions in England, did so at the peril of his life; and whosoever dared to receive absolution at his hands incurred the same penalty, with forfeiture of all his worldly goods besides. As for the fine for not attending church, it remained as before, but the day was coming when the penalties imposed for this offence were to amount to the confiscation of the property of all but the wealthiest proprietors.

Rome had sown the wind, the whirlwind followed. On the 2d of June of the following year the Duke of Norfolk was beheaded at the Tower,—a flimsy dupe, whom more cunning conspirators had put forward as the leader of the Romish cause, and whose misfortune was that he had been born to a station to which in those rough times he was unequal. On the 22d of August, the Earl of Northumberland, whom the Scots had sold, suffered, at York, the tardy penalty of that Northern Rebellion of which we have already heard. Two days after his execution the unparalleled enormity of the St. Bartholomew massacre occurred at Paris, and the tidings were not slow in crossing the Channel. The indignation of every generous heart blazed forth in flames of wrath, horror, and resentment; every heart, that is, in which the moral sense had not become perverted by the insane infatuation which religious fanaticism engenders. From that day the Catholics in England began to have a hard time of it, though the worst had not come yet. For the present it would seem that the Queen's ministers proceeded with some moderation against the Romanising gentry, and I cannot find that any general pressure was put upon the Recusants; nor does it appear that the publication of the Papal Bull had had any great effect in adding to their number or confirming them in their resolution. ([3]) Nevertheless there was no intention of sparing those who, after time given for amendment, should still persist in siding with the Pope against the Queen. The Council, busied with the complications of Elizabeth's foreign policy and the matrimonial farces which were for ever being discussed, proposed, initiated, and dismissed, were content to hang up the scourge that was ready at hand, and could be used at any moment if it were wanted: for the present it was not wanted, and while the burning indignation which the Bartholomew horror had aroused was still hot, there was little to fear from the smouldering discontent and stubborn refusal "to keep their church" by the country squires and some few perverse enthusiasts in the smaller towns.

As though to deepen the impression which the Bartholomew massacre had produced, scarce four years after its occurrence came the horrible sack of Antwerp, and the frightful atrocities of Spanish ruffians in Belgium. ([4]) There was no need to exaggerate barbarities so revolting and inhuman, but the pulpit and the ballad-mongers, and subsequently the stage, severally turned them to account, the Pope being credited with his full share of the blame. While these events were succeeding one another so rapidly, and while the people at large were drawing their inferences from them, the politicians could afford to wait and hold their hands. But that the Romanising gentry were not forgotten, and that a sharp eye was kept upon them, is plain enough from the following curious episode.

In July 1578, the Queen started upon a "Progress."[5] Her first intention was to receive the members of the University of Cambridge at Audley End, to proceed to Long Melford Hall in Suffolk, and to return by Cambridge, and thence through Hunts, Beds, and Bucks to Windsor. The plan was for some reason or other suddenly changed. On the 4th of August she slept at Melford; next morning she rode on to Lawshall Hall near Bury St. Edmund's, and thence to Hawstead.[6] On the 7th she was at Bury; and on Sunday, the 10th, she was entertained at a house called Euston Hall, near Thetford, by a gentleman of the name of Edward Rookwood, who had but lately come of age, and was newly married.[7] The house was of no great size, and confessedly unfit for the entertainment of the royal party. There were several far larger mansions in the neighbourhood, and yet Her Majesty was persuaded to visit it, for reasons which will be apparent presently. When the Queen took leave, Mr. Rookwood was admitted in the usual course to kiss Her Majesty's hand: no sooner had he done so than the Lord Chamberlain bade him stand aside, and in no measured terms charged him with being a recusant, who was unfit to be in the presence, much less touch the sacred person of his sovereign. The unlucky man, quite unprepared for so sudden and unexpected an attack, appears to have made no reply; and the scene ended by his being required to attend the Council under surveillance. When he reached Norwich, he was committed to the castle.

Four days after this incident the royal retinue crossed over into Norfolk; and on the 16th we find the Queen dining with the "Lady Style" at Braconash, about six miles from Norwich. (⁸) Lady Style was the "Lady Elizabeth Style" of the Braconash parish register, who was at this time wife of Thomas Townshend, a man of large possessions in the county of Norfolk. (⁹) He appears to have kept considerable state at Braconash, and to have lived on a scale of baronial hospitality. But Mr. Townshend was under suspicion. A cousin of his, who lived a few miles off, was actually a recusant, and was repeatedly fined for his offence; and though Thomas Townshend had himself conformed, his wife, "the Lady Style," had refused to do so. This time the Queen's host was spared, not so the guests. Nine of the neighbouring gentry, who presumably had come to show their respect for their sovereign, but who hitherto had declined the oath from conscientious scruples, were forthwith arrested, as Rookwood had been, dragged to Norwich, and were either sent to gaol or bound over under a bond of £200 a piece to keep to their lodgings in Norwich until further notice. (¹⁰) Nor was this all: from Braconash the cortege pushed on to Norwich. About a mile from the city it was met by a gentleman of the name of Downes, lord of the manor of Erlham, which was held under the crown by Petit Serjeantry or service of a cross-bow and a pair of spurs. Mr. Downes presented the Queen with a pair of gold spurs, and in offering them addressed her in some English verses, which have been preserved. But he too was a recusant, and had not "kept his church." He was not more fortunate than the others: he was bidden to stand aside, and followed the Council into the city of Norwich, where he was committed to gaol. (¹¹)

At Norwich the Queen lodged at the bishop's palace, and spent her time, as far as the bad weather would allow, in listening to absurd speeches and witnessing grotesque pageants; but on the 19th August (*i.e.*, with the dog-days just ended) she suddenly resolved to *go a hunting* in the park of Cossey, five miles from Norwich, which belonged to Mr. Henry Jernegan, ancestor of the present Lord Stafford. Cossey was at this time occupied by Lady Jernegan, widow of Sir Henry Jernegan, who had been one of the most active adherents of Queen Mary, and who had made himself very conspicuous in opposing the abominable attempt to set aside Mary and Elizabeth as heirs to the crown at the death of Edward VI. In return for his loyalty he had received this very domain of Cossey at Queen Mary's hands. It would have been a little too bad, even in those times, for the widow of a man to whom Elizabeth herself must have felt that she lay under deep obligations, to be in her old age molested and persecuted for her religious convictions; nor, indeed was her son, who was now living at Wingfield Castle, interfered with for the present, though his time was coming; and so when, three days after, the Council met and made order for the committal to gaol of such of the Norfolk gentry as had not kept their church, and upon whom the hand of power had begun to press heavily, Mr. Jernegan's name was omitted, though his kinsman Mr. Bedingfeld's name figures on the list, and appears again and again hereafter.

These were the vexations which drove men mad, and irritated them when they were beginning to acquiesce in the inevitable. But the truth is, a detestable system had now begun to spring up, under which no one with any conscience or any religious scruples could hold himself safe for an hour. An army of spies and common informers were prowling about the length and breadth of the land, living by their wits, and feeding partly upon the terrors of others and partly upon the letter of the law as laid down in the recent Acts—wretches who had everything to gain by straining the penalties to the utmost, for they claimed their share of the spoil. Armed with warrants from weak magistrates, who themselves were afraid of suspicion, or, failing these, armed with an order from the Privy Council, which was only too easily to be obtained, they sallied forth on their mission of treachery. They were nothing better than bandits protected by the law, let loose upon that portion of the community which might be harried and robbed with impunity. In some cases the pursuivants, after arresting their victims and appropriating their money, were content to let them alone, and save themselves further trouble; in others they kept them till a ransom might come from friends; in any case there was always the fun of half-scuttling a big house and living at free quarters during a search, and the chance of securing a handsome bribe in consideration of being left unmolested for the future. ([12])

Chief among these miscreants, of whom we hear so much ten years after, was one Richard Topcliffe. He was of an old Lincolnshire family, son and heir of Robert Topcliffe of Somerly, by Margaret, daughter of Thomas Lord Borough. He married Joan, daughter of Sir Edward Willoughby of Wollarton, co. Notts. He was born, according to his own account, some time in 1532, and early in life seems to have attached himself to the Court. The first notice I find of him is shortly after the collapse of the Northern Rebellion, when he is a suitor for the lands of old Richard Norton of Norton Conyers, co. York, who had made himself so conspicuous in Durham cathedral. Three years after this he appears to have been regularly in Burghley's pay, or at any rate employed by him, but in what capacity does not transpire; and he comes out first in his character of scourge and persecutor of Catholics during this same Norfolk Progress. ([13])

The cruelties of this monster during the next quarter of a century would fill a volume, and the expedients he resorted to to hunt down Recusants, Seminary Priests, and Jesuits would be absolutely incredible were it not that the evidence of even his own admission is too strong to be controverted. In the case of poor Robert Southwell, it is certain that he seduced the daughter of one of his victims, and used her for playing upon her own father, in whose house Southwell was apprehended.([14]) In November, 1594, he sued an accomplice of his own, Thomas Fitzherbert, in the Court of Chancery in a bond for £3000.

"For whereas Fitzherbert entered into bonds to give £5000 unto Topcliffe, *if he would persecute his father and uncle to death, together with Mr. Bassett*. Fitzherbert pleaded that the conditions were not fulfilled, *because they died naturally*, and Bassett was in prosperity. Bassett gave witness what treacherous devices he had made to entrap him, and Coke, the Queen's Attorney, gave testimony openly that he very well had proved how effectually Topcliffe had sought to inform him against them contrary to all equity and conscience."[15] This was rather too disgraceful a business to be discussed in open court, and "the matter was put over for secret hearing," when it would seem that Topcliffe, standing somewhat stiffly to his claim, lost his temper, and let fall some expressions which were supposed to reflect upon the Lord Keeper and some members of the Privy Council, whereupon he was committed to the Marshalsea for contempt, and kept there for some months. While he was incarcerated, he addressed two letters to the Queen, which have been preserved, and two more detestable compositions it would be difficult to find. In one of them, dated "Good or evil Friday, 1595," he says, " . . . I have helpt more traitors [to Tyburn] than all the noblemen and gentlemen of the court, your counsellors excepted. And now by this disgrace I am in fair way and made apt to adventure my life every night to murderers, for since I was committed, wine in Westminster hath been given for joy of that news. In all prisons rejoicings; *and it is like that the fresh dead bones of Father Southwell at Tyburn and Father Walpole at York, executed both since Shrovetide*, will dance for joy!"[16]

The scoundrel was out of prison again and at his old tricks in October, the restless ferocity of the man never allowing his persecuting mania to cease for an hour. The last time I meet with him is in 1598, when one Jones, a Franciscan, was executed with the usual cruelties on the 12th July, having been hunted to his death by Topcliffe's means.[17] What became of him at last it is not worth while to inquire, though it is the fate of such monsters of iniquity that their names can hardly go down to oblivion. Even enormous crime insures a measure, if not of fame, yet of infamy.(¹⁸)

But besides and beyond the pressure exercised by those two great levers for acting upon the Catholics, the oath of allegiance and the compulsory attendance at church, soon came another vexation. When, shortly after Elizabeth had come to the crown, the Roman ritual was put down, the bench of bishops displaced, and the oath of allegiance in its obnoxious form was exacted of all who held office in Church or State, the same result had followed which followed when Mary began to reign; there was a very serious exodus of the most learned and most conscientious of the clergy and of the most distinguished members of both universities. Of the deprived bishops, all, except Scott, Bishop of Chichester, and Goldwell of St. Asaph, who slipped away across the Channel, were suffered to remain unmolested, though under surveillance, and, as far as I know, absolutely unprovided for. Ten deans of English cathedrals and nearly fifty canons were deprived. Fifteen heads of colleges of Oxford and Cambridge, driven out for the most part into banishment; a host of beneficed clergymen, whose number it is impossible to ascertain; and some of the most learned scholars, professors, and fellows of colleges at both universities, bravely gave up their emoluments rather than act against their consciences by taking an engagement which they were persuaded it was unlawful to be bound by.(¹⁹) In many cases these refugees had taken with them across the seas the sons of the discontented gentry, who accompanied them as their pupils; and in not a few instances the reputation of an exiled scholar attracted the children of parents who, though conforming, yet felt a deep dislike for the new regime, and an intense longing for a restoration of the old faith, to which in their hearts they clung so fondly. The exiles were not content with themselves being sufferers; they were perpetually acting the part of proselytisers. By every available opportunity letters of impassioned remonstrance and earnest warning were addressed to friends and relatives at home, calling upon those who still clung to their fatherland to renounce it and join their exiled brethren, describing in glowing terms the blessedness and peace of such as had "left all for the kingdom of heaven," and putting forward every conceivable argument to bring over those who were hesitating to take the step which they felt to be irrevocable.([20])

Prodigious force and point were added to these appeals, and a material guarantee was given of some hope of maintenance for the exiles, by the foundation of Cardinal Allen's splendid college at Douay, which they who enter the town from the present railway station cannot fail to see, the immense buildings still existing being used to-day as a barrack for seven hundred men. Douay College was founded in 1568. During the first two years its success seemed a matter of uncertainty, but the reputation of the scholars who repaired thither and constituted the tuitional staff soon dispelled whatever doubt had existed, and the influence which it was likely to exercise in supplying England with priests strongly impregnated with ultramontane sentiment, and animated by a genuine enthusiasm to "labour in the English vineyard," or to win for themselves the martyr's crown, began to be felt as a real danger which must be met by uncompromising and remorseless severity. The first victim was Cuthbert Mayne. He had been fellow of St. John's College, Oxford, at the time that Campion was in residence there, and, yielding to the solicitations of his friends, had fled across the seas, and after going through a course of preparatory study at Douay, had returned to England. He took refuge with a gentleman in Cornwall, Francis Tregian by name, a man of wealth and high birth, and continued with him for some time, ostensibly as steward. The spies were soon upon his track, and in the summer of 1577 he himself was apprehended, and, what was more to the purpose from the informer's point of view, Mr. Tregian was a ruined man, and his estate forfeited. Cuthbert Mayne was hung, drawn, and quartered at Launceston on the 29th November, the protomartyr of the English College of Douay, as he has since been reckoned and designated. But in that same year no less than twenty-four priests were ordained at the college, and the next spring two of these "Seminarists" were executed at Tyburn; John Nelson on the 3rd, and Thomas Sherwood on the 7th of February.[21]

By this time the English Government had begun to be thoroughly alarmed. It was well known that the education of the country was in a very unsatisfactory state; that not only was there a serious deficiency in the number of candidates for Holy Orders, but the character and ability of these candidates were very much below what was needed. Elizabeth had been now twenty years upon the throne, but things had not much improved among the rank and file of the clergy. Cartwright again and again charges Archbishop Whitgift with the undeniable fact that "there be admitted into the ministry of the basest sort ... such as suddenly are changed out of a serving-man's coat into a minister's cloak, making for the most part the ministry their last refuge."[22] Some of the best of them were ignorant ranters, utterly unfit to cope with the trained dialecticians who were being reared so carefully beyond the seas; and when the time for disputation came, as it did so frequently, the fervent but uneducated Gospeller proved to his own astonishment no match at all for the gladiator of the seminaries, whose skill and success in such encounters confirmed him in his belief that the cause was good and the reasoning unanswerable which appeared, so far, to be easily and triumphantly defensible.[23] If the clergy were ignorant and socially unpresentable, and so had little to teach, the condition of the schools was hardly more satisfactory. It is difficult to understand how the rising generation during the early years of Elizabeth's reign received any education at all. Up to the time of the dissolution of the monasteries there were not seventy schools in England unconnected with monastic institutions. How important a part these latter played in the education of the country is evident from the necessity which was acknowledged of making provision for the training of youth out of the suppressed abbeys; and in the last twelve years of the reign of Henry VIII. no less than thirty-eight grammar-schools were founded, partly out of the abbey lands and partly by the munificence of private benefactors. In Edward VI.'s short reign the number was increased by fifty-one, of which twenty-seven claim the King as their founder; seventeen more were established in the following reign; and about eighty more were built and endowed during the first thirty years of Queen Elizabeth.[24]

Thus the whole number of schools in England, even in the latter half of the Queen's reign, scarcely reached two hundred, and these, with the Universities and the Inns of Court, represented the whole educational machinery of the country; for as for the private schoolmaster, he was a person who in those days had scarcely any existence. No man might exercise the vocation of schoolmaster at all except he were duly licensed by the bishop of the diocese in which he resided, and at any moment he was liable to be called to account for his opinions, political and theological. Meanwhile, considerable efforts were made from time to time to raise the standard of education at the schools, and extraordinary favour was shown to schoolmasters in various ways. They were regarded as a privileged class, and their social status appears to have been higher as a rule than that of the beneficed clergy: they were exempted from the payment of taxes of all kinds, and from many burdens which pressed upon other members of the commonwealth, and the favour shown to them on many occasions was conspicuous.[25] But there was no unanimity in the teaching of English schools; each one had his own tricks which he called his system, and each was only too ready to rush into print and publish some new primer or elementary book, whereby he hoped to get for himself notice, reward, or fame. The whole state of education in England was chaotic, and to this must be added the fact that there was a great deal of coarse brutality in the discipline. Ascham's beautiful "Schole master" lets us into a great deal, and shows the interest that was taken in the subject of education among the upper classes in Elizabeth's reign; but it shows us too that the good schoolmasters were few and the books bad, and the commonest feeling among schoolboys was "the butcherlie fear in making Latines" which their pedagogues inspired of malice prepense. On the other hand, prodigious reforms had been wrought in education on the Continent. In Saxony, Wurtemburg—above all at Strasburg—normal schools had been established, whose reputation had spread over Europe. Their "directors" were men not only of profound learning but of immense earnestness and enthusiasm, who contrived to animate their scholars with a thirst for knowledge and the higher culture which knew no bounds. In England, the pedagogues knew only one way of getting their pupils to learn anything, viz., by an unsparing use of the rod. In Germany, this engine was almost banished from the schools which flourished so marvellously. There, too, the books were incomparably superior to our own: we were as yet in the barbaric stage.([26]) Nor while the Protestant schools were gaining for themselves renown, were the Jesuits idle: it is in the domain of education that the Society of Jesus has achieved its most solid triumphs. Little inclined as Lord Bacon was to look with favour upon the followers of Loyola, he yet has left us a generous testimony to the excellence of their schools and colleges. The organisation of these seminaries in the sixteenth century was far in advance of anything known on our side of the Channel. Their school-books were confessedly far superior to our own, and their discipline was vigilant and protective beyond anything that had ever been known in England.([27])

Though Cardinal Allen's colleges were not meant to be Jesuit colleges, and were as a rule under the government and direction of secular clergy, yet they were, of course, organised after the most approved Jesuit model, and it was not long before they became deservedly celebrated for the quality of the instruction they imparted, and the high tone which their scholars exhibited. They were "gentlemanly" places of education; a man could hardly send a son to Douay or St. Omer if he were not a man of fortune. Moreover, he certainly would not send him there if he were satisfied with what he could find nearer home; every English lad who crossed the sea to get his education elsewhere was, by the very fact of his leaving the kingdom, shown to be the son of a malcontent—of one who at best was not content with the education patronised, fostered, and sanctioned by the Queen's ministers, and who almost certainly had strong leanings towards Roman doctrine, and favoured Rome's claims. For a while no notice was taken of the new colleges. No great difficulty seems to have been experienced by the gentry in getting licences for their children to travel abroad, and one after another they crossed over, usually in small companies, and often under the care of a trusty tutor, who in many cases went in the disguise of a merchant or trader engaged in commercial undertakings. But when Douay College began to assume more formidable proportions, and when from small beginnings it grew into an institution which aimed at supplying England with a regular succession of missionary clergy, every one of whom was bound to do his utmost to convert the "heretics," and to bring them back to the bosom of the Catholic Church, then the existence of this Douay College became a standing menace, and to ignore it was no longer possible. The irritation of the government was extreme; the provocations offered by the Catholic exiles and their supporters abroad never ceased; and just when the Queen's ministers were most perplexed, the tidings came that the Society of Jesus was to enter upon a mission to England, and that Fathers Parsons and Campion had set out from Rome.

# NOTES TO CHAPTER III.

(1) *Page* 59, *line* 32. Wright's *Queen Elizabeth and her Times*, i. 331. Froude's *History of England*, ix. c. 18.

(2) *Page* 60, *line* 35. Lingard, vi. 110. The text of the Bull may be seen in Tierney's *Dodd*, vol. iii. Appendix, and a translation of it in Fuller's *Church History*, b. ix. cent. xvi. sect. ii. § 24.

(3) *Page* 66, *line* 19. This is the impression left upon my mind after much reading on the subject and much careful weighing of evidence, printed and in MS. Tierney's note in *Dodd*, vol. iii. p. 12, does not satisfy me, or in any way shake the conviction I have arrived at. But see Fuller's *Church History, u.s;* Berington's *Memoirs of Panzani, Int.* p. 15; and especially Simpson's *Life of Campion*, p. 62.

(4) *Page* 66, *line* 35. See Mr. Simpson's valuable reprint, "A Larum for London, or the Siege of Antwerp," with its wonderfully learned Introduction. It is surprising that this notable contribution to Shaksperian literature should have attracted such little notice.

(5) *Page* 67, *line* 10. See Nichols's *Progresses and Public Processions of Queen Elizabeth*, vol. ii. p. 108–225. The dates given in the text are from the *MS. Records of the Privy Council*, to which I was allowed access in 1875.

(6) *Page* 67, *line* 17. Lawshall was the seat of HENRY DRURY, second son of Sir WILLIAM DRURY, of Hawstead; his elder brother ROBERT had died during his father's lifetime, leaving, by Audrey, daughter of Richard Lord Rich, WILLIAM DRURY, his son and heir; this WILLIAM was living at Hawstead when Queen Elizabeth was on her progress. The Drurys were suspected, not without reason, of having no love for the 'new learning.' It is clear that Sir WILLIAM DRURY, who died in 1557, was a devout Catholic. In his will, besides other bequests which indicate his leanings, he leaves a "vestiment with the Albe and all that belongeth to it, for a priest to sing in."—(Cullum's *Hawstead*, p. 149.) His son HENRY had been returned as absent abroad, without a licence, in 1576, and must have lately come back to Lawshall when the Queen visited his house; two of his daughters, DOROTHY and FRANCES, were married respectively to ROBERT ROOKWOOD of

Coldham Hall, co. Suffolk, and JAMES HUBBARD of Hailes Hall, co. Norfolk, and are frequently *presented* with their husbands as obstinate Recusants. JOHN DRURY of Godwick, co. Norfolk, another of the family, figures as a Recusant again and again. Cullum is certainly wrong in supposing that Sir WILLIAM DRURY, the younger, lived at Lawshall; he had just rebuilt Hawstead House. His *uncle* HENRY is described as of Lawshall in the list of Suffolk Recusants as late as 1594.—*Harl. MSS.* 6998, No. 165.

(7) *Page* 67, *line* 21. There were two families of the name of Rookwood in Suffolk—
(1) *Rookwood of Staningfield*, to which family belonged *Ambrose Rookwood*, who was hung for complicity in the Gunpowder Plot.
(2) *Rookwood of Euston*, whose representative, *Edward Rookwood*, was Queen Elizabeth's host.

The two families bore different arms, but both were staunch and devoted Catholics, and suffered severely during the whole of Elizabeth's reign. When James I.'s accession brought no alleviation to the Catholics, who had looked to him to relieve them from the pressure of the penal laws, such men as *Ambrose Rookwood* grew desperate and were ready for anything. EDWARD ROOKWOOD of Euston was utterly beggared by the exactions levied upon him, and I find him in the Fleet Prison for debt in 1619; how long he continued there I know not, but he died in 1634, æt. 79. There is a very fair account of the Euston Rookwoods in Page's *Supplement to the Suffolk Traveller*, p. 775, and a very minute account of both families in Davy's *MSS. in the British Museum*.

The following is extracted from Topcliffe's letter giving an account of this Royal Progress, and is too characteristic to be omitted here. Topcliffe's spelling is so original that I cannot but reproduce it. "This Rookewoode is a Papyste of kynde newly crept out of his layt wardeshipp. Her Ma'*y*, by some meanes I know not, was lodged at his house, Ewston, farre unmeet for her Highness, but fitter for the blacke garde; nevertheles (the gentilman brought into her Ma'*y*'* presence by lyke device) her excell*t* Ma'*y* gave to Rookewoode ordenary thanks for his badd house, and her fayre hand to kysse; after w*ch* it was brayved at: But my Lo. Chamberlayn, noblye and gravely understandinge that Rookewoode was excommunicated for Papistrie, cawled him before him; demanded of him how he durst presume to attempt her reall presence, he, unfytt to accompany any Chrystyan person; forthewith sayd he was fytter for a payre of stocks; comanded hym out of the Coort, and yet to attende her Counsell's pleasure; and at Norwyche he was comytted. And, to dissyffer the gent. to the full; a peyce of plaite being missed in the Coorte, and serched for in his hay house, in the hay rycke suche an immaydge of o*r* Lady was ther fownd, as for greatnes, for gaynes, and woorkemanshipp, I did never see a match; and, after a sort of cuntree daunces ended, in her Ma'*y*'* sighte the idoll was sett behinde the people, who avoyeded : She rather seemed a beast, raysed uppon a sudden from hell by conjewringe, than the picture for whome it had bene so often and longe abused. Her Ma⁷ comanded it to the fyer, w^{ch} in her sight by the cuntrie folks was quickly done, to her content, and unspeakable joy of every one but some one or two who had sucked of the idoll's poysoned mylke."

(8) *Page* 68, *line* 4. She was the daughter of George Perient, Gent., of Digswell, co. Hertford, and widow of Sir Humphrey Style of Bekenham, co. Kent. THOMAS TOWNSHEND, Esq., was son and heir of Sir ROBERT TOWNSHEND, Knt., Chief-Justice of Chester. MERGATE HALL, where Queen Elizabeth dined, is still a house of some pretension, and part of the old oak avenue down which the Queen rode remains, though the hand of time is upon the trees, and they are dying fast. Captain Lacon, the present occupant of the house, tells me that there is still a tradition of one of the rooms having been inhabited by a priest. There are some indications of the house having been at one time larger than it is now, but it was not necessary that a house in which the Queen dined should be one of any great size. It must be borne in mind that on the occasion of these "Progresses" the royal retinue were usually compelled to encamp in the neighbourhood of a halting-place. These royal visits were a dreadful infliction upon any but the very rich gentry : even so considerable a person as Sir William More of Losely spared no pains to get relieved from the costly and burdensome honour, and in the *Losely MSS.*, Kemp, p. 265 *et seq.*, are several letters on the subject.

Lady Style died in January 1580, but five years after her death I find her name on a list of recusants "dead and not resident in Norff." There was another THOMAS TOWNSHEND living at WEARHAM, who with his wife, MARIAN TOWNSHEND, was presented to the bishop as a recusant in June 1597, and frequently afterwards. They were living at WEARHAM in the second year of James I. ; and his son [?] THOMAS is returned as late as 20 Charles I., when he paid £6, 13s. 4d. for recusancy.—(*MSS. in the Episcopal Registry at Norwich, and Recusant Roll, penes me.*) The cousin referred to in the text was EDMUND TOWNSHEND of LONG STRATTON.

(9) *Page* 68, *line* 7. Blomefield's account of the Townshend family (vii. 132) is hopelessly confused and full of inaccuracies. He makes this THOMAS to be son of a HENRY TOWNSHEND (ii. 84) ; he was really son and heir of Sir ROBERT TOWNSHEND of Ludlow, co. Salop. There is a good account of him, and a tolerably successful attempt to unravel Blomefield's tangle, by an American gentleman, Mr. Charles Hervey Townshend of New Haven, Connecticut, in the *New England Historic Genealogical Register* for January 1875. Some light is thrown upon Mr. Townshend's state and lordly way of life by the will of RICHARD WALPOLE (*supra*, p. 20, l. 10), who in his will, dated 20th March 1568–9, leaves behind him a consider-

able estate, and among other legacies bequeaths "to my good master, THOMAS TOWNSHEND, Esquire, in token of my poor heart and duty, a piece of gold of thirty shillings, and another piece of gold of lyke value to my good lady my mistress. Item, I give to master ROGER TOWNSHEND my master his son £10 to make him a little chain withal in remembrance of me. . . . Item, To THOMAS BARKER my fellow in household ten shillings." He leaves his brother, TERRY WALPOLE, and THOMAS TOWNSHEND, Esq., his executors. It is clear that he and THOMAS BARKER were *gentlemen in waiting* to Mr. Townshend. In the sixteenth century this position was looked upon as quite an honourable position for the younger sons even of men of distinction.

(10) *Page* 68, *line* 20. This daye there appeared before their LL as warned by the Sheriffe of Norff. by authority given to him by the said LL . . . [*sic*] ROOKWOOD, ROBERT DOWNES, HUMFREY BENINGFIELD DE QUIDENHAM, gent, ROBERT DE GREY DE MARTIN, Esq., JOHN DOWNES de Boughton, gent., JOHN DRURY de Goodwik', gent. And being sev'ally called one by one, the Bishoppe of the Diocesse and S$^r$ Christopher Heydon and S$^r$ Will$^m$ Butts Knights being p̃nt they were particularly charged that contrary to all good Lawes and orders and against the dutie of good subjects they refused to come to the Churche at the tymes of prayer Sermons and other Devine s'vices. Ev'y one of them confessed y$^t$ it was true that they did absent themselves from the Churche as aforesaid. And being demaunded by their LL whither they wold not be contented to conforme themselves to order, and like good subjects to come to the Church ev'y one of them likewise refused so to do, uppon w$^{ch}$ their refusall they were commanded to stand apart. And after their LL had thus passed throughe them all and had conferred w$^{th}$ the B. to understond howe many of them had ben formerly dealt withall to be induced to conformitye and howe many not. There was called again . . . ROOCKWOOD and for as much as it appeared that he had not only bene conferred withal but for his continuance in y$^e$ case stood excommunicate, he was ordered by their LL to be committed prisoñ to the Goale of the Countie of Norff. there to remayne w$^{th}$out conference saving of such as shold be thought meet by the B. either for his better instructions or for direction of his necessary businesses of his living and family. Next there was called againe ROB'T DOWNES, and for that it appeared that he had also been form̃ly dealt w$^{th}$all and stood obstinate, it was ordered that he shold be committed p̃ison' to the Goale of the Citty of Norwich to remaine there in like sorte in all poynts as . . . . . ROCKWOOD was appoynted to remaine in the goale of the Countie. And where it appeared that HUMFREY BENINGFIELD, ROB'T DE GREY, JOHN DOWNES, JOHN DRURY had not bene aforetyme dealt with by the B. in that case they foure being called altogether before their LL were ordered that they shold ev'y of them enter into bonds to her Ma$^{ties}$ use in 200$^{li}$ a peece, that they shold not depart from their

lodgings appoynted unto them in the Citty of Norwich and that they shold once ev'y day as often as they shalbe sent conferre w<sup>th</sup> the L. B. or such as he shall appoynt for their better Instructions to bring them to conformitye.

And like as their LL required the L. B. to use all good meanes that he might by himselfe and his learned Preache<sup>r</sup>s to recov' them to good order. So by their LL he was authorized that in case he shold find any of them willing to give him assurance for his obedience and conformitye in this case, that they were charged w<sup>th</sup> his L. shold give order for the deliv'aunce of any such as shewed himselfe so conformable. And on the other syde if they w<sup>ch</sup> were appoynted to remayne within the Cittye out of the Goales do not before the feast of St. Michaell next coming yeld themselves upon such instruction as shalbe given unto them to conformitie and be contented to deliv' assurance to the B. for the same, His L. by this order shall have authoritie to committ them that shall stand so obstinate to th'one goale or th'other at his discretion there to remaine in such mann̄ as . . . Roockwood and Robert Downes are appoynted to do: untill uppon their reformation he shall find cause of their deliv'aunce, and he shall thereof advertise the LL of the Counsell to receave order for further proceading against them.

The next daye following there were called before their LL for the cause aforesaid Tho. Lovell of East Harling, Robert Lovell de Bechamwell, and Ferdinando Paris de Norton Armig' Who standing uppon like obstinacye were in like sort committed to remayne at their lodginge in the Citty of Norw<sup>ch</sup> as Bedingfield and the rest were, And the like bonds taken of them as of the otheres and to be used in all poyntes as th'other.

| | | |
|---|---|---|
| The presence of | The L. Treasurer<br>The L. Chamberlaine<br>The E. of Warwicke<br>The E. of Leycester<br>S<sup>r</sup> Chr. Hatton<br>S<sup>r</sup> Fra. Knollys<br>S<sup>r</sup> James Crofte<br>M<sup>r</sup> Secr. Wilson | at the making of the said order. |

(Endorsed.) An order taken by the LL touching the Recusants in Norff. 22 August, 1578.

*Cotton MSS.* Titus, B. iii. No. 66.

(11) *Page* 68, *line* 30. Nichols' *Progresses of Queen Elizabeth*, ii. p. 132. It is not to be wondered at that Nichols should have made the mistake he has made in the Christian names of the Downes family; trusting as he did to Blomefield, he could hardly avoid being led astray, for here Blomefield

exhibits inextricable confusion. ROBERT DOWNES was of Great Melton, Esq. By his wife DOROTHY he had a son EDWARD, who was baptized 6th April 1574 (P. R.), and a daughter BRIDGET, who with her mother is returned upon the Recusant Rolls as owing money for recusancy in 1597. This ROBERT appears to have had a brother JOHN, who is presented for recusancy while living at BABINGLEY from 1592 till 1603. In his offer of compounding for his fines in 1585, he describes himself as "a poor younger brother." ROBERT DOWNES, who suffered such hard treatment in 1578, built Great Melton Hall, in which the Rev. H. Evans Lombe now resides (Blomefield, v. 21), and was a man of large property in the county. Blomefield says that his son EDWARD married CATHERINE, relict of Sir THOS. KNYVETT of BUCKENHAM CASTLE. Lady KNYVETT is presented for recusancy in 1597, being then described as wife of EDWARD DOWNES, Esq., of BUCKENHAM, when she must have been a woman of forty at least. Melton Hall must have been in Queen Elizabeth's time one of the noblest mansions in the county, but its first owner was so impoverished by the remorseless exactions levied upon him that he was compelled to sell the estate in 1609. It seems that the purchaser, THOS. ANGUISH, bought the house with all its contents, for there was still to be seen a bedstead of Mr. Downes' in the house in Blomefield's time (Bl., v. 21). Mr. DOWNES was in the city gaol at Norwich in 1580, where he was incarcerated with MICHAEL HARE of STOW BARDOLPH, ROGER MARTIN of Long Melford, co. Suffolk, HUMPHREY BEDINGFIELD of QUIDENHAM, and EDWARD SULYARD, Esqs. The five gentleman "had a common chamber and table, where they met and eat their meals together." Strype tells a very curious story of Mr. DOWNES' receiving a letter from a certain SOLOMON ELDRED at Rome, urging him to leave England and come to Italy, where he would be received with distinction, &c. The gentlemen "could not but laugh, and it became some matter of mirth to them." They appear to have taken to romping, and at last DOWNES snatched the letter out of Mr. HARE's hand and threw it in the fire. "This presently made a noise, and the report came to the Bishop's ears." The affair ended by an inquiry which resulted in some letters and statements signed by the gentlemen being sent to the bishop, copies of which may be read in Strype, *Annals*, II. ii. 343 and 676.

(12) *Page* 70, *line* 9. See the pitiful account in Morris's *Condition of Catholics under James I.*, pp. 35-39. See, too, Lingard, vi. 162 ; but instances might be adduced by the score. The third volume of Tierney's *Dodd* may be referred to as easily accessible, but by far the most complete account of the suffering of the Catholics in Queen Elizabeth's reign, until the appearance of Mr. Morris's *Troubles of our Catholic Forefathers*, was to be found in Yepez, *Historia Particular de la Persecusion de Inglaterra*, published at Madrid in 1596.

(13) *Page 70, line 24.* See Froude, vol. ix. p. 515. The authority for the statements in the text are to be found among the MSS. at the Record Office, *Domestic, Elizabeth*, vol. lxxv. n. 31, vol. xcii. n. 31.

(14) *Page 70, line 32.* The affidavits and correspondence bearing upon this dreadful business are to be seen in *Harleian MSS.* 6998, n. 19. A little while after this, Topcliffe compelled his servant, one Nicholas Jones, to marry the girl, and when her father refused to settle a manor upon her as a jointure, he kept the wretched man in prison for upwards of ten years, persecuting him with extreme barbarity.—*Lansdowne MSS.* lxxiii. art. 47. Tierney's *Dodd*, vol. iii. App. p. 197.

(15) *Page 71, line 8. Stonyhurst MSS.* Angl. A. n. 83. It appears by *Harleian MSS.* 6998, n. 50, that the bond was for £3000.

(16) *Page 71, line 27. Harleian MSS.* u.s. p. 185. The editor of the Harleian Catalogue, who usually describes minutely the contents of every document contained in the several volumes, dismisses this one with a notice of six lines, though, as he tells us, "the book contains 251 leaves."

(17) *Page 71, line 33.* Challoner's *Missionary Priests*, i. 361.

(18) *Page 72, line 2.* Topcliffe's name became in his own days a byeword. See the following letter from Standen to Anthony Bacon, 2d March 1593-4. " . . . Yet thanks be to God his [Robert, Earl of Essex] carriage hath been such now, as her Majesty hath found the rareness of his parts, and all with such mildness and affability, *contrary to our Topcliffian customs*, as he hath won with words *more than others would ever do with racks*."—Birch's *Elizabeth*, i. 160. In a letter to Verstegan among the Bp. of Southwark's MSS. there is an account of the apprehension of SOUTHWELL. The writer says, "*Because the often exercise of the rack in the Tower was so odious and so much spoken of of the people, Topcliffe hath authority to torment priests in his own house* in such sort as he shall think good." . . . The date of this letter is 3rd August 1592.

(19) *Page 72, line 27.* There is a list of them given in Cardinal Allen's tract, *De Justitia Britannica*, but it is, of course, very incomplete.

(20) *Page 73, line 8.* See Simpson's *Campion*, p. 45 *et seq.*

(21) *Page 74, line 8.* Morris's *Troubles*, 1st series, p. 61 *et seq.*; Challoner's *Miss. Priests;* Lingard, vol. vi. 163. For the number of ordinations my authority is the *Douai Diary*, lately published by the Fathers of the Oratory. There is a careful account of the various colleges and seminaries

which were founded for the English Catholics in Tierney's *Dodd*, and a brief but sufficient one in the Hon. Edward Petre's *Notices of the English Colleges and Convents Established on the Continent*. The book was edited by the late Dr. HUSENBETH. See, too, Lingard, vi. 162.

(22) *Page* 74, *line* 21. See the remarkable discussion between Archbishop Whitgift and Cartwright. *Answer to Admonition*, chap i. div. ix. and div. xi.; *Whitgift's Works, Parker Society;* and the important paper quoted by Froude, xi. 323, n. PARSONS (*Responsio ad duo Edicta*) treats this subject in his usual caustic fashion and with his usual power. While this note was passing through the press, Harrison's *Description of England* was issued by the *New Shakspere Society*. His account of the clergy of his time is in their favour at page 3, but I am inclined to think that his own words at p. 21 represent a truer state of the case.

(23) *Page* 74, *line* 30. Simpson's *Campion*, p. 163-4.

(24) *Page* 75, *line* 13. *Commissioners' Report upon the Endowed Schools*, Chronological Tables, p. 36 *et seq.* On the other hand it is evident that when any of the older schools in out-of-the-way districts were possessed of landed estates, such estates were by no means safe from spoliation. A flagrant case is that of Sedbergh School.—Baker's *History of St. John's*, by Professor Mayor, p. 371.

(25) *Page* 75, *line* 32. See the curious instance of BROWN the Separatist, *East Anglian*, vol. i. p. 180; and on the whole subject, Strype, *Annals*, III. i. 76. Conspicuous examples of the favour shown to schoolmasters are Camden, Simon Hayward, and Mulcaster. Many others might be named.

(26) *Page* 76, *line* 23. *Von Raumer Geschichte der Pädagogik*, Stuttgart, 1857.

(27) *Page* 76, *line* 33. "The liberal education of youth passed almost entirely into their hands, and was conducted by them with conspicuous ability. They appear to have discovered the precise point to which intellectual culture can be carried without risk of intellectual emancipation. Enmity itself was compelled to own that, in the art of managing and forming the tender mind, they had no equals."—Macaulay, *History of England*, c. vi. There is a curious notice of their schools in Sir Edwin Sandys' *Travels*, but I have not the book at hand. The passage in Bacon referred to in the text is *Advancement of Learning*, B. I. c. iii. § 4.

## CHAPTER IV.

# THE JESUIT MISSION TO ENGLAND.

"Not only the number, but the severity of these laws, is very considerable: How often do we meet with new-minted treasons, and unaccountable felonies in them? Here is hanging, drawing, and quartering; here is bridewelling, banishing, and selling of people to slavery; here is forfeiting of lands, goods, common right, and all the natural privileges of free-born Englishmen; people convicted in an arbitrary way, without trial by their peers; one man punished for the act of another. The poor distressed widow and the helpless orphan not escaping their fury. And for what all this? Not for any disloyalty, conspiracy, or disturbing the public peace: not for injuring any of our neighbours or fellow-subjects: for nothing criminal by any law, moral or divine; but only for worshipping our Almighty Creator, according to our light, after the best manner we can (after a serious inquiry) apprehend to be acceptable unto Him. Or for not joining in certain rituals and ceremonies, which the imposers themselves confess to be indifferent, and the dissenters conceive to be either sinful or unwarrantable."—HENRY CARE'S *Draconica* [1688].

THE Bull of Pope Paul III., *Regimini militantis Ecclesiæ*, which confirmed the Society of Jesus, was published on the 27th September 1540. So little did men anticipate the importance and magnitude of the work that the new Order was destined to do, and the wonderful part which it was to play in the history of the world, that the new Society was expressly limited at first to sixty members, and not till a new Bull (*Injunctum nobis*) was promulgated three years later was this limit exceeded. The Society in the first years of its activity numbered few Englishmen among its fathers, and the only one who appears to have been admitted during Loyola's lifetime was Thomas Lith, a Londoner, of whom we know no more than that he was received, probably as a Novice, in June 1555. (¹)

St. Ignatius died in the following year, having survived four of his original associates, and leaving behind him five (and these by far the most learned) apostles of the new Order. It was not till after Queen Mary's death had driven across the Channel that army of scholars and enthusiasts, upon whom the rigour of Elizabeth's enactments pressed so hard, that the Jesuits' ranks were at all recruited from England. During the first ten years of the Catholic exodus I find between twenty and thirty names admitted to the Society, though, with the exception of those of Eliseus and Jasper Heywood, there is scarcely one which is anything more than a name. (²) Though it be indisputable that the excommunication of the Queen, followed as it was by the events alluded to in the previous chapter, produced upon the townsfolk and the great middle class precisely the contrary effect to that which was hoped and intended, yet among the Academics of either university, and among the more highly-educated of the youth of England, the perplexity was considerable. The young scholars of Oxford were still trained in a great measure according to the old fashion. Anglican theology had as yet no existence. Hooker had not written a line. Andrewes was lecturing to crowded audiences at Cambridge, but his fame was but beginning. Jewel, the great anti-papal champion, had died in 1571, leaving no one who was at all qualified to take his place; and though he had left a valuable legacy behind him in his *Apology*, yet that work was only an apology after all, and from its negative character and the unimpassioned style of its composition it could never convince any one, still less "carry away" a reader.

Meanwhile the other side were exhibiting a dialectic ability which has rarely been surpassed. Young men, whose intellects were alert, excited, and eager, plunged into the great questions of the day with a zest which was apt to lead them on to side with the persecuted party. The fact that the plebeian was given over to Calvin and Puritanism was reason enough to make the 'gentleman' lean to the Romish cause. When he looked about for sources of information on the great questions at issue, he preferred to bury himself in the elaborate treatises of Laynez or Salmeron, composed in the scholars' own language, or to read what Bristowe or that great master of Latin, Stapleton,[3] had to say in periods which did not jar against the fastidious Ciceronian's ear. He left to the 'mob' the cumbrous heaviness of Fulke and Cranmer. Then, as now, the members of the common room were of the Pharisees' mind,—"this people that knoweth not the law are cursed." And thus it came to pass that notwithstanding all the errors and crimes of the Catholic party at home and abroad, notwithstanding that every career was sternly barred to the ambitious Academic who had any fond clinging to the old learning, and was not prepared to throw himself heart and soul into the party of progress and theological revolution, there yet was a very numerous minority whose sympathies were wholly with the Roman divines, and who were preparing themselves silently and unconsciously for great sacrifices when they should be called on finally to make their choice.

Such men were William Holt of Oriel, Henry Garnet and John Pitts of New College, and, among those elders whose university position was established and their reputation made, Gregory Martin and Edmund Campion of St. John's, and Robert Parsons of Balliol. Any party that had won over from its opponents such adherents as these in the course of a year or two might be pardoned a little exultation in its tone; and however remarkable these converts were, and however conspicuous for learning, culture, and ability, they were but the representatives of a much larger band of zealots, who were ready to follow wherever they led. Prominent among them all, not so much for his learning or eloquence as for a dauntless force of character, which compelled submission to his will, was Robert Parsons, fellow of Balliol. Of plebeian birth—calumny was loud in asserting something more—he was early taken by the hand by his uncle, "a virtuous good priest," named James Hayward, Vicar of Nether Stowey, and sent to Balliol, of which college he became fellow, and eventually Bursar and Dean. At Oxford he had won a high reputation as an able and successful tutor, though in his own college there were those who watched him with jealousy and suspicion. A formidable disputant, unsparing in conflict, and incapable of tolerating contradiction, he was one of those who are born to rule, who when they occupy any position but the highest become arrogant and domineering by their excess of energy; and who rarely fail to get for themselves the implacable hatred of their opponents. The life of Robert Parsons has not yet been written: his career and character demand a more careful study than they have yet received, and the place which he filled in the history of his time has been very much under-estimated by historians; but his is a career perplexing to follow and a character difficult to estimate: the salient points are his enormous capacity of work, his rugged directness of style, the ferocious violence of his rhetoric, and yet withal a certain vein of rollicking humour, the expression of that amazing exuberance of vigour which marks him as one of the Titans of his age. Side by side with some coarseness in the grain, and no little vulgarity in the manner of the man, with a combativeness that repelled and irritated but never convinced, there were associated some very lofty and noble qualities. He was a courtier, whose success was patent to all; his ascendancy over Philip II. was unbounded; his influence at Rome was scarcely less than at the Escurial; the English Jesuits, for a time, he seems to have held in the hollow of his hand; we shall mistake him much if we think of him as a mere man of the world, animated by any mean and common ambition. If there ever were a real enthusiast, absorbed by a genuine fanaticism in a cause which he believed to be the cause of God, Robert Parsons was one; mere petty selfishness appears to have been a vice he could not understand. Nor was this all: he was a pietist of the most ecstatic school. His *Christian Directory* was, for a century at least, one of the most popular and widely-circulated religious manuals in Europe, and was the book which made so deep an impression upon Richard Baxter that he dated the beginning of his religious life from the time when he first became awakened by its fervid and soul-stirring appeal to the conscience. And yet, with all his prodigious force and vehemence, and with all the immense agencies which he had at his command, Parsons' generalship was flagrantly bad. Restlessly aggressive, he never seemed to be able to understand what conciliation meant: he would have all or nothing; he could never bide his time; he could never temporise; he could never even economise his resources. Knowing as he did that for a Jesuit father to land in England during the latter years of Queen Elizabeth's reign was to court almost certain death, he yet hurled man after man against the hosts that were waiting for them, with a recklessness almost horrible to recall. We are tempted to regard him as a monomaniac, mastered by an idea which had got such entire possession of his whole nature, that his judgment was not only perverted but even smitten with the blindness of insanity. What was that idea? To me it seems Parsons' delusion was that the English Jesuits were destined to reconvert England, and to hand back to the Papacy a nation saved from "heresy," humbled by remorse, and seeking reconcilement once again on bended knees at the hands of the Bishop of Rome. A delusion indeed! but such a delusion as no logic of facts could dispel. Facts, however strong, were lost upon him, just because of the strength of that delusion. But let no man attempt to understand Parsons' enormous blunders, or his desperate ventures, or his extravagant arrogance, on the hypothesis of his being a cool politician, with far-sighted sagacity and astute diplomacy,—these things were exactly what he was deficient in. Say rather he was a passionate partisan, without a glimmer of sentiment, without romance, with few moments of tenderness or pity, and absolutely deficient in those qualities which are the main constituents of the poetic temperament. Such characters may be Titanic, audacious, terrible, but nations and men are not converted by them; and in the great conflict of opinions, in that "bridal dawn of thunder peals," when the deepest convictions of mankind are to be reached and swayed, the enthusiasm of mere obstinate determination repels and scares, it is the enthusiasm of love and self-sacrifice which prevails. (4)

A very different man was Edmund Campion of St. John's. He, too, could boast but little of his birth. His father, we are told, was a bookseller and citizen of London, a man of no large means, though there is some reason to believe he was connected by marriage with people who moved in a higher social circle than his own. He had given early promise of remarkable ability, was sent to Oxford, and became in process of time fellow of St. John's College. Here he gained for himself the character of being the most brilliant scholar in the university—conspicuous for his extraordinary readiness in debate, and for oratorical powers of a very high order. When Amy Robsart's funeral was celebrated at St. Mary's in 1560, Campion, though little more than twenty years of age, was one of those chosen to pronounce a funeral oration in her honour; five years later he performed the same task at the funeral of Sir Thomas White, the founder of his college, and when in 1566 Queen Elizabeth paid her visit to Oxford, Campion was one of those chosen to 'dispute' before the Queen, and acquitted himself so well that he made a very favourable impression, and attracted the special notice of Her Majesty, who commended him to the patronage of Leicester, while even Cecil admired and applauded. He was Proctor in 1568, but by this time his position at the university had become untenable. The oath of allegiance was pressed upon him; he took it, but his conscience would not suffer him to be at ease. Scruples crowded upon him till he could find no peace. Under the protection of Sir Henry Sidney, the Lord-Deputy, he crossed over to Ireland; but he was a marked man. The pursuivants were soon let loose upon him. He managed to elude their vigilance, and after one or two narrow escapes, he succeeded in crossing over to Calais, in the summer of 1571. Making his way to Douay, he remained for a year at the new college, and then set out for Rome. Next year he offered himself to the Society of Jesus, and was at once accepted. For the next four years his sphere of labour was in Bohemia.

It had been for some time a scheme of the Court party in Bohemia to revive the waning glory of the University of Prague, and by its instrumentality, through the Jesuits, to recover for the Pope the ascendancy which had been lost since the days of Huss and Jerome. The emperor, Rudolph II., and his mother the dowager empress, sister of Philip II. and mother of his fourth wife, were deeply interested in the success of the plan, and spared no pains to bring it about. Campion was appointed Professor of Rhetoric, and became the leading spirit of the university. He threw himself with ardour into his work, and won for himself on all sides admiration, affection, and esteem. The university prospered, and the fame of the English professor grew and travelled far. Young Englishmen on their journeys turned from the beaten track to confer with the exile, whose reputation had followed him from Oxford to the distant land. Some came with minds disturbed by doubts and questionings; some from mere curiosity; one, Sir Philip Sidney, the pearl of English chivalry, to renew an old acquaintance, and to exchange kind courtesies with his father's friend. But Bohemia was, after all, a banishment, and Campion could not be left to spend his life there, though in the sunshine of a court. This was mere trifling: there was something greater for him to do; let scholars and students teach the lads in the lecture-room, the martyr's crown was meant for other brows. In December 1579, Campion was summoned to Rome.

In the summer of that year Dr. Allen had been disturbed by tidings regarding the state of affairs in the English College at Rome, which moved him to set out for that city. In the College there had been serious quarrels, and the scandal which these had aroused had been made the most of by all who watched the doings of the refugees with jealousy and suspicion. Dr. Allen came as a peacemaker, and his mediation was effectual, at any rate for a while; but while engaged in this work, the thought which had long been slumbering in his mind acquired a distinctness and power which no longer allowed of its remaining inoperative, and he arrived at last at the conviction that the time had come when an effort should be made, and made upon a large scale, for recovering the English people from their lapse into heresy and schism, and bringing them once again into communion with the See of Rome.

Hitherto, as I have said, the Jesuits were unknown in England. From the Continent accounts had come of their immense success as educational reformers, as indefatigable missionaries, as proselytisers whose persuasive powers were said to be almost more than human. They seemed to be labouring everywhere, and wherever they came they prospered unaccountably. The amazing rapidity of growth, and the more amazing influence exercised by the Society, startled and perplexed men least inclined to be scared by vague rumours; and all over Europe the Protestant reformers began to ask themselves with some anxiety where this astonishing ascendancy of the new Order was to end.

When Dr. Allen arrived in Rome in 1579, three of St. Ignatius' original associates were still living—Simon Rodriguez, who died at Lisbon in the August of this year; Alphonsus Salmeron, then about sixty-four years old; and Nicholas Bobadilla, ten years his senior; the General of the Order being Everard Mercurianus, who had been elected on the 1st October

1572. Campion had been his first "Postulant," and he appears to have felt a special interest in English affairs. When Dr. Allen began to urge the necessity of a mission to England, he did not lack supporters nor cogent arguments. 'Had not the priests of his own seminaries shown a noble example of heroism and courageous self-sacrifice? Could they not already boast of their martyrs? Had not Cuthbert Maine obtained for himself the crown that fadeth not away, and were there not multitudes who were ready to follow his steps? What had the Jesuits done for England that could compare with the labours of the Seminarists? They had written enough; let them practise as they preached.' But wilier counsellors took a different view of the situation: they doubted whether the Jesuit training was exactly the best to prepare men for the rough work which the more fanatical Seminary priests were doing, on the whole, so successfully. They hesitated to send away men of high culture and great gifts to run the gauntlet of spies and informers, to slink into hiding-places and assume disguises, to resort to every kind of cunning trick for baffling the vigilance of coarse and brutal detectives. If the Seminarists did not shrink from these things, it did not follow that the Jesuits were called upon to emulate them. The Church could not afford to squander such precious material in times like these, and the experiment was too hazardous to justify the cost of the venture. But the counsels of Dr. Allen and his supporters prevailed, and before the spring of 1580, Pope Gregory XIII. had been induced to sanction the new crusade. It was decided that the Society of Jesus should take its part in a mission to England.

This is not the place to enter minutely into the history of the strange expedition which started from Rome on the 18th April 1580; and the less needful as it has been told once for all by Campion's English biographer.

The whole company numbered, it seems, fourteen, and at its starting was led by Bishop Goldwell of St. Asaph, Laurence Vaux, the Prior of Manchester, Dr. Morton, Penitentiary of St.

Peter's, and four old priests from the English Hospital at Rome. These, however, never crossed the Channel. It was soon found that men far advanced in life, though they might give a certain dignity and importance to the expedition, were not fitted for the labours and dangers which had to be encountered; and the real "missioners" were the Jesuit fathers and the younger priests from Cardinal Allen's colleges, who were associated with them as fellow-workers.

From the first Father Parsons was the manager and moving spirit of the little band. Of commanding stature and big of bone, never losing his presence of mind, ready of speech, and perfectly fearless, always cheerful and fertile in resource, he proved himself on every occasion an able leader, whom others might trust without hesitation and follow without misgiving.[5] Campion was the preacher and pietist, whose place was in the pulpit or the professor's chair. With the two Jesuit priests there went a Jesuit lay brother, Ralph Emerson, afterwards apprehended with Father Weston,[6] who suffered an imprisonment of twenty years for his companionship. Their departure from Rome was celebrated with no little enthusiasm, and, though professedly secret, the mission was actually heralded by rumour all over Europe, and their every movement was watched by English spies. They marched on foot, only the old and feeble using horses; and on the whole journey we hear that Campion rode but once. They passed through Bologna, Milan, Turin; crossed the Alps in July by the Mont Cenis, and at Geneva first adopted disguises. But their appearance was too remarkable to escape notice, and once they were in some danger from a cry arising in the streets that they were monks or priests. The temptation to beard Beza in his study was too great, and thither Parsons went, and Campion as his servant. The details of the interview are exceedingly interesting—how he admitted them with reluctance—how he came forth at last "in his long black gown and round cap, with ruffs about his neck, and his fair long beard, and saluted them courteously"—

how they tried to drag him into an argument which he declined to continue, 'for he was busy'—and how at last the old man with difficulty got rid of them, and bowed them out by the help of his wife. But the lust of controversy was strong among them, and with a somewhat Quixotic zeal Parsons and Campion sent poor Beza a challenge to a public disputation which never came off; for the challenge was never delivered.

The little band arrived at St. Omer's in the beginning of June, and here they learnt that the Queen of England had particular information of their movements, and had issued proclamations especially directed against them and their plans. This and other serious news made them hesitate for awhile; but Parsons was not to be turned back, and by some dexterous diplomacy he managed to reassure the rest, and to bear down the opposition that was being made to any advance. Bishop Goldwell, who was verging on eighty years of age, though animated with all the zeal and a great deal of the energy of youth, found on arriving at Rheims that it would be madness for him to continue the journey. His health had suffered already from the fatigues of the last two months, and after addressing a letter to the Pope, and stating that in view of his intended journey to England being well known to the government, it would be difficult and dangerous for him to land, but yet if the Pope ordered him he was still prepared to go, he relinquished the attempt, and in the beginning of August returned to Rome. [7] At Rheims the company separated into five smaller bands, each intending to enter England by a different port. There, too, another Jesuit father, Thomas Cottam, joined them, so that there were three Jesuit fathers and one lay brother in all.

Arrived at Calais, Parsons as usual took the lead, and on the 11th June he crossed over to Dover, disguised as a soldier from the Low Countries, his ready audacity carrying him almost unchallenged through the searchers who were actually on the lookout for him and his friends. Campion did not cross till the

24th. He was disguised as a merchant of jewels, and Emerson passed as his servant. Less fortunate than Parsons, he was stopped, brought before the Mayor of Dover, and narrowly escaped being sent up to the Lords of the Council; but the Mayor released him, and he arrived safely at last at the house of the Catholic Club in Chancery Lane, on the 26th June 1580.

Then began such an outburst of Catholic fervour as England had not known for many a day. The researches of Mr. Simpson have disclosed to us the fact that, some time before the arrival of Parsons and his coadjutors, a large and carefully-organised society had been formed, with the special object of co-operating with the missionary priests, and furnishing them the means of carrying on their work. A number of young men of property, all of them belonging to the upper classes, and some of them possessed of great wealth, banded themselves together to devote their time and substance to the Catholic cause, and to act as guides, protectors, and supporters of the priests who were coming to "reduce" England. We know the names of some of these young men, but it is quite certain that we know only a few; it is evident that Catholic sympathisers were very much more numerous than has been generally believed. Wherever Campion went he found an eager audience. Five days after his landing he preached in a house in Smithfield, which had been hired by Lord Paget, "gentlemen of worship and honour" standing at the doors and guarding the approaches. The effect of the sermon was very great, the audience breaking forth into tears and expressions of strong emotion. Sanguine people began to believe that their fondest dreams would be realised, and they talked wildly and foolishly. The Queen's Council were kept informed of all that was going on; but so powerful was the combination of the "Comforters," as they were called, that though the spies and informers did their work sedulously, it was necessary to proceed with caution, and not precipitate a crisis. Campion continued to lurk about London and the neighbourhood for some time; his movements were watched, but for the present it seemed unadvisable to attempt his apprehension. At the end of August he was persuaded to write his famous Challenge. It was intrusted to a Hampshire gentleman of large means, Pound by name, who at one time had been a courtier, but, being strongly impressed by his religious convictions, had retired from the world, and given himself up to the exercises of devotion. He had been thrown into prison more than once for his recusancy, and apparently, whilst in the Marshalsea in 1578, had applied to be admitted into the Society of Jesus. But Pound was an impulsive person, and very soon this paper of Campion's became as widely circulated as a royal proclamation. Meanwhile Campion had left London, and was wandering about the country, handed from house to house by the agency of the Catholic Club, and carefully watched over lest the pursuivants should come upon him unawares. The myrmidons of the law were outwitted and baffled, the Lords of the Council became irritated and angry; proclamation followed proclamation, but months passed, and Parsons and Campion were still at large. The Catholics set up a printing press, and published one book after another, the Government tried their utmost to lay their hands upon it, but in vain. At last the rack was resorted to, and seven of those who at various times had been apprehended during the Jesuits' campaign were cruelly tortured in the last month of 1580, but marvellously little was extorted from them; even one of the printers was apprehended, but the press was still undiscovered. Campion continued his labours, preaching and writing incessantly, Parsons remaining in London under the protection of the Spanish ambassador, who treated him as one of his own retinue. But Campion's time came at last, and on Sunday, the 16th July 1581, he was taken at Lyford in Oxfordshire, just after he had preached to a congregation of more than sixty persons, of whom a large proportion were young Oxford students. On the 22nd he was committed close prisoner to the Tower: a week after he was placed upon the rack, to force him if possible to criminate himself, and under the intolerable torture he appears to have given up the names of some of those who had befriended him. The information was not sufficient or not satisfactory, and as soon as he could bear it he was racked again. Then followed certain "controversies," which were held in the chapel of the Tower; the Jesuit father, worn with agony and all the miserable adjuncts of his imprisonment, being called upon to defend himself against all comers. To the wonder of those who flocked to see him—for the controversies were held in public—this Jesuit priest, spite of all he had gone through, comported himself with dignity and courage, and was quite able to hold his own. The tide of popular feeling seemed likely to turn in his favour, for the people hated the torture-chamber, and they always love the man who stands up boldly for himself against odds. The patterers began to sing about the streets doggerels which made Campion a hero, and the controversies were abruptly stopped. For another month after this he was kept close prisoner in his cell; then another order came that he was to be racked for the third time. When, three weeks after this, he was put upon his trial, he had not sufficiently recovered from the effects of his torture to lift his hand at the bar. Of course he was condemned to die. On the 1st December 1581 he was executed at Tyburn, little more than seventeen months after he had landed at Dover. Whoever will may read in Mr. Simpson's work the hideous details of that last tragic scene,—the dreary rainy morning, the motley procession, the dragging of the wretched victims—for there were three of them—through the deep mire of the London streets, the hanging and the cutting down, and the ghastly mutilation that followed; the plunging of the executioner's knife into the quivering bodies, the flinging of the bleeding members into the cauldron that stood by, so that the blood was splashed into the faces of the crowd that pressed round.

. . . . . . . .

Among those who stood nearest to the executioner were many who had been deeply moved by Campion's preaching, and had ministered to his wants in various ways; for Campion was one of those who, animated by a real enthusiasm themselves, are sure to kindle a fire in the hearts of the young and ardent. A man's personal influence depends but little upon the goodness of his cause. It was over young men, above all, that Campion's career exercised an irresistible fascination. His life appeared to them a life of heroic self-sacrifice—his death, a glorious martyrdom. When they stood beside his scaffold and witnessed all the horrors of that barbarous butchery, they could not but be deeply moved. It was a scene to make the most callous shudder; but in those who sympathised with the sufferers it must have aroused a tumult of anger, grief, and passionate revolt, under the force of which it was hard to follow the dictates of prudence. Foremost among that throng who pressed nearer and nearer to catch the martyr's last words, or if possible to obtain some relic of him to keep as a peculiar treasure, was young Henry Walpole, whom we heard of last as having gone up to Gray's Inn about a year before Campion's arrival. Of his life in London we know little or nothing, but we do know that Gray's Inn was at this time a favourite haunt of all who were "Catholicly" inclined—that he was a member of that Society which has been referred to is highly probable—that his leanings were all in favour of the mission is certain. When the executioner had finished his bloody work and flung Campion's quarters into the cauldron that was simmering hard by, the blood spurted out upon Henry Walpole, and bespattered his garment. The beating heart of the young enthusiast throbbed with a new emotion; every impulse of indignation and horror stirred within him; and it seemed that there had come to him a call from Heaven to take up the work which had been so cruelly cut short, and to follow that path which Campion had trodden. From that moment his course was determined on, and from that day he resolved to devote himself to the cause for which Edmund Campion had died.([8])

The crowd dispersed, and each man went to his home. Henry

Walpole returned to his chambers: his excited feelings would not let him remain idle nor silent; and violently agitated as he was, he sought relief for his emotion by pouring out his thoughts in verse. Not many days after there was handed about in manuscript " An Epitaph of the Life and Death of the most famous Clerk and virtuous Priest, Edmund Campion, a Reverend Father of the meek society of the blessed name of Jesus." It is a poem of thirty stanzas, by no means lacking in sweetness and delicacy of feeling; and in the temper of men's minds at the time of its composition, was calculated to produce a profound sensation.'([9]) Copies could not be multiplied fast enough for the demand, and at last it was privately printed by one Vallenger, together with some other poetical effusions on the same subject. Vallenger was soon called to account for his audacity, he was censured in the Star Chamber, and condemned to lose his ears and pay a fine of £100, but he did not give up the author's name, and bravely suffered alone. ([10])

But though Vallenger kept his secret with unusual courage, it was not long before whispers went abroad that the true author of the poem was Henry Walpole, who forthwith became an object of suspicion: he had been notoriously at Cambridge an associate with the Romanist malcontents; he had taken no degree; the oath of allegiance he had declined to be bound by; at Gray's Inn he had already become famous by his uncompromising habit of standing up for his own opinions, and had the character of being a far better theologian than lawyer; at the disputations between Campion and the English divines in the Tower he had been a constant attendant; he had been present at his trial in Westminster Hall, and had stood by his side at the execution; ([11]) he had taken no pains to conceal his sentiments, and rather appears to have exhibited something like a spirit of bravado. His biographers assert that he had made himself obnoxious by "converting" more than twenty young men who were his associates, and that his activity as a proselytiser drew upon him at last the notice of the Council; it is certain that his cousin, Edward Walpole of Houghton, was powerfully influenced by him, and induced to refuse the oath of allegiance, and certain, too, that this circumstance had something to do with his finding it necessary to go away from London, where a warrant was out against him; even the precincts of Gray's Inn would soon become unsafe, and he rode off to his Norfolk home to escape the pursuivants. But there was a danger that by remaining in his native county he should compromise his relations, and after some delays he managed to get a passage on board a vessel sailing for France. ([12]) Where he landed is unknown, but he passed through Rouen, stayed some time in Paris, arrived at Rheims on the 7th July 1582, and enrolled himself among the students of Theology. Here he remained for nine or ten months, and then set out for Rome. He was received as a student into the English college on the 28th April 1583, and in the October of that year was admitted to minor orders. In the following January he left the English college and offered himself to the Society of Jesus. On the 2nd February 1584 he was admitted among the Probationers. After little more than a year his health broke down; change of air and climate was necessary, and he was sent to France and completed his two years of probation at Verdun. The next two years and a half he spent at Pont à Mousson, during which time he was "Prefect of the Convictors." At last he received a summons to proceed to Belgium, and by order of the General of the Society he was ordained Priest at Paris on the 17th December 1588. ([13]) From this time till his death we can follow his movements pretty closely; but for the present we must leave him, and turn our attention to other scenes than those in which he personally took part.

# NOTES TO CHAPTER IV.

(1) *Page* 87, *line* 7. *Oliver's Collections*, sub voc.

(2) *Page* 87, *line* 18. The brothers Eliseus (or Elisha) and Jasper Heywood were the sons of John Heywood the epigrammatist, who, after enjoying the patronage and favour of Sir Thomas More during the reign of Henry VIII., was "much valued" by his daughter, Queen Mary, and appears to have been admitted to her presence even during her last illness. On the accession of Elizabeth he joined the "Catholic exodus," and died in banishment at Malines in 1565. Of his two sons, Eliseus the elder was elected a Fellow of All Souls in 1547, but quitting England with his father, he spent some years in travelling, and finally joined the Society of Jesus in 1574. Jasper, the younger brother, was a far more considerable personage. He, too, was Fellow of All Souls, and was still a Fellow of the college in 1560, when he published a translation of the *Thyestes* of Seneca in small 8vo, which is now extremely rare. In the following year he left England, and entered the Society on the 21st May 1562. He became eventually a prominent person among the Jesuits in England, and for a while was even Superior, having been sent over in 1581, shortly after Campion's death. He was apprehended in 1583, and thrown into the Clink, and from thence sent to the Tower, where he was kept till January 1584-5, when he was banished. While in the Tower "he was permitted to receive visits from his sister, who was able to bestow upon him some care and nursing." This sister was Elizabeth, *mother of John Donne, afterwards Dean of St. Paul's*, whom Ben Jonson calls "a noted Jesuit." Jasper Heywood was celebrated for his proficiency in Hebrew and for his learning generally. See Wood, *Ath. Oxon.; The Athenæum*, No. 2508, p. 673; *Troubles of our Catholic Forefathers*, second series, pp. 34, 68, &c.

(3) *Page* 88, *line* 11. Bellarmine was one of Stapleton's scholars when he was professor of Divinity at Louvain.

(4) *Page* 91, *line* 11. For an account of Parsons see Wood's *Ath. Oxon.*, by Bliss; Oliver's *Collections;* De Backer, *Bibliothèque des Ecrivains de la Compagnie de Jésus*, iii. 564. For Campion, see the exhaustive Life of him published by the late Mr. Richard Simpson. Williams & Norgate., 1867.

(5) *Page* 95, *line* 14. Among the *Yelverton MSS.* in the possession of Lord Calthorpe there is one which is of peculiar interest for the student of the history of the Jesuit mission. It is in vol. xxxiiii., and is entitled "A generall discourse of the popes holines and preists with th$^{re}$ deuices for y$^e$ maintenance of ther religion." It is written in a very minute hand and with great care, by one who evidently had gone to Rome and spent several months there, with the object of making money by giving valuable intelligence to the English government on his return. It is probably the most complete and elaborate account of the persons and habits of the English exiles in existence, and well deserves to be printed. The names, addresses, antecedents, and description of no less than 295 Englishmen are given, who were living in banishment in 1581. The spy describes minutely the appearance and habits of all the members of the Mission, except Campion, who, because he had but very lately come to Rome, he appears never to have seen. His account of Parsons is as follows : " Robarte Persones, preste and Jesuite penitencer for the nacione, some tymes a student of Phisicke, and at the finding of [obliterated] about 40 yeres of adge, talle and bige of statur, full faced and smooth of countenance, his beard thicke of an abrome [*sic*] collore and cute shorte." The fellow arrived at Rome 5th July 1579, and lodged at the house of Solomon Aldred [see above, p. 83, n. 11], and thence removed to the English College, where he was received with confidence, and treated with kindness and hospitality. He stayed at Rome till the following year, and he tells us that " the 17th May 1580, Tuesday, I arrived at London in the morning, and after noon came to the court, where by means of Mr. Frauch [*sic*] Myles I came to the speach of Mr. Secretary Walsingham his ho$^r$." There is a glorious portrait of Parsons in the third volume of Hazart, *Kerckelycke Historie van de Geheele Wereldt*. Fol. Antwerp, 1669. The book is common enough without the portraits (which give it its value), but very rare in its complete form. Dr. Bliss had never seen this portrait, and I am indebted to Father Remy de Buck for procuring for me the copy of Hazart in which it occurs. In the same volume is a magnificently engraved portrait of Sir Thomas More and a scarcely less brilliant one of Campion.

I take this opportunity of expressing my obligations to Lord Calthorpe for his great kindness and hospitality when allowing me to have access to his precious MSS. in January 1876.

(6) *Page* 95, *line* 18. The apprehension of Emerson is one of the many exciting incidents in Mr. Morris's *Troubles of our Catholic Forefathers*, 2nd series, p. 40.

(7) *Page* 96, *line* 26. The particulars regarding Bishop Goldwell have come to light only very recently. My authority is Mr. Maziere Brady's work, *The Episcopal Succession in England, Scotland, and Ireland, A.D.* 1400 *to* 1875. 2 vols. 8vo. Rome, 1876. Mr. Brady refers for a great deal of his information to *The Month* for January and February 1876.

(8) *Page* 100, *line* 34. From a MS. in the Burgundian Library at Brussels (No. 4554) it appears that Henry Walpole himself gave the account in the text of his presence at Campion's execution, and of its profound effect upon him, to Father Ignatius Basselier, shortly after its occurrence. Cresswell, whose *Histoire de la Vie et ferme Constance du Père Henry Walpole* was written eight months after he suffered at York, had not apparently heard the story of Campion's blood spurting out upon him; but he and Yepez mention the fact of his being present at Campion's death and at the conferences in Westminster Hall. Bartoli (*Dell' Istoria della Campagnia di Giesu l'Inghilterra*, 4to, 1676, p. 411) refers to the story; Morus does not (*Hist. Prov. Angl.*, p. 202). For those who have access to *Holinshed's Chronicle*, it will repay them to read his account of Campion's execution. It is valuable as showing the very great excitement that that event occasioned. As to the *manner* in which the story is related in Holinshed, Hallam says, "The trials and deaths of Campion and his associates are told in the Continuation of Holinshed with a savageness and bigotry which I am very sure no scribe for the Inquisition could have surpassed. . . . See particularly p. 448, for the insulting manner in which this writer describes the pious fortitude of these butchered ecclesiastics."—*Constitutional History*, vol. i. p. 146, n. i. p. 3, tenth edition, post 8vo.

(9) *Page* 101, *line* 11. The only contemporary copy of the poem which is believed to be in existence is now in the Bodleian Library, from which the following transcript has been made. I believe it has never yet been printed in full, though Dr. Oliver mentions the fact of four "sonnets" having been printed "in a book of about fifty pages, entituled 'A true Report of the Martyrdome of Mr. Campian, written by a Catholic Priest,' no place or year mentioned in the title." This appears to be the work mentioned by Mr. Simpson in his Bibliographical Appendix to the *Life of Campion*, p. 350, No. 7. I have never seen the book.

How much importance was attached to the following poem is plain, not only from the fact of the government having made great, and apparently successful, exertions to suppress it, and destroy all copies printed or in manuscript, but from a curious collateral piece of evidence which I was fortunate enough to stumble upon some years ago. On the 21st March 1594, *i.e.*, thirteen years after Campion's death, "John Bolt, yeoman, late of Thornden, Essex," was brought up for examination before Sir Edward Coke, then Solicitor-General. Among other things laid to his charge, and for which he had to give account, he was made to confess "that certain leaves containing verses, beginning with '*Why do I use my paper, pen, and ink*, &c.,' are in his handwriting, wrote them in London five years since from a paper given to him by Henry Souche, servant to Mr. Morgan of Finsbury Fields, and has read them five or six times since." . . .— P. R. O., *Domestic, Eliz.*, vol. 248, n. 38.

ELLIOTT, SLEDD, and MUNDAY were three professional spies and informers who were witnesses at Campion's trial. On these worthies see Simpson's *Life of Campion.*

NORTON was the "rack master," who was committed to prison for a few days when an outcry was raised against him for his atrocious cruelty. He was soon set at liberty, and lived to ply his odious vocation upon many another sufferer in after years.

LEE was WILLIAM LEE, foreman of the Jury which tried Campion.

There is a good deal about ELDERTON and MUNDAY in WARTON'S *History of English Poetry, edited by Hazlitt,* 1871, vol. iv. p. 391.

Vita Edmundi Campiani, Ang. vers. Laud. Rot. 2, supra E. C. (in Bibl. Bodl., Oxon.)

✠ ✠ ✠

## Jhesus Maria.

AN Epitaphe of the lyfe and deathe of the most famouse clerke and vertuouse priest Edmñd Campian, and reverend father of the meeke societie of the blessed name of Jesus.

" Whie do y vse my papire yncke and penne ?
　or call my witts to counseil what to saie ?
such memories were made for mortall men,
　I speake of saynts, whose names can not decay.
An angells trumpe were meeter far to sounde
　theire gloriouse deathes, yf such on earth were founde.

" pardon my wants. y offer nawght but wyll.
　theire register remayneth safe above,
Campian exceades the cūpasse of my skyll.
　yet let me vse the measure of my love,
and geave me leave yn lowe and homelie verse,
　this highe attempte in Ingland to rehearse.

" he came by vow. The cawse, to conquyre synne,
　his armour, praier. the word his terdge & shielde,
his cūfort heaven, his spoile our sowles to wyñe.
　the devyll his foe, the wicked worlde his fielde.
his triumphe ioy. his wage æternall blysse,
　his capteine Christe, wich ever durying ys.

" from ease to payne, from honour to disgrace,
　from love to hate, to daynger, beyng well.
from safe abrode, to feares yn euerie place.
　contemnyng deathe, to save our sowles from hell.
our new apostle cumyng to restore
　the feith, wich Austen planted here before.

" hys native flowres were myxte with hearbe of grace.
    his mylde behaveour tempered well wyth skylL
A lowlye mynde possest a learned place.
    A sugred speache, a rare and vertuouse wyll.
A saynt lyke mā was sett in earth belowe
    the seede of trewth yn hearyng harts to sowe.

" Wyth tounge and pēne the trewth he tawght and wrote,
    by force whereof they came to Christe apace,
But when it pleased God it was his lote,
    he shuld be thrall, he leant hym so much grace,
his pacience there dyd worke so much nor more,
    as had his heavenlie speaches done before.

" his fare was harde, yet mylde and sweate his cheare.
    his prison close, yet free and loose his mynde.
his torture greate, yet scant or none his feare.
    his offers large, yet no thyng culd him blynde.
ô constant mā, ô mynde, ô vertew straynge,
    whome want, nor woe, nor feare, nor hope culd chaynge.

"from racke in towre they browght hym to dispute,
    bokelesse, alone, to answere all that came,
yet Christe gave grace, he dyd them all confute
    so sweately there yn glorie of his name,
that evyn the adverse part are forst to saie,
    that Campians cawse dyd beare the bell awaie.

" This foyle enragde the mynds of sū so farre,
    they thowght it best to take hys lyfe awaye,
becawse they sawe he wuld theire matter marre,
    and leave them schortly nawght at all to saie.
Traytour he was wyth manie a seely sleighte
    yet was a ieurie packt, that cried gyltie streight.

" Religion there was treason to the quene,
    Preachyng of penaunce warre agaynst the land,
priests were such dayngerouse men, as hath not bene,
    praiers and beedes were fyght and force of hand.
Cases of cōscience bane vnto the state.
    So blynde ys errour, so false a wittnes hate.

" And yet behold theise lambes are drawen to dye,
    treasons proclaymed, the quene ys putt yn feare,
Owt vpon Satan, phie malice, phie.
    Speakest thow to them that dyd the gyltlesse heare?
Can humble sowles departyng now to Christe,
    protest vntrew? Avaunt foule fende, thou lyest.

"My sovereigne Liege, beholde yo<sup>r</sup> subiects end.
  Yo<sup>r</sup> secrete fooes do mysinfoorme yo<sup>r</sup> grace.
Who yn yo<sup>r</sup> cawse theire holie lyfes wuld spende,
  As traytours dye ? a rare and monstruouse case.
the bloodie wolfe condemnes the harmelesse sheepe,
  before the dogge, the while the sheepards sleape.

"Ingland loke vp. thie soyle ys steinde wyth bloode,
  thow hast made martyrs manie of thine owne,
yf thow hadst grace, theire deathes wuld do thee good.
  The seede wyll take, wich yn such blood ys sowne,
And Campians learnyng fertile so before,
  thus watred too, must neades of force be more.

"Repent thee, *Eliott*, of thie Judas kysse,
  I wysshe thie penaunce, not thie desperate end.
Let *Norton* thynke, wich now yn prison ys,
  to whome was seid, he was not Cæsars frend,
And let the Judge consyder well yn feare,
  that Pilate wasshte his hands, and was not cleare.

"The wittnes false, *Sledd*, *Munday*, and the rest
  Wich had yo<sup>r</sup> slaunders noted yn yo<sup>r</sup> bokes,
Confesse yo<sup>r</sup> fault beforehand, it were best,
  lest God do fynde it writen, when he lookes
In dreadfull doome vpon the sowles of men,
  It wyll be late, alâs, to mende it then.

"Yow bloodie Jewrie, *Lee*, and all the leven,
  take heede, yo<sup>r</sup> verdite wich was geaven yn hast
do not exclude yo<sup>u</sup> from the ioyes of heaven,
  and cawse yo<sup>u</sup> rew itt, when the tyme ys past,
and euerie one whose malice cawsde hym saie
  crucifye, let hym dreade the terrour of that day.

"fond *Elderton* call yn thie foolishe ryme,
  thie scurrile balades are too bad to sell.
Let good men rest, and mend thie selfe yn tyme.
  Confesse yn prose, thou hast not metred well.
Or yf thie folie cã not choose but fayne
  Write alehowse ioies, blaspheme thou not yn vayne.

"Remember yo<sup>u</sup> that wulde oppresse the cawse,
  The churche ys Christes, his honour cã not dye,
thowgh hell it selfe wreste her gryslye iawes,
  and ioyne yn leage wyth schisme and hæresie,
thowgh crafte devise and cruell rage oppresse,
  yet skyll wyll wryte, and martyrdome confesse.

"yo$^u$ thowght perhapps, when learned Campian dyes,
    his pene must cease, his sugred tounge be styll.
But yo$^u$ forgeatt how lowde his death it cries.
    how far beyonde the sounde of tounge and guyll.
yo$^u$ dyd not know how rare and greate a good
    it was to wryte hys pretiouse gyfts yn blood.

"Lyvyng he spake to them, wich præsent weare,
    his wrytyng toke the censure of the view.
Now fame reportes his learnyng far and neare,
    And now his deathe confirmes his doctrine trew.
His vertues now are writen yn the skyes,
    and often read wyth holie watred eyes.

"All Europe wonders at so rare a man,
    Ingland ys filled wyth rumour of his end.
London must neades, for it was present than
    When constantly .iij. saynts theire lyfes dyd spend,
the streates, the stones, the steapps, they hale them by,
    proclayme the cawse, for wich theise martyrs dye.

"The towre saies, the trewth he dyd defende,
    The barre beares wittnes of his gyltelesse mynde,
Tiburne doth tell, he made a pacient end.
    In everie gate his martyrdome we fynde.
In vayne yo$^u$ wroghte, that wuld obscure his name,
    for heaven and earthe wyll styll recorde the same.

"yo$^r$ sentence wronge pronounced of hym here,
    Exemptes hym from the iudgement for to come.
ô happie he that ys not iudged there!
    God graunte me too, to haue an earthlie doome.
yo$^r$ wittnes false and lewdely taken yn,
    doth cawse he ys not now accusde of synne.

"his prison now, the citie of the kynge,
    his racke and torture ioies and heavenlie blysse,
for mēs reproche wyth angells he doth synge
    a sacred songe, wich euerlastyng ys.
for shame but schort, and losse of small renowne,
    he purchast hath an ever duryng crowne.

"his quartered lymmes shall ioyne wyth ioye agayne,
    and ryse a bodie bryghter then the sonne,
yo$^r$ bloodie malice tormēted hym yn vayne,
    for euerie wrynche sū glorie hath hym woñe.
And euerie droppe of blood, wich he dyd spende,
    hath reapte a ioye, wich never shall haue ende.

"Can drerye death then daunt our feith, or payne?
　　Leste lyngryng lyfe we feare to loose our ease?
No. no. such death procureth lyfe agayne.
　　Tis onely god, we tremble to displease,
who kylles but onse, and euer synce we dye.
　　whose hole revenge torments æternally.

" We cā not feare a mortall tormente. we.
　　theise martyrs bloods hath moistened all our harts,
whose parted quarters when we chawnce to see
　　we learne to plaie the constant Christian parts.
his head doth speake, and heavenlie precepts gyve,
　　how we y$^t$ looke, shuld frame our selfs to lyve.

" his yougthe instructes vs how to spend our daies.
　　his fleying bydds vs learne to bañyshe synne.
his streight profession schewes the narrowgh waies,
　　wich they must walke that loke to enter yn.
his home returne by daynger and distresse,
　　emboldeth vs, our conscience to professe.

" his hurdle drawes vs wyth hym to the crosse.
　　his speaches there provokes vs for to dye.
his death doth saie, this lyfe ys but a losse.
　　his martryd blood from heaven to vs doth crye.
his fyrst and last, and all conspire yn this,
　　to schew the waye that leadeth vs to blysse.

"blessed be God, wich lent hym so much grace,
　　thanked be Christ, wich blest hys martyr so,
happie ys he, wich seeth his masters face,
　　Cursed all they, that thowght to worke hym woe,
bounden be we, to geave æternall praise,
　　to Jesus name, wich such a man dyd rayse.

(10) *Page* 101, *line* 17. Henry Vallenger appears to have been a Norfolk man. There were several members of the family settled at King's Lynn and the neighbourhood in the sixteenth century, and it is probable that Vallenger and Walpole were old friends.

(11) *Page* 101, *line* 30. See above, note (8).

(12) *Page* 102, *line* 10. Bartoli tells us that an order was issued for his apprehension by the Council; and expressly mentions Robert, Earl of Leicester, as having been incensed against him in consequence of his having

converted his cousin Edward Walpole. This is a highly probable story, as Leicester can hardly have failed to take some interest in one who, after his own death, would succeed to Amy Robsart's estates in Norfolk. Bartoli goes on to say that Henry Walpole slipped away to Norfolk, and was actually concealed in a hiding-place (*in un fedel nascondiglio della sua medesima casa*) at ANMER HALL; that he escaped with difficulty from the pursuivants, and concealed himself in the woods by day and pursued his journey by night; that he managed to reach Newcastle, and thence took ship for France. —Bartoli, *u. s.*, p. 413.

(13) *Page* 102, *line* 27. "1582, 7 die [Julii] ex Anglia ad nos venit D. Hen. Walpole disertus gravis et pius."
"1583, 2° Martii, Româ missi sunt D. Henricus Walpoole, D. Tho. Lovelace, &c. . . . quibuscum Verduno profecit D. Ric. Singleton."—*Douay Diary*, printed by the Fathers of the Oratory, Brompton.

"MDLXXXIII. Henricus Walpolus, Anglus, Norfolgiensis, annorum 24, aptus ad Theologiam, receptus fuit in hoc Anglorum Collegium inter alumnos S$^{mi}$ D. N. Gregorii, a P. Alfonso Agazzario, Rectore, *de expresso mandato Ill$^{mi}$ D. Cardinalis Boncompagni, Protectoris*, sub die 28 Aprilis 1583.

"Mense Octobris ejusdem anni fuit cum illo dispensatum in [*sic*] irregularitate propter heresim contracta ab Ill$^{mo}$ Cardinale S. Severinæ, et eodem mense accepit minores ordines a R$^{mo}$ Asafensi [Bishop Goldwell of St. Asaph].

"Discessit e Collegio antequam faceret juramentum in mense Januarii 1584."—*Ex Archivio Collegii Anglicani de Urbe, MS.* No. 303, fo. 16 b.

What follows is written with his own hand in the Album of the Tournay Noviciate, which is still preserved among the MSS. of the Burgundian Library at Brussels.

"Ego Henricus Walpolus Nordvincensis Anglus, natus in Octobri anno 1558. In Anglia dedi operam humanioribus litteris aliquandiu in patria, deinde in Academia Cantabrigiensi annis tribus.

"Londini fere quadriennio legibus Anglicanis.

"Postea Rhemis theologiæ scholasticæ simul et positivæ per annum unum, Romæ similiter fere per annum ante ingressum Societatis; post ingressum vero duobus annis et medio theologiæ Scholasticæ Mussiponti, quo tempore fere toto Prefectum egi apud Conuictores.

"Admissus in Societatem Jesu Romæ a R. P. N. Claudio Aquaviva Generali Societatis Jesu 2 februarii A° 1584, ibidem in domo probationis fui tredecim mensibus, inde ob adversam valetudinem in Francia [m] missus, fere per annum mansi in domo Probationis Virdunensi, ubi etiam absoluto probationis biennio uota Scholasticorum emisi, sacrum celebrante R$^{do}$ P. Benedicto Nigrio magistro Novitiorum.

"Mussiponto in Belgium missus R$^d$ P. N. Generalis mandato, Parisiis in transitu factus fui Sacerdos 17 decembris A° 1588, cum antea a R$^{dmo}$ D°

Suffraganeo Metensi promotus fuissem ad ordinem Subdiaconatus pridie Pascatis 26 Aprilis, et ad ordinem Diaconatus 21 Maii eiusdem anni.

"Bruxellis et in castris officia Societatis prestiti per tres annos; denique a R⁴⁰ P. Oliverio Manaræo Societatis Jesu in Belgio Provinciali, uocatus fui ad Domum Probationis Tornacensem, ubi inchoavi tertium annum probationis 22 octobris A⁰ 1591 et examinatus fui a P. Joanne Bargio iuxta examen Scholasticorum, qui studia in Societate absoluerunt, respondique firmum in mea deliberatione et uotis et promissione Deo oblatis antequam ad studia me conferrem, me permanere, eique reddidi rationem vitæ meæ, inchoando ab eo tempore quo eam reddideram, quando ad studia missus fui.

"Actum Tornaci in domo probationis Societatis Jesu. Circa Natalem Dñi° a 1591. Ita est Henricus Walpolus."

## CHAPTER V.

# THE KINSMEN.

"A rampart of my fellows; it would seem
Impossible for me to fail, so watched
By gentle friends who made my cause their own."
— *Paracelsus.*

WITH the execution of Campion the Jesuit mission for a while collapsed. Of all that band of men who in the winter of 1580 set forth with such high hopes to "reduce" England to the old Faith, only one escaped either the scaffold or the dungeon, and that one was Robert Parsons. Of the rest, such as were not hung were kept in jail for a year or two, and then, to the number of twenty-one, were shipped off to the coast of Normandy.(¹)

Whatever effect Campion's preaching and death may have produced upon the more earnest sympathisers with his views, the immediate consequences of the mission were eminently disastrous. The Excommunication had been Rome's first challenge: it had been answered by the legislation of 1570. The Jesuit invasion was the second: it was replied to by the Act of the 23rd Elizabeth; and it will be worth while at this point briefly to trace the development of that penal legislation which from this time began to be put in force with dreadful severity, and which, whether necessary or not, became during the remainder of the Queen's reign a whip of scorpions for the unhappy votaries of the see of Rome.

The Act of 1st Elizabeth was mainly concerned with enforcing the use of the Book of Common Prayer, and providing against the employment of any form of worship except such as that book prescribed. The penalties of that Act were rather negative than positive, attendance at church was compulsory, yet the fine for staying away, although vexatious, could hardly be regarded as intolerable; to say mass in public or private was illegal, but the mass was not mentioned specifically by name.

After the Bull of Excommunication was published, the Act of the 13th Elizabeth treated the breach between England and the Papacy as a fact that could no longer be ignored, and the penalties of that Act were directed against all communion or intercourse with the Church of Rome or its emissaries, and the acceptance of absolution at the hands of its priesthood was declared to be criminal and treasonable. But when the Jesuit mission assumed the character of an actual invasion, the new aggression gave occasion for the passing of the famous "Act to retain the Queen's Majesty's Subjects in their due obedience;" with the rigorous enforcement of which that odious course of cruelty and oppression began, which has been called by continental historians "the English persecution."

Hitherto the Catholic gentry had received some measure of toleration, though regarded with disfavour and suspicion. Henceforth they had to choose between conformity and something like ruin or death. By the first clause of this Act, to persuade any one to embrace "the Romish religion" or to yield to such persuasion, was to incur the penalties of high treason. By the fourth clause, "every person which shall *say or sing* mass" shall forfeit the sum of two hundred marks, and be imprisoned for a year; and "every person which shall willingly *hear* mass" is to forfeit one hundred marks and suffer a like imprisonment. But the most terrible clause was the fifth, which from this time became the real instrument of oppression and robbery upon the unhappy Recusants, and which, in lieu of the old fine for non-attendance at church, provided "that every person above the age of sixteen years, which shall not repair to some church, chapel, or usual place of common prayer, but forbear the same ... shall forfeit to the Queen's Majesty, for every month ... which he or she shall so forbear, *twenty pounds of lawful English money;* and besides over and above the said forfeitures, ... be bound with two sufficient sureties, in the sum of two hundred pounds at least, to their good behaviour."

Finally, lest the very severity of this clause should defeat its object, and lest it should appear that only the Crown or the great lords would benefit by the exactions to be levied on the Recusants, it was enacted by the eleventh clause that all monies forfeited by this statute should be divided into three parts; one part to go to the Queen, one-third to *the poor of the parish where the offence was committed,* the remaining third to the informer. I have never met with the faintest trace of evidence that the poor of the parish in any one case benefited directly or indirectly by the fines that were levied. Some portion undoubtedly did find its way into the Exchequer, but they who got the lion's share of the spoil were the pursuivants and informers.

From this time the persecution of the Catholics in England began in earnest, and men with scruples of conscience had to make up their minds either to sacrifice their dearest convictions or to suffer for them.

When Henry Walpole made his choice, and without a licence crossed the Channel, he left behind him in the Norfolk home five brothers, the eldest of whom was in his twenty-second year, the youngest a schoolboy of twelve.([2]) The second of these brothers, Richard Walpole, had been baptized at Docking on the 8th of October 1564. Just a fortnight before his elder

brother had left Cambridge, to commence his studies at Gray's Inn, Richard Walpole had matriculated at Cambridge, having been nominated to one of the scholarships at St. Peter's College, lately founded by Edward, Lord North. (³) He continued to
5 reside at the university for the next three years, and evidently made good use of his time; but the influence of his brother was strong upon him, and when Henry found it necessary to make his escape from England, Richard soon followed him. He left England in the summer of 1584, and reached Rheims on the
10 3rd of June. He stayed there until the following spring, and presented himself at the English College at Rome in April. (⁴) But the influence of Henry Walpole was not confined to the circle of his brothers. It seems to have made itself felt even upon the remoter branches of the Walpole family. We have
15 seen in the previous chapter how it was directly through his persuasion that his cousin Edward Walpole of Houghton was prevailed on to take up a decided line, and openly to join the party of the Recusants. There was another cousin upon whom, though his influence was apparently only indirect, yet it was so
20 potent and effectual as to prove in the sequel of great importance to the future career of the whole family.

When Serjeant John Walpole of Harpley died, on the 1st November 1557, he left, as has been said, one son, William Walpole, heir to his large possessions. (⁵) The boy, at the time
25 of the taking his father's inquisition on the 14th April 1558, was declared to be of the age of thirteen years, eight months, and six days, *i.e.*, he was born on the 8th August 1544. We have seen that he had already been entered at Gray's Inn, and that by his father's will his education had been intrusted to
30 Thomas Thirlby, Bishop of Ely, to which see he had been transferred from Norwich in July 1554. By all accounts Thirlby is described to us as one of the most accomplished and graceful scholars of his age. He had been a fellow of Trinity Hall, Cambridge, and his rooms were under those of Bilney, the fervent preacher who converted Latimer, and who was burnt

for heresy at the Lollard's Pit, near Norwich, in August 1531. Whilst an undergraduate, Thirlby's frequent " playing upon his recorder for his diversion" seems to have annoyed Bilney, who was " driven to his prayers" by the music which disturbed his reading. Archbishop Cranmer conceived an almost romantic attachment for Thirlby, " so that some thought that if he would have demanded any finger or other member of his, he would have cut it off to have gratified him ; " and this affection of the archbishop soon brought him preferment and notice. In 1538 he had been sent on an embassy to France, and from this time till the beginning of Queen Elizabeth's reign he was constantly employed as ambassador to foreign courts, and in that capacity was at various times despatched to Spain, Scotland, the Low Countries, and Germany. He was concerned in the compilation of the Book of Common Prayer, and was one of the revisers of the translation of the Great Bible. He was one of the executors of Queen Mary's will, and one of the supervisors of Cardinal Pole's. When Mary died he was absent from England, having been appointed to treat with France for the restoration of Calais, and he returned from that mission in April 1559, when Queen Elizabeth had already been three months on the throne. When the new Oath of Supremacy was tendered to him, he refused to take it, and was immediately deprived of his bishopric, but at first left unmolested. Courtier though he was, and a man apparently by no means of a stubborn nature, yet the form of the oath appeared to him so offensive that he felt called upon to preach against it, although warned to desist. For his contumacy he was excommunicated, and in June 1560 was committed to the Tower. After a while he was removed to the custody of Archbishop Parker, with whom he lived at Lambeth and Bekesbourne till his death in 1570, and, though under surveillance and nominally a prisoner, was always treated with marked respect and consideration.([6])

When young William Walpole, on his father's death, was handed over to Thirlby's guardianship, the bishop adopted him as

a member of his own household, and as such he remained until the bishop's imprisonment, when he was received into the family of Mr. Blackwell, a cousin of Thirlby's, Town Clerk of the city of London, and a man of great wealth and considera-
tion. When the bishop was sent to the Tower, and it seemed probable he would suffer in substance as well as in person for his recusancy, he disposed of his property, and sold or made over to this Mr. Blackwell a large mansion which he had either purchased or built in the parish of St. Andrew in the ward of Castle Baynard, and it was here he lived while William Walpole made his home with him.[7] Three months after he attained his majority, Walpole married Mr. Blackwell's youngest daughter at St. Andrew's church, and soon afterwards appears to have settled at Fittleworth in Sussex, though frequently visiting at the house of his father-in-law.[8]

When Bishop Thirlby's health began to decline he begged for permission to take up his residence at Mr. Blackwell's, but he died at Lambeth before he could remove.[9] Mr. Blackwell survived him only a few months, and in his will, left the bulk of his large fortune to his widow.[10] After his death, Mrs. Blackwell lived sometimes at the London mansion and sometimes on her estate at North Chapel in Sussex, where she had some large iron works which her son-in-law William Walpole managed for her. He himself was largely concerned in the manufacture of iron in the neighbourhood, and the Sussex ironmasters exhibited so much activity that the attention of the Government was drawn to them, and an Act of Parliament passed restricting their power of cutting down the woods for fuel, and putting other difficulties in their way. Walpole's iron works must have been upon a large scale, for he had attracted the notice of the Council by casting cannon, which had been exported to the Continent, and in February 1574, he was compelled to give a bond in the sum of £2000 to make no more "cast pieces of ordnance without special licence, and in case of such licence being granted," not to "sell them to any stranger," unless the name of the buyer and the number and description of the ordnance were expressed in the said licence.([11]) This appears to have proved the ruin of the trade for a time, for we hear no more of the Sussex iron works, and a year or two after this Mr. Walpole appears to have left Fittleworth, and removed to his native county.

When Parsons and Campion came over to England in 1580, Mrs. Blackwell was still living in London. She was one of those who conformed, and attended her parish church of St. Andrew; but it is scarcely to be wondered at that she was looked upon with some suspicion. Her husband had died a Catholic; she herself was the daughter of Thomas Campion, a citizen of London, who was related to the Jesuit father, and as a natural consequence was more than once subjected to annoyance. In 1584 the Lords of the Council issued an order that the Countess of Northumberland should be received at Mrs. Blackwell's house at her coming to town, and next year she was presented as a recusant, though upon her protesting she succeeded in excusing herself from paying the exaction attempted to be levied upon her. ([12]) Whether her house was one of those many places in and about London to which Campion resorted —whether there he met young Henry Walpole or his cousin William—it is almost idle to ask, and yet the probability of the Jesuit father's receiving some recognition from his wealthy kinswoman is so great that we are tempted to conjecture that it must have been so.

It was probably in consequence of the interference of the Government with the Sussex iron works that William Walpole, about the year 1580, left Fittleworth. He had purchased another estate in Norfolk not far from Dereham—the manor of St. Cleres in North Tuddenham, with a large tract of land extending into three or four of the adjoining parishes. ([13]) Here he lived as a country gentleman, keeping up a large establishment; and in February, 1582, he bought from Bishop Thirlby's nephew Henry a house in Norwich. It had a frontage opposite the Bishop's palace, with gardens abutting on the river, and had formerly been the residence of one of the city aldermen. (14) There had been no offspring from his marriage, an unhappy disagreement arose between him and his wife, which ended at last in a separation, and when Mrs. Blackwell made her will in May 1585, she expressly orders that her son-in-law be called upon to repay all sums of money that were due to her; and she leaves an annuity to her daughter, to be paid "during the time of any breach between her and her husband, William Walpole." (15)

Just about this time Edward Walpole of Houghton came to reside with his cousin at Tuddenham. His position at home had become a painful one: his parents were by no means inclined to side with the Catholic party, but on the contrary were said to be Puritans, as most probably his grandfather, Mr. Calibut, was. There is some reason for thinking that Edward Walpole had adopted decided views on the religious questions of the day some years earlier than his Catholic biographers have stated; at any rate his name is never once mentioned in the wills of any members of the family who died about this time, and the omission is especially remarkable in his uncle Richard's will, inasmuch as some legacy is left to every one of his other nephews and nieces. (16) More tells us that his parents were so irritated by his obstinate opposition to their views and persistence in his own that at last his mother fairly turned him out of doors; that he took refuge with a relation in the county; that he changed his name to Poor or Pauper, and attempted to slip away to the Continent as Henry Walpole had done two or three years before. He was stopped at the port he was intending to sail from and sent up to the Council; but he could have had little difficulty in getting released while Leicester was at the zenith of his power. Foiled in his attempt to leave England, he returned to Norfolk, and William Walpole offered him a home at St. Cleres. (17) Here he set himself to bring about a reconciliation between the husband and wife, who had been living for some time apart, and was fortunate enough to succeed in his object. (¹⁸) Mrs. Walpole returned to her husband, and appears to have regained his confidence and affection, though they were not destined to continue long united. Perhaps William Walpole's state of health may have had something to do with his removal from Sussex into his native air; at any rate he had only been at Tuddenham three or four years when he felt his end was near, and a few days before he had completed his forty-third year he made his will, and arranged for the disposition of his property after his decease. If the last act of a man's life, and the only act which is irrevocable, may be accepted as a trustworthy index to his character, William Walpole's will proves him to have been a man of remarkable generosity, kindliness, and largeness of heart. He had, as we have seen, no child, but he leaves to his widow a splendid provision during her lifetime, with no mean condition to hinder her marrying again: his mother, his sisters, his uncles, his cousins, every servant in his large establishment, are all remembered and named, and legacies are bequeathed to them with a princely liberality. His real heir is his cousin Edward Walpole, to whom he leaves, on the death of his wife, the great bulk of his large property; and by the way in which he more than once connects his cousin's name with that of his wife, it is evident that in making this disposition of his estates he does so in recognition of the service he had rendered him in bringing to an end that unhappy domestic difference that has been referred to. (¹⁹)

It is almost impossible to estimate the amount of a country gentleman's income in the sixteenth century, and almost as difficult to arrive at the acreage of an estate with anything like accuracy; but the lands and manors bequeathed to Edward Walpole by his cousin's will represented a rental which would now amount to at least £7000 a year; and when he eventually abjured the realm, it was said that he had sacrificed more than £800 a year, even after he had sold his reversionary interest in the Tuddenham property. Just six months after the death of William Walpole, Edward's father, John Walpole of Houghton,

died. ([20]) In his will he does not so much as name his eldest
son, but leaves every acre of land which he had the power to
bequeath to his second son, Calibut. The entailed property at
Houghton, Walpole, and Weybread, in Suffolk, descended to
Edward as his heir, though subject to a life interest reserved to
his widow. In the following November Robert Earl of Leicester
died, and all the Robsart estates descended to the heir of
Houghton, but as John Walpole in his will had left them to his
son Calibut, Edward at once made them over to him, and renounced the claim he might have put forth as heir-at-law. ([21])

Thus at the close of the year 1588 the two brothers, Edward
and Calibut Walpole, were seized as tenants for life or in fee
simple of lands and tenements in no less than nineteen parishes
in the counties of Norfolk and Suffolk, and were the lords of
ten manors, extending over several thousand acres. The fortunes of the house seemed in the ascendant, and it needed
only a little exercise of ordinary prudence and a little worldly
wisdom to assure to the Walpoles a position among the
wealthiest families in the east of England; but, on the other
hand, it required only a very little contumacy and a very little
display of religious fanaticism to bring upon them the full force
of the Government, which would not spare where there was so
much to fall a prey to the spoiler. Henry and Richard Walpole
had already shown how lightly they held by any worldly prospects that might be before them. They had turned their backs
upon their native country, and their cousin Edward was more
than half inclined to follow them into exile.

# NOTES TO CHAPTER V.

(1) *Page* 113, *line* 8. *Rishton's Diary*, which is the authority usually cited for this statement, was first printed at the end of Sanders's *De Origine et Progressu Schismatis Anglicani*, Rome, 1690. It is given in English in Tierney's *Dodd*, vol. ii. p. 148. For additional particulars see Morris's *Troubles*, second series, p. 70. Besides the twenty-one who were banished in January 1585, twenty-two more were sent from York, and thirty-two from London, in September of the same year, making up a total of seventy-two priests and three laymen.—*Douay Diary*, p. 12.

(2) *Page* 115, *line* 33. The following entries are extracted from the Parish Register of Docking :—
1561, y$^e$ xviij daye of Maye, was DOROTHY WALPOLE, y$^e$ daughter of CHRISTOPHER WALPOLE, christened.
1562, the vi$^{th}$ daye of June, was GALFERYE WALPOLE .... christened.
1564, the viij$^{th}$ daye of October, was RICHARD WALPOLE .... christened.
the viij$^{th}$ of December, was MARGARETE WALPOLE .... christened.
1566, the xxv$^{th}$ of August, was THOMAS WALPOLE, y$^e$ sonne of MR. CHRISTOPHER WALPOLE and MARGEREYE his wife, cristned.
1567, 1$^{st}$ November, ALICE WALPOLE ....
1568, 23$^{rd}$ October, CHRISTOPHER WALPOLE ....
1570, 1$^{st}$ October, MICHAEL WALPOLE ....

(3) *Page* 116, *line* 4. He matriculated as a scholar of Peterhouse, 1st April 1579.—*Matriculation Book* in the Registry of the University of Cambridge.

(4) *Page* 116, *line* 11. The dates are given from the *Douay Diary* and from the MS. Records in the English College at Rome.

(5) *Page* 116, *line* 24. Machyn in his *Diary [Camden Society*, 1847], gives the following account of Serjeant Walpole's funeral, p. 156.
☞ [1557]. "The 3 day of November was buried in the parish of St. Dunstan's in the West, Serjeant Wallpoll (*sic*), a Norfolk man, with a pennon and a coat of arms borne with a herald of arms; and there was all the Judges and Serjeants of the coif, and men of the law, a two hundred, with two white branches, twelve staff torches, and four great tapers, and

priests and clerks; and the morrow, the mass of requiem." [Spelling modernised.]

SERJEANT WALPOLE married JANE, daughter of EDMUND KNYVETT, of ASHWELLTHORPE, Esq., Serjeant Porter to King Henry VIII., by JANE, daughter and heir of Sir JOHN BOURCHIER, Knt., who was summoned to Parliament as LORD BERNERS. The Barony of Berners came to the Knyvetts through this alliance.

JANE WALPOLE, the Serjeant's widow, survived him many years. She married (2dly) her husband's friend and executor, THOMAS SCARLETT [ch. i. n. 18], and by him had a second family of four daughters.

(6) *Page* 117, *line* 33. Most of the details given are taken from Cooper's *Athenæ Cantab*. See, too, *Camden Society's Wills* (1863), pp. 46 and 52; *Original Papers, Norfolk Archæological Society*, v. p. 75.

(7) *Page* 118, *line* 11. "1562-3. The — day of February was christened at St. Andrew's in the Wardrobe, GEORGE BACON, the son of Master Bacon, Esquire, some time Serjeant of the Acatry by Queen Mary's days. His godfathers were young Master GEORGE BLACKWELL and Master WALPOLE." . . . [Mr. George Bacon had married one of the daughters of Mr. BLACKWELL.]—Machyn, p. 300. See, too, the next page for the notice of the churching of Mrs. Bacon : " . . . . and after, she went home to her father's house, Mr. Blackwell. . . . "

(8) *Page* 118, *line* 15. "1565, 25° Nov., WILLIAM WALPOLE and MARY BLACKWELL were married at St. Andrew's in the Wardrobe."—From the P. R. communicated by COLONEL CHESTER.

Among the Close Rolls in the P. R. O. is one dated 11th May, 17° Elizabeth, in which WILLIAM WALPOLE, of Fittleworth, co. Sussex, Esq., enters into recognisances to pay RICHARD BUTTERWICK, of Bury, co. Sussex, Gent., £350 on the 24th November next ensuing, "at and in the mansion house of one MARGARET BLACKWELL." Mr. Butterwick married William Walpole's sister CATHARINE.

(9) *Page* 118, *line* 18. Bishop THIRLBY died in August 1570.

(10) *Page* 118, *line* 20. Mr. BLACKWELL's will is at Somerset House. It is dated 7th June 1567, but was not proved till the 17th October 1570. I subjoin the notes I took of it. " . . . My soul to God and to the most blessed and immaculate mother of our Lord Jesus Christ, our Lady St. Mary the Virgin, and to all the Holy Company of Heaven ; . . . to the parson of the parish of St. Andrew in the ward of Castle Baynard, where I am a parishioner ; . . . to every poor godchild ; . . . to my brother-in-law Edward Warton, Gent. . . . Executrix shall give and bestow for me xij black gowns with hoods, vj to the men, viz., my son EDWARD BLACKWELL, my son BACON, my son DRAPER, my son WALPOLE, and my brother

CAMPION, to be given if it shall please them to be at my funeral as mourners; the other vj to the women hereunder named, viz., my son EDWARD's wife, my daughter BACON, my daughter DRAPER, my daughter WALPOLE, my cousin URSULA PATRICK, and my sister CAMPION. . . . To the prisoners of either of the Compters in London ; . . . to the prisoners of Ludgate ; . . . to the prisoners of Newgate. . . . To the poor people of Edgeware in the county of Middlesex, where I was born ; . . . to the poor of Hendon, co. Middlesex. . . . To the Right Rev. Father in God, and my most singular good Lord THOMAS THIRLBY, late Bishop of Ely, for a poor remembrance of good heart and will towards his lordship, a gold ring value five marks. . . . To my cousin HENRY THIRLBY, son of my cousin THOMAS THIRLBY [sic], his lordship's *brother*. . . . To every of my sons, THOMAS, WILLIAM, GEORGE, and RICHARD, £100. . . . To my daughter MARGARET (unmarried) £100. . . . To MARGARET my wife . . . landed property, &c., in Hendon, co. Middlesex ; the manor of 'Campions' in Epping, co. Essex ; . . . my mansion in the parish of St. Andrew in the ward of Castle Baynard. . . . Residue to be divided 'according to the laudable custom of the city of London.' MARGARET BLACKWELL sole executrix, THOMAS BLACKWELL supervisor."—P. C. C., " Lyon," f. 30.

(11) *Page* 119, *line* 11. In the P. R. O., *Domestic*, Elizabeth, vol. 95. No. 21, there is a list of persons who own iron forges and furnaces in the county of Sussex, dated 15th February 1573-4. Among those mentioned are the following :—" The late Earl of Northumberland one forge and one furnace in Petworth great park, in the hands of Mrs. BLACKWELL. Mrs. BLACKWELL a forge and a furnace in NORTH CHAPPELL."

In the same volume (No. 79), under the date of 22nd February, I find "WILLIAM WALPOLE having the occupying of a furnace and a forge in the parish of Petworth in the county of Sussex, belonging to one MARGARET BLACKWELL of London city, wife to WILLIAM BLACKWELL, Town Clerk of the said city, by the grant of the said MARGARET during pleasure, having married one of her daughters."

The bond referred to in the text is dated Hampton Court, 22nd February, 16° Eliz. " The condition that the above-named WILLIAM WALPOLE shall hereafter make no manner of cast pieces of Ordnance of Iron without special licence, and in case of such licence being granted, shall not sell them to any stranger unless the said stranger's name and quality and the number and name of the said Ordnance to be sold shall be expressed in the said licence." The bond is signed and sealed with the Walpole arms, on which is a label with a crescent for the second house.

The iron works in Sussex were carried on for many years after this, and on a large scale. By the Act of 23° Eliz. c. v., certain restrictions are laid upon the cutting down of "woods growing within a certain compass of London . . . to be converted into coals for iron works." Four years after another Act was passed, 27° Eliz. c. xix., entitled "An Act for the preservation of timber in the wealds of the counties of Sussex, Surrey, and Kent, and for the amendment of highways decayed by carriages to and from iron mills there." Even as late as the middle of the eighteenth century the manufacture of iron was carried on extensively in this district, and the iron railings which surrounded St. Paul's churchyard, and which have only been recently removed, were made of Sussex iron.

(12) *Page* 119, *line* 20. P. R. O. *Domestic*, Elizabeth, vol. 184, No. 46. Mrs. Blackwell's petition to the Lords of the Council is dated 26th November 1585.

(13) *Page* 119, *line* 32. The neighbourhood was densely wooded a century ago, and I have talked with an old inhabitant of the village, whose father used to tell him of the fabulous sums of money realised by felling *the old oaks*, which were cut down in great numbers when the then owner of the property got into pecuniary difficulties. The old manor-house was standing ten or twelve years ago, and then inhabited by a farmer. The foundations and a portion of the walls still remain, and the ground-plan of the mansion is easily traceable. It was a house of no great size, with a frontage of about seventy feet, and surrounded by a double moat, which still exists. By certain deeds in my possession it appears that Mrs. Blackwell held lands in North Tuddenham before William Walpole came to reside there.

(14) *Page* 120, *line* 2. This appears by an indenture, made the 14th February in the 24th year of Elizabeth, between HENRY THIRLBY, of Hendon, co. Middlesex, Gent., of the one part, and WILLIAM WALPOLE of NORTH TUDDENHAM in the county of Norfolk, Esq., on the other part, . . . HENRY THIRLBY sells to WILLIAM WALPOLE "All that the Messuage, &c., . . . in Norwich, in the Parish of St. Martin before the Gates of the Palace of the Bishop of Norwich, as they lie between the common lane on the west part and the tenement sometime ROBERT GREEN'S, Citizen and Alderman of Norwich, and late RICHARD CATLYN, Gentleman, on the east part, and it abutteth upon the king's river towards the north, and upon the king's highway towards the south, &c., &c."—*P. R. O. Close Rolls*, 24° Elizabeth, pt. 13.

(15) *Page* 120, *line* 9. Her will is dated 14th May 1585, and was proved on the 4th July 1586. . . . To Sir THOMAS BROMLEY, Knight, Lord Chancellor of England, and to the LADY ELIZABETH his wife, my especial good lord and lady, as a poor token . . . of my hearty good will and love. . . . To ANNE BACON my daughter, my now mansion and dwelling-house, with all the messuages and tenements thereto adjoining, . . . situate and being in the parish of St. Andrew in the ward of Castle Baynard, . . . which

said mansion my husband WILLIAM BLACKWELL bought of my honoured Father in God THOMAS THIRLBY, late Bishop of Ely . . . [ANNE BACON to hold it for three years, and then to be sold, and the proceeds to be divided between her and her brother WILLIAM BLACKWELL] . . . "and for the help and succour which my will is she shall be to her sister MARY WALPOLE another of my daughters, if occasion shall so require, viz., to allow her yearly xx*li.* during the time of any breach between her and her husband WILLIAM WALPOLE. . . . To WILLIAM BLACKWELL all my debts and money whatsoever which my son-in-law WILLIAM WALPOLE doth owe unto me at this present, or which shall hereafter grow to be due unto me from my said son William Walpole " . . .—P. C. C. " Windsor," f. 37. The property bequeathed in the counties of Sussex, Hants, Surrey, Essex, and Middlesex is very large. The will affords a curious and important confirmation of the story first told by Dr. Henry More of the estrangement between WILLIAM WALPOLE and his wife.

(16) *Page* 120, *line* 22. The omission is the more remarkable, because RICHARD WALPOLE's will was proved in London on the 10th May 1568, when his nephew William could not have been more than ten years old.— See c. iii. n. (9)

(17) *Page* 120, *line* 33. Yepez, writing in 1599 (and at a time when one or other of the three brothers RICHARD, CHRISTOPHER, or MICHAEL WALPOLE must have been in Spain, and pretty sure to be in communication with him), says distinctly that HENRY WALPOLE *laboured for more than two years to convert his cousin:* EDWARD WALPOLE certainly did not take any degree at Cambridge, which in the natural course of things he could have done in 1579. It looks as if his refusal to proceed to the B.A., which necessitated the taking of the oath, had been the cause of the indignation of his parents, who by all accounts acted in a violent and indiscreet manner. More tells us that, after having been unsettled for a long time, the reading of Fulke's answer to Cardinal Allen's book on Purgatory produced a profound effect upon his mind. Dr. Fulke's *Confutation of the Popish Churches Doctrine touching Purgatory and Prayers for the Dead* was published in 1577, so that it was after this year.—Yepez, *Hist. Partic. de la Persec. de Inglaterra,* p. 668. *Historia Missionis Anglicanæ . . . Collectore Henrico Moro,* folio, St. Omer, 1660, f. 202.

(18) *Page* 121, *line* 1. See n. (15). More mentions the circumstance without naming the cousins whom he had succeeded in reconciling; and until the discovery of Mrs. Blackwell's will nothing was known of the affair.

(19) *Page* 121, *line* 25. His will is in *Register* " Spencer " f. 80, P. C. C.

... I WILLIAM WALPOLE, of NORTH TUDDENHAM in the County of Norfolk, Esquire. ... my Manor of NORTH TUDDENHAM alias ST. CLERE'S, ... and all my lands, tenements, &c., in NORTH TUDDENHAM, ELSING, HOCKERING, and MATTISHALL, ... and my Manor of FELTHAMS in GREAT MASSINGHAM, ... and all my lands and tenements ... in GREAT MASSINGHAM and LITTLE MASSINGHAM unto Mary my well-beloved wife for term of her life ... the remainder thereof unto my cousin EDWARD WALPOLE; ... to WILLIAM BETTICE my servant, house and land in GREAT MASSINGHAM; ... to MARTIN DIAT my servant, messuage, lands, and tenement in LITTLE MASSINGHAM; ... to my cousin JOHN WALPOLE the son of my uncle THOMAS WALPOLE, deceased, my Manor of CALIS alias PORTERS in HOUGHTON, ... and all my lands, &c., &c., in HARPLEY, HOUGHTON, BIRCHAM, and RUDHAM, to him and his heirs, and in default of issue, *or if it shall happen the said JOHN WALPOLE or any the heirs of his body ... to commit, do, or suffer any act ... to discontinue ... the foresaid estate to the said John or any the heirs males of his body ... whereby the said estate in tail shall be discontinued ... then I will the said manors, &c., shall remain to my said cousin* EDWARD WALPOLE; ... to Katherine my well-beloved mother, certain lands in HARPLEY and DENTON ... remainder to EDWARD WALPOLE ... Manor of BOROUGH HALL in HILLINGTON and lands, &c., in HILLINGTON, CONGHAM, and EAST DEREHAM, and all lands and houses, &c., in NORWICH, to be sold for purposes of will; ... to my sisters URSULA SCARLETT and MARTHA SCARLETT, lands and tenements in BRANCASTER; ... to MARY HOUGHTON my sister; ... to JANE RYVETT my sister; ... to BRIDGETT HOUGHELL my sister; ... to ANNE STEAD my sister; ... I ordain executors ... Sir THOMAS KNYVETT, Knt., and THOMAS FARMOUR, Esq. ... Whereas WILLIAM YELVERTON, Esq., deceased ... willed recompense to be made to me for certain lands in ROUGHAM, containing about XXV. acres, which in right appertained to me ... such recompense to go to EDWARD WALPOLE my cousin ... to "ANTHONY BROWNE, Esq., and ANNE his wife, my two Spanish bowls of silver parcel gilt, and one pair of andirons, and a back of a chimney of castiron standing in the hall" (*probably made at the Sussex Iron Works*); ... to EDMUND CALL my late servant ... ; to JAMES HOWES; ... to the residue of my men servants ten shillings a piece; ... to every of my women servants five shillings a piece, except to CATHERINE HULE, to whom four marks; ... to WILLIAM MICHELL, my godson, and MARY his wife, eight acres in LITTLE MASSINGHAM; ... to the poor of NORTH TUDDENHAM, HARPLEY, GREAT MASSINGHAM, and HILLINGTON; ... to my uncle EDMUND KNYVETT.—Executed 8 October 1587. ... Witnesses, WILLIAM BROWNE, ANTHONY BROWNE, CHARLES YELVERTON.—Here follows a "Testament" or Codicil :—I do clearly forgive my servant EDWARD PARHAM all such sums of money and other things as he have of mine in his hands; ... to the children of my brother BUTTERWICK and of my late sister CATHERINE his wife ;—to AGNES MICHELL my late nurse . . . ;—Residue to be divided into four parts ;—one part unto MARY my wife and my said cousin EDWARD WALPOLE ;—the second part to my uncle CHRISTOPHER WALPOLE and his children ;—the third part to my brother-in-law THOMAS RYVETT and JANE his wife, my sister ;—the fourth part to my cousin JOHN WALPOLE of HOUGHTON, Esq., and to his children. All to submit to the advice of RICHARD HOWELL, whose costs are to be assured him. To THOMAS SCARLETT, Gent. (his step-father). . . . Revokes appointment of Sir THOMAS KNYVETT as executor and appoints in his room JOHN WALPOLE, Esq., of HOUGHTON.

(20) *Page* 122, *line* 1. His will was proved at Norwich 13th April 1588, *Consistory* 'Homes,' f. 206.

(21) *Page* 122, *line* 10. This appears from the case laid before Sir Matthew Hale, that has been already referred to.

## CHAPTER VI.

# JOHN GERARD.

"Surely, Sir,
There's in him stuff that puts him to these ends."—*Henry VIII.*

A FEW weeks after the annihilation of the great Armada, when the heart of England was stirred with exultant gratitude for the deliverance wrought and the victory gained—when, too, with the rising tide of indignation against the arrogance of Spain, there had come a wave of very angry feeling and resentment against the Pope of Rome and all who were disposed to listen to his claims—a young Englishman of gentle birth, rare tact, courage, and ability, landed by night on the coast of Norfolk, his desire and ambition being to labour for the conversion of England, to administer the sacraments to faithful Catholics spite of all the terrors of the law, and to act as a missionary of what he believed to be the truth, wherever the opportunity should be offered him.

John Gerard was the son of Sir Thomas Gerard of Bryn, in Lancashire, a gentleman of great wealth and consideration in his native county; boasting of a long line of ancestors, and connected by blood or marriage with many of the most powerful houses in the North of England; his brother Thomas was created a baronet on the first institution of the order in 1611 by James I., and from him the present Lord Gerard is lineally descended. For generations the Gerards had been numbered among the knightly families, but in Queen Elizabeth's time they were pronounced and uncompromising Recusants. Sir Thomas had suffered a long imprisonment for conscience' sake, and his estate had been heavily burdened by the charges and fines levied upon him. His son John's earliest recollections were associated with his father either being thrown into jail or being released; and he himself had had the experience of more than a year's imprisonment in the Marshalsea, whither he had been sent, shortly after coming of age, for attempting to leave the country without a licence from the Crown. (¹)

He was born in 1564, and brought up at home by a private tutor, who resided in the house, and who appears to have taught him very little. This deficiency in his early training proved a serious hindrance to him in after life, and the inconvenience of it he has himself deplored. But if he never became a man of learning or a scholar, if the habits of a student seem never to have been much to his taste, he learned other accomplishments in his boyhood, which in the sequel served his purpose better than any scholarship could have done. He learned to sit a horse and train a falcon, knew all the tricks and terms and slang of the hunting field, became an adept at field sports, and was familiar with the pastimes and polite accomplishments of town and country life. A year before Campion and Parsons had landed, young Gerard was sent to Exeter College, Oxford, but apparently in consequence of the increased strictness in forcing the oath and exacting conformity while the excitement of the first Jesuit mission was at its height, he left Oxford after a little more than a year's residence, and seems to have passed the next year or two in idling or amusing himself. While at Oxford he had been placed under the tuition of a Mr. Leutner, or Lucknor, a devout and zealous Catholic, one of the fellows of Exeter, and who subsequently resigned his fellowship and retired to Belgium, where he died. Gerard accompanied his old tutor to the Continent, being desirous of gaining a mastery over the French language, and of otherwise improving himself. He took up his residence at Rheims, and for three years attended the lectures at the English college, although he did not enter himself as a regular student, and was left to pursue his own method of study as he chose. The result was that he read a great deal, but in a desultory and random way; his tastes leading him to attend the divinity lectures, and to spend his time upon the works of the mystical writers of the Middle Ages. While leading this aimless and unsatisfactory life, he formed a friendship with a young man whose name he does not give, which proved a crisis in his career; and under this influence his religious convictions became profoundly intensified. He was living with his new friend in lodgings at Rheims, when, to use his own words, "about twenty years of age I heard the call of God's infinite mercy and loving kindness, inviting me from the crooked ways of the world to the straight path, to the perfect following of Christ in His holy Society." It is a significant fact, explain it as we may, that in the latter half of the sixteenth century the "call of God" for young Englishmen of culture and birth, who were Catholics, meant almost invariably a call to enter the Society of Jesus; so completely had the new order attracted to itself all the choice and lofty spirits among the Catholics, and so wonderfully had the fathers of the society impressed the minds of men with a belief in their sanctity, self-abnegation, and the sincerity of their devotion to a great cause.([2])

Shortly after this crisis in his life, he was seized with a dangerous illness while at Claremont College in Paris, and on his recovery he put himself in communication with Father Parsons, explaining to him his desire to join the society. Parsons, with characteristic astuteness, advised him before taking the final step to return to England and settle his affairs, as he had some property it was necessary to dispose of. He took his advice, and went, and, having finished his business, he attempted to slip out of the country, but the vessel he sailed in was compelled to put back by stress of weather, and he was arrested, sent up to London, and thrown into prison. After an incarceration of more than a year he managed to get free, and made the best of his way to France, and thence to Rome. Cardinal Allen had the sagacity to see how much there was in this young zealot, and at once made choice of him as a valuable emissary to use in England; and although he was some months under the canonical age, he obtained a dispensation from the Pope, and procured his admission to priest's orders in the summer of 1588. On the 15th of August in the same year he was received as a novice into the society, and a few weeks afterwards was sent upon his mission to England. ([3])

John Gerard was now twenty-four years of age. In person he was tall, erect, and well set; his complexion dark, his eyes with a strange piercing look in them, a prominent nose, full lips, and hair that hung in long curls; "his beard cut close, saving little mustachios and a little tuft under his lower lip." He was particular in his dress, and rather affected gay clothing. At his ease in any society, he could accommodate himself with consummate adroitness to whatever company he found himself in; always courteous, he yet knew when to assert himself with decision; in speech deliberate, and not voluble, he had the gift of holding his tongue when it was the time to be silent: when it was the time to speak he weighed his words and could use them well. Such was this remarkable man, a man whose influence was destined to make itself felt to an extraordinary extent in the upper ranks of English society for the next seventeen years, and who, though he was dogged and hunted by a legion of spies, with a price set upon his head, yet died quietly in his bed at last. Meantime, however, he passed through imminent perils and hairbreadth escapes; he was apprehended in 1594, and flung into the Tower; here he was exposed to the horrible agony of being hung up by the wrists to the roof of his dungeon for hours, and when he fainted under the cruel torture, he was let down and restored to consciousness only to be tortured again and again. The amazing nerve and courage of the man did not fail him for a moment in this fearful ordeal; and although the strain was so fierce that he lost the use of his hands for months, and the very jailors were moved at the sight of his sufferings, not a word could be wrung from him to implicate or compromise associate or friend. He escaped from the Tower in 1597, and at once returned to what he believed to be his duty,—comforting the persecuted, confessing the penitent, visiting the desolate whose convictions were opposed to the dominant creed, administering the sacraments, although to do so was, *ipso facto*, to incur the penalty of death; holding his life in his hand, yet always cheerful, fearless, and unwearied; never swerving from the path which seemed to him a path that God had marked out for him; if under a delusion and in error, yet true to his convictions and consistent in his aims,—an example so far, and a reproach to most of us who think our faith so much purer than his, while our lives can bear so much less to be tried and weighed in the balance.([4])

When Gerard wrote the account of himself and his mission to England, the events he recorded were so recent that it was necessary to conceal the names of many of his friends, who were still alive in England and liable to be called to account at any moment for having befriended him ten or fifteen years before; but by careful study of his narrative, and by the help of documents which have only lately come to light, we are able to follow his movements pretty closely, so far as his sojourn in Norfolk is concerned. He landed, as has been said, in the end of October 1588, at a point on the Norfolk coast, between Happisburgh and Bacton, and after passing the night with his companion, Father Oldcorne, in a wood, where they were soaked with the rain and half perished with the cold, the two separated at dawn, Father Oldcorne keeping to the coast until he arrived at Mundesley, where he joined a company of sailors who were making their way to London, and, casting in his lot with them, was allowed to pass unchallenged by the searchers and officers who were everywhere on the lookout for Seminarists and Jesuits from abroad. Gerard turned his back upon the sea, made for the nearest village, and after dexterously getting all the information he could pick up from labourers in the fields and any one he met, he at last boldly went to a village inn, probably at Sloley or Stalham, where he passed the night, and ingratiated himself with the innkeeper by buying a pony which the man wanted to sell. Next morning he rode off on his new purchase, and while passing through a village, probably Worstead, he was stopped and told that he must give an account of himself to the constable and the beadle of the place. Here he was in great danger of being taken before a magistrate, but as this would have involved some trouble to the officials, for there evidently was no magistrate in the immediate neighbourhood, and as he adopted a defiant and imperious manner, the beadle let him go on his road, the man of birth and education proving too much for the plebeian, who was only accustomed to deal with members of his own class.

Gerard trotted away on his pony, well pleased to have escaped his first peril. The place of his landing had been singularly favourable for him. If he had left the ship ten miles further to the northward he would have been compelled to pass through North Walsham or Aylsham on his way to Norwich, and would have been almost infallibly detained by the searchers at either of these towns; but as it was he had only inconsiderable villages to go through, and had very little to fear until he should arrive at the cathedral city. On the high road he caught up a packman who was also journeying to Norwich, and the two rode together for some miles. Gerard got from him all the information he required, and taking the advice of his new friend he avoided entering the city by St. Augustine's Gates, and crossing the river at Hellesdon he made a circuit of the walls, entered by the Brazen Doors, close to the present Militia Barracks, and came to an inn which the packman had told him of—one of the many inns on the Market Hill "within a stone's throw of the castle."(⁵) Here he put up, and while he was sitting in the chimney corner his next piece of good fortune happened to him. The Recusants who had been committed to the castle ten years before were still incarcerated there, subject to every kind of vexation and imposition, and suffering severely in their estates by their long detention. They were, however, occasionally allowed to go out of the prison for a few days at a time, and it chanced that when Gerard had arrived in Norwich one of them had just received his liberty for a brief interval to look after some matters of private business.(⁶) He came to the inn where Gerard was staying, and attracted his attention by naming a gentleman who had been a fellow-prisoner with Gerard in the Marshalsea some years before. Gerard inquired who he was, and found out that he was a stubborn Recusant who had been in prison for many years for his religion. This was enough: it was not long before he had told his new acquaintance that he was a Catholic like himself, and anxious to make his way to London. Could he help him? Of course the man who himself had been in jail for ten years could hardly assist another at so critical a moment, but he would tell him of some one who could, and would introduce him to one whose power was greater and inclination no less sincere than his own. That very day a gentleman was coming into Norwich, as zealous an enthusiast as himself, and who, although he had not yet suffered for his opinions, was prepared to do so if the times should require the sacrifice.

Gerard has concealed the name of this friend, but there is now no difficulty in identifying him as Edward Yelverton, son of William Yelverton, Esquire of Rougham, and as the circumstances of his meeting Gerard and his subsequent close connection with him produced important results, not only to the fortunes of the Walpole family, but to the interests of the Catholic party in Norfolk for the next twenty years, it may be advisable here to give some account of so conspicuous a personage.

William Yelverton of Rougham was one of the richest men in the county of Norfolk. He was twice married, and by both wives had a large family. (⁷) His children had almost all married into the wealthiest and most influential families in the Eastern Counties. From his second son, Sir Christopher Yelverton, who was one of the Justices of the King's Bench, the Viscounts Longueville and Earls of Sussex are descended, from a daughter of which noble house the present Lord Calthorpe traces his lineage. His eldest son, Henry, had married a daughter of Sir William Drury of Halstead, whose son was created a baronet in 1620. Another son, Charles, was knighted by Queen Elizabeth, and one of his daughters, who had first married Thomas Le Strange of Hunstanton, had allied herself two years before Gerard's arrival with Philip Wodehouse, son and heir of Sir Roger Wodehouse of Kimberley, ancestor of the present Earl. (⁸) Edward Yelverton was the eldest son of his father's second wife, Jane, daughter of Edmund Cocket of Hempton, co. Suffolk, Esq., and had inherited at his father's death, by virtue of a marriage settlement, a considerable estate in Grimston and the adjoining parishes, extending over between two and three thousand acres. Here he lived according to the fashion of the time, keeping open house, and having as inmates, besides his own family, a younger brother, a sister who had lately been left a widow, who acted as his housekeeper, and a brother-in-law whose name I have as yet failed to discover. (⁹) As has been said, he had been at Cambridge with the two cousins Edward and Henry Walpole, and was a little their senior, being now about thirty years of age. He had lost his first wife shortly after his marriage, and when his sister Jane was left a widow by the death of Edward Lummer of Mannington, co. Norfolk, in 1588, with a very scanty provision and with her marriage portion squandered, he had offered her a home, although she did not sympathise in his enthusiasm for the Roman doctrine and ritual. He had taken his bachelor's degree at Cambridge, but never proceeded further, and it is not improbable that his leaving the university may have been due to the same influences which led so many at this time to give up their hopes of a university career, and to content themselves with the obscurity of a country gentleman's life. ([10])

5 When Gerard's first acquaintance in Norwich parted from him, he went in search of Mr. Yelverton, and according to appointment, met him in the nave of the cathedral. ([11]) In the course of the interview Gerard frankly confessed himself a priest of the Society of Jesus, and explained his desire to 10 present himself before his superior in London with the least possible delay. Mr. Yelverton, instead of furthering this plan, insisted on taking him to Grimston, mounting him on the horse which his servant had been riding, and leaving the man to follow with Gerard's pony. From Norwich to 15 Grimston was too long a ride for one day, and they put up for the night at one of the country houses on the road, possibly Tuddenham, where William Walpole's widow was now living, or Elsing Hall, the seat of Mr., afterwards Sir Anthony, Brown. ([12]) Next day they arrived at Mr. Yelverton's, and 20 Gerard was introduced as a friend who had come to spend some time with him. Though the secret of his priesthood was kept with the utmost jealousy, Gerard never concealed the fact of his being a Catholic; he was in about as safe a neighbourhood as there was in England south of the Humber; the squires 25 in this part of Norfolk had by no means moved with the times, they were Catholics almost to a man. People discussed the great questions between the Churches of England and Rome freely and openly, and scarcely a single one of the old county families was without some prominent members who 30 were already or were soon about to be sufferers for their faith. The Townshends of Rainham, the Cobbs of Sandringham, the Bastards of Dunham, the Bozouns of Whissonsett, the Kerviles of Wiggenhall, and many others of less note and importance, all figure in the Recusant Rolls, and all were within a ten miles' ride of Grimston; the county swarmed with squires who, though

they "kept their church," yet had small love for the new order of things, and would have welcomed a change to the old regime with something more than equanimity. (¹³)

When Gerard dropped down into the midst of this neighbourhood of malcontent gentlemen who were quite inclined to attribute all the inconveniences they might experience from the natural course of events or their own extravagance to the effects of the persecution, which they were not likely to under-estimate, it is not surprising that his success as a proselytiser surpassed his most sanguine expectations. He tells us that his new friend carried him about with him "to nearly every gentleman's house in the county," Yelverton having the sagacity to see that Gerard was no ordinary man, and that he could take care of himself with tact and discretion. Doubtless among the inner circle of the faithful it was soon suspected that this Mr. Thompson, for this was the name he went by, must needs be something else than he professed to be. How if this captivating young gentleman with the courtly manners and charming address were—might they whisper it ?—a priest, or something worse ? To be sure he could hold his own with the squire in the hunting field, or slip a hawk from his wrist with the best of them; take a hand at the card table, or enjoy a seemly joke with a frolic glee that made him welcome wherever he came; but what did that flash of the dark eyes mean when the ribald tongue broke out into blasphemy and filthy language ?(¹⁴) At times how grave he was and silent; with all this gaiety and vivacity, his mind was clearly always running upon serious things. Other men talked on matters of controversy as if such themes were outside of themselves, he spoke with a solemn earnestness that impressed his hearers most profoundly.

Nor was this all: in accounting, or attempting to account, for the effect which a man produces upon others, we mistake the matter much if we allow ourselves to believe that the proselytiser's success is even mainly due to his skilful use of cunningly-constructed syllogisms and all the tricks of logic. Converts are not made by arguments, and none knew this better than the Jesuits themselves. Conviction is the result of a very complex process, and he who leaves out of account the personal element from his calculations will never be able to understand the secret of many a strong man's failure or weak man's triumphs. In these matters it has again and again been proved that the main factor must always be that subtle and indefinable something which can only be classed under the head of personal influence, and which some, in their despair of explaining its potency, have designated as "mesmeric force." It is abundantly clear that Gerard possessed this strange power of attraction and persuasion to a marvellous extent. During the few years of his sojourn in Norfolk and Suffolk, the number of converts of both sexes which he made would appear absolutely incredible, if the evidence were not so conclusive, and the proofs had not come to us from so many different quarters. At least ten young men of birth, and belonging to the most considerable families in the two counties, left England and joined the Society of Jesus before the close of Elizabeth's reign, and in every instance we can distinctly trace his influence; and, indeed in the majority of cases they themselves attribute their conversion to Gerard by name. He has indeed so much understated the importance of his own work, that it looks as if he had scarcely been aware how great was the effect of his labours; and it is only very recently, after the lapse of three centuries, that modern research has enabled us to form a truer estimate of the extent of his influence.

Among the first who found their way to Grimston was Edward Walpole, drawn back to Houghton by his father's death, to look after his affairs. Between him and Edward Yelverton there had long been a perfect understanding, and Yelverton was not likely to keep the great secret from one who was so sure not to betray it. Ever since Henry Walpole had fled the country he had kept up a correspondence with his relatives at home, and letters had passed by every available opportunity. Of course he had been careful not to let his cousin's enthusiasm cool, and the blundering policy of the Government which attempted to crush out all fanaticism, whether in the Romanist or the Sectary, as heinous crime, and which yet did not allow the criminal the resource of running away from his persecutor, had in the meantime continued as vexatious as ever. The rigour had not abated and the irritation had intensified.

So far Edward Walpole had been only a Nonconformist; at worst he had absented himself from church, and thereby rendered himself liable to the fine for Recusancy, but he had not been formally "reconciled" to the Church of Rome. When he heard of Gerard he soon presented himself at Grimston, which was only five miles from Houghton, and with little delay embraced the opportunity of giving in his adhesion to the Jesuit emissary.

At Anmer Hall, too, Henry Walpole's youngest brother, Michael, was now living with no very definite plans for his future career,—restless, discontented, and ready for any venture,—of ardent and enthusiastic temperament,—just at that age and just in that mood in which a youth is readiest to surrender himself to the sway and direction of a powerful mind. There was no need for any conversion in his case. Had not his brother, that hero of the house, stood by Campion's side at the gallows? had he not had already to hide from the pursuivants, to run for his life? and was he not now a exile for the faith which the mob were howling at? Was not that same brother himself a Jesuit Father, from whom over the sea came letters of earnest pleading, and the fervent words which told of inward peace and a trust that knew no doubt or any thought of wavering? And lo! here, on the other side of Grimston heath, in the house of his brother's friend, it was whispered that a Jesuit priest was staying as a guest. He had come none knew whence, and they scarce knew how—the witchery of a certain mystery and romance was round him. Perhaps he might prove a second Campion; perhaps he too was ambitious of the martyr's crown. Certainly he was living every hour of the day holding his life in his hand, and sure, if detected, of being dragged away to horrible torture and death. And yet he went in and out as gay and fearless as the country squires with whom he mixed familiarly on terms of equality, and as much at his ease as if there were no penal law upon the statute book. It is easy to see for a young man of chivalrous nature, with the love of adventure strong in him, all this must have exercised an overpowering fascination. And accordingly we find that young Michael threw himself into Gerard's arms and attached himself to him with entire devotion. From the first he became his trusty companion and constant attendant, shared his perils, acted as his messenger, served him as his esquire in his journeys, clung to his side wherever he went, and proved a most valuable coadjutor and friend.([15])

There were two other brothers of the Anmer family who, as time went on, became subject to the Gerard influence. Geoffrey Walpole, the second son, never seems to have been troubled by any scruples of conscience. There is not the slightest evidence that he had any sympathy with the uneasiness and discontent which troubled the minds of other members of the household. Whether he was more phlegmatic or less romantic, more stable or less earnest, we shall never know; it is, however, certain that he was the only one of the six sons who never suffered for his religious opinions.

Just a year before the arrival of Gerard in Norfolk, Christopher, the fourth son, had entered at Caius College, Cambridge. He was then nineteen, and therefore several years older then the usual age at which at this time freshmen went up to the university. He had passed the previous two years under a scholar of some eminence, Thomas Speght, master of Ely school, and one of the earliest editors of Chaucer. Speght was a Peterhouse man, and had been there under Dr.

Perne, and was probably, like him, a latitudinarian, with more taste for literature than theology.([16])  It is probable that young Christopher Walpole had not been originally intended for one of the learned professions, and that it had been decided to send him to Cambridge only after his brother Richard had relinquished his hopes of a university career;. but we are assured that he made the best use of his time, and that he was a diligent student.  When he came home to Anmer for the long vacation of 1589, he must have made Gerard's acquaintance for the first time, and he was the next to succumb to the fascination of the young Jesuit priest. He never returned to Cambridge.  More than half disposed to throw in his lot with his two exiled brothers, he was ready enough to yield to Father Gerard's persuasive powers.  His position at the university was henceforth no longer tenable. He could not rest where he was.  Oaths and declarations, sermons in the university pulpit, which he was bound to listen to, attendance at the college chapel, and compulsory communion with heretics,—all these things were threatening him.  He could not conscientiously face them, and the time had come when he believed that he must needs make his choice—remain in England and conform, or leave it, and enjoy that liberty of conscience which was not possible at home.

There was still one other brother, Thomas Walpole, a young man of twenty-two, who without any occupation, and apparently without any taste for learning and study, was at this time idling at home.  He, too, it seems, could not make up his mind to conform, and be content with things as they were.  But what could he do?  These Walpoles clung together with a stubborn pride of family that disdained to purchase advancement by bowing in the house of Rimmon; and when his brothers were already so deeply compromised, Thomas Walpole would not be disloyal to his kin.  As for the polemical questions in dispute, he would leave them to others to wrangle about, but his brothers' cause should be his cause, and with them he would stand or fall.

And thus round the hearth at Anmer, five miles or so from Father Gerard's retreat, five young men, the eldest of them six and twenty years of age, might be seen sitting moodily in that winter of 1589, with no future before them, and no career open, living under a ban. At any moment some emissary from the Government might knock rudely at the door, some pursuivant might come to call them to account and press the oath upon them, some spy might report that they no longer put in an appearance at that parish church which was almost contiguous to their hall; every message from the outer world was full of threatening, there was no field for their ambition, no outlet for their enthusiasm, no scope for the exercise of such powers as they were conscious of possessing. *Of course* they became fanatics; *of course* they became more and more possessed by one idea; of course the sense of wrong and injustice mastered their reason and judgment; the rites of a religion which was proscribed seemed to them to be the only things that were worth living for, and became in their eyes all the dearer and more precious because every time that they took part in them they were running a tremendous risk, and braving the terrors of the persecuting laws.

In the midst of this condition of affairs, news came from across the sea which burst upon the brothers with fresh dismay —Henry Walpole had been arrested at Flushing, and was now lying in a dungeon in imminent peril of his life. His captors demanded a ransom. Who would come to his side and bring the deliverance?

# NOTES TO CHAPTER VI.

(1) *Page* 131, *line* 12. The main authority for all statements regarding Father John Gerard and his family, is Mr. Morris's *Condition of Catholics under James I.*, with its able life of Gerard, derived chiefly from his own autobiography, and illustrated by very copious extracts from MSS. in the Record Office and elsewhere. Gerard was imprisoned in the Marshalsea "from the beginning of one Lent" (1584) to the end of the following (1585).

(2) *Page* 132, *line* 27. On the New Religious Orders founded in the sixteenth century, see Ranke's *History of the Popes*, Book ii. sect. 4.

(3) *Page* 133, *line* 13. Morris, p. 11. There are several descriptions of Gerard's person, dress, &c. The following has been given by Mr. Morris, but it will bear reprinting here, affording, as it does, so good an instance of the wretch Topcliffe's peculiar style of composition and more peculiar spelling.

"Jhon Gerrarde, yᵉ Jhezewᵗ is about 30 years oulde Of a good stature sumwhat higheʳ then Sʳ Tho Layton & upright in his paysse and countenance sum what stayring in his look or Eyes Currilde heire by Nature & blackyshe & not apt to have much heire of his bearde. I thincke his noase sum what wide and turning Upp Blubarde Lipps turninge outwards Especially the over Lipps most Uppwards toward the Noase Kewryoos in speetche If he do now contynewe his custome And in his speetche he flourrethe and smyles much & a falteringe or Lispinge, or dooblinge of his Tonge in his speeche."

Another description of him from the MSS. at Hatfield will be found in the Appendix.

(4) *Page* 134, *line* 19. Horrible as the details are, Gerard's account of his torture in the Tower is so vivid and so powerful that I cannot refrain from giving it here in his own words.

"Then we proceeded to the place appointed for the torture. We went in a sort of solemn procession ; the attendants preceding us with lighted candles, because the place was underground and very dark, especially about the entrance. It was a place of immense extent, and in it were ranged divers sorts of racks and other instruments of torture. Some of these they

K

displayed before me, and told me I should have to taste them every one. Then again they asked me if I was willing to satisfy them on the points on which they had questioned me. 'It is out of my power to satisfy you,' I answered; and throwing myself on my knees, I said a prayer or two.

"Then they led me to a great upright beam, or pillar of wood, which was one of the supports of this vast crypt. At the summit of this column were fixed certain iron staples for supporting weights. Here they placed on my wrists manacles of iron, and ordered me to mount upon two or three wicker steps; then raising my arms, they inserted an iron bar through the rings of the manacles, and then through the staples in the pillar, putting a pin through the bar so that it could not slip. My arms being thus fixed above my head, they withdrew those wicker steps I spoke of, one by one, from beneath my feet, so that I hung by my hands and arms. The tips of my toes, however, still touched the ground; so they dug away the ground beneath, as they could not raise me higher, for they had suspended me from the topmost staples in the pillar.

"Thus hanging by my wrists, I began to pray, while those gentlemen standing round asked me again if I was willing to confess. I replied, 'I neither can nor will.' But so terrible a pain began to oppress me, that I was scarce able to speak the words. The worst pain was in my breast and belly, my arms and hands. It seemed to me that all the blood in my body rushed up my arms into my hands; and I was under the impression at the time that the blood actually burst forth from my fingers and at the back of my hands. This was, however, a mistake; the sensation was caused by the swelling of the flesh over the iron that bound it.

"I felt now such intense pain (and the effect was probably heightened by an interior temptation), that it seemed to me impossible to continue enduring it. It did not, however, go so far as to make me feel any inclination or real disposition to give the information they wanted. For as the eyes of our merciful Lord had seen my imperfection, He did 'not suffer me to be tempted above what I was able, but with the temptation made also a way of escape.' Seeing me therefore in this agony of pain and this interior distress, His infinite mercy sent me this thought: 'The very furthest and utmost they can do is to take away thy life; and often hast thou desired to give thy life for God: thou art in God's hands, Who knoweth well what thou sufferest, and is all-powerful to sustain thee.' With this thought our good God gave me also out of His immense bounty the grace to resign myself, and offer myself utterly to His good pleasure, together with some hope and desire of dying for His sake. From that moment I felt no more trouble in my soul, and even the bodily pain seemed to be more bearable than before, although I doubt not that it really increased, from the continued strain that was exercised on every part of my body.

"Hereupon those gentlemen, seeing that I gave them no further answer, departed to the Lieutenant's house; and there they waited, sending now and then to know how things were going on in the crypt. There were left with me three or four strong men, to superintend my torture. My gaoler also remained, I fully believe out of kindness to me, and kept wiping away with a handkerchief the sweat that ran down from my face the whole time, as indeed it did from my whole body. So far, indeed, he did me a service; but by his words he rather added to my distress, for he never stopped beseeching and entreating me to have pity on myself, and tell these gentlemen what they wanted to know; and so many human reasons did he allege that I verily believe he was either instigated directly by the devil under pretence of affection for me, or had been left there purposely by the persecutors to influence me by his show of sympathy. In any case, these shafts of the enemy seemed to be spent before they reached me, for though annoying, they did me no real hurt, nor did they seem to touch my soul, or move it in the least. I said, therefore, to him, 'I pray you to say no more on that point, for I am not minded to lose my soul for the sake of my body, and you pain me by what you say.' Yet I could not prevail with him to be silent. The others also who stood by said: 'He will be a cripple all his life, if he lives through it; but he will have to be tortured daily till he confesses.' But I kept praying in a low voice, and continually uttered the holy names of Jesus and Mary.

"I had hung in this way till after one of the clock, as I think, when I fainted. How long I was in the faint I know not; perhaps not long; for the men who stood by lifted me up, or replaced those wicker steps under my feet, until I came to myself; and immediately they heard me praying, they let me down again. This they did over and over again when the faint came on, eight or nine times before five of the clock. Somewhat before five came Wade again, and drawing near said, 'Will you yet obey the commands of the Queen and the Council?'

"'No,' said I, 'what you ask is unlawful, therefore I will never do it.'

"'At least, then,' said Wade, 'say that you would like to speak to Secretary Cecil.'

"'I have nothing to say to him,' I replied, 'more than I have said already; and if I were to ask to speak to him, scandal would be caused, for people would imagine that I was yielding at length, and wished to give information.'

"Upon this Wade suddenly turned his back in a rage, and departed, saying in a loud and angry tone, 'Hang there, then, till you rot!'

"So he went away, and I think all the Commissioners then left the Tower! for at five of the clock the great bell of the Tower sounds, as a signal for all to leave who do not wish to be locked in all night. Soon after this they took me down from my cross, and though neither foot nor leg was injured, yet I could hardly stand."

(5) *Page* 136, *line* 2. Any reader of Gerard's narrative, with some local

knowledge, will be able to follow him in his route to Norwich by the help of my account in the text. BACTON is the furthest northern point at which the landing could have taken place. Had the vessel put him ashore at Mundesley, Sheringham, or Cromer, he would have almost necessarily had to pass through North Walsham or Aylsham, where he would have been at once brought before a magistrate. On the other hand, had he landed at Bacton itself, he could scarcely have failed to mention Bromholm Priory, which was then not quite in ruins. It is clear that the place of landing must have been *between* Happisburgh and Bacton, and that Father Oldcorne, "keeping to the coast," must have fallen in with the sailors at or near MUNDESLEY. The bridge over the river at Hellesdon existed certainly as early as the middle of the fifteenth century, and the fields outside Norwich at this time were all open. Gerard seems to have crossed the Dereham Road, and to have "made his circuit of the city," till he found himself on one of the main London roads, and, avoiding the long street from St. Stephen's gates, which would have exposed him to observation, to have crossed what was then the common land outside the walls, and entered by the "Brazen Doors."

Not many days before Gerard's arrival in Norfolk, an order had been sent down to the Sheriff of Norfolk (Sir John Peyton of Isleham, co. Cambridge) ". . . for that their L.L. understand that the Recusants that are prisoners in the Common Jail within that county do much harm, and infect the county, *by the liberty which they enjoy there*, their L.L. have thought good to have such of them whose names are contained in the enclosed Schedule to be removed from thence to Wisbech, and therefore did will and require him to cause them to be immediately delivered to the charge of this bearer [        ] George, keeper of the same house, and also to be assisting unto him in the safe conveyance of them thereto."—*Privy Council Records*.

Then follow the names :—1. WALTER NORTON. 2. GEORGE ( a mistake for ROBERT) DOWNES. 3. ROBERT LOVELL. 4. FERDINAND PARIS. 5. HUMPHREY BEDINGFELD. 6. ROBERT GRAYE.

It appears that a complaint had been sent up to the Council in August, against JAMES BRADSHAW, keeper of the Castle at Norwich, "being complained of to have given more liberty to such [as] are obstinate Recusants than is fit," and in consequence a letter was sent down to FREAKE, Bishop of Norwich, ordering him "to inform himself of the behaviour of JAMES BRADSHAW . . . and of his disposition in religion, and how he hath kept the same Recusants, and what liberty they have had," &c.

Of the gentlemen named, FERDINAND PARIS was of Pudding Norton, Co. Norfolk; he had large estates also in Cambridgeshire, but he seems to have been at last ruined by the exactions levied upon him and his family.

ROBERT LOVELL was a younger brother of Sir THOMAS LOVELL of Harling.

HUMPHREY BEDINGFELD, of Quidenham, was a younger brother of Sir HENRY BEDINGFELD of Oxburgh. In another order in the Privy Council Book, dated 20th March, 1588-89, the Sheriff of the County is instructed that, "Whereas HUMPHREY BEDINGFELD, Gent., hath been long time a prisoner for recusancy in Norwich Jail; forasmuch as there is good [hope] of his conformity in religion if he might have conference with some such as are given [sic] therein and for his health's sake. He was required to take order that BEDINGFELD might be delivered to the *custody of* MR. ROWE, *parson of Quidenham*, to remain with him in his charge for the purpose aforesaid until he shall have order for the contrary. Causing good bonds to be taken of BEDINGFELD that during the time of his commitment as aforesaid, he depart not above two miles distant from the house or dwelling-place of the said ROWE."

On ROBERT DOWNES, see Notes 10 and 11 to Chapter III.: he was an uncle of FRANCIS DOWNES of Lavenham, who was ancestor of LORD DOWNES, in the Peerage of Ireland.

ROBERT GRAYE, of Merton, had married a sister of MR. LOVELL'S. His epitaph in Merton church is given in Blomefield, ii. 305. He was ancestor of the present LORD WALSINGHAM.

The order for the removal of these gentlemen to Wisbech was not carried out till April 1590. A month before, a letter had been ordered to be written to "Richard Archenstall, Esq., with a copy of the orders sent down by their L.L. for the keeping of the Recusants."

"1. First the knights and principal gents are to be allowed two men apiece for their necessary service, if they require it, and the others but one man apiece.

"2. It is meet that they shall be placed in the Bishop's Palace in Ely, in such rooms as by him to whom the charge is committed shall be thought most meet and convenient for that purpose.

"3. They are to be used with all courtesy, but not to suffer them to have conference with any stranger but in his own presence, or some such trusty person as he shall depute.

"4. For their bedding, hangings, and such like furniture, the parties themselves to furnish the same, to whom the keeper shall give notice thereof to the end they make provision accordingly.

"5. He shall make them acquainted with the diet that is set down in the Fleet, whereof a note is set down herewithal, both for the allowance and the number of the dishes, and if they shall desire any increase, then are they to compound with him for the same.

"6. It is meant that they shall be permitted to converse together at their meals and at such other times as by him to whom the charge of them is committed shall be thought meet, so as they do forbear formal speeches unfit for good subjects against the Queen's Majesty or any States of the Realm having governance thereto. (?)

"7. So likewise they are to be permitted to walk together at such times as by their keeper's discretion shall be thought meet, in such places as are not open to the town of Ely.

"8. Order may be taken that some of the watchmen of the town of Ely be appointed to watch about the house, in such places as by the keepers shall be thought most meet and needful, and so it is to be referred to his own discretion to consider what number of men he shall think sufficient to keep both for their better safeguard and service.

"9. Every night they are to be shut up in their chamber at a convenient hour.

"Orders to the same effect to Mr. Fynes for Recusants to be placed under his charge at Banbury Castle or Broughton, Mr. Fynes his house, &c., &c."

Doubtless the same orders held good at Wisbech.

(6) *Page* 136, *line* 111. In these same Records of the Privy Council, I found two instances of 'leave of absence' being granted to the Recusant gentry :—

1. "7th January 1587–88. A warrant to the keeper of Norwich Jail to take bonds of WALTER NORTON, Gent., remaining prisoner under his custody, with two sufficient sureties in the sum of £1000 to Her Majesty's use, with condition to return himself prisoner at the end of one month following into his custody, and thereupon to set him forthwith at liberty."

2. "19th June 1589. A letter to Sir Edward Clere, to take good bonds of GEORGE WILLOUGHBY, of St. Mary Magdalen in Marshland, Esq., to Her Majesty's use, for his forthcoming upon notice given him at his house in Marshland, and for his good demeanour and well-usage of himself during the time he shall be employed about the repairing of the sea banks, drains, and draining of marshes ; thereupon to give order for his liberty and releasement from the custody of ROBERT BOZUN, Esq., to whose keeping he was the last year committed for recusancy, that he might remain within the circuit of sixteen miles about his said house in Marshland."

(7) *Page* 137, *line* 3. In the answers given by one of his grandchildren CHARLES YELVERTON, to the usual interrogatories presented to him on his entering the English College at Rome, on the 14th December 1601—copies of which are now in the archives of the Rolls House—he says that his grandfather had twenty children. Some of these may have died young ; I know of only fifteen, and there are only fifteen figured upon his brass, still existing in Rougham church ; these are, however, all represented as men and women : the following scheme gives them at a glance :—

1. Anne, daughter of Henry  ├ WILLIAM YELVERTON of Roug- ┬ 2. JOAN, da. of EDM. COCKET of
   Farmor of Basham.           │ ham, died 12 August 1586.    │ Cocket, Esq., co. Suffolk.

—1. HENRY YELVERTON of Rougham, died 26 April 1601 (p.m. inq.)=Bridget, da. of Sir W. Drury of Halstead.
—2. WILLIAM YELVERTON, B.A., Pembroke Coll. Camb. 1573, said to have settled in Ireland ; but query did he not die young —v. patr. ?
—3. SIR CHRISTOPHER YELVERTON, one of the Judges of the King's Bench=MARY, da of THOS. CATESBY of Whiston, co. Northants. He died 1607.
—4. LAUNCELOT YELVERTON, Clerk, Rector of the parishes of Sculthorpe, Geist, and Castle Rising, died 1577 ?
—5. HUMPHREY YELVERTON of Bawsie.= ELIZABETH, da. of FRANCIS BASTARD of Grimstone, Esq. He died Nov. 1585 ; she, March 1591.
—6. WINIFRED. =OWEN DUCKET of Worthing.
—7. ANNE. =(1) THOS. REDE of Wisbeach.
   (2) JOHN HAWKINS of ...., co. Essex.
—8. MARTHA. =(1) THOMAS FINCHAM of Fincham, Esq. (2) JOHN HEIGHAM of Giffords, co. Suff.
—9. FRANCES.
—10. JANE=EDWARD LUMNER of Mannington, Esq. He died 1588.

—11. EDWARD YELVERTON of Grimstone. =(1)..........? (2) NAZARETH, da. of EDM. BEDINGFELD. He died 1623.
—12. WILLIAM YELVERTON of Hertford. =GRACE, da. of .... NEWPORT of ...., co. Bucks. He died 1616 ; she in 1624.
—13. SIR CHARLES YELVERTON, Knt. Ho died in debt, 1629.
—14. FERDINAND. Query died v.p. ?
—15. GRISELL. =(1) THOS. LE STRANGE.
    (2) SIR PHILIP WOODHOUSE.

(8) *Page* 137, *line* 16. Thomas, eldest son of Hamon Lestrange of Hunstanton, Esq., died in the eighteenth year of his age, February 1st, in the 23rd year of Elizabeth (1582), without any issue by Grisell his wife, daughter of William Yelverton of Rougham.—Blomefield, x. 319.

In the muniment room at Hunstanton (A. 60) are deposited "Articles of agreement made the 19th March, in the 25th year of Elizabeth, by the arbitrament and good mediation of Henry Doyly, Thomas Farmor, Nathaniel Bacon, and Charles Cornwallis, Esquires, as well by the full and mutual consent of Sir Roger Woodhouse, Knight, for and on behalf of Philip Woodhouse, Esq., his son and heir apparent, and Grisell his wife, of the one part ; and John Peyton, Esq., for and on behalf of Nicholas Lestrange, Esq., on the other part ... " In accordance with which arbitration made on the 15th August, 27 Elizabeth, the manors of East Lexham, with West Lexham, Dunham, &c., were made over to Grisell Woodhouse for her life (A. 61).

(9) *Page* 139, *line* 25. The brother and sister present no difficulty. The brother was almost certainly CHARLES YELVERTON, who had been a witness to WILLIAM WALPOLE'S will at Tuddenham a year before, and who shortly afterwards obtained some office at Court, though what that office was I have not yet discovered. The sister, JANE LUMNER, had been left very scantily provided for by her husband, who died very much in debt, as appears by

her petition to the Court of Chancery in 1597, where she speaks of herself as "being very well descended, and having also received a good portion in marriage." (See Original Papers of the Norfolk and Norwich Archæological Society, vol viii. pt. iv.)

She continued "an obstinate Recusant," as she is frequently described to be upon the Lists of Presentments made to the Bishop of Norwich annually. She had two daughters, who sympathised with their mother and suffered with her. I find her name always included in the Recusant Lists down to 1615. During the twenty years, more or less, when her name appears on the rolls, she changed her residence three or four times, and it looks as if she had become poorer and poorer under the pressure of the exactions levied upon her. The license for 'EDWARD [sic] Lumner de Mannington' to marry 'JANE YELVERTON de Rougham' is dated 5th July 1569.

(10) *Page* 138, *line* 4. EDWARD YELVERTON took his B.A. degree in 1579, being then of Peterhouse, Cambridge (MS. Records in the Registry of the University). During his undergraduate days his future brother-in-law PHILIP WOODHOUSE, DUDLEY FENNER, and CHRISTOPHER HEYDON, were among the fellow commoners, and EDWARD WALPOLE, HENRY WALPOLE, BARTLEY (alias BERNARD) GARDINER, and PHILIP PARIS, probably a son of FERDINANDO PARIS of Pudding Norton, were among the pensioners. See, too, n. (33), chap. ii.

That EDWARD YELVERTON was twice married is asserted in the *Visitation of Norfolk*, now in course of publication by the Norfolk and Norwich Archæological Society, p. 269. Who his first wife was I have been unable to discover. His second wife was NAZARETH, daughter of EDMUND BEDINGFELD of Oxburgh. She is frequently described in the Presentments as "*An obstinate Recusant.*"

Blomefield has confounded EDWARD YELVERTON with his son EDWARD YELVERTON, M.D.

The Grimeston and Blackborough estates were settled by indenture, dated 12th Jan., 10 Elizabeth, upon WILLIAM YELVERTON and JANE his wife for life, and after their death on EDWARD YELVERTON their eldest son, in fee tail.—Chancery Inq. p.m., S. P. O. The p.m., inquisition on WILLIAM YELVERTON was held at Walsingham, 4th October, 30 Elizabeth.

(11) *Page* 138, *line* 7. Though no Recusant would enter a church where divine service could be carried on, the *naves of our cathedrals were regarded as no more than within the precincts*. The uses to which the nave of St. Paul's was put may be seen in Dean Milman's work, and elsewhere.

(12) *Page* 138, *line* 19. By a *Subsidy Roll* (P. R. O.) for the 35th Eliz. 1593, 1597, I find that WILLIAM WALPOLE's widow was still unmarried, and living at Tuddenham. The chapel is still in existence at Elsing Hall.

The Brownes of Elsing were conscientious Catholics, but appear to have taken the oath, and so were regarded by the stricter Romanists as 'schismatics.' The following letter, dated Elsing, 29th April 1876, is from the rector of that parish, and deserves to be placed on record here.

"At Elsing Hall, between the grand hall and the withdrawing-room, *in the thick of the wall, is a well, evidently the well of a staircase leading downwards.* The curious part of this is that the opening was in the side of the room ; it was therefore no cellar, but most probably a place of concealment. The plastered wall of the well against the hall was broken into during the repairs some twenty years ago, and then I saw it."

There can be no doubt that this was one of the many instances of a place of concealment specially constructed as a hiding hole.

(13) *Page* 139, *line* 3. Far the ablest sketch which has yet been written of the condition of feeling among the upper classes on the questions at issue between England and the Papacy, is to be found in the seventh chapter of Mr. Simpson's *Life of Campion*. It is all the more valuable and suggestive because it comes from one who was himself a convert to the Church of Rome, and who, in seceding from the Church of his baptism, made some real sacrifices.

(14) *Page* 139, *line* 25. "He [Father Southwell] frequently got me to instruct him in the technical terms of sport, and used to complain of his bad memory for such things, for on many occasions when he fell in with Protestant gentlemen he found it necessary to speak of these matters, which are the sole topics of their conversation save when they talk obscenity, or break out into blasphemies and abuse of the Saints or the Catholic Faith."—Morris, u s. p. xxiv.

(15) *Page* 142, *line* 17. [EDWARD WALPOLE of Houghton] "persuaded his cousin MICHAEL WALPOLE . . . to accompany him. At this period of my story [1589] the latter was my assistant, and used to go with me as my confidential servant, to the houses of those gentlemen with whom it was necessary for me to maintain such a position."—Gerard's *Autobiography*. See, too, Morris's *Condition of Catholics*, p. lxv.; and Oliver's *Collections sub voc.* '*Michael Walpole*.'

(16) *Page* 143, *line* 2. "Christopherus Walpole, filius Christopheri Walpole, generosi, ex oppido Anmyre oriundus in comitatu Norfolciæ, litteris grammaticis institut s in Schola communi Eliensi sub mago Sypght. Per licenciam, adolescens annorum 19, admissus est in collegium ñrum litterarum gratia pensionarius minor commeat' scolar. 25 Octobris 1587, fidejuss. et pro eo magr. Christoph. Grimston, art. mag. et hujus collegii socius."—*Matriculation Book, Caius Coll., Cambridge.*

There is a good account of Speght in Cooper's *Athenæ Cantabrig.* Cooper, in his account of Christopher Walpole (u. s.), has confounded him with his brother Richard.

## CHAPTER VII.

## THE MISSIO CASTRENSIS.

WHEN Robert Earl of Leicester set sail from Harwich on his disastrous expedition to the Low Countries, the avowed object of his going was to wrest the United Provinces from the grasp of the Spaniards, and to free
5 from Spanish domination the much-enduring and much-struggling people whose heroic determination and courage had long attracted the amazement and admiration of Europe. But the Earl of Leicester had over-estimated his own powers: his royal mistress knew him better than he knew himself; she had her
10 own misgivings of her favourite, and had taken a true measure of his qualifications for the mission he was so eager to discharge. What was he that he should aspire to lead armies, and play the sovereign over a stubborn people with a passion for freedom and a hatred of foreign control? When the Queen yielded
15 to the earl's importunity, she yielded with the worst possible grace, and left him to support the honour of England and to pay his ragged followers from his own very limited resources.[1] At war a novice, at diplomacy a child, Leciester had as his antagonist in the field the most consummate captain of the age,
20 and in statecraft, the astute and high-minded patriot, John of Barneveldt. His failure was predicted from the first; but few

could have anticipated the disgraceful rebuffs he received, or foreseen the contemptible incapacity he exhibited, till humiliation after humiliation discovered his utter shallowness, and made it evident that under no circumstances could that handsome fop, the darling of the drawing-room, have proved himself worthy to be a leader of armies. Character, principle, and mental force were needed, not mere personal grace, prettiness, and the languishing accomplishments of a perfect ladies' man.

On his first arrival, Leicester was welcomed with enthusiasm, and almost immediately elected Governor-General of the United Provinces; but his popularity was short-lived; deficient in tact, temper, courtesy and knowledge of men, his arrogance became every day more offensive, and his lack of all soldierly qualities more glaringly manifest. After eight months of absolute inaction, he made the abortive attempt to intercept a convoy at Zutphen; in this attempt Sir Philip Sydney—Leicester's nephew—lost his life while recklessly charging the enemy, a mad and riotous proceeding such as could only have occurred under a general who had no proper control over his officers.([2]) In four months more Leicester was back again in England, having effected nothing. Nay! not quite nothing. He had won the fort which was a formidable menace to Zutphen; he had secured Deventer, one of the most important cities of the United Provinces.

Deventer had been wavering in its allegiance. There was a very powerful Catholic faction there. The religious sympathies of its leading inhabitants were strongly in favour of the old religion, and the magistrates were almost to a man not only deeply discontented with the English domination, but in heart tending more and more towards the Spanish side. On the 20th October, 1587, Sir William Pelham, "the stout marshal," as Motley calls him, made his entry into the city, summoned the magistrates into his presence, and on the following day removed them from their office, demanded the keys of the gates, imprisoned the old officials, and created new ones, staunch

Protestants all of them. Deventer was safe, and Zutphen's fate sealed; for though the fort was gone the town still held out against the English besiegers. The next question to settle was, who should be the new governor of Deventer?

There were in Leicester's army a strange assemblage of soldiers of fortune—men of reckless daring, absolutely without principle; adventurers who were free lances, and ready to serve on either side for plunder or pay; fellows who were no more to be trusted than common blacklegs or banditti. Such a creature was Rowland Yorke. His career pointed him out as a man with the ferocious courage of a wild beast when his blood was up, but who seems to have had no single virtue except an absence of all fear of God or man. One less worthy of a post of confidence it would have been impossible to pick out from the whole force under Leicester's command; and yet to him was committed the duty of holding the fort of Zutphen against the Spaniard, and of ensuring the capture of the beleagured town, which that fort now commanded. This was a bad enough blunder, but a worse blunder followed.

There was another leading captain in the army,—Sir William Stanley,—a restless and ambitious soldier, son and heir of a stubborn Recusant in Cheshire, who had long rendered himself conspicuous by his determined opposition to the Protestant cause in his own neighbourhood, and had given the Earl of Huntingdon in the north of England a great deal of trouble by his factious activity in support of the Romanists, and his vigilance in thwarting every attempt to prejudice the cause to which he was attached. Such as the father was such was the son. First, and above all things, a religious zealot, whose passionate hatred of everything in the shape of Protestantism, and whose intense 'Vaticanism' blinded his judgment and smote his conscience with a stupid palsy. He too had served on both sides, for patriotism he had none. The sentiment of loyalty to one's native country was, in Queen Elizabeth's days, incomparably weaker than, thank God, it has become among us since; and the frenzy of religious bigotry thrust into the background, if it did not quite overpower and extinguish, the sacred associations of fatherland.(3)

It may seem to some a paradox, but it is nevertheless a fact, the truth of which becomes more and more evident as we study the history of Europe in the sixteenth century, that patriotism, as we now understand the term, was a sentiment but feebly apprehended under the last of the Tudors, indeed it was a sentiment that as yet had scarcely any existence. In France men were not Frenchmen but "Leaguers" or "Huguenots" in the sixteenth century, as they had been "Armagnacs" or "Burgundians" in the fifteenth. It was Michel de l'Hôpital who first inspired his countrymen with any enthusiasm for France as France: the party of the "Politiques" were the earliest representatives of French patriotism. In Germany the national sentiment was even fainter. The Reformation had done a great deal to divide men into rival factions quite irrespective of their birthplace. The opposite feeling, where it existed, was not so much national as feudal, and where allegiance to the 'dominus' had faded, it had tended to transfer itself, less to the temporal sovereign than to the shadowy power that represented the idea of religion,—the Church and its head. It was not till after the tremendous catastrophe of the Armada, and when the restlessness of Spanish ambition had familiarised men's minds with the prospect of an actual invasion of *their country*, that they began to appreciate the glory of being Englishmen, and recognised distinctly the paramount claim upon their loyalty which England, as a nationality, demanded of them, whatever their religious convictions or whatever their creed.

Sir William Stanley had not risen to such a standing-point as this. He had persuaded himself that a heretic queen was no queen over him. Enough, that she had been pronounced excommunicate, and by the Pope deposed. Others might split hairs, if they pleased, on the question whether that excommunication were published with due formalities; for him, he accepted it as final, and with that acceptance the foundation of his loyalty to the sovereign crumbled away. Henceforth he seemed to himself set free from every engagement which could bind a man of honour. Cut adrift from his anchorage upon the fundamental principles of moral obligation, right and wrong were tossed about in his mind in a hopeless embroglio; and so treachery had come to be regarded in the light of a sacrifice, and the huge proportions of some monstrous villany, in the misty chambers of his darkened brain, grew into an image of heroism surrounded by a halo of lurid glory. No more conspicuous instance can be pointed to in this time of a man thoroughly saturated with the detestable doctrine that the end justifies the means.

And here it seems to me that we are brought face to face with that bad side of sixteenth century polemics which all the special pleading in the world can never avail to excuse; the tendency, viz., to exalt the claims of a creed above those of morality,—a tendency to sever the one from the other, even to the verge of antagonism,—a tendency to defend the interests of religion at the expense of her principles, in common with all those who enclose the essence of religion in the nutshell of a dogma. With upright and earnest natures the devotional element for the most part absorbed the factious and immoral perversions which reckless disputants were even then beginning to foist upon the theology and ethics of the age; but with men of narrow intellect and low *morale*, cursed as they so often are with a passion for intrigue, the interests were the essence, and all else was form. Such men gave their lives to the one; they accommodated themselves on occasion to the other. Stanley had come to regard the interests of the Church as the idol which he was bound to propitiate by any and every means: with a mind perplexed and confused by problems that fascinated all the more because he had not the wit to solve them; a spurious pietism goading him on he knew not whither; wounded of late in his pride by certain untoward slights that stung him sorely; disappointed in his ambition, too, for he had been passed over by less meritorious commanders; and with visions of a more brilliant career—he was just the man, sooner or later, to make his name infamous to posterity by some act of flagrant and eccentric villany. When Leicester left him at Deventer with almost irresponsible power, he felt that his opportunity had come, and he lost no time in availing himself of it.

Mr. Motley has described in his own vivid way the incidents of the shameful treason in which Stanley and Rowland Yorke were the chief actors. In his pages the whole story may be read in its minutest details. Here it is enough to say that, by a plan cunningly concerted between the two traitors, the fort of Zutphen was delivered up by Yorke, and Deventer surrendered by Stanley, to Tassis, the commander of the Spanish force, on the selfsame day (29th January 1587). Sir William Stanley could sell himself; he could not sell the honour of his officers. As to the Irish *kernes* who formed the rank and file, it was an easy matter with them to change sides. They cared nothing for heretic England and her excommunicate Queen: they cared very much for their own religion, which they had some reason for believing was to be mercilessly persecuted and proscribed. They were almost savages, the terror even of their own side; wild marauders to whom war meant unlicensed pillage; uncouth of look, barbaric in speech, hardly at all amenable to discipline, they rejoiced that they were rid of all control from the English yoke, and exulted in being soldiers now of the "Most Catholic King;" but the regiment came rapidly disorganised, it became necessary to find new officers at any rate, and that without delay.

There were in Belgium no small number of English gentlemen who had taken refuge with the Spanish governor from time to time, when their religious convictions or political partizanship had rendered their stay in their own country dangerous or impossible. The exodus at the beginning of the Queen's reign has been mentioned before—it was an exodus then of men of real learning, piety, and accomplishments—men who had made great sacrifices, and who desired only to live in undisturbed enjoyment of their religion; but when the rebellion in the north collapsed, a very different company crossed the Channel—this time no zealots, but mere malcontents who had raised the standard of revolt, and in many cases actually borne arms against their sovereign; adherents of the northern earls and of the Duke of Norfolk; men deeply implicated in plots and treasons, and bitterly and personally hostile to the Government at home. Making common cause with these, too, there had come over many an ardent supporter of Mary Stuart —some of them sincerely and loyally devoted to her cause— some of them professional conspirators who took up that cause as a party cry—but in either case equally vehement in denouncing the wickedness of those who had compassed her death upon the scaffold. All these were the political exiles. There were others again, who were merely eager for any military employment, and cared not to which side they lent their swords. War was the trade they chose, and if they were Catholics, they preferred the Spanish service to that under any Protestant power. When Stanley's captains threw up their commissions, the difficulty was got over by accepting the services of the unemployed and hungry volunteers, idling about the purlieus of the Brussels Court. It took less time than might have been expected to supply the place of the English officers. It was perhaps less easy to fill up the blanks which death and disease made in the rank and file. There could be little or no hope of any more Irish recruits; the new soldiers must needs be of very mixed nationality, some were Italians, some French, some Flemings, some few Spaniards; it mattered little where they came from, for the Irish *kernes* spoke a tongue which none could understand but themselves. There was one thing, however, that was essential. In the Irish regiment there could be no difference in religion allowable; that at any rate was a thing not to be endured; for if the strongest tie which bound these wild soldiers together was a unanimity in their creed, it was needful that all due precautions should be used to keep up that fanaticism which went far to make them fiery zealots in the shock of war. In those days army chaplains were absolutely unknown; men went forth to battle, or died after it,

> "Unhouseled, disappointed, unannealed,
> No reckoning made, but sent to their account
> With all their imperfections on their heads."

The priest had no place in the camp, and it was assumed that he was better away; but to the honour of the Jesuits be it said, the first organised attempt to introduce the recognition of religion into an army in the field originated with them.

In the autumn of 1586, the Prince of Parma had been very powerfully impressed by a Jesuit father, Thomas Sailly, a native of Brussels, whose health had broken down during his labours in Russia, and who had been sent home to recruit, bearing important despatches and commendatory letters from Stephen Battor, King of Poland. With this introduction, he soon acquired a remarkable ascendancy over the Viceroy, became his confessor, and after a while induced him to establish what may be termed a Missionary Staff of Jesuit fathers, entrusted with the spiritual welfare of the soldiery.([4]) Sailly and his little band of missioners set themselves to their work with heroic energy—preaching in the camp at every opportunity; attending day and night upon the sick and wounded in the hospitals: on the battlefield comforting and shriving the dying; doing all those offices of charity which have been undertaken so nobly in our own time by those devoted philanthropists who unconsciously, during the German campaign in France, were splendid imitators of the Jesuit fathers of three hundred years ago. In the hottest fight these men were to be seen carrying the wounded to the rear, and bending over the dying to catch their last words of

L

penitence or prayer; in the furious turmoil of some town stormed and sacked, they were foremost in rescuing women and children from the brutal lust and cruelty of frenzied ruffians who had lost all self-control. More than one or two fell victims, sometimes to disease, sometimes to their excessive rashness in exposing themselves to fire, sometimes to their unwearied exertions, which were more than flesh and blood could bear; but the admiration and profound respect which their unselfish labours earned for them, and the novelty of the work they gave themselves to do, and did so well, added enormously to the estimation in which the Jesuits were held in Belgium then and long afterwards.

The Missio Castrensis had been established about two years when Henry Walpole was sent to join it. His readiness of speech and abundant culture, his captivating manner and extraordinary facility as a linguist, his long and careful training, and perhaps, too, his birth and connection with some who were conspicuous in the army, marked him out as an eminently fit man for work of this kind. He himself, in his examinations, tells us that his business was to hear confessions in French and English, Spanish and Italian, of all which he was a master, and we may be sure that he threw himself into his new duties with no half-heartedness. But he had not long entered upon this career before misfortune overtook him. Flushing was one of the towns which, in 1589, was held by a garrison chiefly of Englishmen. Its commander was Sir Robert Sydney, a brother of Sir Philip Sydney, and so nephew of the Earl of Leicester, to which earldom he was himself raised by James I. in 1618. In one of Henry Walpole's journeys to minister to the soldiery, or it may be in some attempt to confer with friends in the town,—for friends there he certainly had,—he was taken prisoner and committed to close custody.([5]) We are told that he was confined in the common prison of the town in the depth of winter, with nothing but his soutane to cover himself with, nothing but filthy straw to lie on, and associated with a herd of the vilest criminals incarcerated in the loathsome jail for every sort of atrocity,—wretches who were ready to strangle him for the sake of his scanty garments, and who, if the story be true, actually had a design of murdering him and making it appear that he had committed suicide. But even in this pitiful condition he did not lose heart or suffer his zeal to grow cold. There is a touching incident which comes to our notice during this the first great trial of his earnestness, which shows that his religious enthusiasm had not been extinguished or diminished during his confinement. It appears that after a time the rigour of Henry Walpole's imprisonment was to some extent relaxed, and that he was granted some sort of liberty on parole. The indulgence so accorded him was turned to account, and at once he set himself to exercise his ministry in the town. There was a poor Flushing man named George Nachtegael, who had been originally apprenticed to a tailor, and afterwards had travelled to Madeira as a merchant's clerk. He had returned to his native place after an absence of four years, and was there when Henry Walpole was captured. What brought the two together we are not told, but before long the impression produced by the Jesuit father upon the poor mechanic was so profound that when the order of release arrived, Nachtegael resolved to pursue a religious life, and to offer himself as a lay brother to the Society. He seems to have followed Henry Walpole to Brussels, where he was received as temporal coadjutor to Father Oliver Manareus, in November 1592; and when, two years after, Edward Walpole was passing his time of probation at Tournay, Nachtegael was sent to the same house of noviciate, and doubtless furnished him with many of those particulars of his cousin's imprisonment which have been preserved.([6])

Among the English officers serving at Flushing was one Captain Russel, a Norfolk man. He was one of the Russels of West Rudham, a parish contiguous to Houghton; and was a cousin of the Walpoles. It would have been dangerous for any recognition to pass between the kinsmen under the circumstances, but the soldier soon managed to find means of alleviating the suffering of the priest, to provide him with additional clothing, and, what was of more importance, to communicate with his Norfolk friends, and give them intelligence of his perilous position. The news had no sooner reached England than Michael Walpole determined at once to cross the seas, and go to his brother's side. His training under such a wary diplomatist as John Gerard, and the practice he had already had, fitted him admirably for a mission which required caution, tact, and presence of mind; and the young man had already, it seems, determined to offer himself to the Society, and to forsake his country at the earliest possible opportunity. Slipping away accordingly, in December 1589, without a licence, he made his way to Flushing, and before long managed to get access to his brother, and to confer with him in his prison. Already it had been intimated that a ransom would be accepted for his release, and the money having been found, partly by his relatives and partly by his Brussels friends, he was at length set at liberty in January 1590, having learned, as he himself says, by his imprisonment, " to know better both God, the world, and himself."

It is at this point that the important series of letters contained in the archives of Stonyhurst College comes in. They cover a period of fifteen months, and furnish us with a very valuable picture of the deplorable state of affairs among the English refugees in Belgium during the two years after the Armada. They corroborate in the minutest particulars the miserable account which Lewknor (?) gave of them in 1591, and they show us the petty jealousies, quarrels, intrigues, and poverty of the deluded pensioners of the Spanish king, whose allowances were always coming and always in arrear.(7) They tell us of the gradual dwindling away of the wretched Irish rabble—by courtesy called a regiment—till it almost seemed likely to disband from lack of commanders. They give us notices of the coming and going of Jesuit priests and political agents and Spanish generals. Now and then there are scraps of news from home, and sometimes faint whispers of dark intrigues going on, or of wars and rumours of wars that might be imminent. But free and unrestrained as these letters are, and written as they are in full confidence and affection by one Jesuit to another (Cresswell), there is not from beginning to end one single word or hint which indicates anything approaching, I will not say to treasonable designs, but even to an acquaintance with the existence of such designs on the writer's part. Setting aside such religious views as we should of course expect to meet with, these letters exhibit to us a man of intense enthusiasm, of lofty piety, of fanaticism if you will, but one whose faith was the very life of his life, and the mainspring of his every act and thought and word. As literary compositions they are of little value; as contributions to the history of the time they possess an interest only for the professed student, whose business is to pursue research below the surface of perfunctory manuals; but, as faithful representations of the habits of thought and tone of feeling prevalent among a whole class of able, devout, mistaken men, whose lives were marred and whose minds were unbalanced by the hideous tyranny under which they suffered, these letters have a value of their own. The last of them is dated from Brussels, the 17th October 1591; the first from the same place, 31st January 1590. I am inclined to regard this as the most useful, and at the same time the happiest, period of Henry Walpole's life. He was actively employed, after having been for several years in a condition of tutelage. He was called upon to exercise his priestly function, a prospect to which he must have looked forward for years. He was set free from the restraints of such tuition work as in the case of a man of ambition and active intellect is apt to become irksome, and he was once more brought into close intercourse with his old connections and friends. I am not sure that there is not some slight difference in tone between the earlier and the later of these letters: in the later there is more of the man of the world, more of human sympathy, and more interest in the old associations from which he had been for some time removed.

But if these two years were memorable years to Henry Walpole himself, because of the active employments in which he was engaged, they were more memorable as they affected other members of his family. Michael Walpole, as has been seen, left England in December 1589, and after remaining apparently for some months with his brother, proceeded to Rome in the spring of the following year, and entered at the English college there on the 12th May, accompanied by another Norfolk gentleman, Thomas Goodrich.(⁸) About the same time the youngest brother, Thomas, also crossed over into Flanders, and obtained a commission in the Spanish army. A few months after this Edward Walpole of Houghton, too, "abjured the realm," taking with him his cousin Bernard Gardiner, the two men being received into the English college on the 20th October, and before another year had passed Christopher Walpole, accompanied by two other Norfolk gentlemen, Thomas Lucie [query Lacy?] and Anthony Rouse arrived at Rheims.(⁹) Of all those six sons of Christopher Walpole of Anmer, only one was left in England to represent the family. Meanwhile with every new arrival in Belgium came fresh tidings of the wonderful religious excitement that prevailed among the upper stratum of society in the Eastern Counties, and the news of this one and that one whom he had known in his youth, having been induced to surrender home and country for what he regarded as the good cause, evidently disturbed Henry Walpole not a little. Oh! if he too might be once again at home, labouring in the mission field. The yearning grew, till he became unsettled. The discipline of all those years of self-denial and self-control could not avail to keep him quite silent as to his wishes. "Gerard doeth much good!" he writes to his friend Cresswell. Was there any hope that he might be called to join him? His heart turned to England—to the old Norfolk home—to the old hall under the shadow of the old church tower. "Gerard doeth much good!" Might not he do some work too, and take again his father's blessing, and see his mother's grey hairs, and the sisters that had passed from childhood to womanhood during those years of his absence? Was there danger in the venture? Gerard had braved it and was still unharmed, and if the worst should come the risk was as nothing to the prize—the prize of the martyr's crown. While thoughts like these were flitting through his brain, suddenly in the October of 1591 he received a summons to present himself at the noviciate at Tournai.

# NOTES TO CHAPTER VII.

(1) *Page* 154, *line* 17. Motley's *Rise of the Dutch Republic* is, and must always remain, the chief authority on all matters connected with the history of the Low Countries during the sixteenth century, and I must therefore content myself with a general reference here to that most able and exhaustive work. In Captain Devereux *Lives and Letters of the Devereux, Earls of Essex*, vol. i. ch. vii., there is a letter of Sir F. Knollys to Robert Earl of Essex, from which it appears that Leicester was not the only man who embarrassed himself considerably by the immense outlay incurred in his expedition. On the treatment of Leicester by Queen Elizabeth, see Froude, vol. xii. c. 33.

(2) *Page* 155, *line* 20. There is a very spirited account of the affair, given by Stowe in his *Chronicle*, which has been extracted by Mr. Wright, *Queen Elizabeth and her Times*, vol. ii. p. 316.

(3) *Page* 157, *line* 3. A careful history of the events leading up to the surrender of Deventer, and a very satisfactory account of Sir William Stanley's life and family history, is to be read in Mr. Heywood's *Introduction to Cardinal Allen's Defence of Sir William Stanley*, edited for the Chetham Society, 1851.

(4) *Page* 161, *line* 25. See *Imago Primi Sæculi Societatis Jesu*, folio, Antwerp, 1640, p. 804 et seq.

(5) *Page* 162, *line* 32. Father CRESSWELL (to whom almost all the letters of Henry Walpole are addressed which have come down to us) thus tells the story, ". . . un iour allant à pied d'un College à aultre par ordonnance de ses superieurs, il fut prins par les soldats de l'ennemy, & emené captif en la ville de Flessingne en Zelåde, qui est en la puissãce des rebelles, & à guarnison de soldats Anglois, lesquelz le retindrent plus d'un an entier, le traictant fort mal : Et par ce qu'ilz ne le peurent tuer comme ilz desiroient, pour estre la prison en la main & puissance du Magistrat naturel du pays, ilz offrirent à aucuns larrons qui estoient captifz avec luy, la vie & liberté pour de nuict le mettre à mort : dequoy le pera se doubta, & pour eschapper de ceste mort il eut necessairement besoing de veiller

plusieurs mois presque toutes les nuictz, ce qui luy causa un perpetuel tourment, comme luy mesmes depuis l'a racõté Il a aussi souffert extreme froidure, pour navoir eu aultre vestemẽt qu'une seul vielle soutane : dont ayant compassion certain Capitaine heretique nõmé Rusel qui l'avoit cogneu en Angleterre, se despouilla d'un pourpoint de rase qu'il portoit, & luy donna pour le revestir : En ceste maniere passa le serviteur de Dieu sa captivité iusque à ce que nostre Seigneur y remedia par aultre voye, qui fut en inspirant un sien frere qui estoit en Angleterre de venir à Flessingue, ou changeant son propre nõ, il entra au service du mesme Capitaine qui tenoit son frere prisonnier, par ou il eut commodité de le veoir & traicter avec luy, mesmes le pourveoit de tout ce que luy estoit necessaire. D'avantage il procura que les catholiques Anglois estans en Flandres le racheptassent, comme ils feiret le renvoyans à Bruxelles : & fut si grand la devotion que eut ce ieune iouvenceau son frere, voyant la vertu & patience du pere Henry, que au mesme instant il delibera de quicter le monde, & d'aller à Rome pour entrer en religion, comme il feit par effect."

I have been careful to quote this passage and to print it exactly as I find it, because the little book from which I make the extract is one of the very greatest rarity, and is certainly not to be met with twice in any man's lifetime. In 1874 I heard of the existence of a copy of the book which Father Possoz had seen and consulted at the Public Library of Tournai ; thereupon I started off to get a sight of the precious volume. On my arrival I found, to my extreme mortification, that Father Possoz was dead, and *Cresswell's book had disappeared*. The librarians knew nothing of the book, and had never heard of it ; it was not in the catalogue, and they declared that Father Possoz must have been mistaken. On the other hand, M. Casterman, the very intelligent bookseller and publisher of Tournai, insisted that Father Possoz could never have made the positive assertion he did, [*nous l'avons* enfin trouvé dans celle (la bibliothèque) de Tournai] without being sure of his facts, especially as he was known to be an extremely accurate person, and wrote and published his own little *Vie du Père Henry Walpole* while at Tournai. As there was, however, no chance of seeing the book at Tournai, after staying there three days I gave up the search as hopeless. Some time after this, by a curious accident, in looking over some MSS. that had been entrusted to my care, I found a note which led me to believe there was a copy at the Noviciate at Tronchiennes, and this copy, by the great kindness of the Rector, now lies before me. The book is a little volume in 12mo, of 164 pages. From the dedicatory epistle, addressed " Aux Peres et Freres de la Compagnie de Jesus, & aux Pensionnaires des Seminaires Anglois en Espaigne,",it appears that Father CRESSWELL wrote the work at Madrid, and finished it on the 19th December 1595, *i.e.*, just eight months after the execution of Henry Walpole. The licence to print the Spanish original is dated at Madrid 15th February 1596 ; the licence for the French translation at Arras, 9th [Sep] embro 1596. Though

Oliver asserts that there was an English version of the book published, I very much doubt the truth of the statement. A work of which such men as P. P. Augustin de Backer and Victor de Buck could declare, as they both did to me, that they had never met with or heard of a copy, except on the authority of Oliver, may pretty safely be classed among those which were intended to be printed, as we know it was, but never saw the light.

In a letter of Verstegan's of the date of 1595, now at Stonyhurst (*Angl. A.* vol. ii. n. 13), the writer says, "I wrote long since into Spain the manner of Fa. Southwell his apprehension, and partly how he was tortured by Topclif. It were good that his apprehension, together with his arraignment and death, were printed for the present by itself in the Spanish tongue. As also Father Walpole his history when it cometh, and afterwards they may be put together in Latin with others the like, *and in the meantime it would move much to be in the vulgar tongue.*"

The mistake of Father Cresswell in saying Henry Walpole was in prison for upwards of a year, and which all the biographers repeat, is inexplicable. It certainly is a mistake, for he was ordained in May 1589, by his own showing, and he was out of prison and at Brussels on the 15th January 1590 (Roman style).—*Walpole Letters,* p. 2.

There remains to point out another mistake which *Bartoli* has fallen into, and which others have copied from him. He says that it was CHRISTOPHER WALPOLE who effected his brother's deliverance. Neither *Cresswell* nor *Yepez* (1599) give the brother's name, and it certainly was MICHAEL and not Christopher who was the instrument for effecting his liberation. MICHAEL arrived at Rome on the 12th May 1590 (*Liber Peregrinorum*). Christopher did not enter at the English College till the 22d February 1592.

(6) *Page* 163, *line* 32. The following is from the *Album of the Tournai Noviciate,* MS. 1016, (*Bibliothèque Royale de Belgique,* f. 236). "Je George Nachtegael natif de Vlissinghe, né l'an 1563, envers le Pentecoste. Mon Pere Pierre Nachtegael marronier, ma mere Jacquenine George, tous deux trespassés. J'ay appris à coudre l'espace de deux ans. J'ay servy depuis à un marchand aux Isles de Madère quatre ans. Je scay lire et escrire. Estant recu à la Societé de Jesus à Bruxelles le 16 Novembre 1592, pour estre Coadjuteur temporel du R. P. Oliv. Man. Prov. és Pays Bas, j'ay exercé mains offices de Coadjuteur à la maison de la susditte Soc<sup>te</sup> en Bruxelles, jusqu'à ce qu'on m'a envoyé à la maison de Probation en Tournay à la quelle ie suis venu le 29<sup>e</sup> d'Apuril l'an 1594. Et pour ce que i'avoy fait la premiere Probation à Bruxelles en entrant la Societé, et on m'avoit illic examiné . . . le R. P. Jean Bargius m'a examiné generalement, et j'ay respondu que . . . le 22 d'Apuril, 1594.

George Nachtegael."

The following is extracted from a *Brussels MS*. 3166, pars ii. n. 20. ". . . Hic [H. Walpole] fuit olim Castrensis Missionis fidissimus socius et ad cohortes Anglicas a suo superiore destinatus inter quas, more aliorum patrum, utilem semper navaverat operam. Ad stationem Aulæ, quæ Brugis tunc temporis erat constituta, cum redire statuerat in itinere a siccariis, quos Vreebuteros (!) voant, captus est, et ad Vlussingamun Carcerem deductus. In quo nunquam zelum deposuit quem pro animabus a Deo conceperat et ut erat arctissime ligatus corpore, linquam tamen ita servavit liberam ut Sanctâ eloquentiâ custodem carceris Catholicam redderet ac se [sic] ex curiositate aut misericordiâ visitante in avitâ fide confirmaret . . . Adolescentem quoque inter dum eleemosynas adferentem ita solidâ pietate instruxit, ut non diu post nomen daret Societati. Is erat GEORGIUS NACHTEGAEL olim hic pluribus annis Sacrista et nunc Bergis S. Winnoci sedem fixit . . ."

(7) *Page* 164, *line* 33. There is a doubt who was the author of the remarkable tract printed in the *Appendix to the Sadler Papers*, vol. ii. p. 478, entitled *The Estate of the English Fugitives*.

(8) *Page* 166, *line* 14. He was probably from North Creake, co. Norfolk. THOMAS GOODRICK, Gent., of North Creake, married Suzan daughter of ROGER BOZOUNE, of Wissingsett, Esq., early in the reign of James I. (Blomefield, x. 34). In 1614 I find a NICHOLAS GOODRICH, living in the capacity of private tutor in the house of LADY SULYARD at HAUGHLEY, returned as a "Popish Recusant." In 1615 I find on the Recusant Roll, "Wyverston, JOHN GOODRICH, Sen., WILLIAM GOODRICH, Jun., and his wife UNICA GOODRICH, Spinster, daughter to W$^m$ GOODRICH." [sic.]

(9) *Page* 166, *line* 22. It appears that EDWARD WALPOLE of HOUGHTON had made preparations for leaving England as early as the summer of 1590, and was at Brussels about August of that year (*Walpole Letters*, pp. 10 and 12). Writing from thence on the 5th September 1590, to CRESSWELL, Henry Walpole says, "By the next convoy to Namur my kinsman Edward Walpole cometh towards you, of whom I wrote before and sent his letters to my brother RICHARD. I desire particular favour in his behalf, either for the college or toward my Lord Cardinal if you think meet. He hath hope of exhibition yearly out of England, and hath left an £100 in Father Southwell's hands, whereof some part must be for Mr. Gardiner who was released out of prison by my Lord Cardinal's letters to the prince [Parma] who will needs come to Rome, and desireth either to serve the Lord Cardinal or to study in the college. For the first, by reason *some have imagined amiss of him, and he hath been with such as are suspect*, I dare not commend him, although I have great cause to think him trusty; for the second, I remit [him] to your good disposition and collegiate order and present estate there now; hoping you will have an

eye if ought should be: but indeed, if the general good made me not more suspicious, for my particular experience of him and occasion to wish him well I desire all favour, and that he may be bestowed some way .... Gardiner did once make the vow of our Society, but for some impediment Father Oliverius, our provincial, dispensed with him. (*Walpole Letters*, p. 15.) In the *Liber Peregrinorum* of the English College at Rome, occurs the following entry, "1590 Dominus Eduardus Walpolus et dominus Bernardus Gardnerus, diocis Nordovicensis ambo, excepti sunt hospitio die 20 Octobris: manserunt diebus 3."

In another letter, dated Brussels, 22d August 1591, Henry Walpole says, "Our cousin John Walpole, in Holland [Lincolnshire], is departed, leaving his wife all that .I hear, excepting xx$^{li}$ a year to Thomas and Christopher, who now by God's grace have left that and all other hopes for His service. Christopher related these things unto me, and is on his way with Mr. Hubbard's brother-in-law [Anthony Rouse] and another at Rheims."

This cousin is JOHN WALPOLE, of Whaplode, co. Lincoln, Esq. His will is in the P. C. C. (dated 1st July 1590). His executors are to sell all his lands in Norfolk and Lincoln within one year of his death ..... "to Jane my wife all my lands which I bought since the making of my great Book of Feoffment set before by this my last will devised during her life .... and after her death to my brother ROBERT WELBY." To said Robert Welby after decease of wife ... an annuity of 100 marks per annum *for ever* out of lands in Whaplode and Holbeach late Harwells, Haltofte, Knevetts, and Wythipols. "Item to THOMAS and CHRISTOPHER WALPOLE sonnes of my uncle, *after decease of Jane my wife*," each £10 a year for life out of said lands .... The lands I had by my mother's will to go to Jane my wife for life .... To the churchwardens of Whaplode £4 yearly for ever out of lands in Whaplode and Holbeach "for the finding of a learned preacher for the preaching of the Word of God to His glorie *so long as the inhabitants of Whaplode do give him yearly £20 over and besides*." By a codicil, dated 7th October 1590, he leaves " .... to my uncle Walpole [CHRISTOPHER WALPOLE of ANMER] forty shillings to buy a ring." His wife residuary legatee. This wife JANE was daughter and heir of JOHN ROBARTS of Woollaston, co. Northants, Esq., by CASSANDRA daughter of William Apreece of Washingleys, co. Hunts., Esq. She married (2) JOHN MARKHAM of Sedgebrook, co. Lincoln, Esq. (High Sheriff in 1590). He died 9th February, 159¾. She married (3) SIR WILLIAM SKIPWORTH of Cotes, co. Leicester, who died 3d May 1610; she survived her third husband twenty years. Her will is in P. C. C., and was proved 2d December 1630. In it she leaves "£20 for a tomb in Sleaford for JOHN WALPOLE, Esq., my first husband." Her own monument is at Prestwold. It would appear that THOMAS WALPOLE lived long enough to come in for the annuity, which in Queen Elizabeth's time was, in HARRISON's judgment, a sufficient maintenance for a gentleman.

## CHAPTER VIII.

# THE RETURN TO ENGLAND.

"Come back, come back, more eager than the breeze
The flying fancies sweep across the seas,
And lighter far than ocean's flying foam,
The heart's fond message hurries to its home.
Come back, come back!"

WRITING to Cresswell on the 17th October 1591, Henry Walpole had favoured his correspondent with a strange piece of news. From "divers captains and gentlemen, come from the Earl of Essex in France," who had been "reconciled to the Church" by his means, he had learnt— vain and idle rumour—that there was "great hope and inclination to the Catholic faith of late in England, in court, camp, and country." And this three years after the Armada.

Looking back as we now can do, "with larger, other eyes," upon the state of feeling which prevailed in England at this time, and upon the intense irritation and bitterness against Spain and Rome, which had grown up in all classes as a consequence of the attempt at invasion, few things strike us as more curious than the childish credulity of the English exiles, who still deceived themselves into the belief that they had a strong party of sympathisers and supporters at home. It was not only that the age was uncritical, and that sifting evidence was contrary to the habits of the time, it was much more than this: the exiles were led astray by their earnest longings to believe firmly what they wished for ardently: they became the ready dupes of shallow gossip that reached them from every point of the compass; and though they found themselves taken in every day of the week, nothing could teach them the commonest caution. They were surrounded by a legion of spies receiving Burleigh's pay at so much a quarter, *and they knew it*; they were playing a game of hide-and-seek in which the stake was their own lives; their words were repeated as soon as uttered; their letters were intercepted, and delivered into the hands of the Lord Treasurer to be duly deposited in process of time among the archives at Hatfield or the Public Records, for future generations to read. Their elaborate cyphers were sent to the regular experts who read them at their leisure; their lodgings were watched, their persons accurately described, their every movement known, their plans divulged almost as soon as formed; and yet these Jesuit fathers and Seminary priests, whom historians delight to represent as the wariest and wiliest of conspirators, proved themselves as deficient in craft, cunning, or sagacity, and as little a match for their persecutors in the arts of chicane and espionage as the kingfisher is said to be a match for the village ploughboy, when she deposits her eggs year after year in the same hole, though her nest be robbed as regularly as the summer comes round.([1])

"Great hope for the Catholic faith in England" in the year 1591! "I could wish myself there, if all were answerable," he adds pathetically; and he really believed that there was a career before him, and that it required only a little band of devoted missioners to stem the current of heresy, and to lead back England into the right way once more! From across the sea Southwell and Gerard seemed to beckon, and a voice from friends and kindred to be calling, "Come over and help us!"

Five days after he wrote this letter to Cresswell, I find him at Tournai, entering upon the third year of his probation.([2])

The original college of the Jesuits at Tournai is used at the present day as the Athenée, or Public School, of the town; it has remained unaltered in its main features since its first foundation. One enters by the selfsame porter's lodge through which Henry Walpole passed; the old quadrangle is intact; the old refectory, which could easily have accommodated three hundred students, has been divided into three; the old oratory, which continued to be used as an oratory till fifteen years ago, has been converted into a dormitory, though there never have been scholars to fill it; a portion of the stately cloister still stands; the vaults in which many of the Jesuit fathers lie buried were only bricked up in 1870; the extensive gardens and grounds, shorn of all their picturesqueness, still grow vegetables for the household; the old kitchen is used to the present day. One passes into the chapel: the venerable altar is as it was, but the glory of the stained-glass windows, still faintly remembered by living men, has departed, and the whole place is dreary, desolate, and decaying. The good people of Tournai have broken with the priesthood, and are bitter against them. They have made immense exertions, and incurred very considerable expense, in pushing their Athenée, and subsidising it very heavily; but though there be room in the building for at least two hundred boarders—*one hundred and twenty are offered a separate room about sixteen feet square*—the place languishes dismally, and the school is never half filled with scholars.

How little does persecution and spoliation effect! In this very town of Tournai, at this very day, there stands the modern Jesuit college in the more modern quarter. It has become so much too small for the accommodation of the numbers who apply for admission, that in 1875 arrangements had been made for the erection of extensive new buildings, though in those already constructed there were one hundred and fifty students, provided for on the most liberal scale, and presided over by thirty Jesuit fathers; whilst the charges for each of these students were more than double of those paid at the secular school at the other end of the town.

Henry Walpole had now been seven years a Jesuit; nearly ten years had passed since he left his country and his home. He was in the prime of his manhood; some of the buoyancy of youth had passed, some of its impulsiveness been repressed, some of its romance, its sanguine hopes, its passionate chivalry, its inordinate confidence in a future that was to do so much and triumph so surely; but his consuming enthusiasm had not cooled down one whit; on the contrary, it seems to have been as ardent and as intense as ever. "Gerard doeth much good!" That, doubtless, was the thought which haunted him. Visions of Gerard riding over Dersingham Heath, and sitting in the well-known chimney-corner of Sandringham Hall—warily picking his way to Houghton or Harpley in the gloom of evening, and holding serious converse with anxious inquirers in many a manor-house whose every closet the sad exile knew so well—rose before his mind's eye, and made him long for home. How could it be otherwise? But the way seemed barred to him. The rigid discipline of that wonderful society, of which he was a devoted member, demanded the sacrifice of his own inclinations, and he made that sacrifice as a matter of course; and so he was kept month after month teaching boys, or at Tournai going through the strict routine without a murmur, saying his mass in the early morning in the college chapel, and in the evening pouring out his soul to God in his chamber, begging for—what? For nothing worse, that I can find, than the glory of being used in his Master's service and gaining that Master's guerdon.

Surely the time has come when we can afford to be generous, at least fair, to these men. Think of them as we will, they had no mean personal motives; they had everything to lose, in most cases they had actually sacrificed everything; they had nothing to gain—nothing that worldly men would value or desire. There is only one way of explaining their vehement zeal, their reckless bravery, their dauntless persistence in the cause to which they pledged themselves. Give them the credit of earnestness, and allow that they were sincere, and the history of the world can furnish us with countless parallels of the same heroic devotion in a better or a worse cause : but assume them to have been mere politicians and selfish schemers—false, cunning, and hypocritical—and these Jesuit emissaries and missionary priests, who endured so much and who fought their grim fight so stubbornly, present us with a problem which the experience of mankind will not help us to solve. We shall never understand the religious conflict of the sixteenth century, or indeed of any century, if we put ourselves below the enthusiasm of the time.

For ten months Henry Walpole remained at Tournai: on the 15th July 1592, he was called to the college at Bruges.(³) At this point it will be necessary to make a short digression, in order to understand the significance of much that follows.

The English College at Douai was opened, as has already been shown, in 1568. Ten years of remarkable success had rewarded the efforts of those who had started it; but after it had sent forth fifty-two priests to pursue their vocation in England, its work was rudely interfered with, and its progress received a temporary check, when the course of events necessitated the removal of the tuitional staff and of the whole body of students to Rheims. Here the college went on as before; but once more, at the end of another ten years, the clouds began to gather, and the community at Rheims conceived some anxious fears for the future. The political horizon was indeed sufficiently dark. The "Invincible Armada" had collapsed, Montmorenci had joined the Huguenots, the Duke of Guise was dead, Prince Maurice was doing much more than holding his own, and Henry III. had made truce with the King of Navarre. April For Spain—and Spain meant the cause of Catholicism in

M

Europe—the outlook was very gloomy and menacing. It became evident that, as things stood, it would be impossible to leave the dreaded Parma much longer in the Low Countries, and if he were recalled and his sword employed elsewhere, what might not happen in Belgium and the north of France?

Accordingly, Father Parsons began to look about him for an opportunity of providing some substitute for the College at Rheims in case it should be compelled to dissolve, and it was doubtless a part of his plan to supplant the *Secular* College and to found in its place a *Jesuit* College, which should be exclusively under the control of the Society. It was only natural that Parsons should think of Spain as the best place for setting up a new Educational Establishment: his enormous influence with Philip II. and his court, would of itself have been enough to justify the plan, and there may have been some pardonable ambition to emulate Cardinal Allen in the foundation of colleges which might rival the glory of those older institutions that had prospered so vastly and produced such wonderful results. In the spring of 1589 Parsons wrote to Allen suggesting that in view of the dangers that appeared imminent, an attempt should be made to set up a college in Spain.(4) The matter was debated at Rome and, without delay—not to say without due inquiry and precaution—three young scholars, Henry Floyd, a Cambridgeshire man, John Blackfan, and John Boswell, set out with the intention of making a settlement in Spain for training young men for the English mission. They arrived at Corunna at the end of May, and after many hardships made their way to Valladolid, which they reached almost penniless, and apparently without introductions and without friends. Wandering about the streets they fell in with two young Englishmen who were pursuing their studies in the town, and after hiring a humble lodging they spent their time in attending the lectures which were delivered free of charge in the public schools. Their scanty hoard began to diminish wofully, till waxing desperate they applied to a charitable nobleman, Don Alfonso de Quinones, and laid their case before him; with characteristic munificence he relieved their immediate necessities, and supported them for three months out of his own resources. Just at this point Father Parsons arrived at Madrid, and received intelligence of the hardships endured by the little band. He at once made it his business to extricate them from their difficulties, and by diligent canvassing among his powerful supporters at court, before a year had gone by he had purchased a house for a college, altered and enlarged the buildings, and obtained the grant of a permanent "pension" from the Spanish court. By the end of October 1590, nearly thirty students had emigrated from Rheims alone. By the spring of 1591, there were upwards of seventy inmates, and the numbers were said to be still increasing. The example set by Philip was followed with more or less ostentation by his nobles; and just when it looked as if the college of Rheims would have to be dissolved, as the result of the skilful intrigues and diplomacy of Elizabeth's ministers and agents in France, a new nursery for restless "missioners" and "Seminarists" started into being, exactly where they were least assailable. It was a master stroke of policy on Parsons' part, and might well cause the English Government uneasiness. Where was this everlasting plotting to end? How could this hydra be crushed? By this time Elizabeth began to be seriously alarmed for her personal safety. Brave woman she undoubtedly was; none of her race was lacking in personal courage, but there was ground for uneasiness, and her council did their utmost, not only to increase the feeling of insecurity, but actually to establish a panic of assassination at court. Was there not a cause? The Regent Murray had been foully murdered in broad daylight in Edinburgh streets; Henry the Third had been stabbed to the heart by Jacques Clement; Guise had been slain at Blois; William of Orange had fallen a victim to another miscreant, though he had survived the frightful wound which had almost despatched him in 1582. Furious fanatics talked of the Queen of England as the fittest person to be destroyed by fair means or by foul, and rumour, loud of tongue, never ceased asserting that the adherents of Mary Stuart were as ready as ever to avenge the death of the "martyred" Scottish Queen. The Armada had been scattered to the winds and swallowed up by the ocean, but worse might be preparing, and angry men foiled are loud in threats of what they will do some day. And now, as if by magic, here were fresh seminaries springing up, with all their tremendous organisation for turning out emissaries devoted to the cause of winning back England to the Pope's dominion, and of spreading abroad doctrines which Cecil and his compeers believed could only end in hurling him from power and driving Elizabeth from the throne.—"Something must be done!" Something was done accordingly. On the 29th November 1591, the Queen published her famous edict.([5])

The edict had scarcely been promulgated when Father Parsons set himself to compose a reply. His answer was written in Latin, in his usual vigorous and lucid style; for however rugged and vulgar his English may have been, his Latin is always nervous and fluent, not without a certain grace and elegance of manner: the authorship was ascribed to Andreas Philopater, *Presbyter ac Theologus Romanus ex Anglia olim oriundus*, and it was published sometime in the summer of 1592.([6]) Parsons' answer was skilfully conceived; it aimed at showing that the Queen herself was hardly responsible for the cruelty and atrocity of the edict and of the late sanguinary measures against the Seminarists and Jesuits; it charged the guilt and ferocity of all these measures upon the lords of the council, and chiefly and above all upon Cecil their Coryphæus; upon him Parsons poured forth all the vials of his wrath and scorn; it is surprising to see how intimately he was acquainted with every weakness and every vulnerable point of his adversary. Cecil's birth was comparatively obscure, at least he could boast of no forefathers who had belonged to the English gentry. Cecil knew it, and was sore at the thought; but, if his grandfather was nobody, might not his remote ancestors have been princes and nobles? So he gave himself to genealogy, and was for ever hunting for some pedigree which might fit on to himself and his progenitors; this pedigree making was one of the great man's foibles. In the State Paper Office and at Hatfield there are whole volumes full of these genealogical notes, and it appears that Cecil never could shake off the fascination which such researches exercised over his mind.(⁷)

A few months after the publication of the edict, and immediately upon the completion of the first draught of the Answer to it, a copy in MS. was forwarded to the Treasurer by one of his spies in Flanders. Cecil was gratified by the promptitude of his agent, and addressed to him a letter of thanks for his zeal, and at the same time added some comments upon the reply; Parsons had laughed at him for his lowly birth, retorting upon him a sneer which the edict itself contained. Cecil in his letter had betrayed his mortification, and writing to the spy, entered into particulars about his supposed ancestors, claiming descent from Welsh princes, and asserting that his family had originally been settled at Sitsil in Wales. When the Responsio was published, there before the eyes of amazed Europe was Cecil's own letter, translated into Latin, with all its ridiculous pretensions exposed. Parsons was vastly pleased, and made himself infinitely merry; he did not spare his victim: all the resources of sarcasm and irony were used to sting the Treasurer, and Cecil, deeply mortified, writhed under the lash. Doubtless all possible means were used to keep the book out of England; but besides the interest which the Catholics had in giving it a wide circulation, there were too many people in high position, who had no great love to the Lord Treasurer, to allow of such a *bonne bouche* as this bitter and telling attack to remain unknown, unread, and unsold. Vexed and intensely mortified, Cecil was weak enough to betray the pain of the sting; and when Philopater's book could no longer be suppressed, with fidgety ill-temper he printed a sort of reply, trying to make the best of an attack which might more safely have been left alone. This little episode would be unimportant but for one consideration; the English translation of Philopater was executed by Henry Walpole, and this copy, which the spy forwarded to England, must have been made almost immediately after Walpole had completed his version during his stay at Tournai. When, after divers tortures in the Tower in 1594, Henry Walpole in his agony let out all the harm he had to tell about himself, and as little as possible about any others whom he could have injured, one of his confessions was that he had translated Philopater's book. *That* signed his death warrant. Cecil never forgot, never forgave; and the man who had once provoked his resentment, and hit him hard where he felt most tenderly, might escape for long, but if ever he should be hunted down would certainly not be spared.

It was while Henry Walpole was at Bruges that this translation was executed, and he may have been engaged upon this very work when he received his order from Claudius Aquaviva, General of the Society, to join Parsons in Spain. This appears to have come to him late in the autumn. Some delays occurred, which hindered his setting out immediately, but in the end of December we find him at Seville.

The English Seminary at Seville had been formally opened about a month before his arrival, but the chapel had not as yet been consecrated, and he hurried from Belgium to be present at the ceremony. A great deal of importance was attached to this event, and the opening of the chapel, which took place on the 29th December 1592, was celebrated with extraordinary pomp and magnificence, of which an eyewitness has given some account.([8])

At the first High Mass there "were present the Cardinal Archbishop of the city, who was received with a Latin oration, the Assistant and Senators, great store of ecclesiastical prelates and doctors, the superiors of the religious orders and other men of authority, gravity, and nobility, a great number. At the end of the mass, four scholars *took the oath of priesthood and returning into England, according to the manner of the Seminaries.*"

Henry Walpole took part in this ceremony, and the day was rendered especially interesting to him by the presence of his brother Richard, who had recently arrived in Spain from Italy, and whom he had not seen for years. The meeting must have been an affecting one for the brothers in their then condition of mind; each was prepared for any venture or any labour which his sense of duty might urge him to undertake; and Richard had already volunteered to start upon the English mission, to which he would undoubtedly have been sent, but that just on the eve of his intended departure he was kept back for other and very different employment.

The brothers appear to have remained together at Seville for two months, after which Henry was despatched to Valladolid: there at last the long-desired summons came. He himself has told us the brief story.([9])

"I was minister [at Valladolid] till Fa. Parsons coming to Valladolid about June, anno 93, did find me not so apt, as he said, for that office, and told me he was in doubt whether to send me to hear confessions in Seville or to Lisbon, where is a residence begun; *and suddenly he told me he was resolved I should go into England if I did not refuse, having order thereto from the General and Provincial; and so he and the Rector did determine.*"

Father Parsons had been in close communication with Henry Walpole now for nearly a year. It is clear he had been watching him carefully all the time and scrutinising him narrowly. Of Walpole's earnestness and devotion there was no question; of his zeal and courage he had given ample proofs; but whether his learning was extensive and solid enough to be turned to account in the lecture-room, or could be used in the controversial battles that were always going on, was doubtful. What was to be done with this enthusiast of brilliant and versatile talents rather than of commanding intellectual power, who peradventure had mistaken his vocation when he threw himself into the ecclesiastical life, and forsook the career at the bar in which he was qualified to make a mark, as his uncle had done before him?

Parsons must have known only too well what a dreary prospect he was offering this man of thirty-five years old when he proposed to him "hearing confessions at Seville or Lisbon," and how *any* career or venture would appear preferable to one in whom the faintest stirrings of ambition or the least traces of self-will survived. "Suddenly" came the question, "Would he go into England?" "Yes!" Without a moment's doubt or hesitation. Yes! Though a thousand edicts threaten and a thousand deaths deter. "Gerard doeth much good. Why not I?"

So here was another Jesuit father going to be hurled against the ranks prepared to receive him. Ay! but there was something more. It must be remembered that just at this moment it was more than ordinarily advisable, it was almost necessary, that the Society of Jesus should show some signal evidence of its activity, and of the readiness of its members to take part in the English mission. Douai and Rheims could boast of their army of martyrs and confessors, of their recruits always ready to enlist, of their volunteers eager to lead the forlorn hope at an hour's warning. If this new seminary of Valladolid was to emulate the renown of the French college, it must have its baptism of blood and its martyrs with their crown and palm. Parsons must have felt all this, and none knew better than he the danger and the risk. One is almost tempted to believe that the critical question was wrung from him, as if he even at the eleventh hour doubted his man; and as if for himself he would rather have been spared that trial of the superior officer, who, in the discharge of a duty laid upon him, sends his subordinate to what he knows is likely to end in death, even though that death may prove honourable and glorious.

But the decision once arrived at there was no more delay. Henry Walpole had made his choice, and at once he stood forth as a representative man. He was no longer a mere Jesuit father, he was a Jesuit father who was about to enter upon the English mission, and as such he became a very valuable instrument in Father Parson's hands. Liberal as had been the contributions, and lavish as the promises had been, the funds for the new seminaries in Spain had come in, and were coming in, more slowly than could be desired. The buildings, as usual, cost more than had been estimated, and though the scholars were many, the resources for their maintenance ran short. Moreover, it was by no means intended to drop the French and Belgian seminaries, and yet they were in sore distress, with creditors pressing and payments all behind hand. Money was getting scarcer and scarcer. The English vessels were scouring the seas, plundering King Philip's homeward-bound ships, and the enormous booty gained was so much taken from the Spanish treasury and passing into the hands of English pirates. Philip II. and his courtiers promised largely and did their best, and meant to keep their word, but pay-day came and pay was wanting. Meanwhile so persuaded was every Spaniard, and every man who looked to the Spanish king for support, of the unbounded resources at his command, that the thought never suggested itself, that after all Philip was almost bankrupt. If only a petitioner could gain access to this omnipotent dispenser of gold, there could be no limit to the resources at his command: the only difficulty was how to get admission to the awful presence of the potentate before whom common men might well veil their faces. While Henry Walpole was at Valladolid, a certain priest named Thorne had come into Spain to beg for contributions towards the establishment of a Jesuit college at St. Omer. It does not appear that Thorne was a Jesuit himself, or how or by whom he had been accredited, but he was in

Spain as a petitioner. Week passed after week, but he found himself helpless; he could get no audience, and the courtiers appear to have taken no notice of him or his petition. The St. Omer College scheme, however, was one which Parsons had at heart, and though he could allow Thorne to drop out of notice, he was not likely to despair of St. Omer without an effort. What an obscure priest might be powerless to achieve, that might be easily affected by a Jesuit father, who was about to set sail for England, holding his life in his hand.

Accordingly Henry Walpole was put forward as the petitioner who should appeal with more emphasis for the funds that were so grievously needed. He was furnished with letters to the king and to the most powerful nobles of the court, and despatched to the Escurial with all the moral support he could desire. He was received with marked distinction by the courtiers, assured that the king had granted his request, and had already sent letters to St. Omer ordering the money to be paid, and finally was told that he was to be admitted to the august presence of his majesty, whom it would be politic to thank for past favours before begging for their continuance in the future. Don Juan Crestoval de Mora seems to have been specially interested in the English mission, and Henry Walpole thus tells the story of his interview with the great man:—" Don Juan did talk familiarly awhile with me, asking me of F. Parsons and the seminary, and how I would get into England, and he said he heard say that there was a new religion in England of such as refused to go to church; demanding whether they were like the Catholics, and what hope there was of the conversion of England." . . . . He goes on to tell how, not many days after, "by Ruis de Velasco's means I had audience of the K. as daily many have, and told him that being sent into England by my superior to labour to convert some souls there; and having received his Majesty's new letters for St. Omer, I did humbly thank his Majesty for all his liberalities to the poor students of our nation, who all, therefore, would pray to

God for him, and I hoped many other hereafter whom they should convert to the Catholic faith: beseeching him to continue his alms and liberality towards them there: 'Twas the effect of the speech I did speak unto him, and he *very low, being weak*, so as I could scarcely hear him, said only these words that I could understand, *Dios os Encamina* . . .; this done I returned to Valladolid, and from thence to Bilbao."

He set out from the Escurial on the 3rd or 4th August 1593, and reached Bilbao at the end of the month. At Portugaletta he found a vessel bound for Calais, and taking passage in it, embarked on the 3rd September; the voyage was a very tempestuous one, and occupied so long a time that his friends made up their minds that the ship had foundered at sea, so that when he arrived at Douai on the 27th of the month, he was greeted with immense joy by the college authorities.([10])

After a short stay at Douai he returned as far as St. Omer, and here he fell in with one Edward Lingen, whom he had known previously as an officer in Sir W. Stanley's regiment, and who had been living by his wits for some years, after being driven out of England by the penal laws. Lingen was one of those many soldiers of fortune who were at this time wandering over Europe and ready to take service under any master, willing to embark in any enterprise that offered pay or prize-money. In the sixteenth century it was counted no disgrace or reproach to a man that he should place his sword at the disposal of the King of France to-day and the King' of Spain to-morrow. The profession of arms had in those days a cosmopolitan character, and no one thought any the worse of a 'free lance' who in the course of his career changed sides, provided that he was faithful to his engagements during the campaign, and did not violate a trust committed to him. To use his sword against his own country was considered to some extent discreditable, but even this admitted of excuse, and was looked upon pretty much in the same light as for a barrister to defend a prisoner charged with a capital offence; with this difference, that the one course *was* in those days possible, and the other was not. Lingen was a soldier of fortune: for some years he had been a buccaneer, as were Drake and Hawkins and many another dashing sailor from the Cinque Ports: they carried their prizes into Plymouth, he carried his into Dunkirk, and therefore as a matter of course they, when occasion served, preyed upon Flemings and Frenchmen and Spaniards, he upon Flemings and Frenchmen and Englishmen. His success had been but moderate, and he had tired of the game. A yearning to get back to England at all hazards had taken possession of him, and when he learnt that Henry Walpole was preparing for a homeward voyage, he determined to join him. With the usual want of reserve and caution which characterised the proceedings of the missioners, the "secret" of Henry Walpole's intentions soon became generally known, and among others who heard of it was his brother Thomas, who had also held a commission in Stanley's regiment, but had become disgusted with a course which brought neither credit nor pay. Henry Walpole had still some business to carry on in Belgium, which occupied him till the beginning of November; then we find him once more at St. Omer ready and eager for the start. But once again his patience was put to the trial. The plague was raging in London and its environs. "For all this year," says Camden, "London was most grievously afflicted with the pestilence, *Saturn* running through the uttermost point of *Cancer* to the beginning of *Leo*, as in the year 1563, insomuch as there died this year of the pestilence and other diseases, within the city and the suburbs, 17,890 persons, besides William Rowe, Mayor, and three Aldermen." The consequence was that "from Calais no French ship went by reason of the sickness," and when the brothers with Lingen attempted to get a passage from Calais, they failed and returned to St. Omer, waiting for some turn in the tide of affairs.[11]

During his stay there, Henry Walpole was employed in

making some preliminary arrangements for the new Jesuit College, which was opened in the following year. He kept up a correspondence with Parsons, Cresswell, More, &c., during the month of November, and three of his letters have been preserved, and were printed in Cresswell's short biography. Like every other letter of the writer, they breathe a spirit of ecstatic fervour and somewhat passionate devotion. They are full of prayers for success in "winning souls;" but through them all there is a tone of despondency, and more than one indication that the writer had a presentiment of the fate that awaited him, and which, though he foresaw, he was in no wise anxious to escape. In truth, one sees in this man just that perverse and infatuate hankering after the honour of "martyrdom," which Donne, fifteen years after, so earnestly and grandly reproved in his great polemical work, *The Pseudo Martyr*. The missioners were excited, and goaded on to look upon death at the stake as the most glorious end of life that could be desired; and to do them bare justice, it must be confessed that when it came to surrendering their lives they showed no craven reluctance to meet their doom. In the torture chamber they broke down again and again: at the gallows not a single case of cowardice has been recorded.

And so when week passed after week, and the prospect of finding any opportunity of crossing the Channel in the usual way seemed as far off as ever, and when too his business at St. Omer came to an end and tidings arrived that the English Government was more vigilant, strict, and uncompromising than ever—when too the opinion seemed gaining ground that this was no time to be sending fresh Jesuit emissaries to be arrested, imprisoned, and hung, with little chance of their doing any useful work before they were apprehended—Henry Walpole began to be seriously afraid that if he delayed much longer a fresh order might come from head quarters recalling him from the English mission altogether. At Valladolid he had been one of at least three priests who had been set apart for this work: others had already been stopped by their superiors: if he delayed he too might be sent for to hear confessions or perform some other routine work in Belgium or Spain. The thought of such a contingency became unbearable, and he determined to run any risk rather than not get upon English soil once more.

Just at this time there were lying in Dunkirk harbour three "vessels of war," as they were vaguely called in the language of the time; in other words, three pirate craft fitting out for sea; for naval warfare was then carried on in the Channel almost exclusively by private adventurers, who advanced money for the expenses and shared the risk and the profits of success. A bold buccaneer was always sure to find speculators willing to supply the necessary funds, and there was no lack of reckless spirits eager to sail under the flag of any dare-devil captain. There was little or no regard to nationality, and in this particular case we are not told whether the ships called themselves French or Spanish: they were simply "vessels of war," which were about to cruise along the east coast of England, and make what prizes they could pick up; they were to sail in concert, keeping in sight of one another, and to play what havoc they could upon any luckless merchant-ship that fell in their way, it mattered very little whether she were French, English or Dane. Lingen heard of the little fleet, and Henry Walpole determined to secure a passage. He made his arrangements, and stipulating that he and his two companions should be set ashore on the coast of Essex, Suffolk, or Norfolk, he embarked and the ships weighed anchor about the 20th November 1593. They were not the only passengers. Another priest, who travelled under the name of Ingram, and who appears to have been charged with some political mission for Scotland, and had his own plans to carry out, had already bargained for a passage; and a spy of Walsingham's too had secured a berth without the knowledge of the others of the party. Ingram was a nephew of Lingen's, and it was probably through him that the information came of the intended cruise of the "vessels of war." They set sail in very boisterous weather, with a head wind, at the worst season of the year, and had a rough time of it. On the 3rd of December they were off the English coast, and on that day they took a prize; but they had been carried further northwards than Essex or Suffolk or Norfolk, past the Wash and past the Humber, and by the evening of the 4th they were off Flamborough Head. Ingram was bound for Scotland, he would have been quite content to go on. Henry Walpole had far overshot his mark. Anywhere on the coast of Norfolk or even Lincolnshire he would have found himself very soon among friends, but to land in Yorkshire was to rush into the lion's jaws. Nevertheless the weather showed no signs of mending; it was impossible to say where next he might find himself, and as the captain told him, to use his own words, "that he could not touch the land where he would, and the wind they said was not good . . . for very weariness of the sea I desired them to set me on land anywhere, or else carry me back, and so they put me on land." Unfortunately he and his two companions were not the first to leave the ships. The spy, who was a passenger on board another of the vessels, managed to land before them, and slipped away to carry information to York. The three companions were set ashore at Bridlington, and the ships put out to sea again. Henry Walpole was in England once more.([12])

## NOTES TO CHAPTER VIII.

(1) *Page* 174, *line* 27. In the Record Office there is a collection of the ciphers employed by the agents of the Government and their opponents during the reign of Queen Elizabeth. It occupies three thick quarto volumes.

(2) *Page* 175, *line* 2. The letter is dated Brussels, 17th October 1591. (*Walpole Letters*, p. 44.) For his summons to Tournai, cf. supra, p. 111.

(3) *Page* 177, *line* 17. For this statement my authority is the MS. Life in the *Collectanea Anglo Catholica*, vol. i. fo. 149, in the Archives of the Bishop of Southwark; now under the custody of the Fathers of the Oratory. I think this Life must be a translation from some very early document, and I suspect that another translation is the Latin Life now at Stonyhurst, which was discovered some years ago in the archives of the city of Brussels. Both these Lives, if they are not the same, contain some particulars not to be found in Yepez, Bartoli, or Father More.

(4) *Page* 178, *line* 21. For a full account of the matter see Tierney's *Dodd*, vol. ii. p. 176, and the Notes in the Appendix.

(5) *Page* 180, *line* 15. The text of the edict is to be found in Strype, *Annals*, iv. p. 78 et seq.

(6) *Page* 180, *line* 24. See a letter in the *Athenæum* No. 2602, Sept. 8, 1877.

(7) *Page* 181, *line* 8. There is a very curious note given in the *Quarterly Review*, No. 282, p. 22. "Cecil is labouring for peace . . . . He has found a new pedigree by his Grandmother from the WALPOLES . . . . ." This passage occurs in a letter of the 21st July 1599. Just two years before this EDWARD WALPOLE of Houghton had been outlawed "for a supposed treason done at Rome," and his estates forfeited to the crown. It is evident that the attention of the Lord Treasurer had been drawn to the Walpoles for some time past. There are several of Cecil's genealogical and heraldic collections among the *Lambeth MSS*.

(8) *Page* 182, *line* 31. Tierney's *Dodd,* vol. ii. App. ix. No. lxii. A minute account of the reception of Philip II. at the seminary at Valladolid is to be met with in a scarce volume, entitled *Relacion de un Sacerdote Ingles* .... *de la venida de su Magestad a Valladolid, y al Colegio de los Ingleses* .... *Traduzida de Ingles en Castellano, por Tomas Eclesal cavallero Ingles.*—(Madrid, 1592, 12mo.) Orations were delivered in ten languages; *Hebrew, Welsh, Gaelic, and Flemish* among the number. Prize poems were composed, some of them of very respectable merit, and an elaborate pageant was carried out of which a description is given. The little book is in fact precisely like a modern newspaper report.

(9) *Page* 183, *line* 19. P.R.O., *Domestic,* Eliz., vol. 249, No. 12, where the authority for all that is contained in the next two paragraphs is to be found.

(10) *Page* 187, *line* 15. *Yepez,* &c. The two MS. biographies mentioned at n. 3.

(11) *Page* 188, *line* 34. Supra, n. 9.

(12) *Page* 191, *line* 24. Cresswell's *Life,* p. 6; *Yepez,* p. 680, and the *MS. Lives,* n. 3; *Walpole Letters,* p. 47.

## CHAPTER IX.

## FATHER GERARD'S "MUCH GOOD.'

WHAT was the "much good" that Father Gerard had done in Norfolk, and that had produced so profound an impression on Henry Walpole? The researches suggested by this question have resulted in throwing so much light upon the extent of Gerard's influence during the last fifteen years of Queen Elizabeth's reign, and in revealing so many curious facts bearing upon the social and religious history of the time, that I believe my readers will be in a better position to understand the real significance of what still remains to be told, if I turn away once more from the apparently direct course of my narrative and give some account of this notable Jesuit Father's sojourn in Norfolk.

When Gerard dropped down from the high road to Norwich on that memorable afternoon in October 1588, and determined to "make a circuit of the city" before entering the gates, he was almost certainly within sight of Robert Southwell's birthplace at St. Faith's.(1) Below him, on the other side of Hellesdon bridge, stretched a tract of country in which some of the most considerable of the Norfolk landlords whose names were on the roll of Recusants were then living. To his right were the woods of Cossey, and the hall which Sir Henry

Jerningham had built at the beginning of Elizabeth's reign, and where ten years before the time we have now arrived at Sir Henry's widow had entertained the Queen and her courtiers. Scarcely more than two miles off might be seen the new chimneys of Melton Hall, which Robert Downes had very recently erected. And another mile off, and nearer to Norwich, stood Bowthorpe Hall, at the time occupied by Lady Jerningham's son-in-law, Charles Waldegrave, Esq., who rented the house from Mr. Yaxley, a member of one of the great Suffolk families. Southwell's residence at St. Faith's has now quite disappeared. The old hall at Bowthorpe was replaced by a new house about the year 1660, when the property passed away from the Yaxley family, but the hall at Melton still stands, and so does the picturesque old hall at Cossey, though now reduced to insignificance by the glorious modern mansion.([2]) Every one of these county squires was a conscientious Catholic, and every one of them was suffering for the sake of his religion at the time that Gerard passed by on his way to Norwich.

The Recusant gentry in Norfolk were not all treated with equal severity: a great deal depended upon the power of a man's friends in high quarters—not that the Recusants ever escaped altogether from pains and penalties, but that the laws were so outrageously tyrannical that they did not bear being carried out with full rigour against any but a minority, upon whom extreme measures might be tried with safety— with this minority it was only a question of time when they would find themselves stripped of their lands and turned out into the world as beggars. Mr. Downes of Melton was a notable instance of this. As early as the year 1561 he had incurred the grave displeasure of the Queen's ministers by being "present at the saying of a mass—since masses were made illegal." The Mass was said at the house of Sir Edward Waldegrave at Borley in Essex; and there were present at it Sir Edward and Lady Waldegrave and their children, Lady Petre, Lady Jerningham, and others of the Catholic party. It was a matter looked upon by the Government of the day with some suspicion and alarm. Scarcely a year had elapsed since the Act of the 1st Elizabeth had been passed, which had made the use of any form of worship except such as was prescribed by the Book of Common Prayer illegal, whether in public or private; but, as I have before said, the Mass had not been named in the Act, and it may have been that some were in doubt as to the legality of using the old form of worship, and this meeting at Lady Waldegrave's may have been a prearranged one in order to try the lawfulness of saying Mass in private. If this were so, the plan was unwisely conceived, for though in point of fact it was little more than a family meeting, it certainly assumed very much the appearance of a political gathering.(³) Sir Edward Waldegrave had been one of Queen Mary's privy councillors, and was Chancellor of the Duchy of Lancaster; Sir Henry Jerningham had been a member of the Queen's household and a favourite of his royal mistress; (⁴) and Mr. Robert Downes appears in some way to have been connected with the Waldegraves, though in exactly what relation he stood to them I have as yet failed to discover. Little or no secret was made of the matter, and it at once came to the ears of the council; forthwith such of the party as could be laid hold of were arrested, Sir Edward and Lady Waldegrave, the members of their household, their physician Dr. Fryer, and the priests officiating, in all about a dozen, were sent to the Tower; others were apprehended and thrown into jail at Colchester, among whom Robert Downes' name is conspicuous.(⁵) This, as far as I know, was the beginning of his chequered and unhappy career. How long he was detained in jail on this occasion does not appear. Sir Edward Waldegrave was kept long enough in the Tower to die a prisoner there, and Mr. Downes was not likely to have been released before his patron.(⁶) He was, however, probably at large again before the summer of 1563, when, by the death of his brother, Francis Downes, Esq., of Sudbury, he succeeded as heir-at-law to extensive estates in Suffolk, Norfolk,

Sept. 1, 1561.

and elsewhere, some time after which he appears to have taken up his residence at Great Melton, where he occupied himself in building the hall, and lived in a style befitting his large means.(7)

For some unexplained reason Mr. Downes had made himself especially obnoxious to the Queen or her ministers. The Downes' were a very numerous clan at this time in Norfolk, and a very wealthy one; there was another Robert Downes at the other end of the county, who at the beginning of Queen Elizabeth's reign had succeeded his father as lord of the manor of Bodney, near Watton, and had inherited with it a very valuable and extensive tract of land, where he too kept great state and maintained a large household.(8) Other members of the family were living at various houses in the county, and almost all were conspicuous for their stubborn adherence to the old creed. But though Robert Downes of Bodney was left comparatively unmolested—*i.e.*, he had to "compound" for his Recusancy and pay a heavy annual contribution for the privilege of *not* going to church—his cousin at Melton fared very differently. It has been seen that on the occasion of the Queen's visit to Norwich, in July 1578, Mr. Downes was among those who were first arrested. From that time, for at least twenty years, he seems to have been kept in prison in the castle of Norwich, allowed at intervals, it is true, to go home to his wife and children on giving heavy bail for his reappearance, but liable to be summoned to return to prison at any moment that his rents fell due and the time of payment of the heavy exactions made upon him came round, and never allowed to wander further than five miles from his own hall.(9) Year by year he became more heavily embarrassed; his Suffolk property seems to have gone first, then the lands in Kent followed; at last his life interest in the larger part of his Melton estate was surrendered to the Queen in 1602, the consideration for such surrender being expressly mentioned, viz., that he should retain his dwelling-house at

Melton and some few score of acres round it, and enjoy the undisturbed possession of the manor of Paunton in Herefordshire, "without yielding, paying, or rendering any annual or yearly rent or rents . . . for or by reason of his Recusancy, absence from Church or divine service, contrary to the laws of this Realm in that behalf made and provided." ([10])

There is something very affecting in this man's history, and there must have been in his stubborn and immovable character some real magnanimity and heroism to submit without one moment's flinching to the wearing misery of thirty years of persecution and incessant spoliation, although by a single act of conformity he might have freed himself from all this ruinous weight of oppression.

I have given Mr. Downes as an instance of those who felt the full force of the penal laws: his case is an extreme one, but the truth is that only those of the Recusant gentry escaped absolute ruin who managed to obtain some protection from friends in high quarters. Not even then were they altogether spared, and as surely as a man of any substance or position showed any active sympathy with the Roman creed or its missionaries, so surely did he feel the weight of the penal laws: all the power and influence of the Woodhouses of Kimberley could not save their kinsman Francis Woodhouse from dying in poverty in 1605, though at the beginning of Elizabeth's reign he had been one of the most considerable squires in Norfolk, and in 1568 had built the noble hall at Breccles, which still stands as one of the most beautiful monuments of Elizabethan domestic architecture which the county of Norfolk can produce.([11])

So, too, it fared with Edward Yelverton: as long as he "made no sign" he might escape molestation at the expense of a fixed annual charge upon his estates, but all his high connections could not keep him from ruin when once he became suspected of connivance with the movements and designs of proselytisers. He, too, found himself being stripped of his estates acre by acre, till, as many another of his Catholic associates did, he contrived to turn his lands into money before the spoilers had robbed him of all he possessed.(¹²)

Three years before Gerard took up his residence with Mr. Edward Yelverton at Grimston, his half-brother, Mr. Humphrey Yelverton of Bawsie, had died, leaving behind him a widow with five young children, three sons and two daughters, all sufficiently provided for. The widow seems to have removed to Lynn at the death of her husband, though perhaps keeping up the house at Bawsie and occasionally residing there. Bawsie is about four miles from Grimston, and Humphrey Yelverton's eldest son Charles must have been a frequent visitor at the house of his uncle Edward at the time when Gerard was a sojourner there.(¹³) He appears always to have been a favourite with his uncle, spending months at a time with him after the death of his mother in 1591. He entered at Caius College in April 1590, being then scarcely fifteen years old, soon became one of the suspect, and after taking his first degree the early leaven began to work and give him no peace. He had a handsome patrimony which would well reward an informer who could prove him to be "popishly inclined," and he appears to have shown some imprudence in habitually associating with the more conspicuous of the Catholic party. When the time came for him to proceed to the M.A. degree and take the oath, he left Cambridge, being then some months short of twenty-one, at which time he would come into his inheritance. He had no sooner gone from the university, than Redman, Bishop of Norwich, issued a warrant for his apprehension, which, however, he contrived to escape from, and he seems to have passed the next year or two in doubling from house to house in the Eastern Counties like a hunted hare, till at last he managed to get to Dover; here he was arrested, when actually on ship board, and thrown into prison for six weeks. He contrived to escape by bribing his keepers, and slipping across the Channel made his way to Rome, and eventually was admitted a member of the Society of Jesus in October 1601.(¹⁴)

Of his brother Edward we know but little; he, too, entered at Cambridge, and was in residence there when Charles Yelverton left the university. He appears never to have taken a degree, but at the end of Elizabeth's reign he is described as "a Catholic, and domiciled in the household of Lord Morley," and so by the privileges which the retainers of the nobility still enjoyed, protected from molestation on account of his creed.

It is hardly conceivable that these two young men, who were near relations of Mr. Yelverton, and in constant communication with him during the time that Father Gerard was his guest, were not directly influenced by the zealous "Missioner," and the more so as Charles Yelverton asserts positively that his father had died a Catholic, that one of his maternal uncles was a student at Douai in 1601, and that his maternal grandfather, Francis Bastard of Dunham, was then, and had been for forty years past, true to the old creed.

We are not, however, left to inference and conjecture with regard to others of Gerard's converts. It will be remembered that John Walpole, Esq., of Houghton, had married one of the daughters of William Calibut of Coxford Abbey, who at the close of his life took up his residence at Houghton, where he died in 1577. Mr. Calibut had two other daughters; one of them, Ele, had married Henry Russell of West Rudham, she is named by Mr. Calibut in his will; the third daughter, Anna, married first a Cambridgeshire gentleman, Mr. Thomas Gardiner, and by him had a family of four children,— two sons and two daughters. He must have died a year or two after the birth of Barclay or Bernard his second son. The widow married as her second husband Henry Cornwallis (brother of Sir Thomas Cornwallis of Brome) who thereupon settled at Coxford. A second family was the fruit of this marriage, of whom Richard Cornwallis was the eldest son. He was a young man of great

promise and ability; he was sent to the Grammar School at
Norwich for his education, and in his boyhood imbibed a great
many of the Puritan notions of his teacher Mr. Limbert.

From Norwich he went up to Cambridge, where he entered at
Caius College, and was soon elected to a scholarship. In the
list of those proceeding to the degree of B.A. in 1593, his name
appears second in order, and as a matter of course he was
elected to a fellowship, took his M.A. degree, and continued to
reside at the university for some years longer. Meanwhile he
must have been backwards and forwards between Cambridge
and Norfolk, and in the course of his visits home he came under
Gerard's influence. When, exactly, he lost his mother, I have
been unable to discover. The blood of a rigid Puritan was in
her veins, and as she had lived so she died. But his father
succumbed to Gerard's persuasive powers, and was "reconciled,"
and shortly afterwards Richard Cornwallis followed his example,
and became a marked man at Cambridge. Henceforth the
university was no place for him. He was a great deal too
conspicuous a personage to be allowed to live in quiet, and he
made up his mind to cross over to the continent and to visit
Rome. He succeeded in getting safely to the other side of the
Channel, but immediately on his landing at Flushing the
governor arrested him, and after keeping him in prison for six
weeks sent him back to England, where he was formally
deprived of his fellowship and detained in prison for some
months. How he got out does not appear, but after various
detentions and difficulties he managed again to slip across the
sea, and in process of time presented himself at the English
College at Rome in the autumn of 1598.([15])

I may seem to have rather anticipated the course of events
in giving the story of these young men; yet it must be remembered that conversions like these are not wrought in a day,
and before an undergraduate at the university brought himself
to make the immense sacrifices which were implied and indeed
inevitable when he became a declared and avowed Catholic in

Elizabeth's reign, his mind must necessarily have gone through a long conflict and great revulsions of feeling. It was a slow process, and who could exactly trace the beginning of that change which ended in a step that brought with it the severance of the strongest earthly ties, and the surrender of a man's dearest ambition? Boys of twenty take a leap in the dark recklessly, passionately; grown men in their prime stand at the brink and hesitate before making the great plunge; and though Charles Yelverton was hardly of age when he threw up his prospects at Cambridge, Mr. Cornwallis was a man of thirty with a distinguished position in the university, a career before him, and powerful connections to back him if he would but temporise and bide his time. It can hardly be doubted that in his case Gerard had a long task to perform.

It was otherwise with Mr. Cornwallis' half-brother Bernard Gardiner and his cousin Edward Walpole of Houghton. Between these two young men there existed a strong attachment, and both were ready for the great venture before Gerard appeared upon the scene; whether Gardiner had any property in Norfolk I have been unable to make out, but his mother must have been living with her second husband at Coxford while Gerard was in the neighbourhood; and his sister Katherine had married Thomas Cromwell, Esq., brother of Henry Lord Cromwell, on the 17th August 1580, and was now living at North Elmham, within a ride of Gerard's headquarters. ([16]) For some reason Gardiner was regarded with suspicion by the Catholic party. There may have been some indiscretion on his part, or it may have been that the puritanism of his mother and sister gave occasion to the misgivings that undoubtedly were in existence: though he twice offered himself to the Society of Jesus, he was on both occasions rejected after trial.([17])

Edward Walpole had quite made up his mind, and was only on the watch for an opportunity to follow his cousin Henry, and make common cause with him. Gerard simply tells us that Edward Walpole " began to visit him and to frequent the sacraments," and "thus obtained that vocation which he followed a year after, when he went to Rome." Watson, in his *Quodlibets*, with that recklessness of assertion which is so conspicuous in the statements of informers, asserts that Gerard gave Edward Walpole the spiritual exercises; though had he done so, he is not likely to have omitted to mention it.([18]) Once "reconciled" there was no choice left to Gardiner and Edward Walpole but to leave England, which could not afford a safe home to them if their convictions became generally known, and it only remained for them to sell such property as they could turn into money, and make provision for their future maintenance abroad. Accordingly Edward Walpole lost no time in disposing of his Tuddenham estate. His cousin's widow was the tenant for life in possession of the property, and at this time can hardly have been more than forty years of age; the reversionary interest, under all the circumstances, would be a bad purchase for most men, and the sum paid would in all probability give no return for thirty years. The value of money at the time may, in my judgment, be roughly estimated at ten times what it is at the present day, and yet Edward Walpole's reversion fetched the large price of £500. The purchaser was Edward Yelverton. The deed was executed and quittance given, on the 10th July 1590, and in three weeks' time from this the two cousins were in Belgium, applying to Henry Walpole for letters of introduction to carry them to Rome.([19])

So far we have no difficulty in tracing the *direct* influence of Gerard; and if the limits of my work did not forbid my passing over the borders of the county, as little difficulty would be found in tracing his work in Suffolk, Essex, and elsewhere. Nor was his influence limited to the circle of a single family, or to the connections of those who first harboured him.

Among those houses of the Norfolk gentry at which he tells us he was a frequent visitor, was Bowthorpe Hall one? Was some of the relentless persecution which Robert Downes endured to be attributed to information furnished at headquarters, that Father Gerard had been concealed at Melton? How was it that at Sandringham Hall we find "Mary Cobb, wife of William Cobbe, Esq.," returned as an "obstinate Recusant" two or three years after Gerard's arrival, though before then the Cobbs appear all to have conformed? When Mr. Bedingfield's house was searched in 1590, had some spy discovered that Mr. Yelverton and his "man" had been there?[20] Was he a guest at Cossey when Mr. Jerningham's two sons were taken from him and put under the care of Mr. Mulcaster, to be "religiously brought up" at Westminster (?) School and allowed but rarely to visit their parents in the Norfolk home?[21] How soon did he become a guest at Kimberley? How often did he come and go? How long did he stay? To all these questions something like an answer may be given.

When Sir Henry Jerningham died in September 1572, he left the hall at Cossey to his widow for life. She continued to reside there till her death in December 1583.[22] It would seem that her son, Henry Jerningham, Esq., took up his residence in the meanwhile at Wingfield Castle, while her ladyship made a home at Cossey for her daughter Jeronyma, who had married Charles Waldegrave, a son of Sir Edward Waldegrave, mentioned above, by whom she had a numerous family.[23] Shortly before Lady Jerningham's death she had been reported as entertaining in her house at Cossey a popish mass priest, one Mr. Pratt, who however must have died about the time that the intelligence was furnished, for I find that he was buried at Cossey on the 17th April 1582.[24] It was apparently on the death of Lady Jerningham that Mr. Waldegrave removed to Bowthorpe. He had at the time a family of six children, two sons and four daughters, who are all mentioned in Lady Jerningham's will. From Edward, the eldest son, the present Earl of Waldegrave is lineally descended; Charles, the second son, was a child of three when his father removed from Cossey, and a boy of eight when Gerard passed in sight of the house on his way to Norwich. Mr. Charles Waldegrave, though a Catholic by conviction, had taken the oath at the beginning of the Queen's reign, and was therefore classed by the Romanist party, not indeed among the "heretics" but among the "schismatics."(25) But though by his keeping the strict letter of the law so far as the oath was concerned, he had managed to protect himself from spoliation, yet his heart was with the old faith and the old ritual. As to attendance at church, by this time a very simple device had been invented by the Catholic squires, which has hitherto escaped the notice of historians. If there were no church to go to in the parish, the squire could not be presented by the churchwardens as a Nonconformist. It was easy to reduce the fabric to a ruinous condition in any out-of-the-way village where the lord of the manor was all but supreme, where he was resident and the parson was not; accordingly a systematic destruction of the churches in Norfolk commenced and went on to an extent that may well amaze us; foremost among these was the church at Bowthorpe.(26) It was inconvenient to have a clergyman of the new school coming and using the new Prayer-book and reporting absentees at the bishop's visitation, therefore Mr. Yaxley, the lord of the manor, "converted [the church] to a barne, and the steeple to a dove house," and Mr. Waldegrave could no more be returned as "not keeping his church." It could hardly be expected, however, that the family would live like heathens, and it was in houses of this kind that the Missioners found an eager welcome. Certain it is that two sons of Charles Waldegrave—Charles who was born at Cossey in 1580, and John who was born at Bowthorpe about ten years later—became very early moved to make the great venture, and both ended by abjuring the realm and being "reconciled" to the Church of Rome. Charles appears to have been received into the Society of Jesus. John was ordained some time in 1615. Soon after he returned to England, and was buried at Cossey, 3rd March 1616–17.(27)

But the most signal instance of Gerard's success as a proselytiser is to be found in the conversion of Mr. Yelverton's sister Grisel and her husband Sir Philip Wodehouse of Kimberley. Sir Philip had succeeded his father as heir to the Kimberley estate some months before Gerard's arrival. He was one of the most considerable personages in the county of Norfolk, and had been knighted for his services under Robert Earl of Essex in the Cadiz voyage. The Kimberley Wodehouses had given in their adhesion to the new order of things, had accepted the oath on the accession of the Queen, and were in high favour with the Government. A cousin of Sir Philip's, Francis Wodehouse of Breccles Hall, was indeed a conspicuous Recusant, and his wife a very stubborn and consistent one, but the elder branch of the family had never incurred the least suspicion: the Wodehouses were soldiers and courtiers who went with the times. But Lady Wodehouse had been for some time the object of her brother Edward's special solicitude, and before Gerard had arrived in England she had been already influenced by the arguments which had been put forward. Among other houses at which Gerard was received as a guest, Kimberley was certainly one, and I must leave it to himself to tell the story of his doings there.

" I must not omit mentioning an instance of the wonderful efficacy of the Sacraments as shown in the case of the married sister of my host. She had married a man of high rank, and being favourably inclined to the Church, she had been so well prepared by her brother, that it cost me but little labour to make her a child of the Catholic Church. After her conversion she endured much from her husband when he found that she refused to join in heretical worship, but her patience withstood and overcame all. It happened on one occasion that she was so exhausted after a difficult and dangerous labour, that her life was despaired of. A clever physician was at once brought from Cambridge, who on seeing her said that he could indeed give her medicine, but that he could give no hopes of her recovery; and having prescribed some remedies, he left. I was at that time on a visit to the house, having come, as was my wont, in company with her brother. The master of the house was glad to see us, although he well knew we were Catholics, and used in fact to dispute with me on religious subjects. I had nearly convinced his understanding and judgment, but the will was rooted to the earth, 'for he had great possessions.' But being anxious for his wife whom he dearly loved, he allowed his brother to persuade him, as there was no longer any hope for her present life, to allow her all freedom to prepare for the one to come. With his permission then we promised to bring in an old Priest on the following night: for those Priests who were ordained before Elizabeth's reign were not exposed to such dangers and penalties as the others. We therefore made use of his ministry, in order that this lady might receive all the rites of the Church. Having made her confession and been anointed, she received the Holy Viaticum; and behold in half an hour's time she so far recovered as to be wholly out of danger; the disease and its cause had vanished, and she had only to recover her strength. The husband, seeing his wife thus snatched from the jaws of death, wished to know the reason. We told him that it was one of the effects of the holy sacrament of Extreme Unction, that it restored bodily health when Divine Wisdom foresaw that it was expedient for the good of the soul. This was the cause of his conversion; for admiring the power and efficacy of the Sacraments of the true Church, he allowed himself to be persuaded to seek in that Church the health of his own soul. I being eager to strike the iron while it was hot, began without delay to prepare him for confession; but not wishing just then that he should know me for a Priest, I said that I would instruct him as I had been instructed by Priests in my time. He prepared himself, and awaited the Priest's arrival. His brother-in-law told him that this must be at night time. So, having sent away the servants who used to attend him to his chamber, he went into the library, where I left him praying, telling him that I would return directly with the Priest. I went down stairs and put on my soutane, and returned so changed in appearance, that he, never dreaming of any such thing, was speechless with amazement. My friend and I showed him that our conduct was necessary, not so much in order to avoid danger, but in order to cheat the devil and to snatch souls from his clutches. He well knew, I said, that I could in no other way have conversed with him and his equals, and without conversation it was impossible to bring round those who were so ill-disposed. The same considerations served to dispel all anxieties as to the consequences of my sojourn under his roof. I appealed to his own experience, and reminded him, that though I had been in continual contact with him, he had not once suspected my priestly character. He thus became a Catholic; and his lady, grateful to God for this twofold blessing, perseveres still in the Faith, and has endured much since that time from the hands of heretics."[28]

It will be noticed that Gerard in this account, though he speaks of Lady Wodehouse as still "persevering in the faith," leaves it to be inferred that her husband's conversion had not been as complete as he had at first assumed it to be. Recent discoveries in the archives at Rome, and elsewhere, have furnished us with some very curious corroborations of Gerard's story. Gerard wrote his recollections shortly after his return to the continent, about the year 1606. Good as his memory appears to have been, he was writing of what had occurred fifteen or sixteen years before; and there is reason for believing that during the last five or six years of his stay in England, his connection with Norfolk had been, if not wholly broken off, yet very much less intimate than before. He knew that Sir Philip Wodehouse had, as he would have expressed it, "fallen back into heresy;" he had not heard that Lady Wodehouse had been prevailed on to do the same. But when Charles Yelverton wrote his account of himself in the books of the Roman College in 1601, he had already a different tale to tell. His aunt Jane Lumner was still a strict Catholic, but he says the other sister of his father, "wife of Sir Philip Wodehouse, knight . . . on account of the madness of her husband, which very frequently broke out against her, has lately fallen from the Church."[29] It is plain, however, from another of those scraps of evidence, which, as belonging to the class of "undesigned coincidences," are specially valuable, that for a time at any rate Sir Philip must have had strong leanings in the direction of the Roman ritual, and that he did something more than merely connive at the religious practices of his wife and her relations. In the year 1608 one James Roper, a Suffolk gentleman of good connections, who had spent some years at Cambridge, writes his account of himself in the same books of the Roman college, to which I have already had occasion to refer, and among other particulars of his previous life tells us that after leaving the university, he had (apparently in the capacity of private tutor) "lived with Sir Philip Wodehouse, Knt., in the county of Norfolk, where," he adds, "thanks be to God I became a Catholic . . . by the exertions and conversations of Edward Yelverton, Esq., and of Lady Woodhouse, mother of Sir Thomas Woodhouse, Knt. . . ."; this was about the year 1602.

These traces of Gerard's activity and extraordinary success are but stray gleanings which have been gathered in the course of a few years of research, and it must be remembered that I have studiously resisted the temptation of pursuing my inquiries over the borders of the county of Norfolk, but I suspect it would require only a careful scrutiny of letters and papers still existing to disclose information even more startling. When Gerard tells us that he reconciled in Norfolk "more than twenty fathers and mothers of families," whose names "for prudence sake" he had omitted, he evidently has not one whit overstated his remarkable success, and evidently too this was but the beginning of his labours.[30] But how prodigious must have been the effect upon Henry Walpole's imagination and feelings, when letter after letter arrived from home bringing with it always some new tidings of converts made and waverers "reconciled,"

o

and all this, too, among his own friends, and kinsfolk, and schoolfellows! Was this great stirring only the beginning of the harvest? How grand the ingathering would be when he who had been the first to give up all for the kingdom of heaven's sake should take up the work where Gerard left it, and carry it on! High hopes, indeed, if such were his! Destined to be dispelled only too soon.

# NOTES TO CHAPTER IX.

(1) *Page* 194, *line* 17. Richard Southwell, Esq., had been compelled to sell his property at St. Faith's in the very year that Father Gerard arrived in England. He was heavily in debt, and in 1589 I find him in the Fleet at the suit of Henry Doyle, Esq., and one of the Townsends, and appealing to the Privy Council for relief. His affairs were evidently in a hopeless state of embarrassment. He appears to have died in the Fleet at last.—Blomefield's *Norfolk*, x. 441 ; *Records of the Privy Council*, 6th and 7th July 1589.

(2) *Page* 195, *line* 15. The old hall at Cossey bears upon it the date 1564. Sir HENRY JERNEGAN was buried at Cossey 30th September 1572 (P. R.). His will is in P. C. C.; it was dated 15th August 1572, and was proved 27th May 1573. His widow survived him eleven years, and was buried 23rd December 1583 (P. R.).

(3) *Page* 196, *line* 14. See Froude, vol. vii. p. 339 ; *Calender* P. R. O. *Domestic*, 1547–1580, pp. 173, 176, 179; *Addenda*, 1547–1565, No. 7, 8, 9, &c.

(4) *Page* 196, *line* 17. He was Vice-Chamberlain to Queen Mary in 1556, and made Master of the Horse in 1557; his name occurs frequently in the Queen's Household Accounts.—See *Privy Purse Expenses of the Princess Mary*, edited by Sir Fred. Madden, London, 8vo., 1831.

(5) *Page* 196, *line* 27. *Addenda Domestic*, P. R. O., 1547–1565, vol. xi. No. 8.

(6) *Page* 196, *line* 32. Sir EDWARD WALDEGRAVE died in the Tower 1st September 1561. His p. m. inquisition was taken at Brentwood 21st January 1562. His will, dated 13th September 1559, was proved 13th September 1561, P. C. C.—Loftes, 29.

(7) *Page* 197, *line* 4. The will of FRANCIS DOWNES, of Lincoln's Inn Fields, Esq., is to be found in P. C. C., *Reg. Stevenson*, f. 3 ; it is dated 5th July 1563, and was proved 3rd February 1563-64, by ROBERT DOWNES,

testator's brother and executor. Among other legacies he leaves "to the LADY FRANCES WALDEGRAVE 20 of my best oaks in Goldingham Wood in Bulmer, co. Essex, and my crucifix of gold."

(8) *Page* 197, *line* 13.· ROBERT DOWNES of BODNEY succeeded his father, JAMES DOWNES of LANGFORD, ESQ., 1st February, 1 Queen Mary (p.m. inq. Chancery, 4 and 5 Philip and Mary, pt. 3, No. 17). His name appears regularly upon the Recusant Rolls up to the time of his death, 9 Oct. 1594 (p.m. inq. Chancery, 37 Elizabeth, pt. 2, No. 67), after which his widow and her children are as regularly among the "presented" at the Bishop's Visitations.

(9) *Page* 197, *line* 30. Take the following as a sample :—

"WILLIAM YAXLEY, ar.
HUMPHR. BEDINGFIELD, ar.
ROBERT DOWNES, ar.
ROBERT LOVELL, ar.
ROBERT GRAY, ar.

To be kept in jail till they have paid the whole sums of money whereof they have been before convicted, as also the sums whereof they be convicted at these Assizes upon the Statute from the viii$^{th}$ of July to the last of March, viz., ix months.

*Sessions Book*, among the Records of the Clerk of the Peace for the County of Norfolk, 7th April, 26th Elizabeth.

In the Recusant Roll of the 34th Elizabeth, ROBERT DOWNES of Melton appears as owing £1690, 16s. 1¼d. for his Recusancy! In September 1598 he is returned as still in jail at Norwich, while his wife and daughter are living at Melton.

(10) *Page* 198, *line* 6. Patent Roll, 44th Elizabeth (13 Nov.) part x. The poor man died on the 6th of February, 7 James I. (1610.)—P. m. inq. Court of Wards, bundle 60, No. 273.

(11) *Page* 198, *line* 29. FRANCIS WOODHOUSE of Breccles was son and heir of JOHN WOODHOUSE of Breccles by ANNE, relict of WILLIAM SAYVE of Mundford, Gent., and sister of FRANCIS SPYLMAN of Stow Bedon, Gent. He was nephew of SIR ROGER WOODHOUSE of Kimberley, Knt., whose will was proved at Norwich 15th February 1560-61. He married (1) MARGARET REPPS of St. Stephen's, Norwich, and (2) ELEANOR .... He was buried at Cawston 24th March 1604-5, leaving behind him a son JOHN, who was under age at his father's death. FRANCIS WOODHOUSE was for the last twenty years of his life at least a Recusant, and his wife, with her son "JOHN WOODHOUSE, gent.," are returned as "obstinate Recusants" in 1615. He seems to have sold the Breccles estate to Sir Robert Gardiner about 1599, and his wife appears to have parted with the rest of the landed property shortly after her husband's decease, for in 1607 she is described as "nuper de Caston."

(12) *Page* 199, *line* 3. On EDWARD YELVERTON, see pp. 138, 139 supra. His will is in the Registry at Norwich. The original will alone is now producible, the office copy which formerly was to be found in a volume named *Lawson* having disappeared. It is dated 7th May 1623, and was proved at Norwich 2d October of the same year, by the executors, WILLIAM and JOHN PASTON. He calls himself in this will "EDWARD YELVERTON of Appleton in the county of Norfolk, Gent."

(13) *Page* 199, *line* 14. The will of HUMPHREY YELVERTON "of King's Lynn in the county of Norfolk, Gent.," is dated 16 May 1585, and was proved 8th November 1585. In it he names his five children,—Charles, Edward, Humphrey, Martha, and Ann (*P. C. C., Brudenell*, 48). His wife's will is dated 2d March 1589-90 (*P. C. C. Samberbe*, 20). By this it appears that only three out of the five children were then alive, viz., CHARLES, EDWARD, and MARTHA. She leaves the guardianship of her son CHARLES to her brother HENRY BASTARD; of EDWARD to her brother EDWARD BASTARD; of MARTHA to her uncle RICHARD BASTARD of GREAT DUNHAM, Gent. Administration was granted to her brother HENRY BASTARD 17th March 1590-91.

(14) *Page* 200, *line* 2. "CAROLUS YELVERTON filius HUMFREDI YELVERTON generosi ex oppido Bausie in Com. Norff. oriundus puer annorum 15. Adm. 26 April 1590." (*Caius Coll. Matriculation Book*). He appears to have been a scholar of the college. He took the B.A. degree in 1593. (MS. Cat. in the Registry, Cambridge.) He was admitted an Alumnus at the English College at Rome 15th October 1601. See further concerning him and his family, *Records of the English Province, S. J.*, series i. p. 142-146. Burns & Oates, 8vo., 1877.

(15) *Page* 201, *line* 29. See supra, p. 28, n. 13. For the GARDINER descent see *Original Papers of the Norfolk and Norwich Archæological Society*, *Visitation of Norfolk*, p. 342. It will be noticed that Le Neve, in giving the name BARKLEY, adds, "*now called Bartholomew.*" I have no doubt whatever that this is a mistake for BERNARD. It was a common practice at this time among the Catholics to adopt a change of name. Blomefield, always unfortunate in his genealogies, is more than usually inaccurate in his account of the Coxford Calibuts. (*History of Norfolk*, vii. p. 155). RICHARD CORNWALLIS mentions his *two half brothers, sons of his mother*, one of whom he says "exercises the priestly functions in England." This is BERNARD GARDINER, who returned to England about the year 1599; the other is the HUMPHREY GARDINER of the *Norfolk Visitation*.

In the Bishop's Registry at Norwich evidence for the second marriage is still to be seen.

"1567[-8] 4 Februarii Licentia Matrimonialis inter Mrm. HENRICUM

CORNWALLYS genŏs : et ANNAM GARDINER de Estrudham . . . cuicunque Curatori."

HENRY CORNWALLIS, the father, lived only a few months after his son RICHARD had "abjured the realm." He made his will 4th January 1598-99. In it, after leaving his son Richard a legacy in money " towards his furnishing with *books* and apparel," he bequeaths him certain household effects, adding, "All which parcells my desire is shall remain still at Brome *until my said son Richard shall come thither for them.*" He never did come for them. In the course of his wanderings (after being ordained priest 5th June 1599), he took refuge with his cousin, Sir CHARLES CORNWALLIS, who was the English Ambassador at the Court of Spain. Sir CHARLES calls him "a younger son to my dearest uncle HENRY CORNWALLIS, deceased . . ." He adds, "He hath a long time entertained the Religion that suits best with this country, *although he had a mother very earnestly affected to the contrary.*" This was in September 1606. Two months after this, Sir Charles, writing to Lord Salisbury, tells him that his cousin had lately died at the embassy during his own absence.— Winwood's *Memorials*, vol. ii. pp. 260, 278.

The following is Richard Cornwallis' account of himself (*Ex Archivis Coll. Angl. Romæ*, Scrit. Scholar, No. 8, pt. i. vol. xxiv. *Rolls MSS.*),

RICHARDUS CORNWALLYS, 30 Nov. 1598.

1° Resp. Nomen mihi Rich. Cornwaleys annum agens 30$^m$. Natus apud Monasterium COXFORDIENSE in Norfolc. Transacta in paterna domo ætate puerili, *Nordovicum* concessi rudimentis Grammaticis in Schola Publica imbuendus.

2° Resp. Pater mihi est Henricus Cornwaleys, Armiger, non multo abhinc tempore, Dei benignitate, Ecclesiæ Catholicæ restitutus. Mater ANNA CALIBUT oriunda ex antiqua satis familiâ, sed jam emortuâ ac penitus extinctâ, quæ et ipsa non ita pridem supremum diem obiit. Fratrem habeo natu minorem et sorores germanas binas, totidemque *fratres uterinos*, quorum alter sacerdotali munere in Anglia fungitur. E consanguineis eminet præcæteris THOMAS CORNWALEYS, Miles et Catholicus, GULIELMUS CORNWALEYS, Eques auratus . . . et CAROLUS ejus frater *non Catholici*.

3° Resp. Cantabrigiæ in COLLEGIO GUNVILLE et CAII decem plus minus annos moratus . . .

5 Resp. Ab infantiâ hæreticâ pravitate institutus . . . donec Pater misericordiarum . . . *tribus abhinc annis* in gremium sponsæ suæ me suscipere dignatus est, *usus præcipue operâ ministeriis dicti fratris Sacerdotis et Patris Gerardi* ex Soc. Jesu. Ecclesiæ Catholicæ reconciliatus et Romam cogitans cum Flussinghas appulissem Gubernator reginæ, me deprehensum per sex septimanas in custodia detinuit ; demum remissum in Angliam, et Sodalitio ut vocant (quod in Collegio obtinueram) exutum, iterum per sex alias septimanas carceri tradiderunt . . .

(16) *Page* 202, *line* 25. "1580, Thomas Cromwell, Esq"., and M[rs] Katharine Gardyner were marryed ye xvii[th] daye of August." (P. R. North Elmham.) Five children of this marriage are registered among the baptized at North Elmham, the last, Lyonell, 8th January 1591–92.

(17) *Page* 202, *line* 31. On his first attempt, see supra, c. vii, n. 9, p. 157. Seven years after this he tried again; for in Father Greene's *Collect.*, c. p. 206 (*Stonyhurst MSS.*) I find, among the names of those admitted " in domo probat[s] S. Andree ab anno 1590, usque ad 1600," " 1597, P. Bernardinus [ætat] 34, Ex. Coll. Angl. *Dimissus ex Novitiatu*, 1598."

(18) *Page* 203, *line* 6. Watson's *Quodlibets*, p. 91; Gerard's *Autobiography, u. s.*

(19) *Page* 203, *line* 25. P. R. O. *Close Rolls*, 32° *Eliz.*, pt. 26. EDWARD YELVERTON did not come into the Tuddenham estate till 1614, when I find him living there and returned as a Popish Recusant among the presentations at the Bishop's Visitation (*Ep. Reg. Norwic*).

In a case drawn up for the opinion of Sir Matthew Hale in 1653 (*penes me*), I find it stated that MARY, widow of EDWARD WALPOLE of Tuddenham, married a certain JOHN BEADLE, but I have been quite baffled in my attempts to find anything about him, or when or where he or his wife died.

Bernard Gardiner and Edward Walpole arrived in Belgium in August 1590. (*Walpole Letters*, p. 11.)

(20) *Page* 204, *line* 7. For the search at Mr. Bedingfield's house and the anonymous letter which led to it, see *Cal. State Papers, Domestic, Eliz.* 1581 1590, p. 648, No. 76.

In "A trewe Certificat of Popishe recusants within ye Dyoces of Norwich . . . detected by inquisition, made ye first of December 1595 . . ." I find the following entry showing that Father GERARD was at this time in Norfolk. . . . "WOOLVERTON. Edward Yelverton, Gent., kepith a small howse, ROBT. THOMPSON HIS MAN."

*Thompson was the name which Gerard assumed and generally went by while in Norfolk.*

(21) *Page* 204, *line* 11. In a letter among the *Archives at Hatfield*, from a spy named JOHN BYRDE, dated 27th August 1601, and addressed to CECIL, the writer, who bargains for £100 to betray FATHER GERARD, says among other things ". . . which said Gerard's abidings are . . . sometimes (as it is said) *at St. John's with* MR. JERNINGHAM."

The following is from the MSS. at Cossey :—

To our Lovenge Friende Henrye Jerninghame, Esq.

After our hearty commendations, &c.

Whereas upon humble Suit made unto us bye you, That your two Sons remaineng with Mr. Molcastor, might during the time of the Infectiou bee sent to remain with you for one Season. We accordingly have directed That uppon your sending for them, Mr. Molcastor shall send them unto you, to remain and be kept with you untill All hallowstide next. For as much as you now again doe desire (all though God bee thanked the Sickness doth decrease in the City) that your said Children may for some longer space of time remaine in the Country with you, till the Infection be more slacked in the City. We are contented to yield to your request, so as your said Sons may bee delivered again to Mr. Molcastor's charge bye Twelve tide next, to remain with him for their Education as before, the which requiring you to see accordingly performed, we bid you farewell.

From the Court at Whitehall the 26 of October 1593.

Your Loving Friends,

HOWARD.

Wee doe look that in the mean time your Children bee brought up & instructed bye a Schoolmaster known to be well affected to Religion that may give accompt for theer Education, &c.

| Hunsdon. | Jo. Fortescue. |
| Wm. Cobham. | T. Buckhurst. |
| R. Cecil. | J. Wolley. |

(22) *Page* 204, *line* 17. SIR HENRY'S will was proved in P. C. C., 17th September 1577. He was buried at Cossey 30th September 1572 (*P. R.*) I cannot account for the interval that elapsed between his death and the proving his will. Lady JERNINGHAM was buried at Cossey (*P. R.*) 23d December 1583. Her will, interesting in many ways, is especially so for the mention of her *Fool*. This is the latest instance that I have met with of a *Fool being kept as a regular member of the household*.

"In dei nomine Amen. The Twentith day of Auguste," 24th Eliz., "I Fraunces Jernegan of Cossey in the Countie of Norff., widdowe,"—to be buried "where the body of my late husband Henry Jernegan, Knighte [whose soule god pdon] is buried or shall hereafter be transposed;"—£40, amongst other charitable bequests, to be distributed "among the poore prisonners in London by my Exor withe the advise and consente of my sonne Charles Waldegrave, Esquire, and John Derehm, my Surveyors;— s⁴ Exor also (if the same be not donne by mee in my Liefe tyme) to cause some decent Toombe to be made or ells some convenient stone of marble to be laide on the grave of my Layde Kingston his Grandmother, whoe lyeth buried in the parishe Churche of Layton in the Countie of Essex;" * * * to the next heir of William Sterer sometyme possessor of the scite of my

Manno² of Feales in Fressingfeilde, £20;—100 marks to Mʳ Derehm for the aunsweringe of the Debtes of Sʳ Anthony Kingston;—to my Daughter Waldegrave my Pomander of golde ynamyled," &c., &c., for life, remʳ to Fraunces W. her dauʳ;—"Alsoe I give unto her [sᵈ dauʳ W.] my graye nagge, and to her husband a horse, either the graye or the baye, wᶜʰ my Sonne Jernegan shall thinke best; also to Edward Waldegrave his sonne, to Charles W. his seconde Sonne, to Fraunces W. his daughter, to Magdalen and Dorothie W., and to Christian W., . . .—to Henry Jarnegan my Grandchilde, and to Thomas J. his brother, to William J., to George J., to Edward J. and to Anne J., to my Lady Pawlet, to Mrs Anne Bogas, to my sister Sturley, and to my sister Anne," a Ring each;—to Mr. Justice Windham, "to Sʳ Henry Benefeilde, to my cossen Mʳ Edward Audley, to my cossens Mʳ Edward Suliard and Mʳ Thomas S., to my Lady Lovell, to my Ladye Petre, to Mʳˢ Briddiman, to my cozen Andrewes, and to Mʳ Hobard of Hallis Hall;"—to my servaunt John Dereham, gentleman, an Annuity of £20;—to Anne Rucwood my gentlewoman, an Annuity of 4 marks;—to servtᵗ John Powle, Willm. Addamson, and Symon Harrys and Mathewe Harryett, an annuity of 40s. each;—to servᵗ John Freeman;— "Also I doe give unto Joane, foole, four poundes in monney and twenty shillings a yeare as longe as *she* liveth . . . Also from the tyme that John Harvye shall not be kepte and maintayned in my Sonnes howse I doe gyve to the poore foole a yearly Rent towards *his* maintenance of fower markes by yeare;"—to Thomas Freeman, "40s. by yeare until my Sonne maie and shall place him in a Beadmanshippe at Saincte Olaves;"— William Addamson "to enjoy the Bayliewicke of Dages in Rannington;" —Residue of Goods, &c., after payᵗ of debts and funeral expenses to son Harry J. he sole Exᵒʳ. Overseers, Sʳ Thomas Cornwallis, Knighte, Charles Waldegrave, Esquire, and John Derehm, Gentleman;—to one Mʳ Russell, sonne unto Mʳˢ Jane Russell, that was one of the Gentlewomen of Queene Marye's Privye Chamber, £10 "which I borrowed of his Mother;"—to Nicholas Phillippes my servᵗ £4 and a horse;—to my Cozen Anne Bogas; —to Mʳ Marshall;—"to Thomas Harman, the boye wᶜʰ wayteth on mee," 20s. a year for life.

No witnesses given. Proved 15th Feb. 1583.

(23) *Page* 204, *line* 22. It was a common practice among the gentry in the sixteenth century for a young man to bring his bride to his father's house, and to spend the first year or two of his married life with his parents. The separate establishment was not set up until the increase of the family or other circumstances rendered the change necessary. Among the muniments at ROUGHAM HALL there is an indenture, dated 12th October, 1 and 2 Philip and Mary (1554), which sets forth that, "In consideration of a Marriage between Henry, son and heir of William Yelverton of Rougham, Esq., and Bridget, daughter of Sir William Drury, Knt." . . . Sir William

Drury covenants to make certain payments *and to give his daughter " double apparel and the wedding dinner."* William Yelverton covenants to settle certain manors and lands and *" to give two years' board with two servants, and at the end, for two years more, one other maid and a woman, and to pay for his son double apparel.* Among the Earl of Kimberley's muniments there is a marriage contract of this date drawn up in almost precisely similar terms.

(24) *Page* 204, *line* 27. In P. R. O. *Domestic, Elizabeth,* vol. 157, No. 88, is a paper giving "Information of the names and places of residence of certain Recusants . . ." Among them I find under Norfolk, "At Cossey, the LADY JERNINGHAM, MR. CHARLES WALDEGRAVE and his wife, . . . and MR. PRATTE a priest. . . . MR. ROBERT DOWNES and his wife, who doth dwell but a mile off from Cossey [viz., at MELTON HALL] the LADY JERNINGHAM her house." Under Suffolk I find ". . . At Winkfelde Castle, MR. HENRY JARNINGHAM." This paper is ascribed to the year 1581 or 1582. In the P. R. of Cossey I find, "1582, Sepultu fuit RICHARD PRATT, 17° die Aprilis." As this is the only instance of the occurrence of the name of PRATT in the Register, the inference is obvious.

(25) *Page* 205, *line* 3. CHARLES WALDEGRAVE, son and heir of SIR EDWARD WALDEGRAVE of BORLEY, Knight, was, at his father's death on the 1st September 1561, aged ten years forty weeks and three days, *i.e.,* he was born on the 22d November 1550. By patent dated 8 Feb. 1563, ROBERT NOWELL (brother of Dean NOWELL) was appointed his guardian. NOWELL died in 1569, and by his will left to his "good Mr. and freinde MR. SECRETORIE CICILL *the wardeshippe of younge Mr. Walgrave, with all my righte and intereste in the same, payeng such monnye to the quenes ma<sup>tie</sup> as I shoulde* . . ." Immediately after he came of age, viz., on the 25th November 1571, he obtained a license from Parkhurst, Bishop of Norwich, to marry "HIERONIM JERNEGAN . . . anywhere within the diocese of Norwich." Where the marriage was celebrated I have not found. It is clear that he was living with Lady JERNINGHAM, his wife's mother, at COSSEY in 1581, and apparently continued to live there till her death in December 1583. His second son, CHARLES, in his answers to the interrogatories put to him on his admission at the English College at Rome, says that he himself was born at Cossey in 1581. On the other hand, his younger brother, JOHN WALDEGRAVE, says that *he* was born at BOWTHORPE in 1592. When he became possessed of STANNINGHALL I have not been able to discover, but I think it must have been shortly after the birth of John Waldegrave in 1592; for about this time the affairs of FRANCIS WOODHOUSE of STANNINGHALL (nephew of FRANCIS WOODHOUSE, Esq., of BRECCLES HALL) had got into a desperate condition, and he must have been compelled to sell this estate. On the 14th October

41 Eliz. (1599) Mr. Waldegrave settled certain manors and lands upon himself and his wife Jeronyma for life, and after their death on his son and heir Edward Waldegrave, and his wife Eleanor; remainder to *their* son and heir Henry Waldegrave; remainder to *his own second son* CHARLES W.; remainder to *his third son* JOHN; remainder to *his brother* NICHOLAS. He died at Stanninghall on the 10th January, 7 Charles I. (1632), having survived his wife just five years. She was buried at Cossey, 4th February 1626-27.—Chancery p.m. Inq. Suff., 4 Eliz., No. 130; the Townely-Nowell MS., edited by Mr. Grosart, pp. xxxvi. and xlix.; Marriage Licenses in the Reg. Cur. Episcop. Norw.; Answers to Interrogatories at the Engl. Coll. Rome (Rolls, MSS.); see other authorities supra, n. (11).

(26) *Page* 205, *line* 17. See *East Anglian*, vol. i., pp. 340, 370; ii., pp. 75, 89. Very noticeable is the startling return for the Deaneries of HYNGHAM and HUMBLEYARD in 1602. In the contiguous parishes of EARLHAM, BOWTHORPE, COSSEY, EASTON, and RUNHALL *the churches are in ruins, and in all these places the influence of the Recusant gentry was paramount.* This subject requires to be investigated more minutely than would be possible in these notes.

(27) *Page* 205, *line* 33. Rolls MSS., u. s.; *Records of the English Province, S. J.*, series I.; see note (23).—Cossey P. R.

(28) *Page* 208, *line* 16. *Father Gerard's Autobiography*, p. xxvii.

(29) *Page* 209, *line* 3. *Records of the English Province, S. J.*, series I., p. 142.

(30) *Page* 209, *line* 32. The following is from Watson's *Quodlibets*. I give the extract *in extenso*, as the book is a very scarce one, and few of my readers can have the opportunity of referring to it:—

"Another surmised holy father of their society (in whose mouth a man would think butter could not melt) . . . . poor man I pity his simplicity in that, being otherwise of a good nature, he is much blinded and corrupted in his life and manners by being a Jesuit . . . . but I will only enlarge myself with a few golden threads from Fa. Gerard's web . . . . First he was the man that caused Henry Drurie to enter into this exercise and thereby got him to sell the manor of Lozell in Suffolk, and other lands to the value of 3500 pounds and got all the money himself; the said Drurie having chosen to be a lay brother. Afterwards he sent him to Antwerp to have his Noviciate by the Provincial there, by name Oliverius Manerius (for at that time Fa. Garnet had not his full authority to admit any) where after twelve or fourteen days he died, not without suspicion of some indirect dealing. Fa. Holt the Jesuit ascribed it unto the alteration of his diet, saying that he might have lived well enough if he had remained at home and not have come thither.

"Two others had the exercise given them at that time by Fa. Gerard, viz., Master Anthony Rouse, of whom he got about 1000 pounds, and Master Thomas Everard, of whom he had many good books and other things.

"Also he gave the exercise to Edward Walpole, whom he caused to sell the manor of Tuddenham, and had of him about 1000 marks.

"He dealt so in like manner with Master James Linacre, his fellow prisoner in the Clink, from whom he drew there 400 pounds. And afterwards got a promise of him of all his lands; but was prevented thereof by the said Linacre's death.

"Furthermore, under pretence of the said exercise, he cousined Sir Edmund Huddleston's son and heir by sundry sleights of above 1000 pounds; and so he dealt with Master Thomas Wiseman, and by giving him the exercise he got his land, and sent him to Antwerp, where he died.

"He also gave the exercise to the eldest son of Master Walter Hastings. And he hath drawn Master William Wiseman into the said exercise so oft as he hath left him very bare to live.

"He hath so wrought with Master Nicholas King, lately of Gray's Inn, as he hath gotten most of his living and sent him to Rome.

"Master Roger Lee of Buckinghamshire hath been in this exercise likewise, and is also by him sent to Rome.

"In like manner he dealeth with such Gentlewomen as he thinketh fit for his turn and draweth them to his exercise: as the Lady Lovell, Mistress Heywood, and Mistress Wiseman, now prisoner [1602] of whom he got so much as now she feeleth the want of it.

"By drawing Mistress Fortescue, the widow of Master Edmund Fortescue, into his exercise, he got of her a farm worth 50 pounds a year and paid her no rent.

"Another drift he hath by his exercise of cousinage; which is to persuade such gentlewomen as have large portions to their marriage to give the same to him and to his company, and to become nuns.

"So he prevailed with two of M. William Wiseman's daughters of Broddocke; with Elizabeth Sherly born in Leicestershire; with Dorothy Ruckwood, M. Richard Ruckwood's daughter of Suffolk, who had a great portion given her by the Lady Elizabeth Drury her grandmother; with Mistress Tremaine, Master Tremaine's daughter of Cornwall, she having a large portion; with Mistress Mary Tremaine of Dorsetshire, of whom he had 200 pounds; with Mistress Anne Arundell, of whom he got a great portion; with the Lady Mary Percy who is now a nun at Bruxels . . . . . . But this is enough for this time of their practices by fame and report."
—Watson's *Quodlibets*, p. 91.

The following description of Gerard's person is extracted from the archives at HATFIELD :—

"Jerrard's discovery may the better be by observing this description of him and his habit. To be of stature tall, high shouldered, especially when his cope is on his back, black haired, and of complexion swarth, hank nosed, high templed, and for the most part attired costly and defencibly, in buff leather, garnished with gold or silver lace, sattin doublet, and velvet hose of all colours, with cloaks correspondent, and rapiers and daggers gilt or silvered."

Blackwell describes him thus :—

"About 50 years of age, his head brownish, his beard more black, cut after the fashion of a spade, of stature indifferent, and somewhat thick, decently attired in black silk rush hose and doublet, with a silk russet or black cloak, of good length, laced, with a rapier and dagger sanguined or sometimes gilt."

It is quite clear that this Blackwell *did not know Gerard personally*, but had obtained his information at second hand. He could not otherwise have described him as "of stature indifferent, and somewhat thick." Gerard beyond all doubt was above the ordinary stature, and in some circles went by the name of "Long John."

## CHAPTER X.

## CAPTURE AND IMPRISONMENT.

IN no part of England had the suppression of the monasteries caused such deep discontent, and nowhere had the doctrines of the Reformers been regarded with such bitter aversion, as in Yorkshire. By far the most formidable outbreak which occurred in the kingdom during the sixteenth century was the great rebellion of 1536, which for a time seriously threatened the crown of Henry VIII., and numbered among its leaders many persons of wealth and influence in the Northern Counties. The insurrection of the Cornishmen in 1549, and that of Kett in Norfolk, grew to formidable dimensions, mainly through the want of any organised police in the districts in which they originated, the supineness of those in authority, and the panic which the very suddenness of the risings occasioned. The Cornish rebellion was indeed a religious riot, the poor rustics being excited to phrensy by finding themselves debarred from the use of that ritual and those ceremonies which they regarded as infinitely precious and dear. The Norfolk revolt was a purely agrarian movement, a peasant war on a small scale; but though in one case Exeter was menaced, and in the other Norwich was besieged, the insurgent rabble was scattered to the winds almost at the first appearance of a disciplined force, and when the fighting began it was not so much a conflict as a massacre. Nor, indeed, was the rebellion of the northern earls much more important; the malcontents from the first had no chance and little hope of success, the leaders had nothing but their great names to fall back upon, there was not a man among them of any conspicuous ability or any reputation in peace or war, and at no time could the government have had any cause for alarm or grave uneasiness. The power of the nobility had gone for ever long before Queen Elizabeth had been ten years upon the throne. But the Pilgrimage of Grace at one time threatened to develop into an actual revolution, and when the armies of Aske and the Duke of Norfolk faced one another at Doncaster in October 1536, the fate of a kingdom was trembling in the balance. When the king's side came out of that struggle victorious, and affairs took the turn they did, one of the results was the institution of a permanent commission for the better administration of the Northern Counties; a court whose functions, purporting at first to be mainly judicial, became in process of time in large part inquisitorial, and its records, if they should ever be recovered, would present us with one of the bloodiest chapters in the history of England. This was the famous "Council of the North," a name of terror during the later years of the sixteenth century to all who favoured the Romish cause or who had any leaning towards the Papal hierarchy or the Papal authority.([1])

At the suppression of the monasteries St. Mary's Abbey in York had been kept in the king's hands; it was reserved as a royal palace, which might prove useful upon occasion if the disturbances on the Scotch frontier should make it advisable for the sovereign to show himself in the northern parts of the kingdom. It was an imposing and stately building in which a prince might hold his court and maintain a large retinue, and soon after Aske's rebellion collapsed it was made the official residence of the President of the Council. Henry, Earl of Huntingdon, was appointed to this office in the autumn of

1572; for years he had served his mistress faithfully, had deserved her confidence and gained it. He was a man who had always sided with the party of progress in religion, had consistently favoured the Puritans and as consistently set himself to oppose the Romanists. From the hour when he was installed in his office as President, the Yorkshire gentry whose loyalty in religion was at all questionable began to have a very bad time of it. In Sir Thomas Gargrave, who was Vice-President of the Council, Lord Huntingdon found a coadjutor as zealous as himself, a relentless persecutor, and one who, unlike his chief, managed to enrich himself at the expense of his victims. The Earl had scarcely entered upon his office before Gargrave sent up to Burleigh a list of all the principal gentry in Yorkshire, with marks against their several names indicating which were "Protestant," "the worste sorte," "meane or less evyll," and "doubtfull or newtor." It is a suggestive document, and shows how, even at this date, the country gentry in the North were deeply tinged with disaffection, and how much irritation and discontent was smouldering. From the first the Earl of Huntingdon set himself to keep down the malcontents and to maintain a vigilant supervision over them and their concerns; while Sandys, the coarse and miserly Archbishop of York, co-operated with him to the best of his ability, he too having a keen eye to the spoil that might be looked for from the plundered Recusants. Up to Lord Huntingdon's arrival in Yorkshire the Catholic gentry had not had much to complain of; the laws were rarely put into force and the penalties for non-attendance at church were rarely exacted; but there were too many hungry and unscrupulous hangers-on among the retainers of the Lord President, and too much to be made out of those who having manors and houses and lands were known to be men of conscientious convictions, to allow of these latter remaining long unmolested. Very soon a system of espionage grew up, and a regular band of informers was taken into the Lord President's pay. Sir Thomas Gargrave's first list had, it seems, failed in its object of stirring up the government to exercise more severity; but in 1577 Archbishop Sandys himself forwarded another and more elaborate paper to the Lords of the Privy Council, and the campaign against the Recusants began in earnest. The Archbishop's paper purports to be a list of "The names, surnames, additions, and dwelling-places of such within the diocese of York as have been detected to the L. Archbishop of York and other Her Maj. Commissioners in these parts for their disobedience in refusing the Church and public prayers, &c., and do not conform themselves, with a note of their abilities, &c.;" the annual income of all whose names occur is set down minutely, that the fine imposed might be adjusted to the several capacities of the proscribed, and in some cases a note giving further information is added. It was not long before the Recusants began to feel that a new regime had begun. As yet no blood was shed, but the pursuivants were let loose, and the searches at the houses of the suspected gentry began to be carried on with a harshness which up to this time had never been heard of, and the spies vied with one another in their hateful work. Before a single Jesuit had set foot in England, before a score of Cardinal Allen's Seminarists had been sent across the seas, we find Huntingdon writing to Walsingham with a grim boast that on the information of "one of my spialles" he had ridden twenty miles to make a raid upon the houses of certain of the gentry who were reported to be harbourers of such priests as came to say mass and give absolution. Year by year the iron heel of the Lord President pressed more and more heavily. Unhappy gentlemen left their homes and kept in hiding, were sought for, informed against, and hunted down; the terrible fine of £20 a month exacted without mercy, and those who were unable to pay thrown into York Castle and kept at their own charges. But when Campion had been apprehended, racked, and butchered, and it was felt that the Jesuit Mission had produced an important effect, and might lead to important and dangerous results if things were allowed to go on in their course undisturbed, the Lord President thought that the time had come for making an example of some one in a sterner way than he had as yet thought it prudent to pursue.(²)

William Lacey was a Yorkshire gentleman of Great Houghton in the West Riding, of respectable family and moderate means, whose name appears on Archbishop Sandys' list of Recusants as then in prison at Hull for refusing to come to church. He managed to escape from jail and to slip away to France; there he entered at the English College at Rheims, where, and at Pont à Mousson, he pursued his divinity studies for some time, and going from thence to Rome obtained a dispensation (for he was a widower) from the Pope, was ordained priest and returned to England in that capacity about 1580. With the strange imprudence which characterised the Seminarists at all times, he had no sooner got back to his old neighbourhood than he set himself to exercise his functions among the prisoners in York Castle, though he might have known by this time that the spies were on the alert and keeping careful watch around. On the 22nd July, 1582, as he was coming out of the castle, he was arrested, taken before the Archbishop, examined, and thrown into a dungeon, where he was debarred from all converse with his friends, and on the 11th of August was put upon his trial with another Seminarist whose history was almost exactly like his own; both were found guilty as a matter of course, and equally of course were condemned to death, and on the 22nd they were hung as traitors, special care being taken to prevent their addressing the multitude who had assembled at the place of execution. This was the first blood shed by the Lord President, but it was by no means the last. On the 28th November of this same year another lately-ordained priest, James Thompson, was delivered over to the hangman at the same spot where Lacey and Kirkman had suffered. Next year there were two more victims; in 1585, two more, one priest and one layman;

in 1586, one gentleman was hung, drawn, and quartered for being "reconciled," and another for having harboured a priest. But the most memorable incident of this year was the atrocious and almost unexampled barbarity of the 20th March.(³)

Margaret Clitherow was the daughter of Thomas Middleton, a wealthy citizen of York, and sheriff of that city in 1565. On her father's death, her mother had taken as her second husband one Henry Maye, who was Lord Mayor of York this very year, 1586, when his stepdaughter was brought before the council for trial. Margaret was married to John Clitherow in 1571, and had borne him several children, of whom the eldest son had been sent abroad to be educated a year before her last troubles came upon her. As early as 1576, she had been presented as a Recusant and thrown into prison, and I find her in York Castle in the October of the following year. How long she remained there does not appear, but it is evident that some years after this she had made herself notorious by her ascetic life and the uncompromising way in which she had befriended any priest who needed shelter and help. Her husband appears to have been a very thriving tradesman, warm-hearted, open-handed, and easy-going, devotedly attached to his wife in his own rough way, but quite devoid of any religious sentiment or convictions. On the 10th of March, 1586, the Council called Clitherow before them, and apparently the same day ordered a search to be made at his house; the officers arrested everybody upon the premises, and compelled a boy of ten or twelve years of age to give them such information as he was able to communicate. On this evidence Margaret Clitherow was put upon her trial for the crime of concealing priests. When called upon to plead at the bar, she obstinately refused, and as no arguments or threats could make her change her resolution, she was condemned to the *peine forte et dure*, and actually crushed to death in accordance with the hideous sentence.(⁴)

And so the horrible work went on. In 1587 three priests, in

1588 two, in 1589 two more, suffered in this city of York alone for the crime of saying mass or giving absolution, or simply setting foot on English soil. Scarcely a year passed by without these dreadful massacres, the details of which are more revolting and shameful than those who have not given their attention to the subject, or read the accounts written down at the time, could be readily brought to believe. For ten years the butchery had been kept up remorselessly. The victims, as a rule, were not hung by the neck till they were dead, but cut down while they were alive and conscious, then thrown upon their backs, the executioner's knife was plunged into their bowels, and the entrails and heart tossed into a cauldron of water which stood hard by. In more than one instance the victim in his agony and despair struggled with the hangman, but it was only for a moment. In some cases the crowd shouted out to the sheriff to "let him hang." Sometimes a condemned man begged as a special grace that he "might not be bowelled ere he were dead." The rabble looked on terror-struck, but such scenes could not but brutalise them. The appetite for blood is a strange passion, and once yielded to is prone to exercise a horrible fascination on some minds.

But nothing is more sure than that these ghastly tragedies did not help the cause they were meant to serve, or weaken the hands of those who were on the side of the sufferers. Sympathy for the "martyrs" never languished; the Council of the North, with the blind and ferocious infatuation which always characterises persecutors, never allowed pity to grow cold. Men and women, with any spark of chivalry or generous emotion left, could not but feel some remorse and commiseration for the men whose crimes they could not be made to understand, while they saw them suffer for their faith with the courage and constancy of heroes.

It was in this northern province that Henry Walpole found himself cast, with his two companions, on that dark and rainy December night of 1593. The roar of the angry billows sounded hoarsely in the distance; inland were the watchers, and no friendly roof to give them shelter. Ignorant of the neighbourhood, and without plans, they committed the unaccountable blunder of keeping all together instead of separating, as was the almost invariable course with the emissaries at their first landing. They passed the night wandering among the woods or hiding in some outhouse, and early in the morning they found their way to Kilham, a place about nine miles from where they had been put ashore, and took refuge in the village inn.(5)

Before noon the tidings had spread far and wide that three strangers, travel-stained and soaked with rain, had appeared in the neighbourhood, no one knew whence, and had taken up their quarters at the roadside alehouse. The constables, at this time more than ordinarily vigilant, were soon upon the track. Three months before Lord Huntingdon had laid his hands upon a Seminary priest of some note—one John Boast—whom he had been endeavouring for years to get into his power. On his succeeding at last, he had received from the Lords of the Privy Council a special letter of thanks in acknowledgment of the important service rendered.(6) Gratified by this recognition, the Earl had replied to the Council assuring them of his unabated desire to deserve the approbation of his Royal Mistress, and in accordance with his professions the coast had been watched with increased strictness. Every stranger and wayfarer was subjected to search and cross-examination, and the chances of escape for any Seminary priest adrift in Yorkshire had been reduced to a minimum. Before the sun set on that first day after landing on English soil the three returned exiles had been arrested and straightway committed to the castle at York.(7)

According to a document very recently discovered at Rome, Henry Walpole and his companions were apprehended on the 7th of December. No time was lost before subjecting them all to a severe scrutiny and by the 22nd of the month the

Privy Council had not only received from Lord Huntingdon a report of the capture, but had drawn up and forwarded instructions in reply.

The apprehension had come so suddenly that there had been no time for making any concerted plan. In prison the three men were allowed no communication, they all gave their true names, and no attempt was made at disguise or concealment of the purpose of their mission. Henry Walpole at once confessed himself a Jesuit Father, and his brother and Lingen allowed that they had served in Sir William Stanley's regiment in Flanders. But when it came to their being questioned on matters which affected the safety or even the life of others, Henry Walpole and Lingen were obstinately silent, and persuasion, entreaty, and menace were powerless to extort from them a word. It was otherwise with Thomas Walpole; he was not of the stuff that martyrs are made of, and for his religious convictions they cannot have been deeply rooted at this time, whatever they became in the years that followed. He had, to be sure, fought on the Spanish side against the revolted Flemings, but it was as a soldier of fortune that he had joined the wars; his faith had little to do with the matter. If to have served under Stanley was treason, it was a sort of treason that might easily be condoned, and "young Thomas," as Topcliffe calls him, was not disposed to put his life in jeopardy by keeping back information which it was no matter of conscience with him to withhold. Lord Huntingdon saw that the younger man might be worked upon by a little dexterous diplomacy, and he spared no pains to extort from him all he knew. Thomas Walpole made but little difficulty; perhaps he saw that there was no chance for him or his brother except in making an open confession, and having once begun to be communicative he told all he knew: he accompanied the officers to the seashore and dug up the packet of letters which his brother had, on their first landing, hidden in the sand under a stone; and when a short time after another returned priest was arrested, Thomas identified him as one whom he had seen at Antwerp and Brussels years before, and thus became the means of his being sent to the Tower for further and severer handling.([8])

Meanwhile the Earl resorted to other means for working upon the elder brother, who was by this time felt to be a representative man. It would be a great point gained if his convictions could be shaken, or, better, if in open controversy he might be put to the worse by some practised theologians qualified to stand forward as champions for the Protestant faith. There were by this time at York a whole bevy of Romish priests who had been arrested and were in confinement; all had been hard pressed to recant and give information of their former associates, and under promise of their lives being spared they had, in several cases, yielded to the temptation, and having once broken with their old friends, all chance of regaining the confidence of the Romish party being gone, they threw themselves into the arms of their new supporters with the bitterness which usually characterises perverts. Of these men the most conspicuous were Anthony Major, Thomas Bell, and a Mr. Hardesty; they were all "Seminary priests," and all had been betrayed by one of their fellow-Seminarists, George Dingley, about a year before.([9]) At the time of their arrest they were wandering about Yorkshire exercising their functions as priests, and Bell and Major were settled somewhere in the neighbourhood of York. Hardesty had passed through Brussels on his way to Rome at the end of 1590, and had there received some assistance from Henry Walpole; but after his departure news came that he was under grave suspicion, and that even then he "had published articles scarce sound showing himself a cynic and schismatic,"([10]) but he had managed to clear himself of such charges as had been brought against him, and had contrived to get sent to England as an accredited "missioner." All three men on finding themselves in peril appear to have at once turned round, and Bell became afterwards a conspicuous personage and as furious and violent a declaimer against the Papacy as the strongest Puritan could desire to find. Father Parsons, in one of his most caustic books, pours out against him all the vials of his scorn and indignation, and "The dolefull knell of Thomas Bell" is among the most telling and pungent of Parsons' compositions. The three "converted" Seminarists might be presumed to know the weak points of the controversy between the Churches of England and Rome: they all professed to have been themselves convinced of the errors of their ways; they had all been brought to see the falsity of their belief, and it was but fair that they should now be used to bring another back to the true path; accordingly they were summoned to take part in a set controversy with the lately-captured Jesuit, who professed his readiness to defend the truth from the Romish point of view, and if he were vanquished in argument to recant his errors as they had done. But the converted Seminarists were not left to carry on the battle unaided; the Earl's chaplain, Dr. Favour, "a very mild divine," as Topcliffe calls him, who had lately been appointed Vicar of Halifax, and a man of learning and piety, was also invited to take part in the disputation, and along with these were associated some of the leading clergy of York—Dr. Bennet, one of the Prebendaries of the Cathedral, and Mr. Remington, Archdeacon of the East Riding. Archdeacon Remington was a Cambridge man, and while a fellow of Peterhouse had been Henry Walpole's tutor; he seems to have taken little part in the argument, and, indeed, was present but once when, we are told, that "he said they came to make a friendly conference . . . . . . . . . that he had been my tutor at Cambridge and wished me well."([11])

It is difficult to make out whether the conferences which these clergymen carried on with their Jesuit opponent were public or private; the notes which Henry Walpole drew up afterwards, and which he forwarded to the Lord Huntingdon, are now in the Record Office and were printed in the Irish Ecclesiastical Record in 1873, but they leave it uncertain whether any formal debate was held in presence of a general audience, while it is pretty certain that some part of the dispute was carried on in Walpole's own chamber. An appearance of fairness and some kindly consideration for the prisoner was kept up throughout, and he was even allowed access to books, which were supplied to him freely. We are forcibly reminded of Campion's famous disputation in Westminster Hall twelve years before, and it may well be that to Henry Walpole himself that memorable scene recurred, and perhaps the hope suggested itself, that, though the master's fate might be awaiting the scholar, yet before the end he too might win over some disciple who in his turn should take up the mantle that was now upon his own shoulders. Be that as it may, this controversy ended as such controversies usually do: each side perfectly satisfied with itself, neither in the least shaken or influenced by the conflict of words. On the whole the Jesuit seems to have been the better disputant, and in proportion as he had shown himself superior in dialectic skill, in that proportion was he sure to bring upon himself increased animosity from his opponents. It soon became evident that this man was not of the Bell and Hardesty stamp—one who had his price, and that a very low price, easily set down at its money value; but that though he were never so misguided, obstinate or vain, he was certainly in earnest, and that if these endless controversies did nothing else they were having the dangerous effect of gaining for the Jesuit father a character for learning, piety, and devoted zeal. So the controversies were stopped, and Henry Walpole thereupon assumed an aggressive attitude; he actually had the audacity to employ his time in jail in composing a tract with the title "Beware of False Prophets," which was directed against those very ministers who had so lately taken part in the disputation that had been going on. This was too much for the Lord President, and as any further delay in dealing with such a case would be only loss of time, the Earl appointed a jail delivery for the 24th January 1594, when the Walpoles and Lingen were to be put upon their trial.

But here a difficulty was suggested by "the learned of the council." The statute which made it high treason for a Jesuit father to land in England was plain enough, and Henry Walpole might have been tried for his life at first, as he was at last, solely upon this indictment. But in the case of Lingen and Thomas Walpole it was by no means so certain that the law could touch them. They had borne arms under the Queen's enemies to be sure, and Lingen had been a pirate, but these offences had been "committed beyond the seas," and it was very questionable how far they could be reached by any laws that then existed. Hereupon the Earl wrote off in haste to the Lord Keeper Puckering, explaining the nature of the technical objection that had been raised, and suggesting that a special commission should be issued, "the example whereof" (he adds) "will do good in these parts."(12) Astonishing though it be, it is nevertheless almost certain that no such commission was ever issued, *because there was no law to deal with the case of the two laymen.* Piracy and robbery on the high seas were such venal offences that the law took little or no cognisance of them, and for serving in the armies of France or Spain, even against the Crown of England, it appears that no man could be called to account on English soil. The government had too much to do with hunting up priests and putting the screw on Recusants at home to trouble itself with the doings of men who were living by their wits on the other side of the Channel. In the case of a needy adventurer, driven by his necessities to acts of violence, it was no man's interest to hang him, and no man's gain to strip him of his all. Cruel and bloody as the laws were, there were loopholes by which the worst criminals could escape now and then. "Benefit of clergy" still had a meaning; and if a man had friends in high places he could cheat the gallows even at the eleventh hour. It was only the poor wretch who had a conscience, and who dared not go against that conscience, who had no hope of pity or respite. During the three years ending with this year, 1594, I find no less than sixty-one pardons recorded for murder, burglary, highway robbery, and other felonies, but pardons to priests or their harbourers there are none: to such criminals no mercy might be shown.([13])

And so Lingen and Thomas Walpole found themselves scarcely amenable to the law for any offence against its enactments; but inasmuch as all three defendants were apprehended together, the technical objection which had been urged in favour of the two laymen was allowed indirectly, and to some small extent affected the priest with whom they had been so intimately associated. No special commission was sent down to York, "the example whereof might do good in these parts." But a special *commissioner* was sent down by the Lords of the Privy Council, one whose practised hand would be sure to deal skilfully with such a matter as this, and to him the case of the Jesuit father was committed accordingly. Towards the end of January the dreaded Richard Topcliffe appears on the scene. Immediately on his arrival Lingen was examined, and a report of his answers sent up to the Privy Council on the 21st January. He obstinately refused to disclose anything, and what he did say declined to asseverate on oath. Thomas Walpole had little or nothing more to tell; he had already told all; how much that was may appear from Topcliffe's own letter, in which he exultingly praises the young man for his candour, and adds to the Lord Keeper, "By this your Lordship may show unto her Sacred Majesty how GOD blessed her Highness with the uttering of that which I see will turn to her high service for discovering of disloyal men and women both about London, in sundry counties in England, and deeply in Ireland;" and then, after giving a list of some trinkets and tokens with which Henry Walpole had been entrusted to hand to the friends of the exiles if he should be fortunate enough to meet with them on his mission, Topcliffe significantly adds, "Much more lieth hid in these two lewd persons, the Jesuit and Lingen, which wit of man giveth occasion to be suspected that labour of man *without further authority and conference than his Lordship hath here can never be digged out* ...... So the Jesuit and Lingen must be dealt with in *some sharp sort above*, and more will burst out than yet, or otherwise, can be known, *yet see I more in this service than ever I did in any before to her Majesty's benefit both of state and purse.*"(14) Yes, for be it remembered that this same Henry Walpole was his father's eldest son and heir, and it might be that the old man at Anmer Hall could be got at and accused, for such things had been before and might be again, and it might be too that rumours were rife that old Christopher's health was failing, and then whose would the inheritance be?

It seems that Topcliffe's stay at York was short. In a letter of Lord Huntingdon's, dated 12th February, he is spoken of as having gone some time; (15) but while the result of his visit was as yet unknown Henry Walpole found means of communicating with his friends outside, and, through the connivance probably of his jailer or other functionaries in the castle, he managed to keep up a correspondence, considerable portions of which have been preserved.

The original of the following letter was still in existence when Bishop Challoner published his *Missionary Priests* in 1741; but at the French Revolution it disappeared along with thousands of other records of this bloody time :—

'Your Reverence's Letters give me great Comfort; but if I
'could but see you, tho' it were but for one Hour, it would be
'of greater Service to me, than I can possibly express. I hope
'that what is wanting, my sweet Lord *Jesus* will supply by
'other Means, whose heavenly Comfort and Assistance has
'always hitherto stood by me in my greatest Necessities, and, I
'am persuaded, will continue so to do, since his Love for us is
'everlasting.

'If I would write down all Things that have here passed with
'our Adversaries, it would be endless, and the Work of a long
'time. In my Examination I gave in in Writing a long Account
'of my Life beyond the Seas, of the Places where I lived, and
'of my Actions and Designs; which, I assured them, had no
'other Butt than the only Glory of God, and the Increase of the
'holy Catholic Faith. With which View I told them, I returned
'into *England*, with a very great Desire of the Conversion, not
'only of the People, but most of all, of the Queen herself, and
'of the whole *English* Nobility; which I plainly assured them,
'I should ever use my best Endeavours to bring about, with the
'Grace of God.

'To their Queries concerning others, I refused to answer. And
'when *Topliffe* threatned that he would make me answer when
'he had me in *Bridewell*, or in the *Tower*, I told him, *That our
'Lord God, I hoped, would never permit me, for Fear of any
'Torments whatsoever, to do anything against his divine Majesty,
'or against my own Conscience, or to the Prejudice of Justice, and
'the Innocence of others.*

'I have had various Conferences and Disputations with many
'of the Heretics. And whereas I believed I should have been
'tried at the last Assizes in this City [*York*] I sent in Writing
'to the Lord President, all those Conferences and Disputations;
'who had ordered me Pen, Ink, and Paper for that Purpose.
'To which I joined a large Discourse, or Treatise; in which I
'exhorted all to *beware of false Prophets*, and to give Ear to
'the Voice of the holy Church, the Spouse of the King, the
'House, the Vineyard, and the City of *Christ*. One of the
'Ministers complain'd of me much to the President, for being
'so bold as to put down such Things in Writing: But he could
'not refute what was written: And, indeed, they seem to me to
'be much confounded. Blessed be *Jesus, Qui dat os insipienti,
'cui non possunt resistere sapientes.* I want very much to have
'a Book or two for a few Hours; but if I cannot have them,
'*Jesus*, our God and Lord, is at Hand; and he is the eternal

'Wisdom. Your Reverence will be pleased to pray to him, that
'he may always stand by me, and that all Things may turn out
'to his Glory.
'I am much astonished that so vile a Creature as I am should
'be so near, as they tell me, to the Crown of Martyrdom : But
'this I know for certain, that the Blood of my most blessed
'Saviour and Redeemer, and his most sweet Love, is able to
'make me worthy of it, *Omnia possum in eo qui me confortat.*
'Your Reverence, most loving Father, is engag'd in the Midst
'of the Battle. I sit here an idle Spectator of the Field; yet
'King *David* has appointed an equal Portion for us both; and
'Love, Charity, and Union, which unites us together in *Jesus*
'*Christ* our Lord, makes us mutually Partakers of one another's
'Merits: And what can be more closely united than we two,
'who, as your Reverence sees, *Simul segregati sumus in hoc*
'*ministerium.*

'The President inquired of me who was the Superior of our
'Society in this Kingdom? whether it was this, or the other, or
'who it was? *Topliffe* answered, He knew who it was, and
'named him. I beg your Reverence would communicate this
'Letter to all our Friends: I desire to give myself to every one
'of them; and more particularly to all our most dear Fathers
'and Brothers of the *Society of Christ my Jesus*, in whose
'Prayers, Labours, and Sacrifices, as I have a Share, so have I
'a great Confidence. About *Midlent* I hope my Lot will be
'decided, either for Life or Death; for then the Assizes will be
'held here again. In the meanwhile I have Leisure to prepare
'myself, and expect, with good Courage, whatever his divine
'Majesty shall be pleased to appoint for me. I beg your
'Reverence to join your holy Prayers with my poor ones, that I
'may walk worthy of that high and holy Name and Profession
'to which I am called; which I trust in the Mercy of our Lord
'he will grant me, not regarding so much my many Imperfec-
'tions, as the fervent Labours, Prayers, and holy Sacrifices of
'so many Fathers, and my Brothers his Servants, who are

'employed over all the World in his Service: And I hope, 'thro' the Merits of my most sweet Saviour and Lord, that I 'shall be always ready, whether living or dying, to glorify him, 'which will be for my eternal Happiness. And if my Un- 'worthiness and Demerits shall keep me at present at a 'Distance from the Crown, I will strive to deserve it by a 'greater Solicitude and Diligence for the future. And, if in 'his Mercy, our Lord shall grant me now to wash my Garments 'in the Blood of the Lamb, I hope to follow him for ever cloth'd 'in *White*.

'I can never end when I get any Time to write to your 'Reverence, which I have been seldom able to do; and whether, 'as long as I live, I shall ever have another Opportunity, I 'know not. I confess'd in my Examinations, *That I had* '*labour'd for the Encrease of the Two Seminaries in* Spain, *and* '*for that of St.* Omer's; *and that I had returned hearty Thanks* '*to his Catholic Majesty for his great Favours to the Seminary of* '*St.* Omer's: *I also confess'd, that all my Actions had always in* '*View the Good of others, and no one's Harm; the procuring* '*Peace among all, and the propagating our holy Catholic Faith,* '*and the Kingdom of* Christ, *to the utmost of my Power.* This 'was the Sum of my general Confession, which I gave in 'Writing, sign'd by my own Hand, to the President and to '*Topliffe*. They ask'd me, what I would do if the Pope should 'wage War against *England*. I answered, *That the Circum-* '*stances of that Time would give me more Light: and that I* '*should then have Recourse to our Lord God for Counsel, and* '*would think seriously on it before I would any ways intermeddle* '*with Things of War. Hæc & hujusmodi, de quibus postea.* 'May *Jesus* be always with your Reverence. *Oremus pro* '*invicem.*'

If the reader finds in this letter some things which may appear to him distasteful, and some which give him but a mean idea of the intellect or the good sense of the writer, I would beg him to remember that I am in no ways concerned with proving that this Jesuit father was a man at all in advance of his age, but exactly the contrary. What we do want is to put ourselves in a position to estimate rightly the actual state of feeling and habits of thought of the men who set themselves to "reduce" England in the sixteenth century; and if we can afford to smile, as we well may, at their Quixotic venture, at the astonishing ignorance which they displayed of the forces arrayed against them, and at their lack of the most essential agencies for effecting their purpose, we can also afford to give them some little credit for the enthusiasm which animated them, and to regard with abhorrence the ruffians whose trade was to hunt down such victims as these, and whose boast it was to torture and slay them.

While Topcliffe was away in London, and the fate of Henry Walpole was still uncertain, his friends outside determined to make an effort to effect his release. How this was to have been carried out it is now impossible to say; but money could do a great deal in those days among jailors and guards, and the discipline of the prisons was incredibly lax. The management of the whole plot was to be left, of course, to the confederates outside, but it was necessary that the prisoner himself should concur in the arrangements, and be willing to make the attempt, which would be attended with considerable danger and hazard.

By far the most influential man amongst the Catholics of the north at this time was Richard Holtby. He was a Yorkshireman, born at Brayton in the West Riding, and had entered the Society of Jesus in 1583. He seems to have been sent into Yorkshire shortly after Campion's execution, and had been diligently and very warily at work in his own neighbourhood ever since: though frequently mentioned, and more than once informed against, he seemed to bear a charmed life, and, as far as appears, was never once apprehended. Of no other English Jesuit can it be said that he exercised his vocation in England for upwards of fifty years, and that too with extraordinary effect and ceaseless activity, without once being thrown into jail or once falling into the hands of the pursuivants; and quietly died in his bed in extreme old age. Holtby must have had some very powerful friends in Yorkshire, to escape molestation so long. He lived to be the Superior of the English Jesuits after the execution of Garnet, and he took an active part in the matter of the oath of allegiance when the Archpriest Blackwell gave an example of submission to the powers that be in 1608.([16]) At the time we are now concerned with, Holtby seems to have been in and out of York Castle continually, and though denied personal intercourse with Henry Walpole, he managed to keep up with him a frequent correspondence, and acquired a great ascendancy over him; the gentler and more romantic disposition of the younger man yielding itself to the direction of a nature more masculine and vigorous than his own. When, on Topcliffe's departure, Henry Walpole's friends laid their plans for a rescue, and it only remained for the prisoner to throw himself into the plot, he hesitated. Scruples of conscience suggested themselves, and that too eager longing for martyrdom, which has been noticed before, came in to confuse his judgment and to make him exaggerate the risks and to dwell upon the consequences that might result from either success or failure. Perplexed and doubtful, he refused to take the responsibility of the venture till he had consulted Holtby; and he resolved to draw up a "case of conscience," submit the matter to him, and abide by his decision, whatever it might be. Holtby, a man of strong sense and great practical ability, was in point of fact far better able to pronounce upon the feasibility of the proposed plan of escape than Henry Walpole or his friends. He knew the risks which would have to be run and the serious consequences which would ensue in the event of failure; perhaps he judged that Walpole had not the nerve or the cunning to carry him through, and with characteristic shrewdness he decidedly gave it as his opinion that the attempt in this case should not be made.([17]) The freedom of one Jesuit

Father might be purchased too dearly by the blood of others, and how many others it was impossible to say.

When Henry Walpole received this answer he accepted it as the voice of God. He wrote back a letter, which, though it has only reached us in a Latin or Spanish translation, reads like the rhapsody of some excited devotee who has worked himself up to believe that death at the hangman's hands is the most glorious euthanasia. Surrendering himself to the one idea of martyrdom, he had become possessed by it, and henceforth his actions were out of the range of criticism: there was nothing for it but to let matters take their course.

And yet there *was* one chance of escape, one hope of deliverance. Thomas Walpole had thrown himself upon the mercy of the Lord President, might not his brother be induced to do the same? By this time the younger brother had been allowed his liberty, though still apparently kept under *surveillance*, and urged by his strong affection, while at the same time he was unable to sympathise with the fanaticism of his more fervent and enthusiastic brother, at the suggestion of Lord Huntingdon he made one last effort to save him. He addressed a long letter to Henry Walpole which was forwarded to him by the Earl, in which he informed him of all that he had himself disclosed, and pressed upon him the absolute necessity of similar outspokenness, if he would save himself from the rack and the gallows. From the young soldier's point of view all attempt at concealment was now suicidal, there was nothing to hide. It was mere madness to attempt to withhold the names of his friends, or to keep back information which had been given already without reserve; and he was implored to hide nothing which in point of fact was no longer hidden: stubborn silence could only turn to his own ruin.([18])

It was all in vain. For the younger brother to give such information as he was master of was one thing—after all there was but little that he had to tell; it was a very different thing for the elder to act the traitor's part, and betray the friends and kindred with whom for years he had been keeping up a correspondence. The latest news about the seminaries and their scholars,—the particulars about his own labours abroad,—the incidents of his journeys or the details of his interview with the King of Spain,—these were matters that Lord Huntingdon or the Government were welcome to know; but to surrender the names of those at home who had compromised themselves by befriending him would bring beggary upon many a household, and, GOD helping him, where the lives and fortunes of others were at stake he would be silent as the grave. Unmoved by threats, or entreaties, arguments or expostulations, he was prepared to suffer the worst that could befall him; and blinded by that which men call their conscience, but which is often the name for something far less deserving of our respect, and with the emotional side of his nature stimulated to the point of monomania, he prepared to meet his doom with the same determination that an Indian fakir prepares to throw himself before the car of Juggernaut; and the torture chamber and the dungeons of the Tower were the scene of the next act in this miserable drama.

## NOTES TO CHAPTER X.

(1) *Page* 223, *line* 25. Mr. Froude's account of the Pilgrimage of Grace is perhaps the most brilliant production of his skilful pen.—*History of England*, vol. ii. chaps. xiii. and xiv. *Kett's Rebellion in Norfolk*, by the Rev. F. W. Russell, Longmans, 1859, is a respectable compilation, the result of some little research. For the Cornish Rebellion, see *Froude*, vol. v. ch. 26.

(2) *Page* 226, *line* 4. My authorities for the statements in this paragraph are to be found in Mr. Cartwright's *Chapters on the History of Yorkshire*, Wakefield, 1872; Bell's *Huntingdon Peerage Case*, London, 4to. 1820; *Harl. MSS.*, 6992, art. 26, p. 50; Morris' *Troubles of our Catholic Forefathers*, series iii. passim; Challoner's *Missionary Priests*, vol. i.; Fuller's *Church History*, b. vi. a. vi. § 7; *Calendar of State Papers, Domestic*, Add. 1580–1625, p. 11–13.

(3) *Page* 227, *line* 4. Challoner's *Priests*, vol. i. p. 110, 113. Morris, u. s.

(4) *Page* 227, *line* 34. The story of Margaret Clitherow has been investigated with very great labour and research by Mr. Morris, in whose book (*Troubles*, u. s., s. iii.) all the horrible details may be found. The particulars are given from the still existing Records of the City of York.

(5) *Page* 229, *line* 10. Yepez, *Hist. Partic.*, p. 680; *P. R. O. Dom. Eliz.* vol. 249, n. 12, § 15.

(6) *Page* 229, *line* 21. *Harl. MSS.* 6996, art. 19. Lord Huntingdon's letter is dated 2 October 1593.

(7) *Page* 229, *line* 31. Challoner gives the date 4th December 1593, but this is clearly wrong. Topcliffe in his letter to Puckering says it was "about a fortnight before Christmas."

(8) *Page* 231, *line* 4. *Dom. Eliz.* vol. 247, art. 21. *Harl. MSS.* 6996, art. 40, p. 78.

(9) *Page* 231, *line* 23.   Dom. Eliz. vol. 242, arts. 121, 122, 125.

(10) *Page* 231, *line* 32.   *Walpole letters*, p. 19.

(11) *Page* 232, *line* 31.   The conferences were printed in *The Irish Ecclesiastical Record for June* 1873.

(12) *Page* 234, *line* 18.   Harl. MSS. 6996, art. 28.

(13) *Page* 235, *line* 7.   Cal. P. R. O. Dom. Eliz. 1591–1594.

(14) *Page* 236, *line* 9.   Dom. Eliz. vol. 247, art. 21.

(15) *Page* 236, *line* 18.   Harl. MSS. 6996, art. 35.

(16) *Page* 241, *line* 9.   There is a very full account of Holtby in Morris' *Troubles*, series iii. He frequently went under the name of *Duckett*. Some interesting notices of him are to be found in *The Life of Mrs. Dorothy Lawson of St. Antony's*, London, Dolman, 1855.

(17) *Page* 241, *line* 35.   Yepez, *Hist. Particular*, p. 685, et seq. I must remind my readers that *Bp. Yepez* published his work *less than four years after Henry Walpole's execution*. It is astonishing how accurate his information was. In the minutest particulars I have again and again found him corroborated by the evidence lately brought to light from the contemporary documents in the Record Office and elsewhere.

(18) *Page* 242, *line* 31.   Harl. MSS. 6996, art. 37, page 72.

## CHAPTER XI.

# THE TOWER AND THE RACK.

WHILE Henry Walpole was going through his preliminary ordeal in York Castle, disputing with crafty trimmers and sour Puritans on matters of theology one day, and writing flimsy tracts another, but always entangling himself more and more hopelessly in the meshes of the net that had closed around him, a very curious drama was being acted in London, which exercised an important influence upon his fate.

Robert Earl of Essex had for some time past been recognised as the chief favourite of the Queen. He was now in his twenty-sixth year, with a handsome person, abilities of a high order, and many qualifications for ensuring him success as a courtier. Lavish with his money, fond of display, a firm and zealous friend, chivalrous, romantic, and brave to the point of recklessness, he attracted to himself the admiration and regard of generous enthusiasts, while sagacious and wily sycophants knew how to turn to good account the enormous arrogance and immeasurable self-confidence which in the end brought him to the scaffold. At his father's death in 1576 the young earl was in his eighth year, and at that father's special request he was committed to the guardianship of Lord Burghley, of whose house he continued for some time an inmate, having as his constant playmate young Robert Cecil, then a lad of some twelve or thirteen.(¹) In 1584 he made his first appearance at court, and at once became the darling of the Queen. But his royal mistress' caresses, showered upon him in season and out of season, not without some scandal, could not content him long, and he was hardly eighteen when he became a suitor for the Mastership of the Horse, which he obtained, not so much by reason of any fitness for the post which the Queen had observed in him, but rather by his ceaseless and petulant importunity. Passionately eager to win some renown in war, he vainly applied for military command, and on this being refused him he slipped away from court when the Portugal expedition sailed in 1589, and putting out to sea from Falmouth about the same time as the fleet weighed anchor at Plymouth, he fell in with it at last off the coast of Portugal, and when the attack upon Peniche was made, Essex was the first to land, leaping into the surf, and wading breast high under the fire of the enemy's guns. At Lisbon he loudly challenged any of the garrison to come forth and "break a lance" with him; at Cascaes he "sent a cartel" offering himself against any Spaniard of equal quality; on the 4th of June he was summoned to return to England by a peremptory and indignant letter from the Queen. No sooner had he got back to court than he picked a quarrel with Sir Charles Blount, for no other reason than because Sir Charles was rising in favour at court, and in the encounter that ensued he was disarmed and wounded in the thigh. In 1591 he obtained at last the desire of his heart, and was sent with an auxiliary force to assist Henry IV. in Normandy. When in obedience to orders he was preparing once more for his return from an expedition which had brought little honour and no profit, he again sent a challenge to Villars, the Governor of Rouen, couched in terms not a whit less ridiculous than the Knight of La Mancha might have used. (²)

Thus far his career had been other than successful, and he began to suspect that for him the road to fame was not to be carved out by the sword. A new direction was given to his ambition when, at the death of his father-in-law, the Secretary Walsingham, it became clear that Lord Burghley and his son Sir Robert Cecil were at the council table almost supreme. Death had played sad havoc among the great men who had lived through the danger of the "Invincible Armada." Leicester had survived it but a few weeks, Walsingham died in April 1590, in November of the same year George Talbot Earl of Shrewsbury died, and a year after Sir Christopher Hatton. Lord Shrewsbury was Earl Marshall, Hatton was Chancellor of the University of Oxford; Essex with passionate eagerness claimed both posts of honour. He gained neither the one nor the other; Lord Buckhurst succeeded to the chancellorship, the other office was kept vacant for years. Essex was stung to the quick; his pride was wounded, and he thought the Cecils were alone to blame for his failure. How had they foiled him?—How but by intrigue?—Henceforth he would turn their own weapons against them and try to outwit them in policy.

The Secretary Walsingham had for years had a little army of spies in his pay—wretches of blasted character and broken fortunes, fellows who were adepts at inventing plots or worming out secrets, their trade eavesdropping, their daily bread gained by scenting out "murders, stratagems, and crimes;" where true intelligence was not to be gained, false rumours and slanders of the blackest hue served their turn as well. Sometimes they were hot in the chase of a cracked-brained Familist; sometimes they were dogging the steps of decrepit old "Queen Mary's priests;" sometimes they were busy in forging letters from people in high station; but always sleepless, suspicious, unscrupulous—men of infinite resources in the base expedients of the informer's trade.([3]) Walsingham's death had been a sad blow to this miserable gang, and the execution of Mary Stuart had even before his death lessened the demand for their services. When Essex determined to play his new rôle, there was a stir among the band of "intelligencers," as they called themselves, who were on the look-out for an employer. Essex with his usual rashness took man after man into his pay, and set himself to outdo his rivals by attempting to get such secret information from abroad as should anticipate that supplied to his rivals. He spared no expense; lavish as ever he imagined it was only a question of money, and that, provided he paid liberally, he might dispense with the necessity of all caution and of the sagacity in discriminating between the true and the false, which only long practice and years of training in diplomacy can supply. Again he found himself foiled; the cool judgment and long discipline of Lord Burghley and his son were more than a match for him. Lord Burghley's health failed, and his long career of statesmanship came to an end, but his son had not served his apprenticeship in vain; Sir Robert Cecil held his ground, and proved the abler man. Irritated beyond endurance, and in a mood to believe anything that might establish his character for acuteness, Essex was in that excited state when a man's judgment is least to be trusted, and when the burning desire to make some discovery leads him to see all things through a false medium. At last the hour came when he was sure that he had possessed himself of a real secret, and that he had found out a real plot.

There was a certain Roderigo Lopez, a Portuguese, who for some years had practised as a medical man in London, and had attained to such eminence in his profession that he had been sworn physician to the Queen. He had already amassed a considerable fortune, and no breath of suspicion had hitherto lighted upon him. (⁴) In November 1593, certain of Essex's gang of intelligencers cast their eyes upon this Lopez, and denounced him to the Earl as one engaged in an attempt to assassinate his royal mistress. Manuel Andrada, a miscreant "discovered to have practised the death of Don Antonio," and whose life Lopez had himself saved; Manuel Lewis Tinoco, "one that had twice betrayed the King Don Antonio his master;" Ferera de Gama, "sometimes a man of great livelihood and wealth in Portugal, which he did forego in adhering to Don Antonio, .... but some years since secretly won to the service of the King of Spain"—these were the witnesses upon whom Essex's spies relied. In January 1594, Lopez was arrested and examined by Essex and the Cecils, and his house searched. Lord Burghley and his son reported decidedly in Lopez's favour; Elizabeth laughed at the whole story, and with some scorn called Essex "a rash and temerarious youth." Essex was furious. He shut himself up in his chamber, and refused to come forth; swore that some "atonement" should be made for the wrong done him, and insisted that another inquiry should be instituted, and that the Lord High Admiral should be associated with him and the Cecils in the next examination.(5) He gained his point. The three witnesses deserved hanging as much as any men in Europe, yet they vehemently denied *at the outset* that they were in any way cognisant of any plot, and knew nothing of Lopez's guilt; but then the "manacles were shown" to Tinoco, and with a shudder of fear he was ready for any confession that might be put into his mouth. The rest followed. Lopez shrieked forth in an agony of terror his protestations of innocence till his vehemence provoked the laughter of the court of inquiry.(6) Ferera and Andrada strove only to save themselves, and Lopez, in the vain hope of his life being spared, made foolish admissions, and in his desperation and horror became more and more entangled. His doom was sealed, and Essex had his way; the four men were kept in prison for three long months, in the hope of some further discoveries; when these failed three of them were sent to the scaffold without remorse. Of course Lopez's property was confiscated, but Ferera was spared to accompany Essex into Spain some years after, and in a memorial which he addressed to his patron in 1597, "desired his lordship to remember the words which he had said to him in the Tower of London, upon the confession of Lopez."(7)

As I have said, this business of Roderigo Lopez could not but exercise an important influence upon Henry Walpole's fate; he had but lately returned from Spain, he had been admitted to the presence of Philip II., he had enjoyed familiar intercourse with all the nobles of the Spanish court, whose names had been brought forward and made dexterous use of in the accounts of the conspiracy; if this Jesuit father, clearly a man of mark, could not throw some light upon this business, who could ?— If the "plot" was genuine, it could hardly have been kept so very secret, when the emissaries were broken-down adventurers and common informers with no characters to lose. A confession was extorted from the wretched Lopez on the 25th February. On that very day Henry Walpole started on his journey to London, he was placed under the custody of Topcliffe, and at this point his real sufferings began. Topcliffe's coarse brutality showed itself from the first; the journey to London appears to have been made with all possible haste, probably with the intention of producing Walpole as a witness upon the trial of Lopez, which took place upon the 28th. All along the road Topcliffe gave out that he had got under his charge a notable Jesuit, who was privy to the plot to assassinate the Queen; and no insult or outrage was omitted which might aggravate his sufferings. Lopez's trial was over before they reached London, and Walpole was at once committed to the Tower. [8]

There were in the Tower at this time fifteen or sixteen notable prisoners, of whom five at least had been already condemned to death. Philip Howard, Earl of Arundel, had been put upon his trial just five years before, his crime being that he had attempted to abjure the realm, in the hope of obtaining liberty of conscience elsewhere. This was enough to serve as the ground for arraigning him upon a charge of high treason; and in those days to be charged with such a crime was to be condemned. The earl was, however, never executed; for six years he was kept in close confinement, his health gradually failing, and he died in his prison on the 19th October 1595. Dr. Lopez, too, was lying there under sentence of death, and with him the men who had been induced to accuse him; and "John Annias, an Irishman, who came over *under pretence of killing* (*sic*) Antonio Perez;" and James Fitzgerald, son of the unfortunate Earl of Desmond; and Peter Wentworth "committed from the Parliament," his offence being that he had presumed to speak in the House of Commons on the subject of the succession to the crown. ([9])

But the prisoner whom of all others Henry Walpole would most have wished to hold converse with at such a time, if it had been permitted him, was Robert Southwell: he, too, the son of a substantial Norfolk squire, who in 1578 had entered the Society of Jesus, had returned to England in 1586, and since then had spent five years in the house of the Countess of Arundel. Southwell had been in the Tower for about two years, after being barbarously tortured in Topcliffe's house in Westminster, and was now lying in daily expectation of being tried;—for his torture and his long imprisonment had been before any such trial. ([10]) Whether he and Walpole ever met we cannot tell, but the probability is that both men were kept in too close custody to allow of their exchanging many words, though there is some presumption that they did contrive to communicate with one another, and that this communication had its influence upon the confessions which were in the end extorted.

Henry Walpole remained for nearly two months in solitary confinement; the "close prisoners" were permitted to hold no intercourse with the outer world; they were subject to be treated with infinite brutality by their jailors; allowed nothing but mouldy straw to lie on; liable to be robbed of anything upon their persons that was worth taking, and furnished with scarcely sufficient to keep life in their bodies. ([11]) Two months of such treatment were usually long enough to break even a brave man's spirit, and to weaken whatever resolution and courage he might have been able to summon to his aid in better times. With a constitution shaken, and with an emaciated frame, the man who could hold out against the terrors of the torture chamber or the physical agony of the rack, the scavenger's daughter, or the gauntlets, would be a man of very extraordinary powers indeed, both of body and mind.

At last, on the 14th of April, the notorious Richard Young, a creature whose life was spent in hunting up priests and torturing them, and who disputed the palm of cruelty with Topcliffe, wrote to the Lord Keeper Puckering, suggesting that an order should be given him to examine certain prisoners in the Tower, who had "long lain in oblivion, and by delay and lingering matters of great importance are hurt and hid."([12]) In Southwell's case Topcliffe had got himself into trouble by torturing his victim to the extent of getting talked about. Young had the cunning to provide against any chance of incurring blame; and in this same letter he begs that Mr. Beale and Sir Thomas Wilkes, clerks of the Privy Council, might be associated with him in the work, together with some counsel at law. The suggestion was not immediately acted on, but on the 27th of the mouth Henry Walpole was subjected to his first examination, not before Richard Young, but before Serjeant Drewe, Sir Edward Coke the Attorney-General, and Richard Topcliffe.([13]) The inquisitors, as they may well be called, appear to have conducted their examination in a very methodical manner. They had before them the previous admissions which Henry Walpole had made at York, the information furnished by Thomas Walpole, and the confessions of one of the many vagabond informers. This man was an Irishman named Hugh Cahill: he had fallen in with the Walpoles at Calais, and, being in bad health and great poverty, had applied to the brothers for assistance, and thrown himself upon their compassion. Of course he had pretended to be a Catholic who was suffering for his religion, and of course he had been relieved: equally of course he had made the best of his way across the Channel, and presented himself at Burghley House with such information as he had to give, supplementing it with such additions and embellishments as he could invent. The fellow could not write his name, but he was ready to add his mark to any document which Topcliffe might think proper to lay before him. There was another scoundrel of the same type, a confederate of Cahill's, who was also ready with his contribution of information. He too had fallen in with the Walpoles and been assisted by them, and he too was anxious to make his account out of his previous acquaintance with a prisoner against whom it was desirable to collect some damaging evidence.([14])

The inquiries addressed to the prisoner in the Tower on this 27th of April were evidently based upon the admissions and confessions gathered from all these sources. Henry Walpole in reply to the interrogatories admitted that he was a Jesuit, that he had met Cahill at Calais, and lodged at the same inn, the *Plume Blanche;* that he had gone to Spain and had an interview with Philip II. at the Escurial, had talked with this one and that one, noble and gentle, lay and cleric; that he had landed in Yorkshire furnished with letters, the greater part of which he had destroyed—some he had hidden under a stone, as has been already told; and that his only object in returning to England was to preach the doctrines of the proscribed faith and win souls to the Catholic cause. So far so good.—Here was abundance of information, if only the Government could make any use of it. Unfortunately there was not a single item that was not perfectly well known already; and though the "examinate" had told them a great deal about a number of conspicuous personages, these were all far out of harm's way and safe in Spain, or Belgium, or France. But Walpole had been at the new seminary of Valladolid, and had received certain "labels" to serve as a pass from some Englishman at Dunkirk. He had said, too, that at Valladolid there were some forty young Englishmen pursuing their studies; these were the sons of men of substance and position at home. Who were these forty young students?—Who was this Englishman at Dunkirk?—If he answered *these* questions, the prisoner would have been bringing others into jeopardy. Pressed to name these he flatly refused; they could get no more from him.

A formal report of the examination was drawn up—the whole business must have taken some hours—and Henry Walpole and the three commissioners appended their names to the document, and the first examination came to an end. The prisoner was taken back to his cell: he occupied himself in drawing pictures of saints and angels upon the walls and ceiling, and in carving his name on the stone where it remains to the present hour. It is piteous to contrast the bold firm cutting of the first with the ragged and unshapely look of the last letters, as if the hands had gradually lost their power or he who guided them had gradually lost his control.

On the 3rd of May Henry Walpole was again brought up for examination. This time only two commissioners were present, Topcliffe and Serjeant Drewe. The questions addressed to him were aimed almost exclusively at extorting such names as it was in his power to disclose.—What were the contents of the letters destroyed? He would not tell.—What were the names of two gentlemen mentioned in a certain letter, to which allusion had been made? " He knoweth but refuseth to disclose." —He had been directed to a house in Lincoln's Inn Fields, "but he utterly denieth to disclose the name of the owner of the said house, or of the gent. to whom he was directed . . . . refuseth for conscience' sake (as he sayeth) to reveal the same." At this point the first dreadful pressure seems to have been used. The questions were repeated, and Topcliffe had his victim almost to himself. The ghastly instruments of torture were ready at hand—the rack and the manacles—those dreadful manacles that would stretch every sinew and wrench the arms from their sockets. Let him speak, this stubborn Jesuit, who knew so much! Speak or hang till life should be only horrible torment. Was the gentleman's name in Lincoln's Inn Fields,

French?—Was it a white house?—He would not answer. Hang him up again!—"Being asked again of the gentleman which was of acquaintance with this examinate, as with the said Edward Walpole, he refuseth to disclose his name." Again and again the questions were pressed. Was Braddox in Essex one of the houses set down in his directions?—Was Spiller one of his names?—Was Mrs. White?—And so on. Where he could answer that such names were *not* in his list he said so; where he could not, he was obstinately silent or stubbornly refused to tell. The probability is that this examination only came to an end by the prisoner fainting under the torture, or the examiners becoming convinced that nothing more was to be got out of him *that* time. But they could afford to wait. It was only a question of time. Topcliffe's long experience had already made him acquainted with the terrible physiological fact that pain rarely kills, and he had no scruples about trying its power of crushing a man's spirit, and breaking his heart. It is probable that the prisoner was too much exhausted by the effects of his sufferings on the last occasion of his examination to allow of any further torture being applied to him, until some time were given to recover from the frightful strain which his system had endured. At any rate a fortnight elapsed before he was subjected to another ordeal. But on the 18th of May Serjeant Drewe and Topcliffe were once more at the Tower, and Henry Walpole was again brought before them. They began at the point where they had left off—"What those two men were to whom he was directed to use their aid in Ireland?"— The answer was as before, "he refuseth to utter their names." Topcliffe hereupon seems to have produced some of the papers which Thomas Walpole had given up, and upon these papers the examination proceeded. The names of certain gentlemen in Norfolk, Essex, and Suffolk were asked for, and still refused. His Spanish journey was reverted to. On this point he was ready to tell them all he knew, but when again they pressed him to betray the places of residence of certain persons whose names Topcliffe mentioned, and which had been found upon the papers produced, it was as before; they might hang him up by the manacles, but he would not yield. The pair of worthies left their victim, having gained little or nothing. So far he had been able to bear the agony bravely. Another respite was allowed him, but it was plain that flesh and blood could not bear these horrible examinations much longer. This man had been and was ready to sacrifice all hopes of an earthly career, and all that most men value most highly. Honour and fame and wealth had long ceased to have any attraction for him: no bribe that this world could present would have tempted him for a moment; but the horrors of that dark dungeon, the presence of those ghastly instruments of torture, the immeasurable agony of wrenched joints and strained sinews, the spasm succeeding spasm, and the swoon from which he was awakened only to be racked again, the certainty that he was in the power of men in whom there was no more pity than in the stone walls that re-echoed his groans;—all this proved too strong for human resolve, and he gave way. It was, as I have said, only a question of time; each repetition of the torture must needs have weakened the power of resistance. The wonder in such a case is, not that he broke down at last, but that he endured so long.

His next examination was on the 4th June. This time he was not left to the tender mercies of Topcliffe and Drewe alone, nor does it appear that any torture was applied. His two former examiners were present, but they were held in check by the presence of Sir Edward Coke the Attorney-General, "Justice Yung," Robert Beale the Clerk to the Privy Council, Sir Henry Killigrew, and Sir Michael Blount the Lieutenant of the Tower, seven in all. The report to which their names are appended is very short. ([15]) All that Henry Walpole is represented as confessing is, that he had received directions at Valladolid in July 1593, from Claudius Aquaviva, to proceed to England and to put himself under the orders of his superior,

R

Father Garnet; that he had intended to arrive in London, and had actually landed in England in December last. This document was doubtless intended to serve as evidence upon the trial, and it appears that Sir Edward Coke had already made some preparation for the prosecution which it was intended at this time to proceed with. (16)

On the 10th of June Coke addressed a note to the Lord Keeper Puckering, giving an abstract of the depositions which had been laid before him touching the cases of Henry Walpole and half-a-dozen other prisoners. Of course the document is a mere case for the plaintiff, in which all that makes in Walpole's favour is kept back, and all that makes against him is made the most of; but Coke plainly shows that so far there was no case at all against him, except on the ground of his having come back to England, after receiving Orders from the Church of Rome beyond sea. In fact, the attempt to fasten any other charge upon him had quite broken down: but he was now in Topcliffe's hands. On the 13th the commissioners were at the Tower once more,—Drewe, Young, and Topcliffe of course, Miles Sandes, Clerk of the Crown of the King's Bench, and this time, not Sir Edward Coke, but his rival Francis Bacon. Topcliffe, we may be sure, had not spared his victim, and when the examiners appeared, Topcliffe triumphantly handed in a confession which Henry Walpole had written with his own hand; and yet it is a confession which does him some little honour. He tells of Captain Jaques, Sir William Stanley's second in command, having on one occasion sounded him upon the subject of the lawfulness of assassinating the Queen; "to whom," says he, "I answered that for all the good in the world I would not counsel any such attempt." He tells of a conversation with Parsons on the same subject, when Parsons had replied "that Catholics, and chiefly we religious men, ought to suffer violence, but offer none, chiefly to princes; and he added that other means were by persuasion and prayer, and that though it were not presently, yet no doubt the seminaries would at length reduce

England to the faith." And then he adds, " For mine own part I protest before God, as I have often, that I abhor to think thereof, and never did nor would not move any man thereunto for all the good in the world, Jesus is my witness!"

After this he goes on to give a minute account of his life during the last few years, of his journey to Spain, of his return to Flanders, of his interviews with a number of people whom he names, of his commission to go to England and put himself under the direction of Garnet the Superior of the Jesuits, and meanwhile to do his best in bringing over "fitting youths to the seminaries." From this he passes on to tell all he knew of Stanley and his doings. He had not seen him for some years, but he tells how Stanley had written to him "to deal with some priest that might get access to my Lord Strange, now Earl of Derby, to induce him to the Catholic religion . . . . and he added that Mr. John Gerard he thought were a fit man thereunto." More intelligence follows; it is mere gossip of what he had heard in this place and that place, and he expresses his belief that there is nothing to fear from the Spaniards now. And this was all that he had to tell of conspiracies or treasons abroad.—When this confession was handed in, it was accompanied by a running commentary in the margin, which may still be read in Topcliffe's hand. The object is plainly to prejudice the minds of the examiners against Walpole, and to suggest that there was still something kept back. So there was.—Henry Walpole even yet had not betrayed his friends, nor had he yet disclosed even a single name or a single fact which was not perfectly well known to the government. But he was not to be allowed to stop at this point. He had told all he knew of things beyond the sea. What did he know of things at home?—What of Garnet?—What of the Earl of Arundel?—What of those to whom he had brought letters?—Who were those scholars at Seville and Valladolid?—Of Garnet he had still nothing to tell; in fact his apprehension immediately on his arrival had put it out of his power to disclose anything. "*I have heard* he hath been at Mr. Wiseman's at Braddocks." "Of the Earl of Arundel I do not remember anything of moment." "*I was told* that there was one Barnes, &c.," and so on. Pressed for more precise answers on the more important intelligence he could give, he told of Verstegan as the channel of communication between the refugees and their friends in England; ([17]) of Dr. Giffard wishing him to see his mother, and ask for relief; of some of Parsons' writings, and of the chests of books still "lying at St. Omers, which were printed when the Armada was to have come over," six years before; but of any one in Norfolk who had befriended him; of Edward Yelverton or the score of others in Norfolk whom he must have had it in his power to betray, *not one single word*. For himself his agony and despair wrung from him this last affecting appeal: "I desire leave, if you please, to wait upon the most Honourable Her Majesty's Council, and that this act be concealed till it shall please them to dispose of me howsoever to their honours shall seem most to the good of the realm and service of her Majesty, whom I do beseech upon my knees to take pity upon a miserable prisoner and offender; yet now resolve to employ all my forces to her Majesty's service, and to conform myself ever as it shall please her Majesty to appoint me."—Mercy! As though such men as Topcliffe and Young and Drewe understood what the word meant, or had one little spot in their natures where compassion could find a momentary resting-place.

Next day Henry Walpole was examined again, by the same examiners as before. The information given this time consists of a very valuable and particular account of the seminaries in Spain, and the names of all the scholars and priests residing in them at the time. There are between forty and fifty names. After this he appears to have received instructions to write to the Council whatever other information he had to furnish. Some time appears to have elapsed before this letter to the Council was extracted from him, and it was probably not till the beginning of July that it was handed in. Alas! it is a painful document; painful, *i.e.*, to those who would wish to find a man who had endured so much exhibit more heroism than in this case can be claimed for him. But who of us can estimate the power which immeasurable bodily pain must exercise upon a highly sensitive and nervous temperament? Who shall say what could not be wrung from himself, if all the mechanical appliances of ingenious cruelty were paraded before his eyes in ghastly array—his imagination worked upon at one time, his enfeebled frame exposed to intense torment at another, and the recollection of the torture of yesterday craftily made use of to foreshadow the horrors that were prepared for the morrow? Who can imagine the sum of misery, shame, remorse, despair, and self-reproach which those grim solitudes could tell of in the cases of men who could bear their agonies no longer, who broke down and betrayed their dearest friends, and when the respite came from the torturer's manacles or his rack, were left to reflect upon the consequences which their weakness might have brought on others; left to gnash their teeth, and gnaw their hearts, and weep tears of blood, for treachery which none more than they themselves blushed at, and sorrowed for, and abhorred?

It would, however, be an injustice to Henry Walpole to allow my readers to suppose that, even at the very worst, he betrayed any who were not already heavily compromised. A careful reading of this elaborate confession shows plainly enough that he compromises no one *at home* whose life or liberty could have been put in peril by his revelations. If he told of the hundred pounds sent over to Edward Walpole through Father Southwell, he knew that Southwell was at that moment a prisoner in the Tower. If he mentioned the four Rookwoods of Coldham Hall, who were at Douay, he was only speaking of what was a matter of common parlance. If he says that he had heard of Gerard having been harboured by "one of the Woodhouses in Norfolk," he leaves it quite uncertain whether it was Francis Woodhouse of Breccles, who had been a notorious Recusant for years, or Philip Wodehouse of Kimberley, who was in a position to take care of himself. The priests whose names he mentions had been all denounced long before. The Wisemans' house at Braddocks had been lately searched, and its inmates thrown into prison. For the information that Holtby "lieth about York," it was as well known as that Lord Huntingdon was to be found in the same neighbourhood; but *he does not reveal the name by which Holtby was known among the Catholics.* "I think all be known," he says, "which I knew to be Catholics fourteen years ago;" and if he adds the names of "Mr. Hubbard and one Mr. Walgrave, in Suffolk or Essex," this was but to tell what needed no telling, for there were at least three or four Hubbards, and as many Waldegraves, who at this moment were among the suspect. About friends and kinsfolk in Norfolk, and all those among whom he had a year ago learnt that John Gerard had been doing "much good," he tells absolutely nothing. ([18])

But the most remarkable part of this paper addressed to the Lords of the Council is that in which he professes to have been brought to see the errors of his ways and states his readiness to recant and conform. The language he uses is not creditable to him, and there are expressions for which I can offer or find no excuse. When he says, "I never allowed of the ambition of the popes or any their unjust usurpation over princes and their kingdoms," it is difficult to see how he can have been sincere. When he further declares his readiness "to go to the church ... and there preach only such doctrine as my conscience doth tell me, and the Spirit of God, to be manifestly deduced out of the Word of God;" when again he says, "having conferred with divers learned Protestants of the clergy at York I did find much less difference than I thought," it is hard to get rid of the suspicion that his misery and terror had told upon him, and dragged him down to overact the craven's part. It is true he does introduce in the midst of all this a saving clause which reads like an attempt to shelter himself behind a quibble, though here again he can hardly have believed that any recantation would be accepted as sufficient in which he declared that whatever he was prepared to say or do, should be "*without prejudice of the Catholic faith, which I ever profess.*" After all, we must read this document "between the lines," and even so there is much that must to the end remain unexplained.

One thing, however, is certain, viz., that all these confessions and revelations did not save Henry Walpole from far worse torture than he had been subjected to before he made them. On the contrary, the really dreadful ordeal was still to come. In July 1594, he was able to write. It seems that in the next few months Topcliffe was allowed to deal with him as he pleased. What he endured in that terrible time, what he revealed and what he was pressed to invent, and what they tried to make him say or do or promise, will never be known. The curtain drops upon all those horrible scenes which make us shudder as we faintly endeavour to recall them to our minds. We do know that there came a time when he lost the use of his hands altogether; and when he somewhat recovered from the effects of his torturing, his writing had become a tremulous and almost illegible scrawl. ([19]) For nine long months he lay in the Tower, and no further word or whisper concerning him has survived to our time. The grey old walls have many a sad story to tell of those who languished there broken down and desperate, but no sadder one than that of this man, who aspired to be a hero and who failed.

# NOTES TO CHAPTER XI.

(1) *Page* 247, *line* 2. Devereux's *Lives of the Devereux, Earls of Essex*, vol. i. p. 144. Sir Robert Cecil's birth year is usually given as 1563, but there is some uncertainty about it. In a letter to James I. [Camden Society], Sir Robert speaks of "the mutual affection in our tender years" which had existed between him and Essex.

(2) *Page* 247, *line* 33. *Devereux*, i. 172 and seq. For his challenging Sir Walter Raleigh see Edwards' *Life of Raleigh*, vol. i. p. 120. Norreys and Drake sailed from Plymouth on the 14th April; Essex in the Swiftsure joined them on the 13th May 1589. *Devereux*, i. 194, 201, 204, 214. Compare Naunton's *Fragmenta Regalia;* Lingard's *Elizabeth*, chap. viii.; Wright's *Elizabeth and her Times*, vol. ii. p. 400.

(3) *Page* 248, *line* 31. Here is one sample among a hundred. ".... .. We have examined a priest whose name is GREGORY GUNNES, *alias* STONE, being found out here by one EVAN ARDEN, servant unto Mr. Treasurer of the Household, who finding him by his speeches to be but a lewd fellow, *trained him to walk into a lane and causing two honest men to be behind a pale where they might hear their conference*," &c., &c.—P. R. O. Domestic, Eliz., vol. 179, No. 7, 8 June 1585. This Gunnes was a Norfolk man, and I find him indicted in the Guildhall at Norwich in 1596.

(4) *Page* 249, *line* 28. As to his Judaism, see Spedding's *Bacon* (*Life and Letters*) i. 278. The paper in Murdin says nothing about it; Camden asserts it, as of course does Cecil. He had been taken prisoner in DON PEDRO'S business in 1558. He can hardly have been long sworn in physician to the Queen, otherwise it would be difficult to believe that ANTHONY BACON could write of him as he does in Birch, i. 93; yet FRANCIS BACON says he had been physician "several years." See, however, the "*Abstract of the Evidence laid before the Jury on the trial of Lopez.*" —Cal. P. R. O. Domestic, Eliz., 1591-1594, p. 445 and seq.

(5) *Page* 250, *line* 14. See the graphic account of ESSEX'S violence given by STANDISH in Birch, vol. i. p. 149.

(6) *Page* 250, *line* 22. Camden's *Elizabeth*, B. iv. f. 59.

(7) *Page* 250, *line* 34. He adds "that he had ruined his father and mother and himself *by what he had done with regard to Lopez, and the service which he had performed to the Queen.*"—Birch, ii. 268.

(8) *Page* 251, *line* 24. Morus, *Historia Prov. Angl. Soc. Jesu*, lib. v. § 39, p. 212.

(9) *Page* 252, *line* 8. The "*List of Prisoners in the Tower, under the custody of* SIR MICH. BLOUNT, Lieutenant," may be seen in the Cal. Domestic, Eliz., 1591–1594, p. 484. For PHILIP HOWARD, *Earl of Arundel*, see the very curious Life of him published from the original MS. by the DUKE OF NORFOLK in 1857. Why *any* omissions should have been made in printing this very interesting biography, it is difficult to understand. Hallam, *Const. History*, vol. i. c. v. p. 255, gives a good account of WENTWORTH'S *two* offensive speeches. His first committal had taken place in February 1576; "he was by the Queen's special favour restored again to his liberty and place in the House on Monday, the 12th day of March ensuing." D'Ewes has given a full report of his examination, &c.— *Journal of the Houses of Parliament, temp. Eliz.*, p. 241 and seq. On the second occasion of his outspokenness, seventeen years after, "so highly was her Majesty offended that they must needs commit them [WENTWORTH and SIR HENRY BROMLEY]. . . . Whereupon MR. PETER WENTWORTH was sent Prisoner to the Tower. . . . " This was "Sunday, and the 25th February," 1592–93.—D'Ewes, u. s. p. 470.

(10) *Page* 252, *line* 19. The authority for *Southwell's* Life and Sufferings is Mr. Foley's *Record of the English Province, S. J.*, series i. p. 301–386.

(11) *Page* 252, *line* 33. The following extracts from "Questions to be proposed to the Council, touching the sums to be paid to the Lord Lieutenant by prisoners in the Tower, for diet, fees, and other charges," are suggestive: " . . . Now the L. has not the goods or bedding of prisoners . . . is he to have them ? . . . Shall it be taken at entrance or departure of prisoners ? . . . The Porter may claim upper garment . . . *shall it be only upper garment?* . . . Item, whereas the Lieut. is bound to send meat to every close prisoner, he hath invented a new exaction to cause the said prisoners to pay him 5s. a week *for the man that bringeth them meat*, which was never seen before, for a man cannot pay for meat unless he have it, *and a close prisoner cannot go for it nor send his man for it.*"—P. R. O., Dom. Eliz., vol. xvii. No. 46. These questions are dated "June (?) 1561." It is very certain that matters did not get *better* after this time.

(12) *Page* 253, *line* 12. P. R. O. Dom. Eliz., vol. 248, No. 68.

(13) *Page* 253, *line* 23. u. s., No. 78. As Mr. *Jardine's* tract is now rare and seldom met with, I think it well to extract from it the following order of the Privy Council, which will speak for itself.

"25ᵗʰ Oct. 1591.

"A Letter to DOCTOR FLETCHER, RICHARD TOPCLYFFE, RICHARD BRANTHWAYTE, and RICHARD YONGE, Esquers.

"Whereas one EUSTACE WAYTE, a Semynarye Prist, was of late taken, and there was also one BRIAN LASSEY, a dispenser and distributure of letters to papysts and other evyll affected subjects, apprehended in like sorte; Theise shall be therefore to will and require you to take the examynacions and confessions of both the said persons, *and veriestraightly to examyn them uppon soche articles as you*, RICHARD TOPCLYFFE, *shall administer unto them*; and if they shall not declare their knowledges, and answer directly to all soche matters *as you shall think meet and necessary to be propounded unto them*, then shall you by vertue hereof, for the better boulting forthe of the truthe, *cause them to be put to the manacles and soche other tortures as are used in Bridewell*, to th'end they may be compelled to utter soche things as shall concern Her Majestie and the Estate: And their Examynations so taken by you, we pray you to send the same to us."—From the "*Council Book*," in "*A Reading on the Use of Torture in the Criminal Law of England, by David Jardine*," 1837, Appendix No. 34, p. 92.

BRIAN LACEY (spelt Lassey in the Council Book) was brother to RICHARD LACEY of BROCKDISH, CO. NORFOLK. He had been *betrayed by his brother* eight years before this horrible torturing, but had apparently managed to escape apprehension. In RICHARD LACEY's confession, extorted probably under great pressure, he gives some valuable information regarding the Catholic gentry in Norfolk and Suffolk at this time. I hope to print this curious document, with illustrative notes, in the *Original Papers of the Norfolk and Norwich Archæological Society* at no distant date. The original is to be found in vol. 169, No. 19, Domestic, Eliz., P. R. O. It is dated 13th March 1584.

(14) *Page* 254, *line* 11. u. s., vol. 247, No. 78, No. 91.

(15) *Page* 257, *line* 32. u. s., vol. 249, No. 4. I have not thought it necessary to give the references to each of these examinations. The Calendar, Dom. Eliz., 1591–1594, may easily be referred to, but I quote, and have before me, verbatim transcripts from the original documents themselves.

(16) *Page* 258, *line* 6. Sir Edward Coke had just been appointed Attorney-General. For the rivalry between Coke and Bacon at this time see *Spedding*.

(17) *Page* 260, *line* 7. It was perfectly well known to the government that VERSTEGAN was the principal channel of communication between the refugees and their friends at home. As to Braddocks and the WISEMANS, Walpole very probably had heard all about them, the search at their house (Braddocks in Essex) and the break up of their establishment, from his fellow-prisoner SOUTHWELL. See *Foley's Records*, u. s.

(18) *Page* 262, *line* 17. On Sir Philip Wodehouse, see previous chapter. The following is from the Day Book of the "Commissioners for Ecclesiastical Causes within the Diocese of Norwich," now in the Bishop's Registry: "23d March 1597 . . . *In aula infra Palacium Episcopale Norvicense* . . . before WILLIAM, Bishop of Norwich . . . EDM. SUCKLINGE, S.T.P., ROBERT WEST, S.T.P., JOHN MAPLISDON, Archd*. of Suffolk . . . NICHOLAS WILKINSON, Gent., appeared in custody. . . . And being further examined what Conventicles in Matters of Religion he had frequented, he saith that he did not frequent any such unlawful assemblies, neither that he had been at any Popish Recusant's house, *saving only at* BRECCLES *at the house of* MR. FRANCIS WOODHOUSE, ESQ. (whose wife is a Recusant), since his coming from London, and hath made his abode there in that house by the space of three weeks last past before this his Examination. And being secondly required whether he would receive the Holy Communion or not, he answered he was not fully persuaded in his Conscience touching the doctrine of that Sacrament, &c., &c."

(19) *Page* 263, *line* 21. ". . . I can well believe that he (Henry Walpole) was racked that number of times, for he lost through it the proper use of his fingers. This I can vouch for from the following circumstance. He was carried back to York, to be executed in the place where he was taken on his first landing in England, and while in prison there he had a discussion with some ministers, which he wrote out with his own hand A part of this writing was given to me, together with some meditations on the Passion of Christ, which he had written in prison. . . . These writings, however, I could scarcely read at all, not because they were written hastily, but because the hand of the writer could not form the letters. *It seemed more like the first attempts of a child than the handwriting of a scholar and a gentleman such as he was.*"—Gerard's *Autobiography* prefixed to *The Condition of Catholics under James I.*, p. xci.

NOTE A.

HENRY WALPOLE'S CELL IN THE TOWER.

The following account is extracted from a paper in *The Month*, for December 1874, by Mr. Morris, entitled "The Tower of London."

"Father Gerard's account of his escape from the Tower is not likely to be forgotten by any one who has read it. It makes an impression on the imagination second only to his narrative of the torture he endured. It will be interesting therefore to try to identify the cell occupied by him, and the place where he effected his escape by crossing the moat on a rope. He has mentioned a sufficient number of circumstances to make this identification possible, and as far at least as the cells are concerned which were honoured by the imprisonment of Father Henry Walpole and himself, they are happily in excellent condition, and but little changed.

"Sir Richard Barkly, the Lieutenant, conducted him, when he was brought to the Tower of London from the Clink prison, 'to a large high tower of three storeys, with a separate lock-up place in each, one of a number of different towers contained within the whole inclosure. He left me for the night in the lowest part.' The warder, after throwing some straw on the ground, 'fastened the door of my prison, and secured the upper door both with a great bolt and iron bars. The next day I examined the place, for there was some light though dim, and I found the name of Father Henry Walpole, of blessed memory, cut with a knife on the wall, and not far from there I found his oratory, which was a space where there had been a narrow window, now blocked up with stones. There he had written on either side with chalk the names of the different choirs of angels, and on the top, above the cherubim and seraphim, the name of the Mother of God, and over that the name of Jesus, and over that again, in Latin, Greek, and Hebrew, the name of God.'

"The place thus described was the Salt Tower, an ancient tower, the origin of the name of which is unknown, and which seems at one time to have shared with the White Tower the honour of being called after 'Julyus Sesar.' The tower has received a new external face of stone, but the interior is as nearly in its ancient state as is compatible with its present use as a dwelling-house. A door has been opened from the bottom of the tower, which did not exist in Father Gerard's time, when the entrance to it was from the ballium wall or inner line of fortification, of which the Salt Tower formed the south-east angle. Father Gerard took no account of what is now called the cellar, and the interior face of the stones of its walls shows no sign of ever having been scored by a prisoner's knife. Besides this there are three ancient storeys. What we should now call the first floor is the cell to which Father Gerard descended from the door by which he entered, and in which he found Father Walpole's 'oratory.' The room is 'sufficient large and commodious for a prisoner,' being a pentagon about sixteen feet across. It is no longer dimly lighted, for a modern two-light Gothic window has taken the place of one of the ancient loopholes, through which the cell received of old such light and air as it had. There were five of these little openings in the enormously thick walls of the circular tower, and as Father Gerard says that at least one of these was blocked up with stones, the place may well have been dim.

"There are many inscriptions remaining on the walls of the cell, interesting enough in their way; but there was one in particular, that has not been noticed in any of the books written on the Tower, the sight of which made one's heart leap into one's mouth. There were the words, thickly coated with whitewash, that testified that in this cell Henry Walpole had been imprisoned. The name of the martyr is to be seen where Father Gerard saw it, by the window, though of course the holy words that he had written close by in chalk have long ago been effaced. A very fine old fireplace faces you as you enter the cell, and the window once thus sanctified is the next to it on your left."

## CHAPTER XII.

# THE TRIAL AND THE SCAFFOLD.

THERE is a curious story to be found in Henry Walpole's earliest biography (published, it must be remembered, within a year of his death) which professes to account for the sudden decision of the Council to bring their prisoner to trial. We are told that in January 1595, a Jesuit father, whose name does not appear, had been commissioned to take charge of six young Englishmen, who had been spending some time at the seminary of St. Omers, and to transfer them to the new seminary at Valladolid. The vessel in which they set sail was captured by an English cruiser in the Channel, and the whole party was thrown into prison. The boys were the sons of men of birth and position in England, who had sent their children across the sea to be educated—contrary to the statute which had made such a course illegal—and of course they belonged to the class of malcontents who were either Popish Recusants, or at least averse to the dominant creed. The capture of so many young people at once created, says Cresswell, some excitement. They were first brought before the Council, and then sent to Archbishop Whitgift, to be kept under surveillance and to be taught the error of their ways. They are said to have behaved with something like contumacy, but they were compelled to afford information on the condition of the French and Spanish seminaries; and the intelligence gathered from them sufficed to increase the irritation and annoyance of the government, who learnt that the activity of the English Jesuits on the continent was just as great as ever, and their success as remarkable as ever in inducing young Englishmen to leave their homes, and to seek education in the colleges beyond the sea.  These lads had not been long under the Archbishop's charge before their conductor disappeared, and then for the first time, to the mortification of the authorities, it leaked out that this *Naples merchant,* as he was supposed to be, was himself a Jesuit father, and that he had managed to escape the clutches of the law.  This was provoking enough, but when, very shortly after, all the six youths gave their jailors the slip, and succeeded in getting safely to the other side of the Channel, it was only natural that the government should rush to the conclusion that such a remarkable escape, on such a large scale too, must have been the result of some widespread plot, of which many must be cognisant, and the ramifications of which might extend very much further than yet appeared.  We are told that Topcliffe was called in to advise what should be done, and that he reminded the Lords of the Council that there were two notable Jesuits still pining in the Tower—Southwell, who had been lying there nearly three years, and Walpole, who had been in confinement fifteen months.  Topcliffe suggested that these two should be brought to trial without delay, and proceeded with according to the utmost rigour of the law. (¹)

The truth of this story is, that on the 25th January 1595, one of the fathers of the Society named William Baldwin started from St. Omers for Spain, as Cresswell tells us, having six scholars under his charge.  The vessel in which they sailed was captured by an English ship and brought home as a prize; Father Baldwin, who was committed to the custody of Lord Nottingham, the Lord High Admiral, being taken for a Neapolitan merchant, was subsequently sent to Bridewell and there detained as a prisoner of war. The boys were put under the custody of Aylmer, Bishop of London, and first one and then another were let out on bail, their friends, it is to be presumed, giving security for their re-appearance when called on. One and all slipped away and again crossed the Channel. Father Baldwin, after being kept some months in confinement, was exchanged against one Hawkins, an Englishman, who had been a prisoner in Spain. Not till they had all got away safely was it discovered that an active Jesuit emissary had succeeded in outwitting the government; and it is quite conceivable that under the irritation that was aroused, the Lords of the Council resolved upon making an example of such Jesuit fathers as were then in prison, and that thus the trial of Southwell and Walpole was precipitated.

It is, however, hardly worth while to attempt to account for Henry Walpole's trial taking place when it did, nor would it be worth our while to do so at all, but that an impression had got abroad, and a report been circulated, that the Queen had been so shocked at the execution of Campion, that she had vowed never again to put a Jesuit father to death. Certain it is, that though several Jesuits had been captured, none had been executed for more than thirteen years: the unhappy Seminary priests had been butchered by scores, but of the Jesuits who had been hunted down, none had suffered on the scaffold since the day when Campion and Briant had been hung at Tyburn. Whatever may have been the occasion or the motive, the fact alone is what we are now concerned with. In the spring of 1595 it was determined that Henry Walpole should be sent to York for trial.

The judges who held the Lent Assizes at York were Francis Beaumont and Matthew Ewens. Beaumont had been appointed a Justice of the Common Pleas about two years. He was the father of the dramatic poet, and he had himself been a fellow commoner of Peterhouse a few years before Henry Walpole had matriculated at the college. Ewens had been raised to the bench of the Exchequer only a few months, and this was probably his first criminal cause. Associated with these was the Earl of Huntingdon, as a matter of course, and William Hillyard, who had been reader at the Temple some years before, had represented York in the Parliament of 1586, and was now Recorder of the city. (²)

Unhappily the Assize Rolls of this period can no longer be found, and the only details of the trial that have reached us have come down to us in a fragmentary form. But we learn that the prosecution was entrusted to Serjeant Saville, ancestor of the present Earl of Mexborough, (³) and the jury was impanelled on Thursday, the 13th of April 1595. The indictment appears to have contained three counts:—

> 1st. That the prisoner had abjured the realm without a licence.
> 2d. That he had received Holy Orders beyond the seas.
> 3d. That he had returned to England to exercise his priestly functions, he being a Jesuit father and a priest of the Roman Church.

The prisoner pleaded "Not guilty," and Serjeant Saville proceeded to open the case for the prosecution. The speech which he delivered seems to have been a long and elaborate one. He did not spare the Jesuits, we may be sure: he did not spare the prisoner. It was bad enough that he was a priest; it was worse that he had entered the society; but that he should have returned to his country to pervert and corrupt men's minds was worst of all; and this of itself, according to the provisions of the statute, constituted him guilty of the crime of high treason, and deserving of a traitor's death. When the prosecutor had finished, Henry Walpole's own confessions, extracted under torture, or such of them as were pertinent to the occasion, were read by the clerk of the court; and upon the evidence thus adduced the jury were called upon to pronounce their verdict. At this point Henry Walpole begged to be heard in his own

S

defence. It must be borne in mind that no one charged with a capital offence in any English court was allowed, under any circumstances, to employ counsel to defend him for more than two centuries after the time we are now speaking of, and the chances of obtaining an acquittal were almost infinitely small; on this occasion it was even moved by the Recorder Hillyard that the prisoner *should not be heard*. The court, he said, had before it the confessions which had been put in as evidence, and required to hear no more. The prisoner earnestly and humbly appealed against the cruel objection, and Beaumont overruled it, and allowed him to proceed. Then he is reported to have commenced his reply. (⁴)

" I find, my Lords, I am accused of Two or Three Things.

" 1*st*. That I am a *Priest*, ordained by the Authority of the See of *Rome*.

" 2*dly*. That I am a *Jesuit*, or one of the Society of *Jesus*.

" 3*dly*. That I return'd to my Country to exercise the ordinary Acts of these Two Callings; which are no other than to gain Souls to God.

" I will shew that none of these Three Things can be Treason: Not the being a Priest, which is a Dignity and Office instituted by our Lord *Jesus Christ*, and given by Him to His Apostles, who were Priests; as were also the holy Fathers and Doctors of the Church, who converted and instructed the World: And the first Teachers, who brought over the *English* Nation to the Light of the Gospel, were also Priests; so that were it not for Priests, we should all be Heathens; consequently to be a Priest can be no Treason.

" Judge *Beamont* here spoke; *Indeed*, said he, *the merely being a* Priest, *or* Jesuit, *is no treason; but what makes you a Traitor, is your returning into the Kingdom against the Laws.* If to be a Priest, said Father *Walpole*, is no Treason, the executing the Office, or doing the Functions of a Priest, can be no Treason. *But if a Priest*, said the Judge, *should conspire against the*

*Person of his Prince, would not this be Treason?* Yes, said Father *Walpole*; but then neither his being a Priest, nor the following the Duties of his Calling, would make him a Traitor; but the committing of a Crime contrary to the Duty of a Priest; which is far from being my Case.

" *You have been,* said *Beamont, with the King of* Spain, *and you have treated and conversed with* Parsons *and* Holt, *and other Rebels and Traitors to the Kingdom; and you have return'd hither contrary to the Laws; and therefore you cannot deny your being a Traitor.* Father *Walpole* replied, To speak or treat with any Person whatsoever, out of the Kingdom, can make me no Traitor, as long as no proof can be brought, that the Subject about which we treated was Treason; neither can the returning to my native Country be look'd upon as a Treason, since the Cause of my Return was not to do any Evil, either to the Queen or to the Kingdom.

" *Our Laws appoint,* said *Beamont, that a Priest who returns from beyond the Seas, and does not present himself before a Justice, within Three Days, to make the usual Submission to the Queen's Majesty, in Matters of Religion, shall be deem'd a Traitor.* Then I am out of the Case, said Father *Walpole*, who was apprehended before I had been one whole Day on *English* Ground.

" Here *Beamont* being put to a Nonplus, Judge *Elvin* ask'd him, *If he was ready to make that Submission to the Queen, in Matters of Religion, which the Laws of the Kingdom required, viz.,* To acknowledge her Supremacy, and the Pope? Father *Walpole* answered, he did not know Laws they have made in *England* whilst he was abroad, nor what Submission these Laws required; but this he very well knew, that no Law could oblige any one, that is not agreeable to the Law of God; and that the Submission that is to be pay'd to earthly Princes, must always be subordinate to that Submission which we owe to the great King of Heaven and Earth. Then he added, *You, my Lords, sit here at present in Judgment as Men, and judge as such, being subject to Error and Passion; but know* for certain, that there is a sovereign Judge, who will judge righteously; whom, in all Things, we must obey in the first place; and then our lawful Princes, in such Things as are lawful, and no farther.

"Here the Lord President spoke. *We deal very favourably with you, Mr. Walpole*, said he, *when, notwithstanding, all these Treasons and Conspiracies with the Persons aforesaid, we offer you the Benefit of the Law, if you will but make the Submission order'd by the Law; which, if you will not accept of, it is proper you should be punish'd according to the Law*. Father *Walpole* replied, There is nothing, my Lord, in which I would not most willingly submit myself, provided it be not against God: But may His divine Majesty never suffer me to consent to the least Thing, by which He may be dishonour'd, nor you to desire it of me. As to the Queen, I every Day pray for her to our Lord God, that He would bless her with His Holy Spirit, and give her His Grace to do her Duty in all Things in this World, to the End that she may enjoy eternal Glory in the World to come: And God is my Witness, that to all here present, and particularly to my Accusers, and such as desire my Death, I wish as to myself the Salvation of their Souls, and that, to this End, they may live in the true Catholic Faith, the only Way to eternal Happiness."

It was not *for* nothing that Henry Walpole had gone through his legal tr*ai*n*i*ng at Gray's Inn, if he could acquit himself so well on t*h*is s*u*preme occasion. But it need hardly be said that it was all in vain. He had been brought into court, not to obtain a trial, but to hear his sentence, and this was soon to follow. The judge summed up the evidence, and ordered the jury to find the prisoner guilty. They did as they were told, and the prisoner was removed to his cell to await the sentence, which for the present was deferred.

There was another priest, a Gloucestershire man, named Alexander Rawlings, whom it had been determined to make an example of at the same time, who had now to be tried. He had been educated at the English college at Rheims, and had been exercising his priestly functions in Yorkshire for some years before the pursuivants caught him. He had been arrested on Christmas Eve, and had apparently been in York Castle ever since. He had never been connected with the Jesuits, and was a seminary priest of whom very little is known. (⁵) It was too late on the Thursday to proceed with this man's trial, and when it came on, it occupied the whole of the next day. While it was going on, and while Henry Walpole was hourly expecting to hear his doom, he found means to write to his father and some other friends. In his letter to his father, which unhappily has not been preserved, he made one last request, viz., that £80 should be distributed among the officials of the castle in which he had been immured. It is only reasonable to assume that the jailors were made acquainted with the contents of the letter, and took good care that it should be delivered, together with any others that their prisoner might choose to send. One of these other letters has reached us in a Latin translation, and may be seen in extenso in *Henry More's History*, but as the volume is one of excessive rarity, I think it well to give a portion of it here. It was addressed to Father Holtby, of whom we have heard before.

"I am to be executed to-morrow. It appears to me, therefore, needful that I should commend myself to your prayers and those of our fathers and brethren. For the rest, I doubt not that the Holy Spirit has already suggested to you, as to all truly Catholic hearts, with whom I glory in being in communion, to pray to our GOD, Creator, Redeemer, and Sanctifier, that He may be my helper in this last conflict that I have to sustain, for the glory of His name and the edification of His holy Church. That He may vouchsafe to strengthen the inner man against all the suggestions of this fleshly body that we gat from the old Adam! This earthly prison-house which keeps in the soul is about to fall off, but GOD with His mighty hand will raise it up again, glorified and immortal, to place it in its home of eternal felicity, and to make it conformable to the body of our Lord Jesus Christ." Then, after briefly referring to the main points of his defence, he prays for the forgiveness of those who had compassed his death, &c., and brings his letter to a close as follows: "I tell you nothing of all that passed during my year's detention in the Tower of London. I hold my peace, too, on many other details. You will know them in heaven, when we shall see each other again. Let this letter, written in haste, but with cordial affection, suffice. It is time for me to lay my pen aside to employ myself only in prayer to the great God, for whom I am fighting the good fight, with whom I hope to be face to face on the morrow."

But the closing scene was not to come so soon: the trial of Rawlings was protracted till late on Friday evening, and the judges resolved not to call up the prisoners to receive sentence till next day. This was Saturday the 15th, and as the ordinary practice was to allow one night to intervene between the sentence and its execution, and even in those days the susceptibilities of some people would have been shocked if two men had been hung upon the Sunday morning, they were granted another day to live, and the hanging was fixed for the Monday morning. Not even during those two days which preceded the execution, however, was Henry Walpole allowed to remain unmolested. Once again he was subjected to an ordeal which to our minds appears, under the circumstances, eminently shocking and indecent, but which to our forefathers seemed only a proper and commendable proceeding.

Once again the prison was turned into a debating place, and a crowd of polemics presented themselves to dispute on points of controversial divinity with this man who had but a few hours to spend on earth. It is painful to hear of clergymen of learning and character taking part in such an unseemly wrangling, and of a scholar and gentleman like Sir Edwin Sandys putting himself forward and entering the lists; (⁶) but these encounters suited the temper of the age, which, after all, was a cruel and coarse one; and people were attracted in crowds to watch the way in which a criminal met his fate, much in the same spirit that they assembled to look on at a bull-fight or a bear-baiting.

The fatal morning came at last, and with it came the end. The story of that dreadful day has reached us from the pen of one who, if he were not present, could not have been far away; for the letter which follows, and which is still preserved among the archives at Stonyhurst, is, I believe, in Holtby's handwriting. I give it as I find it, neither adding to nor withholding a word: it needs no comment.

"I thought it my dutie bothe to him of whom I have to write & to yourself, to send you worde of that w[ch] I have understood of F. Warp. [sic] by a gentleman whoe was his schoolefellowe and familiar frend in Cambridge and lately felowe prisoner with him in Yorke, who havinge conference with him there hath tould me what himself was there an eye witnesse of. First for his usage in the Tower he would not tell him an[y] further but that he was diverse tymes (my frende thinks 6 or 7) uppon a torture I thinke by his description somewhat like that of F. South[lls] by which means bothe his thums were lamed, so that he had not the use of them; he was not uppon the racke. He was verie austere unto himselfe after his cominge out of the Tower: in all his jorney he neither ley in bed nor came upon any, but laye uppon the flore. In the castle he had a litle matt of a yard longe uppon which he used in the night to kneele, and untill deade sleepe came uppon him he did not sleepe. And he that ley in his chamber w[th] him did affirme that he never wakened but he heard the f[r] either praye or sighe, and some tyms when the comon prisoners in the gaile did sweare and blaspheme, he should heere him softly to saye *Conjuro te Sathan, audio blasphemiam.* Thus saithe my frend he laye uppon the stones (belike his chamber beinge pavd or done with bricke) unlesse he leined uppon his elboe. But beside his praiers much parte of the night he spent in making verses wherof I send you a copie so far as he went untill his deathe. My frend whoe tellethe me this hath his owne copie in Yorkshire which is so ill writt (by the defect of his thums) that he had verie much adoe to reade it thoughe I thinke acquainted with his hand.

"The daye tyme was for the most parte spent in disputation with diverse ministers that came unto him. At on, which was the cheefe, my frend was present. The disputers were on Higgens,(7) a minister, and I thinke a graduate in their kind of divinitie, and on Sands, soñe to the old man of Yorke, deceased, and he the better witt and a fine philosopher, and able to saye more than any there, it is thought, but he is a man of feine livinge and noe minister. The questions were betweene them of Justification, and of the continuance of faith in Peeter's chaire. In the first Higgens was in the begiñinge verie earnest; but as his reasons grewe weaker soe his words, insomuch that afterwards he deferred much unto the F$^r$, and kept of some other ministers when they would interrupt him or be hastie with him, shewinge both with words and with countenance that the man was to be used with reverence. The particulars my frend doth not remember. Sands desired rather to prove his part *perpetua oratione* than otherwise; trustinge to his witt and fine discourse, he made a speeche of an hower and a quarter longe, seekinge to prove that the faithe first might decaye by scriptures, then that it had decayed as well by councills, which he alledged, as by other authorities. When he had doñe, F. Warp. collected all his speeche, recitinge the suñe thereof, and all his arguments so playnly, so truely, and with so good a methode, that both the disputers and others gave him great thanks, and seemed to saye they had not heard the like. Then he answered the particulers with greate facilitie, and as my frend saithe he shewed a greate memories, leinge down unto them the stories of those councells, and declaring how they were never confirmed, &c. Sands would sometyms interrupt him, but still he was satisfied, and drewe neerer and neerer by grauntinge many particulers. Insomuch that in the ende he sayd publicly there was litle difference betweene their opinions, usinge the Greeke wurd, that there diff. was but in Microtrion, I thinke he sayd. On minister standinge by my frend havinge seene the F<sup>r</sup>. stand so still when the other was speakinge so longe together, and afterwards seeinge him speake so fully to the matter and so amply, he sayd softly to himself, *This is a close felowe*, sayd he, affirminge it with an othe. Finally all the companie did shewe greate satisfaction both in his modestie, wisedom, and learninge, and desired him then with greater instancie that he would yeeld but in the least point, or doe somethinge to save his life, which they sayd they greately pittied.

"At the tyme of his execution, first they brought out Mr. Alexander, and the people would have had him lye on the right side, but he refused, seinge that was provided for a better man. There went diverse of the cheefe to F. Warp. to intreate him that they might save him, and stayed him 2 howers all (?), the other lyinge uppon the hurdle. On tyme they asked him what he sayd of the Queene and whether he would praie for her. As I take it this was there question, and he answered he tooke her for his Queene, and honoured her, and would praie for her; with which answer they, being desirous to save him, rañe to the President, but it pleased GOD that He propounded an other question, willinge them to aske him what yf the Pope should excom̃unicate her, &c., and forbid men to praie for her (I doe not well remember this question, but I will inquier better of it), whether then he would doe as before; he answered he might not nor would not. Then they caried him awaye. Mr. Alexander was first put to deathe, whoe beinge taken up went first to F. Warp. to aske his benediction. They had beene leid contrarie ways uppon the hurdle, and F. Warp. head next unto the horses. Mr. Alex<sup>r</sup>. goinge up the ladder kissed it, and the people bad him kisse the rope alsoe. He say'd he would with all his hart, and so did when he came unto it. When he was dead they shewed him to F^r. Warp., still using persuasions. When he was up the ladder they still cried uppon him to yeeld in the least point, but to sey he would confer, and he should be saved. He answered, you knowe I have conferred. They kept him longe with such questions, and satisfied all in fewe words, and prayed muche. At lengthe some (?) asked him what he thought of the Queen's supremacie, he answeared she doth chalenge it, but I maye not graunt it. His last praier was P&#x159; n&#x159;, and he was begiñinge Ave Maria when they turned him over the ladder. They let him hange untill he were dead. There were verie many of the best thier present, and the highe Sherife went with him to his deathe, which was never seene in the contrey before. I am promised a peece of his ha . . . . which was taken out of the fier whole when the people were goñe."[8]

Thus suffered upon the scaffold Henry Walpole in his thirty-sixth year. If he did not deserve a better fate, he could scarcely have met with a worse. His creed was not my creed; his career may well require excuse; his life may seem to some one long mistake; his character was not without defects; there was even in his intense enthusiasm a certain element of effeminacy; he had not that rugged vigour and coarseness of fibre which has enabled some men to bear pain and be silent even unto death, but when there remained for him nothing but to die, he died bravely. Thank God the fires of Smithfield will never be lighted again, nor the hangman's bloody knife again be plunged into the bowels of unhappy priests at York, but, alas! the spirit of intolerance is not dead; and it is against that spirit, and not only against the ghastly exhibitions of its malignity, that we have to protest and be on our guard. Falsehood has had its martyrs as well as truth, and persecution has not been idle in the east or the west: the Saviour told us He came not to send peace but a sword. Even now, with all our boasted advance, we find it hard to extend our charity towards those whose powers of persuasion we have learnt to fear. Even now there is rather a tendency to excuse the atrocities of a bygone age than to condemn them. But let who will plead for the persecutor such palliation as may be found: for me, I do not envy that man or woman who can think of Henry Walpole's sufferings without pity, or of his cruel death without shame.

# NOTES TO CHAPTER XII.

(1) *Page* 271, *line* 28. I have called this a curious story, because, though Cresswell makes a great deal of it in his little book, neither *Yepez* nor *Bartoli* mention it at all, nor, if I remember rightly, does Father *Henry More*. Father Baldwin's apprehension is detailed by *Juvencius* (*Hist. Soc. Jes.*, lib. xiii. pars v., p. 143), who says that his captors, deceived by BALDWIN'S stature and military bearing, believed him to be an Italian soldier of fortune. He for his part pretended to know no English, and kept up the character of a foreigner till he was released. CRESSWELL assures us that the boys were examined before the Lord High Admiral and Archbishop WHITGIFT, and that they were interrogated, among others, by M. DE LA FONTAINE, preacher of the French Church in London, and ADRIAN SARAVIA, who, he says, was at that time a member of WHITGIFT's household. [He did not receive his stall at Canterbury till nearly a year after this.] In both cases he spells the names incorrectly, and evidently did not know who the men were whom he writes about. He adds that he had actually received his account from two of the boys who had escaped, and whom he had talked with at Valladolid. In Mr. Foley's *Records of the English Province*, vol. iii. p. 503, are the names of these boys and an account of FATHER BALDWIN. It appears that at the time of his capture he went by the assumed name of OCTAVIUS FUSCINELLI. Father Baldwin became eventually a very conspicuous character, and Mr. Foley gives a long account of him.—On M. DE LA FONTAINE, see Strype, *Ann.* iv. 549 *et seq.*; and on SARAVIA, *Ann.* I. ii. 223, and Heylin, *History of the Presbyterians*, lib. ix. § 11.

(2) *Page* 273, *line* 7. FRANCIS BEAUMONT—he was never knighted—was made one of the Justices of the Common Pleas 25th January 159⅔. MATTHEW EWENS was made a Baron of the Exchequer 1st February 159⅘. WILLIAM HILLYARD of Winestead, co. York, was Reader to the Temple in 1581, and M.P. for York 1586. He was a member of the Committee for considering whether MARY QUEEN OF SCOTS should be brought to trial, and he appears then to have been Recorder of York.—Cooper's *Athenæ Cant.*; Foss' *Judges*; Dugdale's *Origines*; *The Temple Records* by W. H. Cooke, Q.C.; Sir Simonds D'Ewes' *Journals of Parl.*, Eliz. p. 294. The

reader will notice that Challoner, following his MS., speaks of *Ewens* as
*Elvin*. There was no such judge at this time, and there is no doubt of
Judge *Ewens* being concerned in Henry Walpole's trial.

(3) *Page* 273, *line* 12. SIR JOHN SAVILLE was of a very ancient Yorkshire family. He was made Serjeant 29th November 1592, and Baron of
the Exchequer 1st July 1598. His estates in Yorkshire are still in the
possession of the family. His brother HENRY SAVILLE was the editor of
Chrysostom, one of the translators of the Gospels for King James' Bible,
and the founder of the Savillian Professorship of Mathematics at Oxford.
—Foss' *Judges;* Wood's *Ath. Oxon.;* Cartwright's *Chapters on Yorkshire
Hist.*, p. 202.

(4) *Page* 274, *line* 12. Challoner's *Missionary Priests*, vol. i. p. 347.
Cresswell gives a *resumé* of SIR JOHN SAVILLE'S speech, which is translated
by *Yepez*. The report of the trial in the text is from Challoner, who
appears to have had before him the original document from which Yepez
made his Spanish version. Bartoli makes no mention of the trial.

(5) *Page* 277, *line* 7. He made his appearance at Rheims 23rd
December 1587, and gave his *alias* as FRANCIS FERRIMAN. He was
ordained priest 18th March 1590, and left for England 9th April of the
same year.—*First and Second Diaries of the English College, Douay*, D.
Nutt, 1878.

(6) *Page* 278, *line* 35. SIR EDWIN SANDYS was second son of the Archbishop of York. Though a layman, he was a Prebendary of York from 1582
to 1602, as his brother, SIR MILES SANDYS, was from 1585 to 1601. He was
a pupil of RICHARD HOOKER at Corpus Christi College, Oxford; knighted
by James I. in 1603; treasurer of the Virginian Company 1619. He was
thrown into the Tower with SELDEN in June 1621, but released next
month. In 1625 he, together with PYM, drew up a petition to Charles I.
to enforce the laws against Popish Recusants. His work *Europæ Speculum*
was at one time a book much read.—Wood's *Ath. Oxon.;* Le Neve's *Fasti;*
Gardiner's *Prince Charles and the Spanish Marriage*, vol. ii. 26, 29; and
*England under the Duke of Buckingham and Charles I.*, vol. i. 196. There
is much about him in Gardiner's *History of England*, 1603-1616, and in
Birch's *Court and Times of James I.*

(7) *Page* 280, *line* 10. GEORGE HIGGIN, Prebendary of Eton in the
collegiate church of Southwell from 1588 to 1624.—Le Neve's *Fasti*.

(8) *Page* 282, *line* 15. The word which the binder of this letter (*Stonyhurst MSS.*, Father Greene's '*Anglia A*,' No. 82) has 'cropt' is certainly

*hand.* The hand *was* rescued from the fire, and sent over to EDWARD WALPOLE at Tournai. He appears to have distributed the fingers among friends, retaining the thumb himself and prizing it as a relic. Father JAMES ZELANDER, who had been intimately associated with HENRY WALPOLE in the Missio Castrensis, begged hard for the thumb to be deposited among other relics in the Church of the Jesuits at Brussels; but EDWARD WALPOLE could by no means be prevailed upon to part with it, until great pressure was put upon him by Father WILLIAM HOLT, who appears on his deathbed to have sent to EDWARD WALPOLE, earnestly begging him to surrender the precious relic to the Church. This must have been some time in 1599 or 1600. Shortly after this Father BALDWIN (see n. 1) presented to the same church the halter with which HENRY WALPOLE was hung; and on the 7th February 1604 ZELANDER drew up a formal account of the presentation; which document is now in the Royal Library at Brussels (MS. 3166, pt. ii. c. 41, § 9.) The two relics remained in the treasury of the Church of the Jesuits at Brussels till the Revolution, when they disappeared.

## CHAPTER XIII.

# THE GATHERING OF THE FRAGMENTS.

"Perhaps only those who have endeavoured to throw into a continuous narrative the vast mass of details involved in any one line of historical study, are conscious how easy it is to fall into error."—TODHUNTER, *Whewell,* vol. i. p. 103.

THE dreadful news of Henry Walpole's shameful death was not long in travelling from York to Norfolk. Old Christopher Walpole and his wife may perhaps have hoped against hope even to the last, but it was a gloomy outlook for them now; of their six sons only two remained to them—for the three who had become Jesuits, and been ordained abroad, were as dead to their parents, and could never again venture to set foot in England except at the risk of their lives. Geoffrey Walpole was now the eldest of the family, and was still at his father's side; so was Thomas, who had been released from prison after having told all he knew at York and subsequently again in London. For Geoffrey, I cannot divest myself of the impression that he laboured under some mental or physical infirmity, and thus was saved from the notoriety to which his brothers attained. It is evident that he was a cypher in the family. He was not sent to Cambridge as the others were, nor indeed does he appear ever to have gone far from his paternal home. There is nothing to show that he had any religious scruples about conforming or taking the oath of allegiance; and though I find him assessed upon his lands at Dersingham in 1601, and apparently cultivating those lands still in 1610, yet I cannot find that he ever married, nor has any testamentary disposition of his property or any administration after his decease survived to our time.([1])

When Thomas Walpole returned to Norfolk after his imprisonment, he appears to have quietly settled down as a country gentleman, and taken the management of the Anmer estate; he was wanted at home, for his father had been grievously hit in his pride. The old man's heart was broken and his occupation gone; just a year after the tragedy at York he made his will, and then he turned his face to the wall. On the 19th July 1596, less than fifteen months after his son Henry was executed, he died at Anmer. The Norfolk property was divided between Geoffrey and Thomas: Thomas was to have Anmer, keep up the house, and afford a home to his mother during her life; Geoffrey was to take the outlying lands at Dersingham, lands which are now part of the Norfolk estate of H.R.H. the Prince of Wales.([2])

At this point it will be advisable to trace the career of the other three brothers, who at their father's death were virtually outlaws, and had become exiles from their country for conscience' sake. They all attained to some eminence in the Jesuit body; that "staff corps," as it has been called, of the Church of Rome, every member of which is a picked man, and by the necessity of the case possessed of exceptional intellect, culture, or fervour. It will not escape the notice of those who believe in hereditary genius that in this "Generation of a Norfolk House" there was no lack of that remarkable power of brain, that subtlety and taste for intrigue, that somewhat perverse and reckless tenacity of purpose, and that vigour and force of character, which have been distinctive of the Walpole family in past times, and may very likely thrust some members of it to the front again, to play a leading part in our annals.

   .      .      .      .      .      .      .      .

Of Richard Walpole, the third son of Christopher, we heard last when he met his brother Henry at the opening of the College of Seville, in the winter of 1592. He had at that time volunteered for the English mission, and was actually under orders to start upon the voyage when an opportunity should offer. He had never been connected with any of Cardinal Allen's colleges, and, strictly, did not fall under the designation of a seminary priest; but he had received priest's orders at Rome on the 3d December 1589, and so in the eye of the law had been guilty of high treason. Three years before his ordination he had thoughts of offering himself to the Jesuits, but he either changed his mind then, or if he did offer he was for some reason rejected. When Father Parsons arrived in Spain in 1592, and then, apparently, made the acquaintance of the young priest for the first time, he saw at a glance that here was too valuable a man to send away on the errand which could be discharged by far inferior emissaries: for Richard Walpole was the most learned and perhaps the ablest and most accomplished of the brothers; and now that the old generation of scholars who had fled from England at the accession of Elizabeth was beginning to drop off, it was of supreme importance that their places should be supplied, if possible, by men like Richard Walpole, who had some experience of an English university training, and were qualified to keep up the spirit and tone which the first founders of Rheims and Douay had infused into those seminaries, and which there was some reason to fear might die with them.(³)

Parsons soon acquired a commanding influence over Richard Walpole's mind; the mission to England was given up, and once more his thoughts were directed to entering the Society of Jesus. This time there was no difficulty, whatever there may

T

have been before, and in February 1593 he was admitted into the Society, probably by Parsons himself, at Seville.(⁴)

For the next four years he was employed in various offices at the Spanish colleges, and it was while he was Prefect of Studies at Valladolid that he became the hero of one of the most extravagant stories which was ever circulated, even in an age so credulous and uncritical as the sixteenth century. "A strange story," says Mr. Spedding, "and in some part hard to believe, but .... as a fact in the history of criminal proceedings, it is still a curiosity worth preserving."(⁵)

Edward Squier was the type of a class that is never likely to become extinct as long as there is any room for the *chevalier d'industrie*. With just enough of cleverness to "pick up learning's crumbs," and so receive an education which had given him a distaste for the habits and sentiments of his kindred and associates, and aroused in him a hankering to rise in the social scale, he had received no moral benefit from his schooling, and was wholly without conscience or principle. He had been living for some years by his wits, occasionally employed as a scrivener or accountant, disliking the occupation, and finding it hard to make two ends meet. When Sir Francis Drake was making preparations for his last disastrous voyage, Squier determined to join the expedition, and shipped on board a vessel called the *Francis*, which became separated from the rest of the fleet—for Squier's ill-luck was never relieved by a single gleam of success in his strange career—and was captured with all hands by Don Pedro Tello, one of the Spanish admirals. The crew were carried to Seville and treated as prisoners of war. Squier appears to have been liberated on *parole*, and, always on the look-out for a chance of turning an honest or dishonest penny, he bethought him that he might improve the present opportunity. He soon began to amaze the Spaniards by going about and challenging them to dispute on matters of religion, and put himself forward as a champion for the Church of England as against the creed of the Church of Rome. To do

*Oct. 1595.*

this at Seville in our own days would be, to say the least, somewhat hazardous ; to do it in the Spain of Philip II. was to court imprisonment at least, and to run some danger of being torn to pieces by a fanatical mob. But Squier had no intention of being torn to pieces; he had every intention of being thrown into prison, and thus get for himself the credit of having suffered for truth's sake when his ransom or order of release, on an exchange of prisoners, should arrive from home. As a matter of course he was soon arrested by the Inquisition, and on his case being inquired into, he was sentenced to be confined two years in a monastery of the Carmelites. He had not been long at the monastery before he changed his tone, and gave out that he was a converted character; there were still some points in dispute on which his mind was unsettled and distressed, and he was humbly desirous of having his last doubts resolved by some man of learning, some eminent and gifted Jesuit father,—say such an one as Father Walpole of the English College !

By this time Richard Walpole had become a personage who was attracting a great deal of notice in Spain: he was regarded as a man of profound learning, and one likely to leave his mark behind him ; his brother Henry had recently been hung, and was claimed as the first martyr of the college of Seville. Cresswell's little book had produced a very deep impression, and had especially excited the enthusiasm of a Spanish lady of rank, who was connected with the noblest families of the country, one Doña Luisa de Carvajal, who had been left a widow with a large fortune entirely at her own disposal. She had long been animated by an ardent desire to help forward the English mission, and when Cresswell's biography of Henry Walpole was published, she became consumed by a passionate longing to cross over to England, brave the penal laws, defy the Government and all its cruel enactments, and herself take part in the glorious work of bringing back benighted Englishmen to the Catholic faith once more.([6]) Just when Squier landed at Seville, Doña Luisa had put herself under Richard Walpole as her spiritual adviser, and was preparing to make over to him her whole fortune to bestow in pious uses, having determined to divest herself of all that bound her to this world, and to live henceforth in voluntary poverty. Squier must have heard what every one was talking about, and he thought he saw a chance of retrieving his broken fortunes. Accordingly, he persuaded his Carmelite custodians to carry a message to Richard Walpole begging him to come and hold a conference at the monastery. Walpole assures us in his narrative that he did not obey the summons without some reluctance. He expected nothing but a weary dispute on controversial divinity, and to enter the lists on such subjects with a broken-down scrivener, who might be a crack-brained fanatic or a designing knave, offered very little attraction. But accustomed to obey when duty called, he went at last, and to his surprise found on his arrival at the monastery that Squier had altogether changed his ground, and that he was now begging only to be "reconciled to the Church." Walpole's suspicions were aroused,—for the trick of getting thrown into prison and then running home with "valuable information" had been tried before, and not without success,—and those suspicions were not allayed when he found Squier betraying an ever-increasing impatience under his captivity, and losing no opportunity of asking that he might be furnished with introductions to the Catholic gentry and seminary priests in England, with whom he said he intended to put himself in communication when he should succeed in obtaining his liberty. Richard Walpole was too wary to trust the fellow with such dangerous information as he asked for, and it is evident that he gave him no names and no letters: if he had done so it is quite certain that Squier's confessions would have betrayed them. Suddenly, after being among the Carmelites for about a year, Squier managed to escape, leaving behind him a letter to Walpole which the Inquisitors took possession of, furnishing Walpole with a copy only. Squier made the best of his way to England, having gained nothing by his crafty scheme. Just at the time that he got back, the expedition on what is known as the Island Voyage was about to set sail, and having nothing better to do he joined it, and got a berth on board the Earl of Essex's ship, in what capacity does not appear. Once more he was unfortunate; the voyage was a failure, and brought no profit or prize-money to any of those engaged in it. The fleet returned in the middle of October, and he found himself again at his wit's end for employment. How he managed to exist during the next six months we are not told, nor would it interest us much to know all the ups and downs of such a life of scoundrelism: but on the 4th May 1598, Chamberlain, writing to Dudley Carleton, says, "Here be certain apprehended for a conspiracy against the Queen's person and my Lord of Essex . . . . much buzzing hath been about it, but either the matter is not ripe or there is somewhat else in it, for it is kept very secret." Mr. Spedding has assumed that this passage refers to Squier, and though at a time when buzzings of this kind were the common subject of talk at every tavern and ordinary, it would be rash to assert that the allusion *must* be to this business, yet the probability is that it does refer to it.(7)

We hear no more of Squier during the next four or five months, but on the 23d September 1598 a man named John Stanley was examined before Sir John Peyton, Lieutenant of the Tower, Francis Bacon, and William Waad, Clerk of the Privy Council, and gave an incoherent account of how he and another worthy, named Munday, had contrived to get released from imprisonment at Seville on pretence of their intending the taking of Flushing from the English, and handing it over to the king of Spain. Richard Walpole, they said, had come to them "to persuade them to become Catholics, but *not to do any service against the Queen or the realm.*" (8)

About a month after this, viz., on the 18th October, Stanley was again examined, and though on the previous occasion he had not mentioned Squier's name, and, from all that appears, had never heard of him, now first we read, "*Walpole* told me that Rolls and Squier were employed about Her Majesty's person, and had received money for the same." The man had evidently been tampered with, but clumsily tampered with, since his last examination, for though he had got the name of Squier right enough, he bungled about the poisoning, and instead of accusing *Richard Walpole* of that, he says that it was *Father Cresswell* who told him " to go to Munday and receive of him a perfume which should be cast in the way of Her Majesty, to cut off her life." Next day Squier himself was examined for the first time. Squier had got up his amazing story with some little skill, though in the end he wofully outwitted himself. In his examination in the Tower before Bacon, Coke, Sir John Peyton, Fleming, and Waad—

"He confesseth that at that time that Walpole persuaded this examinant to attempt and be employed against Her Majesty's person, this examinant did take upon him to have some skill in perfuming, and thereupon Walpole asked whether he could compound poisons, and this examinant said no, but said he had skill in perfumes, and said that he had read in Tartalia of a ball, the smoke whereof would make a man in a trance and soon to die, to whom Walpole said that should be done with difficulty, but to apply poison to a certain place is the convenientest way. . . .

" Being demanded what directions he had from Walpole concerning his employment: saith that he had certain directions from Walpole in his own handwriting, which as he saith he threw into the water the same day he came from Seville. And the letter directed to Bagshaw he threw into the sea after he came past Plymouth. And saith that certain poisonous drugs whereof opium was one were to be compounded and beaten together and steeped in white mercury water, and put in an earthen pot, and set it a month in the sun, by Walpole's said directions.

" This examinant demanded of Walpole how he should apply the poison, and he said it should be put in a double bladder, and the bladders to be pricked full of holes in the upper part, and carried in the palm of his hand upon a thick glove for safeguard of his hand; and then to turn the holes downward, and to press it hard upon the pommel of her Highness' saddle; and said that it would lie and tarry long where it was laid, and that it would not be checked by the air. . . . . .

"He further confesseth that he bought two drams of opium and five drams of mercury water, at an apothecary's shop in Paternoster Row, towards the further end, near Dr. Smith's house: one of the residue at an apothecary's in Bucklersbury, at the Plough, and the other two at an apothecary's shop in Newgate Market, beyond the Three Tuns on the left hand. All which he bought in an evening in July was twelvemonth; and saith that he carried them about him six or seven days; and confesseth that he compounded them, and put them in an earthen pot, and set it in a window of his house at Greenwich, where it might take the sun; and saith that he applied part of it to a whelp of one Edwardes of Greenwich, and never saw the whelp after, and thinks it died thereof."

Five days later Squier had more particulars and fuller details to give, and by this time Richard Walpole is not only credited with a plot to assassinate the Queen, but he is further said to have suggested an attempt upon the life of the Earl of Essex; and though his success while experimentalising upon the Earl had not been more encouraging than in the case of "Mr. Edwardes' whelp," yet he had, he says, persisted in his designs notwithstanding.

"He sayeth that the other three drugs or ingredients, whereof he did compound these poisons, were all such as might be beaten to powder; one of which was yellowish, and the other of a brownish colour, and were called by the Latin or Greek names. And sayeth that all three cost eightpence, as he remembereth. And sayeth that all being compounded together, the confection was of a duskish colour, having some sort of yellow in it; and the whole composition was not above the bigness of a bean. . . .

"He confesseth that at the persuasion of Walpole, the Jesuit, he undertook to poison the Earl of Essex, when he should be with him at sea, to the end to defeat the voyage, and that he carried the confection of the poison with him to sea in the Earl's ship, in a little earthen pot of a red colour, glazed within, with a narrow mouth, which he stopped with cork and parchment, made it close with a pack thread, and carried it in his portmanteau, and did apply it to the pommel of the Earl's chair, where he did use to sit and lay his hand, which chair stood under the spare deck, where the Earl used to dine and sup. And this he did in an evening a little before supper-time, when the Earl was at sea between Fayal and St. Michael, and saith that the confection was so clammy as it would stick to the pommel of the chair, and that he rubbed it on with parchment. And soon after the Earl sat in the chair all supper-time, and that the arms of the chair were of wood.

"And now at last confesseth that the Monday seven-night, after his coming home from Spain, and had obtained leave to go with the Earl to sea, understanding that Her Majesty's horses were in preparing for Her Majesty to ride abroad, as her horse stood ready saddled in the stable-yard, this examinant came to the horse, and in the hearing of divers thereabout said, 'God save the Queen,' and therewith laid his hand on the pommel of the saddle, and out of a bladder which he had made full of holes with a big pin, he impoisoned the pommel of the saddle, being covered with velvet, by brushing the poison on it through the holes of the bladder, with his hand, and soon after Her Majesty rode abroad that afternoon."

It was the invariable characteristic of these "plots" that somebody should be put to death; and so as Richard Walpole could not be got at, Squier himself was made the victim. Whatever the luckless creature meddled with seemed always to turn to his harm, and as his life could do no good to any one, they hung him. At the gallows he solemnly repudiated his previous confessions, and did his best to atone for his malignant and stupid slander; but there were too many people interested in keeping up a belief in the story—people who would have been stultified if it had *not* been believed—to allow of its being treated as a hoax, and a great deal of pains was taken to give it credence and importance.  Bacon actually wrote a pamphlet in which he drew up an account of the case with all the ingenuity of a practised advocate.  Coke, ten years after, in his speech at Garnet's trial, made use of the story to point one of his many invectives hurled at the prisoner, against whom he was labouring to get a verdict; and in an "Order for Prayer and Thanksgiving . . . . . for the safety and preservation of Her Majesty and this realm," *set forth by authority*, and printed in 1599, the "Admonition to the Reader" contains an account of the plot in its coarsest form.  Even in our own times Mr. Spedding more than half believes the tale; and in popular histories the attempt to poison Queen Elizabeth's saddle is still repeated, and boys and girls are taught to regard it as true.  To me it seems only a monstrous fiction, which the more closely it is looked into, the more entirely incredible does it appear. (9)

Richard Walpole remained at Seville for two or three years after the "Squier's plot" had been exposed.  I find him next at Rome, employed as secretary to Father Parsons, and his name is attached to an abstract of certain letters lately received from England, dated the 19th June 1602.  In 1605 he was in Spain once more, and causing great annoyance to Sir Charles Cornwallis, the English ambassador, by his zeal in proselytising.  Sir Charles speaks of him as "a countryman of mine (*i.e.*, of the same *county*), one Walpole, a hot-headed fellow, as full of practice as he is of learning, yet therein they say he hath attained much perfection."  About a month after this he made some stir by converting the son and heir of Lord Wotton to become a Catholic; and in December of the same year Sir Charles Cornwallis writes home a report of a long interview he had had with him on the question of granting toleration to the Catholics at home.  At this time he was Vice-Prefect of the English Mission at Valladolid, and while acting in this capacity a disagreement seems to have arisen between him and his old friend Cresswell. The students at the college complained of Richard Walpole in high quarters, and the dispute was still going on when he died at Valladolid, it is said suddenly, in his forty-third year. The exact date of his death has not been recorded, but it took place at the end of the year 1607. ([10])

His brother Christopher, of whom we know less than any of the others, also died at Valladolid about a year before him. Though the last to leave England, he entered the Society before either Richard or Michael, having been admitted at Rome on 27th September 1592. ([11])

Thus at the death of Richard Walpole only one of the Jesuit brothers survived; this was Michael, John Gerard's convert. Though he had not the advantage of such training as an English university could afford—and his father must have had enough experience of that after three of his sons had tried it, and left Cambridge without a degree—yet Michael Walpole was not the least conspicuous among the brothers. When Doña Luisa de Carvajal took up her abode in England, Michael was her confessor, and appears to have had unbounded influence over her. He found time, too, for engaging in the controversies of his time; exhibited some literary activity, and occupied a prominent position among the English Jesuits during the whole of the reign of James I. We have seen that he obtained his brother Henry's release from prison at Flushing, and that after this he went to the English college at Rome in May 1590. On the 8th September 1593 he entered the Society of Jesus: where he passed his novitiate we are not told. We hear no more of him for ten years, but he must have been sent into England either at the close of Queen Elizabeth's reign or shortly after the accession of James I., for when John Gerard slipped away to the continent after the excitement raised by the Gunpowder Plot, he left Michael behind him, and there he seems to have been in May 1606. On 30th August 1607 Doña Luisa mentions him as then at her side, and in 1609 he published *at London* his translation of Boethius. By this time he seems to have acquired great influence in England, and when James I. put forth his apology for the new oath of allegiance, Michael Walpole published an *Admonition to the English Catholics,* of course dissuading them from taking the oath. The book was printed at St. Omers, and does not seem to have attracted much attention, but the author drew upon himself the watchful eye of Archbishop Abbot by his close connection with Doña Luisa, and probably too by his own exertions in proselytising: some time in the spring of 1610 he was caught by the pursuivants, and thrown into prison. The Spanish ambassador, Don Pedro de Zuniga, a great friend of Doña Luisa, succeeded in obtaining his release with some difficulty, and then only on condition that he should at once leave the country, which he did accordingly. ([12]) He retired to Belgium, and employed himself at first in writing an answer to *A Treatise concerning Antichrist,* which had been published some years before by Dr. George Downham, one of James I.'s chaplains and a prebendary of St. Paul's. ([13]) Both books have long since been forgotten. In September 1612 we find him at Douay, employed in arbitrating in some disputes between the Jesuit fathers and the authorities of the English college there. In the autumn of 1613 Don Diego de Sarmiento, the famous Gondomar, came to England as Spanish ambassador, and Michael Walpole appears to have returned to England in his train. Gondomar had not been many weeks in London when Archbishop Abbot, whose irritation at Doña Luisa's fanatical behaviour seems to have gone on constantly increasing, issued a warrant for her apprehension. On the 8th October 1613 the recorder and sheriff of the city of London, with a large band of constables, broke into Doña Luisa's house in the Barbican, and arrested every one they found. Michael Walpole had gone there early in the morning, to hear the confessions of the devotees who kept up a conventual life in the poorly furnished and scantily supplied dwelling, and he fell into the hands of the constables for the second time. The assault upon the Spanish lady's house created a great excitement, and the news was immediately carried to the ears of M. de Boischot, the archduke's ambassador, who was another staunch friend of the Catholics, and who hurried to the assistance of Doña Luisa. She addressed herself to him in Spanish, and told him that at all costs the Jesuit father must be set free, or his life would be in danger; and with ready tact the ambassador turned round to Father Walpole, and treating him as one of his servants, rebuked him strongly for being in the house contrary to his express orders, and bade him at once go home and never come there again. The officials, disarmed by the ambassador's manner, set their prisoner at liberty, and he made the best of his way to a place of safety. When Doña Luisa died, in January 1614, Michael Walpole was again with her, and he accompanied her body on its removal to Spain in August 1615. I think he never returned to his native land. Dr. Oliver says he held the same office as his brother Richard in the college at Valladolid, but I have not found any authority for the statement. About a year after his leaving England he published a translation of Ribadaneyra's *Life of St. Ignatius Loyola*, which is said to have gone through several editions. The last I find of him is a letter of his addressed to Gondomar, who was then in England, in which he intercedes for a certain Jane Mills, who had been one of Doña Luisa's companions in London, and asks for the continuance of an old pension of *a real and a half a day*, which had been formerly awarded to her by the king of Spain. This letter is dated from Seville, 12th August 1624. Michael Walpole must have died soon after this. ([14]) Hitherto it has been maintained that his death occurred in 1620, but this is clearly wrong; and if, as is asserted, the eldest of the brothers, Geoffrey, was buried in 1622, ([15]) and Michael died shortly after the date of his letter to Gondomar, only one of the six sons of Christopher Walpole of Anmer, Topcliffe's "young Thomas," survived to see Charles I. on the throne.

Of Thomas Walpole I have little to tell, but that little is not without interest and significance. He continued to live at Anmer for many years: he married, and seems to have had one son at least: his wife's name was Thomasine. She, too, was a strict and zealous Catholic. In June 1609 she was presented to the Bishop of Norwich as a Popish Recusant, being described as wife of Thomas Walpole, Gent., *he at this time being a conformist.* I find this state of things going on in July 1610, and again in August 1612. In 1613 Thomas Walpole's name appears in the Subsidy Rolls, in which he is assessed *on his goods at Anmer, and on them alone,* from which we may almost assume it as certain that he had made over his land to trustees.

It was just at this time that his brother Michael was in England once more, and under the protection of Gondomar. The presentments for 1614 are missing, but in the lists of Norfolk Recusants for 1615, I find for the first time Thomas Walpole, Gent., of Anmer, *together with his wife* Thomasine; and after this for thirty years I can trace him no more. But some years ago, by a curious chance, the high sheriff's list of recusants for the year 1645 came into my hands, and conspicuous among the names upon the roll I find *the tenants of Thomas Walpole, Gent.,* returned as paying a composition for sums due for his recusancy. He must have been at this time nearly eighty years old, and shortly afterwards the Anmer estate passed to the Pells, from them it went to the Coldhams, by one of whom it is now held. ([16])

We catch one more glimpse of this Anmer family. On the 11th October 1617, Christopher Warner "*alias vero nomine Walpolus Norfolciensis,*" aged nineteen, entered as an alumnus at the English college at Rome, and after pursuing his studies there for some years, he was admitted to priest's orders in May 1622. He was sent in 1624 as a missioner to England, and, apparently while there, was admitted to the Society of Jesus in 1625. We are told that he subsequently served as a Jesuit priest in Devonshire; that after this again he was sent to Belgium, and became Rector of the Jesuit College at Ghent; but, possibly at the Restoration, he returned to his native country once more, and died there on the 1st of December 1664. While in England he passed by the name of Warner only, *i.e.*, retaining the Christian name of his grandfather, he assumed for his surname his grandmother's maiden name. ([17])

I have chronicled all I have to tell of this "one generation" of the Anmer family; I have a few words to add about Edward Walpole, the heir of Houghton. We have seen that Edward Walpole left England soon after his father's death. He crossed over to Belgium with Bernard Gardiner, and there met his cousin Henry Walpole, and, receiving letters of introduction from him, hastened on to Rome, which he reached on the 20th October 1590. ([18]) Father Henry More tells us that he had a license to travel from the Lords of the Council, and he had evidently sufficient money at his disposal to make him quite free from any anxiety on the score of his means of livelihood. Watson was probably right in saying that the proceeds of his Tuddenham estate had been handed over to John Gerard for pious uses, but it is clear that he had disposed of other property; and besides what he must have taken with him, he had arranged for £100 to be sent after him through the agency of Robert Southwell. ([19]) Nor was this all: it has been shown that when John Walpole of Houghton died, in April 1588, he left his interest in the Robsart property to his second son, Calibut. But Edward Walpole, the heir, however little he might wish to press his claim, could not be despoiled legally of his right to a third part of the Newton and Syderston manors; in the autumn of 1588 he sold this interest to his brother Calibut, and he appears to have accepted as an equivalent an annuity or rent-charge of forty marks a year, which in those days was considered a liberal annual allowance for a gentleman of no extravagant tastes. ([20])

Thus placed beyond the reach of the "eternal want of pence," he would not trespass more than three days upon the hospitality of the English college, and on the 23d of October he entered himself as a *convictor, i.e.*, he was pretty much on the same footing as a Gentleman Commoner at Cambridge or Oxford in the days when such students were subjected to very little restraint, and might pursue their studies according to their own tastes. At this time neither Edward Walpole nor Bernard Gardiner seem to have had any definite plans. Gardiner appears to have thought of the military profession. ([21]) We are assured that Walpole shrank with some repugnance from the thought of taking orders, but his cousin's friends, the Jesuits, soon acquired influence over him, and he began to attend their lectures. It ended as we should have expected. We are told that his resolution to take orders was made at last when on one occasion, in company with Father Richard Smith, afterwards Bishop of Chalcedon, he escaped shipwreck after being exposed to great danger, and on the 5th February 1592, he took the decisive step of entering himself as a regular alumnus of the English college, and thereupon pledged himself by an oath to take holy orders, and to exercise his functions as a priest in England whenever called upon to do so by the authorities. That same Lent he received minor Orders, and on Ascension Day, 1592, he was admitted to the priesthood. ([22]) But these things were not done in a corner: he was too conspicuous a personage to escape the vigilance of the spies, who were always on the watch for men worth plundering, and news of his ordination soon reached England. His long residence at Rome must have been a matter of notoriety, and his leave of absence was drawing to a close. If he did not return when that license came to an end, by the statute his estates would be forfeited; and in those days when a man's estates *were* forfeited to the Crown, the rule was that some favoured courtier obtained a grant of them and made his market out of the spoils. It was a vile system; but ever since the suppression of the monasteries, and the enormous confiscations which had then ensued, people had become accustomed to see lands change their owners frequently and suddenly, and grants of forfeited lands and manors were a cheap way of rewarding needy placemen.

Edward Walpole believed that his ordination was a secret, and that he had some hope of being able to save his estates, if only he should return before his license had expired. Some time in the spring of 1593 he seems to have gone back to England, and to have sought out his brother Calibut in London. Calibut had about a year before married Elizabeth, daughter of Edmund Bacon of Hesset in Suffolk, and had now too much at stake to allow of his entangling himself in his brother's concerns. Nevertheless, he received him at first with cordiality; but on becoming aware that he was now actually a seminary priest, to harbour whom was treason, he entreated his brother not to compromise him; and Edward Walpole when he learnt that his ordination was known, and that his life was in real danger, and probably not having made due preparation for any such contingency, hastily recrossed the Channel, and, leaving his business unfinished, he once more sought out his cousin Henry, who was at this time in Belgium, and consulted him upon the course he should pursue. (23) The result was that he offered himself to the Society of Jesus, was admitted by the Provincial, Oliver Manaræus, and entered the Noviciate at Tournai on the 4th July 1593, just a year after Henry Walpole had himself completed his time there. Here he remained for three years, passing his examinations in the ordinary way, though he has left it on record that there were some of his duties which he found it difficult to discharge, from his imperfect command of the French language. He continued at Tournai till the 8th of July 1595, when he was sent to the college at Louvain. (24) But he was a marked man. He had brought himself under the penalties of the penal laws, and there were those who were not likely to forget him. The blow came at last. In Trinity term, 1595, he was indicted in the Court of Queen's Bench, "*for a supposed treason done at Rome on the 1st April* 1593;" and on the 29th May he was outlawed at Norwich. ([25]) Hereupon a special commission was issued for the holding of inquisitions concerning the possessions of the outlaw: they were held at Bury St. Edmunds and at East Dereham in the autumn of the same year; and, as a matter of course, the whole of the settled estates which he had inherited from his ancestors at Houghton, Walpole, Weybread, and elsewhere, as well as those which his cousin William had left him by his will, were at once forfeited to the Crown. ([26]) The family would have been well-nigh beggared, and we should never have heard of the great Sir Robert as the son of a wealthy Norfolk squire but for one circumstance: Edward Walpole's interest in these lands and manors was a reversionary interest, and there were two tenants for life in actual possession; his mother at Houghton, and his cousin William's widow still living at Tuddenham. Either of these ladies might live many years, and in the meantime circumstances might arise to bring about the reversal of the attainder; the grant of the lands might after all prove valueless, and whoever obtained that grant would be prudent if he turned it into money as soon as he could get a price.

Two years passed before the Queen gave away the estates. It was not till the 3rd August, 1597, that they were actually bestowed upon two persons of whom we know little or nothing —James Hussey and John Goodman, Esqrs.—the grant being made in consideration of the services of Sir Anthony Ashley, Clerk of the Privy Council.([27]) It is to be presumed that Calibut Walpole, the next heir to the estates, had due notice given to him of what was coming; for on the 27th of the next month he bought back the estates of the grantees, paying what was, in fact, a fine of £1600, a sum which in those days would be equivalent to a charge upon any estate in Norfolk of at least £20,000.([28]) As far as Edward Walpole was himself concerned, the attainder and the outlawry left him where it found him; he had already broken with all that bound him to the old home:

at the time of his being outlawed he was at Louvain; how long he remained there does not appear, but at the end of 1598 he was once more in England, and was at last regularly commissioned as a Jesuit Father. On his first arrival we hear of him as going down to Norfolk once more in company with Bernard Gardiner; but the pursuivants were on his track—there was a very diligent search of the houses of the Catholic gentry in Suffolk and Norfolk. Edward Yelverton among others was thrown into prison, and the two cousins were in very great peril. They eluded their pursuers, however, and Bernard Gardiner from this time disappears from our notice. Edward Walpole seems never to have left England again. At the end of Queen Elizabeth's reign he was living with "old Mr. Cotton, of Swanborow in Sussex," who may have been perhaps a friend and neighbour of William Walpole at the time that he was settled at Fittleworth.[29]

At the accession of James I. some little less rigour began to be shown to the Catholics, and amongst other instances of the king's leniency was his grant of a pardon to Edward Walpole, dated 4th April 1605, which it is presumed that Calibut obtained through the interest of friends at court.[30] A year or two after this he was stationed somewhere near Oxford, and passing under the name of *Rich*, as he had some years before passed by the name of *Poor*.[31] His mother died in 1612, and by virtue of his pardon he might if he had pleased have entered upon the Houghton estate; but instead of doing so he executed a deed of gift in which he renounced all claim to his paternal estates, and transferred them absolutely and unconditionally to his brother.[32] In 1623 his name appears as one of the "Jesuits in and about London," and again in 1627 we catch a glimpse of him as still there. In London, too, he died, on the 3rd November 1637, in his seventy-eighth year.[33] For thirty-nine years he worked as a Catholic priest in England, liable to be arrested at any moment, to be thrown into jail, and butchered in the barbarous way then in vogue; but he never was taken, and the later years of his life he must have passed in comparative quiet and security. I have seen it stated somewhere that he had a great gift as a preacher, and no one seeing his magnificent handwriting in the album of the Tournai noviciate—where it strikes the eye among that of hundreds of others who have with their own hands recorded their brief and often touching autobiographies—could believe that he was an ordinary man. His only brother Calibut survived him less than nine years, and was buried at Houghton in May 1646, just thirty years before his lineal descendant, the great Sir Robert Walpole, there first saw the light. The heavy fine and the expense inseparable from obtaining the pardon must have seriously taxed Calibut Walpole's resources, though he married an heiress; and the estates must have been encumbered when he entered into possession. Of the next generation we know little or nothing, and it was not till the days of Sir Edward Walpole, Sir Robert's grandfather, that the fortunes of the house began to rise again.([34])

My task is done and my story told. I am not so sanguine as to hope that my readers will take as lively an interest in the results of my researches as I have myself taken in pursuing them. As my work has proceeded, the England of Queen Elizabeth's days has become to me an altogether different land from the England I had formerly imagined it to be: the conflict with Rome has gradually unfolded itself as a problem which must remain unintelligible to the merely political historian: the homes and habits of life and thought of men and women of the gentry class have revealed themselves in quite unexpected forms and colours; and light has gleamed from many a dark corner, whence it was least hoped that any ray could shine. Who that sets forth upon a voyage of discovery ever knows whither he may be carried? A man sooner or later puts into port again, and shows the world his gains, and the world peradventure counts them little worth; but for him, he has visited strange lands and sailed into unknown waters, and in his enlarged experience and the memories of the long quest he finds his best reward.

To some perhaps the chief interest of this family chronicle will lie in the fact that the great minister whose name is a part of England's history, became in the sequel the head of this house, with "one generation" of which we have been concerned; but so to read the story is to miss its true point and lesson. Of course it *is* interesting to reflect that in Sir Robert's boyhood and early manhood the memories and traditions of the persecuting days were still fresh, and matters of common parlance; and that there must have been men still alive at Houghton who had talked with the outlawed Jesuit father, who had voluntarily resigned his inheritance, and with his brother, who had saved the estates from forfeiture; but the real value of the story lies rather in this, that it is one which, *mutatis mutandis*, might be told of fifty families in England, which were rich and prosperous in the first half of the sixteenth century, and were simply reduced to beggary for conscience' sake before James I. came to the throne.

This Norfolk House, whatever it may have been two centuries before, was certainly not one of the great governing families in the sixteenth century, though it seemed on the point of rising to the very first rank. Had Serjeant Walpole lived only a year or two longer, he would have been raised to the Bench in the ordinary course; as it was, to his son any career was open. When that son died childless, and his large possessions were added to those which Edward Walpole, as the heir of Houghton, might one day have enjoyed, a brilliant future seemed to be opening. It is clear that in this generation there was an abundance of energy, ambition, and intellectual power; but wealth and talent and birth and splendid opportunities were sacrificed to that which we call conscientious conviction, and with the ball at their feet these Walpoles resigned the game.

So did others whose prospects were scarcely less promising than theirs,—others whose names have gone down to silence; others from whom no Prime Minister sprung; who were *not* saved from ruin by any fortunate conjunction of circumstances, and whose cup of bitterness was drained to the dregs.

"But they were contumacious, they were perverse, they were wrongheaded, they would not bend to the times, they did not understand the spirit of the age." Be it so! And they counted the cost, and they did not shrink from the penalty and the pain. Living or dying, they did not play the craven. "But their creed was other than ours." Granted again! So was Henry Barrow's and John Greenwood's, and many another's—men whose carcases the hangman outraged, and whose disciples claim them now as glorious martyrs for the truth. These men were of the same stuff that Latimer and Rowland Taylor were made of; they were animated by the same enthusiasm, supported by the same intense earnestness, hurried along by the same fiery zeal, as free from vulgar worldliness, and as sincere. Surely, surely, they deserve at least a portion of the same honour! Let us not grudge it them: it is all the atonement we can make for the cruel wrongs of an age when toleration was looked upon as a crime, and pity for the erring was a sentiment unknown.

# NOTES TO CHAPTER XIII.

(1) *Page* 288, *line* 7.  *Chancery Fine Rolls*, 44° Eliz., Mich. term; *Lay Subsidy Rolls*, 7° James I., P. R. O.

(2) *Page* 288, *line* 21. Christopher Walpole's inq. p. m. was held at Fakenham, 1st September, 38° Eliz. (1596). It sets forth that on the 9th March 1596 he had *made over* to Thomas Walpole his son three messuages and about 500 acres of land, exclusive of two fold-courses in Anmer and Dersingham, reserving his own life interest and "unum conclave et cubiculum parcellam premissorum predictorum in Anmer predicta, ad usum cuiusdam *Margerie* ad tunc uxoris eius pro termino vitæ eiusdem Margerie." His will was made 8th May 1596: in it (according to the inquisition, for the will itself has disappeared) he leaves to Geoffrey a messuage and about 300 acres, together with a fold-course called Eastling Course, in Dersingham. According to this document it appears that the Anmer property made over to Thomas was more than double the value of that in Dersingham bequeathed to Geoffrey. What the acreage or value of the *fold-courses* was it is now quite impossible to determine, as the number of sheep running upon them is not specified.—*Chancery Inq. p. m.*, 38 Eliz., Part I. No. 51.

(3) *Page* 289, *line* 30. "*Richardus Walpolus*, Anglus, Norfolciensis diocesis, annorum 22, aptus ad logicam, receptus fuit in hoc Anglorum Collegium inter Alumnos S$^{ti}$ D. N. Sixti Papæ V., a P. Alfonso Agazario, Societatis Jesu, hujus collegii rectore, de expresso mandato Ill$^{mi}$ D$^{ni}$ Cardinalis S. Sixti, hujus Collegii Protectoris, sub die 25th Aprilis 1585." [He took the College oath, 2d February 1586] .... "Factus est subdiaconus 26. Novemb: Diaconus 30. Novemb: Sacerdos 3. Decemb: 1589. Missus est in Hispaniam, ut inde trajiceret in Angliam."—*Ex Archivis Collegii Anglorum in Urbe*, MS. No. 303, fol. 23.

His desire to enter the Society of Jesus is referred to by his brother Henry, in a letter which bears internal evidence of having been written in the summer of 1585, *i.e.*, at the time when *Richard Walpole* was at the English college.— *Walpole Letters*, xix. n. 3.

(4) *Page* 290, *line* 2.  *Fa. Greene's Collectanea, Stonyhurst MSS.*, Angl. A. II. No. 15.

(5) *Page* 290, *line* 10. Spedding's *Life and Letters of Francis Bacon*, vol. ii., p. 109. For the narrative given in the text I have not only consulted the ordinary authorities, but I have taken some pains to sift all the evidence which recent research has laid open to us. For the benefit of those who choose to test my accuracy, I have at the end of this note subjoined some few references which may be readily turned up by such as have access to any public library. One document, however, though very few living men can have ever seen or are likely to see it, was procured for me by the late Hon. Frederick Walpole several years ago. It is a copy of *Richard Walpole's own letter* to Father Garnett, in reply apparently to a request that he should draw up a vindication of himself from the charges made against him. The original is preserved in the Archives of the College at Valladolid, and is a long and verbose document. After some hesitation I decided that it was not worth printing, though authorised to print it by a letter from Mr. John Guest, whom I assume to have been Rector of the College at Valladolid at the time the transcript was made. No one reading Richard Walpole's own account of the affair could doubt that the story which he gives is the true one, even if it were not corroborated as strongly as it is by the *cumulative* evidence which supports it.

Mr. Spedding is mistaken in supposing that the "*Authentic Memoirs of that exquisitely villainous Jesuit, Father Richard Walpole*," published in 1733, was printed from the original edition which appeared in 1599. Through the kindness of my friend Mr. G. Napier, of Alderley Edge, I have had the opportunity of minutely collating the two editions, and I feel no hesitation in pronouncing that they were printed from two different manuscripts. There is nothing to show, but quite the contrary, that the printer or editor of the 1733 book had ever seen or heard of any earlier printed copy. Unfortunately my edition of Carleton's *Thankful Remembrance* (second edition, 1625) does not contain this tract. Mr. Spedding will be glad to learn that Father Henry More expressly refers to the tract which he has reprinted in his edition of *Bacon's Letters* as "*Baconus in litteris ad amicum Patavii.*"—*Cal. P.R.O. Domestic Eliz.*, 1595–1597, pp. 209, 255; *Ibid* 1598–1601. *See Index;* Foley's *Records*, series ii.–iv.; Spedding's *Life and Letters of Bacon*, vol. ii., book ii., ch. v.; Henry More's *Hist. Prov. Anglice*, Lib. v. § 34, 35; Camden's *Elizabeth*, book iv., p. 132, in Kennett's *Complete History of England*, fol. vol. ii.; Ellis' *Letters*, vol. iii., p. 189, second series; Lingard's *Elizabeth*, App. B.B.B.

(6) *Page* 291, *line* 34. The *Life of* DOÑA LUISA DE CARVAJAL was written by MICHAEL WALPOLE not long after her death, and the original MS. is still preserved in the Convent of the Encarnaçion at Madrid; "it is composed of a series of separate sheets, about two hundred leaves in all,"

and was examined by Dr. Juan Riaño in November 1874, permission having been obtained to inspect it from the Vicario Capitular of Santiago de Galicia, not without considerable difficulty. Large extracts were subsequently made for me and copies taken of letters and contemporary documents, by Dr. Riaño, transcripts of which are in my possession. This biography and the manuscript collections which accompany it were used by the Licenciate LUIS MUÑOZ, and very closely followed in drawing up his *Vida y Virtudes de la Venerable Virgen* Doña *Luisa de Carvaial y Mendoça* . . . . . which was dedicated to Philip IV., and published at Madrid, in 4to., in 1632. The book is one of very great rarity, and it was only after searching for it for years, that I was fortunate enough to procure a copy through the kind offices of DON PASCUALE DE GAYANGOS. From Muñoz' Work LADY GEORGIANA FULLERTON compiled her "*Life of Luisa de Carvajal*," which was published by Burns and Oates in 1873. Of course this latter is one of that class of devotional biographies which are distasteful to some people, but the main facts of the biography are capable of proof. In Southey's *Letters written during a Journey in Spain* (third edition), published in two volumes, 1808, there is (vol. i., pp. 259-302) an abstract of Muñoz' work, and a long account of Doña Luisa characterised by Southey's usual robust good sense ; it is a chapter very well worth reading.

(7) *Page* 293, *line* 20: Spedding, u.s., vol. ii., p. 109.

(8) *Page* 293, *line* 31. The examinations are printed in extenso by Foley, *Records*, *u.s.*

(9) *Page* 297, *line* 18. *Liturgies and Occasional Forms of Prayer set forth in the reign of Queen Elizabeth (Parker Society*, 1847), p. 679.

(10) *Page* 298, *line* 6. The "abstract of certain letters" mentioned in the text is to be seen in Father Greene's *Collect. Angl. A.*, vol. iii., No. 19, *Stonyhurst MSS.* For the authority for RICHARD WALPOLE'S proselytising, &c., in Spain, see Winwood's *Memorials*, vol. ii., pp. 136, 151, 178, &c. For his death Oliver's *Collections.* From Father Greene's *Collect. Angl.*, N. ii., it appears that he translated into Latin PARSON'S *Memorial for the Reformation of England.* The Latin version has never been printed. In a list of Letters of PARSONS in Greene's *Angl.*, P. ii., *Stonyhurst MSS.*, one bearing the date of October 15th 1607, is addressed to Father Cresswell, and treats "Of the great dissension betwixt him and F. Ric. Walpole, that hath caused extreme damage to the seminaries and great disorder in the seminary, which F. Cresswell seemeth to have bin cause or occasion (*sic*) never ending these difficulties with F. Parsons and other fathers . . . . . the disorders were cause that many schollars went to the Benedictines."

(11) *Page* 298, *line* 11. *MS.* No. 303, f. 39, 247; *Ex. Archivis Coll. Anglic in urbe.* He was admitted into the college, 22d February 1592.

(12) *Page* 299, *line* 15. For his entering the Society the authority is the MS. last quoted; for his being in England in 1606 see Morris, *Condition of Catholics under James I.*, p. lxv. For the other statements in this paragraph I must ask my readers to take my word for the fact that they are made on the authority of transcripts from MSS. in the *Bibl. Nacional* and the *Biblioteca de la Academia de la Historia* at Madrid; from *Archives at Simancas,* and the autograph *Life of Doña Luisa* in the Convent of the Encarnaçion. These transcripts (now in my possession) were made by Dr. Riaño, whose name is a sufficient guarantee for their fidelity. I cannot thank that accomplished scholar enough for the masterly way in which the work was done which he so kindly undertook.

(13) *Page* 299, *line* 19. He was a Cambridge man and Fellow of Christ's College. In 1594 he held a stall at Chester; in 1598 he was made a Prebendary of St. Paul's. He was promoted to the See of Derry 6th December 1616.—Le Neve's *Fasti* and Cotton's *Fasti Eccl. Hib.* iii. 317. His *Treatise concerning Antichrist* was published in 4to. 1604. For Michael Walpole's *Answer* to it, see Oliver's *Collect.*

(14) *Page* 300, *line* 29. There is a letter of Abbot's on the subject of the religious services at the Spanish ambassador's house in the P. R. O. An abstract is given in the *Cal. Dom.* 1611–1618, p. 140. *Muñoz*, p. 174, tells the story of the assault on Doña Luisa's house. See too Lady Georgiana Fullerton's *Life of Doña Luisa.* For the other details mentioned in the text I must again refer to MSS. penes me. Michael Walpole's letter to Gondomar is in the library of Don Pascuale de Gayangos.

(15) *Page* 300, *line* 32. *Visitation of Norfolk,* vol. i. p. 373, published by the *Norfolk and Norwich Archæological Society.*

(16) *Page* 301, *line* 27. The *Subsidy Rolls* are in the Record Office. They were formerly kept in the Tower and Exchequer. The *Presentments of Recusants* to the bishop were made annually, and sometimes oftener, by the churchwardens. In the *Ep. Registry* at Norwich there is a very imperfect collection of them bound up into a ragged volume. Two of these lists were printed in the *East Anglian.* I have been through them all: for genealogical purposes they are of some value.

(17) *Page* 302, *line* 7. For the larger part of this paragraph I am indebted to Mr. Foley: see too Oliver's *Collect.* This Christopher

WALPOLE's name appears on a list of Novices, 1625, printed in Foley, *Records*, series i. p. 132.

(18) *Page* 302, *line* 15.  *Walpole Letters*, p. 13.

(19) *Page* 302, *line* 24.  *U. s., Letter VI.* n. 2.

(20) *Page* 302, *line* 34.  *Harrison* says that a gentleman could in his young days live on £10 a year, and many instances might be adduced of an annuity of this amount being left to younger sons by men of large means. For a case in point see ch. vii. n. (9).

(21) *Page* 303, *line* 9.  "I am glad to hear of Bernard Gardiner's oath. God send him constancy and health, if not Rhemes; for I would be sorry he should, from so happy an estate, *return to be a soldier to his own discomfort*."—*Walpole Letters*, p. 29.

(22) *Page* 303, *line* 24.  Father *Henry More* mentions his reluctance to take Holy Orders, and his narrow escape from shipwreck.—*Hist. Prov. Anglic.*, lib. v. § 33. It is plain, too, from the *Letters of* H. WALPOLE, that he did not leave England with any intention of entering the priesthood.— iv. 4, v. 5, vi. 3.

(23) *Page* 304, *line* 22.  "Vulgato itaque reditu cum susque deque quererentur plurimorum apud Norfolcienses et Suffolcienses ædes ut unum hunc reperirent, aliquantâ collectâ pecuniâ rursus trajecit . . . ." Calibut Walpole married in 1591.—More's *Hist. Prov.* v. § 32 ; Collin's *Peerage by Sir Egerton Brydges*, v. 648.

(24) *Page* 304, *line* 31.  The following is a copy of EDWARD WALPOLE's account of himself, written with his own hand in the Album of the Noviciate of Tournai. This MS. is now in the Royal Library at Brussels, in admirable preservation (MS. No. 1016, p. 210). I went carefully through it in 1874.

*Ego Edouardus Walpolus Examinatus fui a P. Joanne Bargio juxta Examen Novitiorum* 18 *Decembris,* 1593. *Rursus* 23 *Junii,* 1594, *et* 16 *Decembris,* 1594, *et rursus* 16 *Junii,* 1595.

Ego EDOUARDUS WALPOLUS Norfolciensis in Anglia natus circiter annum 1562. Patre JOANNE WALPOLO viro nobili vitâ functo, matre CATHERINA CALLIBUTTA adhuc superstite. Studui Grammaticæ et humanioribus litteris in patria circiter 4$^m$ annos et in Academia Cantabrigiensi totidem, Romæ in

*Experimenta hæc feci Exercitia Spiritualia. Secundum et tertium commutata fuerunt in officia humilia, quæ exercui juvando præfectum Refectorii, hebdomadis decem, et postea adhuc quatuor. Quartum ex professo obivi in domo Probationis serviendo coquo hebdomadibus quatuor. Quintum et Sextum, ob ignorantiam linguæ Gallicæ, obire non potui, idcirco eorum loco comitatus sum aliquoties emptorem ad forum, et id genus alia officia humilitatis obivi.*

*Ego Edouardus Walpolus cum venia R. P. Georgii Durœi [?] Provincialis emisi vota privata juxta consuetam Soc$^{tis}$ formulam Sacrum celebrante P. Joanne Bargio in sacello Domus Probationis Tornacensis Soc$^{tis}$ Jesu ipso die Nativitatis Christi Anno 1594.*

Scholis Soc$^{tis}$ Theologiæ Scholasticæ duobus annis, majori ex parte languens, medio anno casubus conscientiæ. Ibidem promotus fui ad tonsuram et 4$^{or}$ minores ordines quinque diversis diebus in quadragesima anno 1592: ad Subdiaconatum Sabbato Sancta: ad Diaconatùm feria secunda Paschatis eodem anno, in Basilica S$^t$ Joannis Lateranensis a Suffraganeo Summi Pontificis: ad Sacerdotium in Festo Ascensionis Domini in Ecclesia Collegii Anglicani a Reverendissimo Dño Odoeno Epõ Cassanensi. Admissus fui ad Soc$^{tem}$ Jesu a R$^{do}$ Patre Oliverio Manareo Præposito Provinciali in Belgio, ex commendatione R$^{di}$ P. N. Generalis Claudii Aquavivæ. Veni Ad domum Probationis Tornacensem 4 Julii anno 1593, et examinatus fui a P. Joanne Bargio juxta examen generale ejusdem Soc$^{tis}$ Diplomate Apostolica instituti. Duas constitutiones ejusdem conformatorias Gregorii 13 et Gregorii 14, et regulas ejusdem Soc$^{tis}$ perlegi. Habeo propositum vivendi et moriendi in Soc$^{te}$ Jesu, et omnia, tam quæ in examine, quam quæ in supradictis, proposita sunt, observare desidero ac propono, nominatim quod ad obedientiam et promptitudinem animi, ad serviendum Deo, ubique et in quavis re, item quæ ad indifferentiam ad quemvis gradum Soc$^{tis}$ et ad reddendam rationem Conscientiæ manifestationemque meorum defectuum pertinet. Contentus sum, ut res quæcunque quæ in me notatæ et observatæ fuerint, per quemvis, qui extra confessionem eas acceperit, superioribus manifestenter. Paratus quoque sum ad correctionem aliorum juvare, aliosque manifestare secundum voluntatem et præscripta superioris ad majorem

*Missus est ad
Collegium Lovaniense
8 Julii 1595.*

Dei gloriam; necnon ad omnia officia Societatis, quæ a superiore injungerentur mihi indifferentem me offero. Promitto autem me relicturum omnia bona post elapsum ab ingressu meo annum, quandocunque id a superiore meo injungetur. In quorum fide hæc mea manu scripsi et subsignavi.

Actum Tornaci in Domo Probationis Societatis Jesu 15 Julii, Anno 1593.
Ita est
EDOUARDUS WALPOLUS.

(25) *Page* 305, *line* 2. *Controlment Roll*, 38° Eliz., P. R. O.

(26) *Page* 305, *line* 10. *Special Commissioners, Suffolk* 37° *Eliz.*, *concerning the possessions of Edw. Walpole, late of Houghton near Harpley*, P. R. O. This inquisition was held at Bury St. Edmunds. The inquisition held at Dereham is missing.

(27) *Page* 305, *line* 27. *Dom. Eliz.*, vol. cclxiv. n. 70.

(28) *Page* 305, *line* 33. The main facts of this business are given in the case drawn up for the opinion of Sir Matthew Hale, which I have before referred to. When it is said that a fine of £1600 would be "equivalent to a charge upon any estate in Norfolk of £20,000," the reader must be warned that I do not mean to dogmatise upon that extremely difficult question of the comparative value of money in the sixteenth century and in the nineteenth; but simply to express my very strong conviction that a charge of £1600 upon a given acreage in 1598 would be *at least* as heavy as a charge of £20,000 upon the same acreage in our own days. This is not the time nor the place to discuss a question which involves so many considerations.

(29) *Page* 306, *line* 16. Foley's *Records*, ser. ii.-iv. p. 265, and ser. i. p. 146; Morris' *Troubles*, ser. i. p. 192.

(30) *Page* 306, *line* 21. On the attitude of James I. towards the Catholic gentry at the beginning of his reign, see Gardiner's *History of England from the Accession of James I. to the Disgrace of Coke*, vol. i., p. 109 and seq. My authority for the granting of the pardon is *Davey add. MSS. Brit. Mus.* 19, 092 (*Hoxne Hundred*). Davey gives the date of the pardon, 4th April, 2° James I.

(31) *Page* 306, *line* 24. *More Hist. Prov. Angl.* says he assumed the name of "*Pauper*" when he first attempted to leave England about 1588; for his assuming the name of "*Rich*" see *Foley* i. 646, quoting Gee's "*Foot out of the Snare.*"

(32) *Page* 306, *line* 29. His mother, CATHERINE WALPOLE'S, will is dated 16th June, 5° J. I., and was proved 11th January 1612, *Cur. Ep. Norvic. Coker*, f. 269. The legacies are numerous and, for the time, unusually large. The original surrender of all claim on the estates by EDWARD to CALIBUT WALPOLE (*penes me*) is dated 2d May 1613, *i.e.*, just a year after their mother's death.

(33) *Page* 306, *line* 32. Foley's *Records*, series ii. p. 264.

(34) *Page* 307, *line* 18. On SIR EDWARD WALPOLE, see Collins, v. 651. His only son ROBERT, father of SIR ROBERT WALPOLE, first Earl of Orford, was a very different man from the rough boor and sot whom *Coxe*, strangely, represents him to have been. DEAN PRIDEAUX, who had very few good words to say of any one, speaks of him as a likely person to succeed the Duke of Norfolk as Lord Lieutenant of the County, "and beside him," he adds, "there is not a man of any parts or interest in all that party. To pitch on him I reckon will be a certain expedient to remove all manner of divisions out of this country."—*Letters of Humphrey Prideaux to John Ellis* (*Camden Society*), p. 195.

# INDEX NOMINUM.

ABBOT, 313.
Addamson, William, 217.
Agazario, Alfonso, 310.
Aldred, Solomon, 83, 104.
Alexander, Mr., 281.
Allen, Cardinal, 76, 93, 94, 133, 225, 289.
Andrada, Manuel, 249, 250.
Andrewes, Launcelot, Bishop, 87.
Anguish, Thos., 83.
Annias, John, 252.
Antonio, Don, 250.
Apreece, Cassandra, 172.
—— William, 172.
Aquaviva, Claudius, 182.
Archenstall, Richard, 149.
Arden, Evan, 264.
Arundell, Earl, 4, 251, 259.
—— Countess, 252.
—— Archbishop, 29.
—— Mrs., 230.
Ashley, Sir A., 305.
Ascham, Roger, 32.
Audley, Mr. E., 217.
Aylmer, Bishop, 41, 272.

BACON, ANNE, 126.
—— Anthony, 49, 84, 239.
—— Edmund, 304.
—— Elizabeth, 304.
—— Francis, 49, 76, 258, 264, 293, 294, 297.
—— George, 124.
—— Lady, 53.
—— Mrs., 124.
—— Nathaniel, 151.
—— Nicholas, 52, 54.
Bagshaw, 294.
Bagster, Margaret, 33.
Bainbrigg, Richard, 49.
Baldwin, William, 271, 284, 286.

Bargius, 170, 314.
Barker, Thomas, 81.
Barkley, Sir R., 268.
Barnes, 260.
Barneveldt, John of, 154.
Barrow, Henry, 309.
Bartoli, 105.
Barton, William, 12.
Basselier, Father, 105.
Basset, 71.
Bastard of Dunham, 138, 200.
—— Edward, 213.
—— Elizabeth, 151.
—— Francis, 151.
—— Henry, 213.
—— Richard, 213.
Battor, Stephen, 161.
Baxter, Richard, 90.
Beadle, John, 215.
Beale, Mr., 253, 257.
Beaumont, 272, 275, 284.
Beckham, Margery, 24.
—— Richard, 24.
Bedingfield, Mr., 69, 81, 83, 148, 204, 212, 215.
—— Edmund, 151.
—— Sir Henry, 149, 217.
—— Nazareth, 151, 152.
Bell, Thomas, 231.
Bellarmine, 103.
Berners, Lord, 124.
Bettice, William, 128.
Beza, 95.
Bilney, 116.
Bird, Henry, 37, 52.
—— John, 12, 215.
Blackfan, John, 178.
Blackwell, Mr., 118.
—— Mrs., 118, 119, 120, 125, 126, 127.
—— Baron, 124.

# INDEX

Blackwell, Campion, 125.
—— Draper, 124.
—— Edward, 124.
—— George, 124.
—— Margaret, 124, 125.
—— Mary, 124.
—— Richard, 125.
—— Thomas, 125.
—— Walpole, 124.
—— William, 125, 127.
—— Archpriest, 241.
Blount, Sir Charles, 247.
—— Sir Michael, 257, 265.
Boast, John, 229.
Bobadilla, Nicholas, 93.
Bogas, Mrs., 217.
Boischot, de, 300.
Boleyn, Bridget, 31.
—— Sir John, 31.
Bolt, John, 105.
Borough, Lord Thomas, 70.
—— Margaret, 70.
Boswell, John, 173.
Bourchier, 124.
Bowes, Sir G., 60.
Bozoun of Whissonsett, 138.
—— Roger, 171.
Bradshaw, 148.
Branthwaite, 266.
Briddiman, 217.
Bromley, Lady Elizabeth, 126.
—— Sir Henry, 265.
—— Sir Thomas, 126.
Browne, Anne, 128.
—— Sir Anthony, 4, 128, 138, 153.
—— Sir Thomas, 56.
—— William, 128.
Buckhurst, Lord, 216, 248.
Bukke, John, 36.
Burghley, William, Lord, 70, 246, 247, v. Cecil.
Bushe, Paul, 12.
Butterweck, Catherine, 124, 129.
—— Richard, 124, 129.
Butts, Sir William, 81.

Cahill, Hugh, 253, 254.
Calibut, Andrew, 32.
—— Anna, 200, 214.
—— Catherine, 22, 314.
—— Edgar, 32.
—— Edward, 32.
—— Ele, 200.
—— Francis, 31.
—— Henry, 32.

Calibut, James, 32.
—— John, 31.
—— Robert, 32.
—— William, 22, 31.
Call, Edmund, 128.
Calthorpe, Lord, 104, 137.
Camden, 85.
Campion, Edmund, 42, 77, 88, 91, 94, 95, 97, 98, 99, 100, 101, 103, 112, 119, 131, 233.
—— Thomas, 119.
Carleton, Dudley, 293.
Cartwright, 74.
Carvajal, Luisa de, 291, 298, 311.
Catesby, Mary, 151.
—— Thomas, 151.
Catline, Richard, 36, 126.
Cecil, William, 33, 180, 181, 192, 215, 216, 218, 247, 248, 265.
Chambers, John, 12.
Clitherow, John, 227.
—— Margaret, 227, 244.
Cobbe, Joan, 21.
—— of Sandringham, 49, 57, 138, 204.
—— Geoffrey, 33.
Cobham, William, 216.
Cocket, Edmund, 137, 151.
—— Jane, 137, 151.
Coke, Sir Edward, 26, 34, 105, 253, 257, 258.
—— Robert, 26, 33, 35, 52, 294, 297.
Cornwallis, Charles, 197, 214, 297.
—— Henry, 200, 214.
—— Richard, 200, 201, 214.
—— Thomas, 200, 214.
—— William, 214.
Cottam, Thomas, 96.
Cotton, Mr., 300.
Cranmer, 117.
Cresswell, Joseph, S. J., 105, 167, 169, 170, 171, 173, 189, 291, 294, 298, 312.
Crestoval de Moro, 186.
Crockett, Ralph, 17.
Croft, Sir James, 82.
Cromwell, Henry, Lord, 202.
—— Thomas, 202, 215.
Curzon, Dorothy, 32.

Daubeny, Arthur, 57.
Derby, Earl, 259.
Dereham, John, 216.
Desmond, Earl of, 252.
Diat, Martin, 128.
Dingley, George, 231.

Donne, John, 103.
—— Elizabeth, 103.
Downes, Bridget, 83.
—— Dorothy, 83.
—— Edward, 83.
—— Francis, 83, 149, 196, 211.
—— James, 212.
—— John, 81, 83.
—— Lord, 149.
—— Mr., 68, 83.
—— Robert, 81, 83, 195, 196, 203, 211, 212.
Downham, Dr. G., 299.
Doyle, Henry, 210.
Doyly, Henry, 151.
Drake, Sir F., 264.
Drewe, Serjeant, 253, 255, 256, 257.
Drury, Bridget, 151, 217.
—— Dorothy, 78.
—— Frances, 78.
—— Henry, 78, 219.
—— John, 79, 81.
—— Lady, 220.
—— Robert, 78.
Ducket, Owen, 151.
Dudley, Amy, 21, 29.
—— Lord Robert, 21, 29.
Dugdale, 23.

ELDERTON, WILLIAM, 106.
Elizabeth, Queen, *passim*.
Elliott, 103.
Emerson, Ralph, 95, 97, 104.
Essex, Robert Devereux, Earl of, 84, 169, 246, 250, 264, 295.
Ewens, Matthew, 272, 284.
Exeter's wife, Marquis of, 4.

FARMOR, ANNE, 151.
—— Henry, 151.
—— Thomas, 128, 151.
Faunt, Nicholas, 37.
—— Robert, 52.
Favour, Dr., 232.
Feckenham, Abbot, 47.
Fenner, Dudley, 48, 57, 152.
Ferriman, Francis, 285.
Fincham, Thomas, 151.
Fitzgerald, 252.
Fitzherbert, Thomas, 70, 71.
Fleet, Thomas, 32.
Fleming, 294.
Fletcher, Dr., 266.
Floyd, H., 178.
Fontaine, de la, 284.

Fortescue, Edmund, 220.
—— Mistress, 220.
Fowle, Thomas, 41.
Fox, John, 54.
Freake, Bishop, 54, 148.
Freeman, John, 217.
—— Thomas, 217.
Fryer, Dr., 196.
Fuscinelli, Octavius, 284.
Fynes, Mr., 150.

GAMA, FERRARA DE, 249.
Gardiner, Bernard, of Coxford Abbey, 49, 52, 152, 166, 200, 202, 213, 215, 303, 306, 314.
—— George, Dr., 39, 40, 42, 52, 54.
—— Humphrey, 213.
—— Katherine, 215.
—— Lyonell, 215.
—— Sir Robert, 212.
—— Thomas, 200.
Gargrave, Sir Thomas, 224.
Garnet, Henry, 88, 241 259, 297, 311.
Gayangos, Don Pascuale de, 313.
George, David, 45.
Gerard, John, 130-144, 145-148, 194, 200, 202, 206, 215, 219-221, 259.
Gerard, Lord, 131.
—— Sir Thomas, 130.
Gifford, Dr., 260.
Goldwell, Bishop, 72, 94, 104, 111.
Gondomar, 299, 300, 313.
Goodman, 5, 16.
—— John, 305.
Goodrich, John, 171.
—— Nicholas, 171.
—— Thomas, 166, 171.
—— William, 171.
—— Unica, 171.
Graye, Robert, 149.
Green, Father, 312.
—— Robert, 37, 53, 126.
Greenwood, John, 309.
Grey, Robert de, 81.
Gunnes, Gregory, 264.

HALE, SIR M., 129, 215.
Hardesty, Mr., 231.
Hare, Michael, 83.
Harman, Thomas, 217.
Harryett, Matthew, 217.
Harrys, Symon, 217.
Harvey, Gabriel, 49.
—— John, 217.
Hastings, Martin, 33.

X

## INDEX.

Hatton, Sir Christopher, 82, 248.
Haugh, or Hawe, 37, 38, 51, 53.
Hawkins, 272.
—— John, 151.
Hayward, James, 89.
—— Simon, 85.
Heigham, John, 151.
Heydon, Sir Christopher, 81, 152.
Heywood, Eliseus, 87, 94.
—— Jasper, 87, 94.
—— John, 94.
—— Mrs., 220.
Higgens, 280, 285.
Hillyard, William, 273, 274, 284.
Hilsey, John, 12, 13.
Hobbard, *see* Hubbard.
Holbech, Henry, 12.
Holgate, Robert, 12.
Holt, William, 88, 219, 275, 286.
Holtby, Richard, 240, 241, 245, 262, 277, 279.
Holtoft, Gilbert, 30.
—— Margaret, 21, 22, 31.
—— William, 31.
Hooper, Bishop, 13.
Hopital, Michel de l', 157.
Horden, 32.
Horne, Charles, 49.
Houghell, Bridget, 128.
Houghton, Adam de, 20.
—— Mary, 128.
Howard, Sir Philip, 251, 265.
Howards, the, 216.
Howell, Richard, 129.
Howes, James, 128.
Hubbard, James, 79, 172, 262.
Huddleston, Edmund, 220.
Hule, Catherine, 128.
Huntingdon, Henry, Earl of, 223, 224, 225, 229, 230, 232, 242.
Hussey, James, 305.

INGRAM, 190.

JACQUES, CAPTAIN, 258.
Jerningham, Anne, 217.
—— Edward, 217.
—— George, 217.
—— Sir Henry, 69, 195, 196, 204, 211, 216.
—— Henry, 217.
—— Jeronyma, 204, 218.
—— Lady, 195, 216, 218.
—— Mr., 204, 215.
—— Thomas, 217.

Jerningham, William, 217.
Jewell, Bishop, 40.
Joan, Queen Mary's fool, 216, 217.
Jones, Nicholas, 84.

KELKE, ROGER, 38.
Kerviles of Wiggenhall, 138.
Killigrew, Sir H., 257.
King, Nicholas, 220.
—— Robert, 12, 13.
Kingston, Sir Anthony, 217.
—— Lady, 216.
Kirkman, 226.
Kitchin, Anthony, 12, 13.
Knollys, Sir F., 82, 169.
Knyvett, Catherine, 22, 83.
—— Edmund, 124, 128.
—— Jane, 124.
—— Sir Thomas, 83, 128.

LACEY, WILLIAM, 226.
Lassey, Brian, 266.
—— Richard, 266.
Lee, William, 106.
—— Roger, 220.
Leicester, Robert Dudley, Earl of, 23, 55, 82, 110, 120, 122, 154, 155, 156, 159, 248.
Le Strange, Grisell, 151.
—— Hamon, 151.
—— Nicholas, 151.
—— Thomas, 137, 151.
Leutner or Lucknor, 131.
Limbert, Stephen, 38, 39, 53.
Linacre, James, 220.
Lingam, George, 18.
Lingen, Edward, 187, 190, 230, 234, 236.
Lith, Thomas, 87.
Longueville, Viscount, 137.
Lopez, Roderigo, 249, 250, 251, 264.
Lovell, Lady, 217, 220.
—— Robert, 82, 148, 212.
—— Thomas, 82, 148.
Lovering, Mr., 51.
Lucie, Thomas, 166.
Lumner, Edward, 137, 151, 152.
—— Jane, 137, 151, 152, 208.

MAJOR, ANTHONY, 231.
Manareus, Oliver, 163, 219, 315.
Maplisdon, John, 267.
Markham, John, 172.
Marshall, Mr., 217.
Martin, Gregory, 88.
—— Roger, 83.

## INDEX.

Mary, Queen, 4, 6, 10.
—— Stuart, 59.
Maye, Henry, 227.
Mayne, Cuthbert, 73, 74, 94.
Michell, William, 128.
Middleton, Thomas, 227.
Mills, Agnes, 300.
—— Jane, 300.
Montford, Simon de, 20.
More, Henry, Dr., 127, 302, 311, 314.
—— Sir Thomas, 63, 103, 104.
—— Sir William, 80.
Morgan, Mr., 105.
Morley, Edward Parker, Lord, 200.
Morton, Dr., 94.
Mulcaster, Mr., 204, 216.
Munday, 105, 293.
Muñoz, Luis, 312.
Myles, Mr. F., 104.

NACHTEGAEL, GEORGE, 163, 170.
Naunton, Robert, 39, 52, 53.
Nelson, John, 74.
Newport, Grace, 151.
Nichols, Degory, 49.
Norfolk, Thomas Howard, 4th Duke of, 29, 65, 265.
Norreys, 264.
North, Edward, Lord, 116.
Northumberland, Henry Percy, 9th Earl of, 54, 66, 125.
Norton, Richard, 70, 106.
—— Walter, 148, 150.
Nottingham, Charles Howard, Lord, 271.
Nowell, Dean, 218.
—— Robert, 218.

OLDCORNE, FATHER, 134, 148.

PAGET, THOMAS, 3d LORD, 97.
Parham, Edward, 128.
Paris, Ferdinand, 82, 148, 152.
—— Philip, 49, 57, 152.
Parker, Archbishop, 37, 39, 44, 117.
Parkhurst, Dr. John, Bishop of Norwich, 39, 40, 53, 54.
Parkyns, 18.
Parma, Prince of, 161.
Parsons, Robt., 77, 88–91, 95–98, 104, 114, 132, 178, 179, 180, 183, 232, 258, 289, 297.
Paston, John, 213.
—— William, 213.
Patrick, Ursula, 125.

Pawlet, Lady, 217.
Pelham, Sir W., 155.
Pells of Anmer, 301.
Pembroke, Earl of, 33.
Percy, Lady Mary, 220.
Perez, Antonio, 252.
Perient, George, 80.
Perne, Dr., 47, 56, 143.
Petre, Lady, 195, 217.
Peyton, Sir John, 148, 151.
Philippes, Michael, 217.
Philopater, Andreas, 180, 182.
Pitts, John, 88.
Pole, Reginald, 1, 117.
Ponet, 16.
Possoz, Father, 169.
Pound, Thomas, 98.
Powle, John, 217.
Pratt, Mr., 204, 218.
Puckering, Lord Keeper, 234, 253.
Pym, 285.

QUINONES, ALFONSO DE, 179.

RAWLINGS, ALEXANDER, 276–281.
Rede, Thomas, 151.
Redington, Mr., 52.
Redman, Bishop, 199.
Remington, Robert, 57, 232.
Repps, Margaret, 212.
Ridley, Bishop, 5.
Rich, Audrey, 78.
—— Lord, 78.
Robarts, Jane, 173.
—— John, 39, 173.
Robsart, Amy, 21, 23, 29, 30, 91, 111, see Dudley.
—— Arthur, 30.
—— Elizabeth, 30.
—— John, 21, 29, 30.
—— Lucy, 21.
—— Sir Terry, 21.
Rodriguez, Simon, 93.
Rolls, 294.
Rookwood, Annie, 217.
—— Ambrose, 79.
—— of Coldham, 261.
—— Dorothy, 220.
—— Edward, 67, 79, 81.
—— of Euston, 79.
—— Richard, 220.
—— Robert, 79.
—— of Stanningfield, 79.
Roper, James, 209.
Rouse, Anthony, 166, 172, 220.

## INDEX.

Rowe, Mr., 149.
—— William, 188.
Rugg, William, 12.
Russell, Mr., 217.
—— Captain, 163.
—— Henry, 200.
—— Jane, 217.
Ryvett, Jane, 128, 129.
—— Thomas, 129.

SAILLY, THOMAS, 161.
Salcot, John, 12.
Salisbury, Dean, 40.
Salmeron, Alphonsus, 93.
Sampson, Abbot, 20.
Sandys, Archbishop, 224, 285.
—— Sir Edwin, 278, 280, 285.
—— Miles, 57, 258, 285.
Saravia, Adrian, 285.
Saville, Serjeant, 273, 285.
Sayve, William, 212.
Scarlett, Martha, 128.
—— Thomas, 26, 33, 35, 129.
—— Ursula, 128.
Scott, Bishop, 72.
Selden, John, 283.
Sherley, Elizabeth, 220.
Sherwood, Thomas, 74.
Shrewsbury, Earl of, 248.
Sidney, Sir H., 92.
Skipwith, Sir William, 172.
Sledd, 105.
Smith, Richard, Father, 303.
—— Thomas, 42, 55, 295.
Souche, Henry, 105.
Southwell, Richard, 211.
—— Robert, 70, 84, 153, 177, 252, 271, 279, 302.
Speght, 142, 153.
Spelman, Sir H., 14, 33.
Spylman, Francis, 212.
Squier, Edward, 290–296.
Standen, 84.
Stanley, John, 293.
—— Sir William, 156–160, 169, 230, 258.
Stapleton, 103.
Stead, Anne, 128.
Sterer, William, 216.
Still, Mr., 55.
Stransham, or Potter, George, 57.
Style, Lady Elizabeth, 68, 80.
Sucklinge, Edmund, 267.
Suliard, Edward, 83, 217.

Suliard, Lady, 171.
—— Thomas, 217.

TELLO, DON PEDRO, 290.
Thexton, Launcelot, 54.
Thirlby, Thomas, Bishop of Ely, 26, 116, 118, 119, 124, 125, 127.
—— Henry, 125, 126.
Thompson Mr. Robert (Gerard), 139, 215.
—— James, 226.
Tinoco, Manuel, Lewis, 249.
Topcliffe, Richard, 70, 71, 79, 84, 145, 235, 236, 239, 255, 256, 266, 271.
—— Robert, 70.
Townshend, Marian, 80.
—— Sir Robert, 80.
—— Thomas, 68, 80.
Traheron, 16.
Tregian, Francis, 73.
Tremaine, Mr., 220.
—— Mistress, 220.
—— Mary, 220.

VALLENGER, 101, 110.
Vaux, Laurence, 94.
Velasco, Ruis de, 186.
Verstegan, 84, 260, 267.

WAAD, WILLIAM, 293.
Wakeman, John, 12.
Waldegrave, Charles, 195, 204, 205, 216, 218.
—— Charles (son), 205.
—— Christian, 217.
—— Dorothy, 217.
—— Edward, 204, 217, 219.
—— Sir Edward, 195, 196, 211.
—— Frances, 217.
—— Henry, 219.
—— John, 205, 219.
—— Lady, 195, 212.
—— Magdalen, 217.
—— Nicholas, 219.
Walker, Dr. John, 41.
Walpole, Alan, 28.
—— Alice, 123.
—— Beatrix, 28.
—— of Brockley, 20.
—— Calibut, 23, 122, 304, 314.
—— Catherine, 31, 124, 128, 317.
—— Clarice, 28.
—— Christopher, 21, 23, 32, 33, 38, 123, 127, 129, 142 153, 166, 170.
—— Christopher (son), 298, 301, 313.

Walpole, Dorothy, 123.
— Edmund, 20.
— Edward, 21, 22, 38, 49, 50, 57, 102, 116, 120, 121, 127, 129, 140, 152, 153, 166, 171, 192, 203, 215, 220, 286, 302, 304, 314, 316.
— Egeline, 28.
— Elizabeth, 31.
— Francis, 32.
— Galferye, 123.
— Geoffrey, 142, 286, 288, 300, 310.
— Henry of Herpley, 22, 23, 32, 33.
— Henry, S. J., *passim.*
— Jane, 124, 172.
— Joceline, 28.
— John, 21, 23, 31, 38, 121, 122, 128, 172, 200, 314.
— Lemare, 28.
— Margaret, 123.
— Margerye, 123.
— Mary, 215.
— Michael, 123, 127, 141, 142, 153, 164, 166, 170, 298, 299, 311.
— Osbert, 28.
— of Pinchbeck, 20.
— Radulphus, 20.
— Reginald, 28,
— Richard, 22, 80, 115, 123, 127, 289, 298, 314, 315.
— Robert, 317.
— Sir Robert, 305, 307, 317.
— Serjeant, 52, 116, 123.
— Simon, 18, 28.
— Terry, 22, 81.
— Thomas, 21, 24, 32, 122, 128.
— Thomas (son), 143, 172, 188, 230, 242, 253, 256, 287, 301, 310.
— Thomasine, 301.
— William, 29
— William of Herpley, 14, 21, 23, 26, 117, 121, 124, 126, 128, 152.
Walsingham, Sir F., 37, 104, 190, 248.
Warner, Edward, 36.
Warton, Edward, 124.
— Robert, 12.
Warwick, John Dudley, Earl of, 21, 29, 82.
Watson, 219, 302.
Wayte, Eustace, 266.
Welby, Robert, 172.

Wendon, Nicholas, 42, 55.
Wentworth, Peter, 252, 265.
— Thomas, Lord, 52.
West, Robert, 267.
White, Sir Thomas, 91.
Whitgift, Archbishop, 74, 85, 270, 284.
Wiltcot, Mr., 18.
Wilson, Matthew, 32.
— Mr. Secretary, 82.
Willoughby, George, 150.
Wilkes, Sir Thomas, 253.
Wilkinson, Michael, 267.
Windham, Mr. Justice, 217.
Wiseman, Mr. T., 220, 235, 267.
— Mrs., 220.
Wodehouse, Francis, of Breccles, 198, 206, 212, 218, 267.
— Grisell, Lady, 151, 206.
— John, 212.
— Philip, of Kimberley, 137, 151, 152, 206, 208.
— Sir Roger, 137 151, 212.
— Sir Thomas, 17, 190.
Wolsey, J., 216.
Wotton, Lord, 297.
Wyatt, Sir Thomas, 16.

YAXLEY, 195, 205, 212.
Yelverton, Anne, 151, 213.
— Charles, 128, 137, 138.
— Sir Charles, 137.
— Sir Christopher, 137.
— Edward, of Rougham, 49, 57, 136-140, 151, 152, 202, 213, 215, 276.
— Ferdinand, 151.
— Frances, 151.
— Grisell, 151, 206.
— Henry, 137, 151.
— Humphrey, 151, 199, 213.
— Jane, 151, 152.
— Launcelot, 151.
— Martha, 151, 213.
— William, 128, 136, 137, 151, 152.
— Winifred, 151.
Yorke, Rowland, 156, 159.
Young, Richard, 253, 257, 266.

ZELANDER, 286.
Zuniga, Pedro de, 299.

www.ingramcontent.com/pod-product-compliance
Lightning Source LLC
Chambersburg PA
CBHW032357230426
43672CB00007B/727